Foundation Units 1 and 2

RECORDING INCOME AND RECEIPTS
MAKING AND RECORDING PAYMENTS

For assessments in December 2003
and June 2004

Interactive Text

In this May 2003 new edition

- For assessments under the new standards
- Layout designed to be easier on the eye – and easy to use
- Clear language and presentation
- Lots of diagrams and flowcharts
- Activities checklist to tie in each activity to specific knowledge and understanding, performance criteria and/or range statement
- Thorough reliable updating of material to 1 April 2003

FOR 2003 AND 2004 SKILLS BASED ASSESSMENTS

First edition May 2003

ISBN 0 7517 1094 6

British Library Cataloguing-in-Publication Data
A catalogue record for this book
is available from the British Library

Published by

BPP Professional Education
Aldine House, Aldine Place
London W12 8AW

www.bpp.com

Printed in Great Britain by WM Print
Frederick Street
Walsall
West Midlands
WS2 9NE

All our rights reserved. No part of this publication may be reproduced, stored in a retrieval system or transmitted, in any form or by any means, electronic, mechanical, photocopying, recording or otherwise, without the prior written permission of BPP Professional Education.

We are grateful to the Lead Body for Accounting for permission to reproduce extracts from the Standards of Competence for Accounting, and to the AAT for permission to reproduce extracts from the mapping and Guidance Notes.

BPP Professional Education
2003

Contents

Introduction

How to use this Interactive Text – Foundation qualification structure – Unit 1 Standards of competence – Unit 2 Standards of competence – Assessment strategy – Building your portfolio

		Page	Answers to activities

PART A — Accounting for sales and purchases

1	Sales invoicing and issuing credit notes	3	475
2	Processing suppliers' invoices and credit notes	41	484
3	Sales and sales returns day books	71	491
4	Purchase and purchase returns day books	85	493
5	Double entry bookkeeping	97	494
6	The sales ledger	135	503
7	The purchase ledger	161	509
8	Communications with debtors	181	512
9	Communications with creditors	211	517

PART B — Accounting for receipts

10	Receiving and checking money	237	520
11	Banking monies received	275	522
12	Recording monies received	307	527

PART C — Accounting for payments

13	Authorising and making payments	329	532
14	Recording payments	367	538
15	Maintaining petty cash records	385	543

Page   Answers
        to activities

PART D Payroll

16   Paying wages and salaries and updating records 425 547

PART E Basic law

17   Business law 449 550

PART F Computerised accounting systems

18   Computerised accounting systems .... 469 .... -

Answers to activities 475

Index 555

Order forms

Review form & free prize draw

IMPORTANT

Most colleges teach Units 1 and 2 together. However to assist those that teach the two units separately, there is a Signpost at the start of each chapter indicating the Unit(s) being covered

---

Introduction

How to use this Interactive Text

Aims of this Interactive Text

> To provide the knowledge and practice to help you succeed in the assessment for Foundation Unit 1 *Recording income and receipts* and Foundation Unit 2 *Making and recording payments*.

To pass the assessment successfully you need a thorough understanding in all areas covered by the standards of competence.

> To tie in with the other components of the BPP Effective Study Package to ensure you have the best possible chance of success.

Interactive Text

This covers all you need to know for the skills based assessment for Unit 1 *Recording income and receipts* and Unit 2 *Making and recording payments*. Icons clearly mark key areas of the text. Numerous activities throughout the text help you practise what you have just learnt.

Assessment Kit

When you have understood and practised the material in the Interactive Text, you will have the knowledge and experience to tackle the Assessment Kit for Unit 1 *Recording income and receipts* and Unit 2 *Making and recording payments*. This aims to get you through the assessment, whether in the form of the AAT simulation or in the workplace.

Passcards

These short memorable notes are focused on key topics for the Foundation Units, designed to remind you of what the Interactive Text has taught you.

INTRODUCTION

Recommended approach to this Interactive Text

(a) To achieve competence in Units 1 and 2 (and all the other units), you need to be able to do **everything** specified by the standards. Study the Interactive Text carefully and do not skip any of it.

(b) Learning is an **active** process. Do **all** the activities as you work through the Interactive Text so you can be sure you really understand what you have read. There is a checklist at the end of each chapter to show which knowledge and understanding, performance criteria and/or range statement is covered by each activity.

(c) After you have covered the material in the Interactive Text, work through the **Assessment Kit**.

(d) Before you take the assessment, check that you still remember the material using the following quick revision plan for each chapter.

   (i) Read and learn the **key learning points**, which are a summary of the chapter. This includes key terms and shows the sort of things likely to come up in an assessment. Are there any gaps in your knowledge? If so, study the section again.

   (ii) Do the **quick quiz** again. If you know what you're doing, it shouldn't take long.

   (iii) Go through the **Passcards** as often as you can in the weeks leading up to your assessment.

This approach is only a suggestion. Your college may well adapt it to suit your needs.

Quick quizzes

These include multiple choice questions, true/false and other formats not used by the AAT. However, these types of questions are usually very familiar to students and are used to help students adjust to otherwise unfamiliar material.

Remember this is a **practical** course.

(a) Try to relate the material to your experience in the workplace or any other work experience you may have had.

(b) Try to make as many links as you can to your study of the other Units at Foundation level.

(c) Keep this text, (hopefully) you will find it invaluable in your everyday work too!

Foundation qualification structure

The competence-based Education and Training Scheme of the Association of Accounting Technicians is based on an analysis of the work of accounting staff in a wide range of industries and types of organisation. The Standards of Competence for Accounting which students are expected to meet are based on this analysis.

The AAT issued new standards of competence in 2002, which take effect from 1 July 2003. This Text reflects the **new standards.**

The Standards identify the key purpose of the accounting occupation, which is to operate, maintain and improve systems to record, plan, monitor and report on the financial activities of an organisation, and a number of key roles of the occupation. Each key role is subdivided into units of competence, which are further divided into elements of competences. By successfully completing assessments in specified units of competence, students can gain qualifications at NVQ/SVQ levels 2, 3 and 4, which correspond to the AAT Foundation, Intermediate and Technician stages of competence respectively.

Whether you are competent in a Unit is demonstrated by means of:

- *Either* an Exam Based Assessment (set and marked by AAT assessors)
- *Or* a Skills Based Assessment (where competence is judged by an Approved Assessment Centre to whom responsibility for this is devolved)
- Or *both* Exam *and* Skills Based Assessment

Below we set out the overall structure of the Foundation (NVQ/SVQ Level 2) stage, indicating how competence in each Unit is assessed. In the next section there is more detail about the Skills Based Assessments for Units 1 and 2.

All units are assessed by Skills Based Assessment, and Unit 3 is also assessed by Exam Based Assessment.

INTRODUCTION

NVQ/SVQ Level 2 – Foundation (all units are mandatory)

All units are mandatory.

Unit 1	Recording Income and Receipts	Element 1.1	Process documents relating to goods and services supplied
		Element 1.2	Process receipts

Unit 2	Making and Recording Payments	Element 2.1	Process documents relating to goods and services received
		Element 2.2	Process payments

Unit 3	Preparing Ledger Balances and an Initial Trial Balance	Element 3.1	Balance bank transactions
		Element 3.2	Prepare ledger balances and control accounts
		Element 3.3	Draft an initial trial balance

Unit 4	Supplying Information for Management Control	Element 4.1	Code and extract information
		Element 4.2	Provide comparisons on costs and income

Unit 21	Working with Computers	Element 21.1	Use computer systems and software
		Element 21.2	Maintain the security of data

Unit 22	Contribute to the Maintenance of a Healthy, Safe and Productive Working Environment	Element 22.1	Contribute to the maintenance of a healthy, safe and productive working environment
		Element 22.2	Monitor and maintain an effective and efficient working environment

Unit 23	Achieving Personal Effectiveness	Element 23.1	Plan and organise your own work
		Element 23.2	Maintain good working relationships
		Element 23.3	Improve your own performance

Unit 1 Standards of competence

The structure of the Standards for Unit 1

The Unit commences with a statement of the **knowledge and understanding** which underpin competence in the Unit's elements.

The Unit of Competence is then divided into **elements of competence** describing activities which the individual should be able to perform.

Each element includes:

(a) A set of **performance criteria.** This defines what constitutes competent performance.

(b) A **range statement.** This defines the situations, contexts, methods etc in which competence should be displayed.

(c) **Evidence requirements.** These state that competence must be demonstrated consistently, over an appropriate time scale with evidence of performance being provided from the appropriate sources.

(d) **Sources of evidence.** These are suggestions of ways in which you can find evidence to demonstrate that competence. These fall under the headings: 'observed performance; work produced by the candidate; authenticated testimonies from relevant witnesses; personal account of competence; other sources of evidence.' They are reproduced in full in our Assessment Kit for Unit 1.

The elements of competence for Unit 1 *Recording income and receipts* are set out below. Knowledge and understanding required for the unit as a whole are listed first, followed by the performance criteria and range statements for each element. Performance criteria are cross-referenced below to chapters in this Unit 1 *Recording income and receipts* Interactive Text.

Unit 1: Recording income and receipts

What is the unit about?

This unit relates to the role of invoicing and receiving payments. The first element involves you in manually preparing and coding invoices and credit notes for goods and services supplied, and entering the details in both a manual and computerised accounting system. The element also requires you to prepare statements of account manually and as computerised output. It is expected that you will communicate with customers politely and effectively in response to their queries or when chasing payments.

The second element is concerned with checking and recording receipts in a manual and computerised system. The element requires you to deal with receipts in a variety of different forms and, therefore, to complete paying-in documents where necessary. You are required to deal with unusual features relating to wrongly completed cheques, out-of-date cheques, debit or credit cards limits exceeded and disagreement with supporting documentation. Where these features are outside of your own area of responsibility the element expects you to refer them to an appropriate person.

INTRODUCTION

Knowledge and understanding

The business environment

1. Types of business transactions and documents involved (Element 1.1)
2. Basic law relating to contract law and Sale of Goods Act (Elements 1.1 & 1.2)
3. Document retention policies (Elements 1.1 & 1.2)
4. General principles of VAT (Element 1.1)
5. Types of discounts (Element 1.1)
6. Cheques, including crossings and endorsements (Element 1.2)
7. The use of banking documentation (Element 1.2)
8. Automated payments (Element 1.2)
9. Credit limits (Elements 1.1 & 1.2)
10. Basic law relating to data protection (Element 1.2)

Accounting methods

11. Double entry bookkeeping, including balancing accounts (Elements 1.1 & 1.2)
12. Accounting for receipts from credit customers and customers without credit accounts (Elements 1.1 & 1.2)
13. Methods of coding data (Element 1.1)
14. Operation of manual accounting systems (Elements 1.1 & 1.2)
15. Operation of computerised accounting systems, including output (Elements 1.1 & 1.2)
16. The use of the cash book and petty cash book as part of the double entry system or as books of prime entry (Elements 1.1 & 1.2)
17. Batch control (Elements 1.1 & 1.2)
18. Relationship between accounting system and the ledger (Elements 1.1 & 1.2)
19. Credit card procedures (Element 1.2)
20. Methods of handling and storing money, including the security aspects (Element 1.2)
21. Petty cash procedures: imprest and non imprest methods; analysis (Elements 1.1 & 1.2)

The organisation

22. Relevant understanding of the organisation's accounting systems and administrative systems and procedures (Elements 1.1 & 1.2)
23. The nature of the organisation's business transactions (Elements 1.1 & 1.2)
24. Organisational procedures for authorisation and coding of sales invoices (Element 1.1)
25. Organisational procedures for filing source documents (Elements 1.1 & 1.2)
26. House style for correspondence (Element 1.1)
27. Banking and personal security procedures (Element 1.2)

INTRODUCTION

Element 1.1 Process documents relating to goods and services supplied

	Performance criteria	Chapters in this Text
A	Accurately prepare **invoices and credit notes** in accordance with organisational requirements and check against **source documents**	1
B	Ensure invoices and credit notes are correctly authorised before being sent to customers	1
C	Ensure invoices and credit notes are correctly **coded**	1, 3
D	Enter invoices and credit notes are entered into **books of prime entry** according to organisational procedures	3, 5
E	Enter invoices and credit notes in the appropriate **ledgers**	3, 5, 6
F	Produce **statements** of account for despatch to debtors	8
G	**Communicate** politely and effectively with customers regarding accounts, using the relevant information from the aged debtors analysis	8

	Range statement	
1	**Invoices and credit notes**: pricing; price extensions; discounts; VAT	1
2	**Source documents**: quotations; purchase orders; delivery notes; sales orders	1
3	**Coded**: manual systems; computerised systems	1, 3
4	**Books of prime entry**: manual sales daybook; manual sales returns daybook; relevant computerised records	3
5	**Ledgers**: manual main ledger; manual subsidiary ledger; computerised ledgers	3, 6
6	**Statements**: manual; computerised	8
7	**Communicate**: in response to queries; chase payments	8

Element 1.2 Process receipts

	Performance criteria	Chapters in this Text
A	Check **receipts** against relevant supporting information	10, 12
B	Enter receipts in appropriate **accounting records**	12
C	Prepare paying-in documents and reconcile to relevant records	11
D	Identify **unusual features** and either resolve or refer to the appropriate person	10, 11, 12

	Range statement	
1	**Receipts**: cash; cheques; an automated payment	10, 12
2	**Accounting records**: manual cash book; manual main ledger and subsidiary ledger; computerised records	12
3	**Unusual features**: wrongly completed cheques; out-of-date cheques; credit and debit card limits exceeded; disagreement with supporting documentation	10, 11, 12

Unit 2 Standards of competence

The structure of the Standards for Unit 2

The Unit commences with a statement of the **knowledge and understanding** which underpin competence in the Unit's elements.

The Unit of Competence is then divided into **elements of competence** describing activities which the individual should be able to perform.

Each element includes:

(a) A set of **performance criteria.** This defines what constitutes competent performance.

(b) A **range statement.** This defines the situations, contexts, methods etc in which competence should be displayed.

(c) **Evidence requirements.** These state that competence must be demonstrated consistently, over an appropriate time scale with evidence of performance being provided from the appropriate sources.

(d) **Sources of evidence.** These are suggestions of ways in which you can find evidence to demonstrate that competence. These fall under the headings: 'observed performance; work produced by the candidate; authenticated testimonies from relevant witnesses; personal account of competence; other sources of evidence.' They are reproduced in full in our Assessment Kit for Unit 2.

The elements of competence for Unit 2 *Making and recording payments* are set out below. Knowledge and understanding required for the unit as a whole are listed first, followed by the performance criteria and range statements for each element. Performance criteria are cross-referenced below to chapters in this Unit 2 *Making and recording payments* Interactive Text.

Unit 2: Making and recording payments

What is the unit about?

This unit relates to the organisation's expenditure. It includes dealing with documentation from suppliers and ordering and delivery documentation, preparing payments, recording expenditure in the appropriate records, and making payments relating to invoices, wages and salaries, and petty cash.

The first element is concerned with ensuring calculations and records of expenditure are correct and deducting available discounts. You are required to code and enter documents in a manual and computerised accounting system. You are also required to handle both verbal and written communications with suppliers in a polite and effective manner. However, you are not expected to deal with goods supplied under leasing or hire purchase contracts at this level.

The second element relates to preparing authorised payments, relating to creditors, payroll and petty cash. This involves you in selecting appropriate payment methods and ensuring that all payments are recorded and entered into the accounting records, both manual and computerised. This element also requires you to take responsibility for ensuring the security of relevant payment methods and to refer queries to the appropriate person.

INTRODUCTION

Knowledge and understanding

The business environment

1. Types of business transactions and documents involved (Element 2.1)
2. Basic law relating to contract law and Sale of Goods Act (Elements 2.1 & 2.2)
3. Document retention policies (Elements 2.1 & 2.2)
4. General principles of VAT (Element 2.1)
5. Types of discounts (Element 2.1)
6. Cheques, including crossing and endorsements (Element 2.2)
7. Automated payments (Elements 2.1 & 2.2)
8. Different ordering systems: Internet, verbal and written (Element 2.1)
9. Documentation for payments (Element 2.2)
10. Basic law relating to data protection (Element 2.2)

Accounting methods

11. Double entry bookkeeping, including balancing accounts (Elements 2.1 & 2.2)
12. Accounting for payments to credit suppliers, and to suppliers where a credit account is not available (Elements 2.1 & 2.2)
13. Capital and revenue expenditure (Elements 2.1 & 2.2)
14. Methods of coding data (Element 2.1)
15. Operation of manual accounting systems (Elements 2.1 & 2.2)
16. Operation of computerised accounting systems, including outputs (Elements 2.1 & 2.2)
17. The use of the cash book and petty cash book as part of the double entry system or as books of prime entry (Elements 2.1 & 2.2)
18. Batch control (Elements 2.1 & 2.2)
19. Relationship between accounting system and ledger (Elements 2.1 & 2.2)
20. Credit card procedures (Elements 2.1 & 2.2)
21. Petty cash procedures: imprest and non imprest methods; analysis (Element 2.2)
22. Payroll accounting procedures: accounting for gross pay and statutory and non-statutory deductions through the wages and salaries control account; payments to external agencies; security and control; simple gross pay to net calculations but excluding the use of tax and NI tables (Element 2.1)
23. Methods of handling and storing money from a security aspect (Element 2.2)

The organisation

24. Relevant understanding of the organisation's accounting systems and administrative systems and procedures (Elements 2.1 & 2.2)
25. The nature of the organisation's business transactions (Elements 2.1 & 2.2)
26. Organisational procedures for authorisation and coding of purchase invoices and payments (Elements 2.1 & 2.2)
27. House style for correspondence (Element 2.1)
28. Organisational procedures for filing source information (Elements 2.1 & 2.2)

xiii

INTRODUCTION

Element 2.1 Process documents relating to goods and services received

	Performance criteria	Chapters in this Text
A	Check suppliers' invoices and credit notes against relevant **documents** for validity	2
B	Check **calculations** on suppliers' invoices and credit notes for accuracy	2
C	Identify and deduct available **discounts**	2
D	Correctly **code** invoices and credit notes	4
E	Correctly enter invoices and credit notes into **books of prime entry** according to organisational procedures	4, 5
F	Enter invoices and credit notes in the appropriate **ledgers**	5, 7
G	Identify **discrepancies** and either resolve or refer to the appropriate person if outside own authority	2, 9
H	**Communicate** appropriately with suppliers regarding accounts	9

	Range statement	
1	**Documents**: orders; suppliers' invoices; delivery notes; credit notes	2
2	**Calculations**: pricing; price extensions and VAT; bulk, trade and settlement discounts	2
3	**Code**: manual systems; computerised systems	4
4	**Discounts**: settlement	2, 7
5	**Books of prime entry**: manual purchases day book; manual purchases returns day book; relevant computerised records	4
6	**Ledgers**: manual main ledger; manual subsidiary ledger; computerised ledgers	7
7	**Discrepancies**: incorrect calculations; non-delivery of goods charged; duplicated invoices; incorrect discounts	2, 9
8	**Communicate**: orally; in writing	9

Element 2.2 Process payments

	Performance criteria	Chapters in this Text
A	Calculate **payments** from relevant **documentation**	13,15,16
B	Schedule payments and obtain authorisation	13,15,16
C	Use the appropriate **payment method** and timescale, in accordance with organisational procedures	13,15,16
D	Enter payments into **accounting records**	14,15,16
E	Identify **queries** and resolve or refer to the appropriate person	13,14,15
F	Ensure security and confidentiality is maintained according to organisational requirements	13,15,16

Range statement

1	**Payments**: payroll; creditors; petty cash	13,15,16
2	**Documentation**: petty cash claims; suppliers' statements; payslips; cheque requisitions	13,15,16
3	**Payment method**: cash; cheques; an automated payment	13,15,16
4	**Accounting records**: manual cash book; manual petty cash book; manual main ledger; manual subsidiary ledger; computerised records	14,15
5	**Queries relating to**: unauthorised claims for payment; insufficient supporting evidence; claims exceeding authorised limit	13,15

Assessment strategy

Unit 1 and Unit 2 are assessed by **skills based assessment**.

Skills based assessment is a means of collecting evidence of your ability to carry out practical activities and to **operate effectively in the conditions of the workplace** to the standards required. Evidence may be collected at your place of work or at an Approved Assessment Centre by means of simulations of workplace activity, or by a combination of these methods.

If the Approved Assessment Centre is a **workplace** you may be observed carrying out accounting activities as part of your normal work routine. You should collect documentary evidence of the work you have done, or contributed, in an **accounting portfolio**. Evidence collected in a portfolio can be assessed in addition to observed performance or where it is not possible to assess by observation.

Where the Approved Assessment Centre is a **college or training organisation**, assessment will be by means of a combination of the following.

- (a) Documentary evidence of activities carried out at the workplace, collected by you in an **accounting portfolio**
- (b) Realistic **simulations** of workplace activities; these simulations may take the form of case studies and in-tray exercises and involve the use of primary documents and reference sources
- (c) **Projects and assignments** designed to assess the Standards of Competence

If you are unable to provide workplace evidence, you will be able to complete the assessment requirements by the alternative methods listed above.

Building your portfolio

What is a portfolio?

A portfolio is a collection of work that demonstrates what the owner can do. In AAT language the portfolio demonstrates **competence**.

A painter will have a collection of his paintings to exhibit in a gallery, an advertising executive will have a range of advertisements and ideas that she has produced to show to a prospective client. Both the collection of paintings and the advertisements form the portfolio of that artist or advertising executive.

Your portfolio will be unique to you just as the portfolio of the artist will be unique because no one will paint the same range of pictures in the same way. It is a very personal collection of your work and should be treated as a **confidential** record.

What evidence should a portfolio include?

No two portfolios will be the same but by following some simple guidelines you can decide which of the following suggestions will be appropriate in your case.

(a) **Your current CV**

This should be at the front. It will give your personal details as well as brief descriptions of posts you have held with the most recent one shown first.

(b) **References and testimonials**

References from previous employers may be included especially those of which you are particularly proud.

(c) **Your current job description**

You should emphasise financial **responsibilities and duties**.

(d) **Your student record sheets**

These should be supplied by AAT when you begin your studies, and your training provider should also have some if necessary.

(e) **Evidence from your current workplace**

This could take many forms including **letters, memos, reports** you have written, **copies of accounts** or **reconciliations** you have prepared, **discrepancies** you have investigated etc. Remember to obtain permission to include the evidence from your line manager because some records may be sensitive. Discuss the performance criteria that are listed in your Student Record Sheets with your training provider and employer, and think of other evidence that could be appropriate to you.

(f) **Evidence from your social activities**

For example you may be the treasurer of a club in which case examples of your cash and banking records could be appropriate.

(g) **Evidence from your studies**

Few students are able to satisfy all the requirements of competence by workplace evidence alone. They therefore rely on simulations to provide the remaining evidence to complete a unit. If you are not working or not working in a relevant post, then you may need to rely more heavily on simulations as a source of evidence.

INTRODUCTION

(h) **Additional work**

Your training provider may give you work that specifically targets one or a group of performance criteria in order to complete a unit. It could take the form of questions, presentations or demonstrations. Each training provider will approach this in a different way.

(i) **Evidence from a previous workplace**

This evidence may be difficult to obtain and should be used with caution because it must satisfy the 'rules' of evidence, that is it must be current. Only rely on this as evidence if you have changed jobs recently.

(j) **Prior achievements**

For example you may have already completed the health and safety unit during a previous course of study, and therefore there is no need to repeat this work. Advise your training provider who will check to ensure that it is the same unit and record it as complete if appropriate.

How should it be presented?

As you assemble the evidence remember to **make a note** of it on your Student Record Sheet in the space provided and **cross reference** it. In this way it is easy to check to see if your evidence is **appropriate**. Remember one piece of evidence may satisfy a number of performance criteria so remember to check this thoroughly and discuss it with your training provider if in doubt.

To keep all your evidence together a ring binder or lever arch file is a good means of storage.

When should evidence be assembled?

You should begin to assemble evidence **as soon as you have registered as a student**. **Don't leave it all** until the last few weeks of your studies, because you may miss vital deadlines and your resulting certificate sent by the AAT may not include all the units you have completed. Give yourself and your training provider time to examine your portfolio and report your results to AAT at regular intervals. In this way the task of assembling the portfolio will be spread out over a longer period of time and will be presented in a more professional manner.

What are the key criteria that the portfolio must fulfil?

As you assemble your evidence bear in mind that it must be:

- **Valid**. It must relate to the Standards.
- **Authentic**. It must be your own work.
- **Current**. It must refer to your current or most recent job.
- **Sufficient**. It must meet all the performance criteria by the time you have completed your portfolio.

What are the most important elements in a portfolio that covers Units 1 and 2?

You should remember that the units are about **receipts** and **payments**. Therefore you need to produce evidence to demonstrate that you can carry out certain tasks.

For Element 1.1 *Process documents relating to goods and services supplied* you need to show that you have prepared invoices and credit notes in accordance with your organisation's procedures and that you have **checked** them prior to despatch. If you have a checklist, this could be attached to copy invoices that you have prepared. You will also need evidence of source documents, such as a purchase order and delivery note. Reports and memos can provide evidence of communications with debtors.

The main evidence that you need for Element 1.2 *Process receipts* relates to paying-in cheques, etc and recording the receipt in the cash book and sales ledger.

Element 2.1 *Process documents relating to goods and services received* is similar to Element 1.1. You need copy purchase orders, delivery notes and service book records; and evidence that suppliers' invoices have been checked to these source documents eg by completion of a stamp on the invoice.

With Element 2.2 *Process payments*, the emphasis is on authorisation. You will need evidence that cheque payments have been authorised eg invoice marked 'approved for payment' or whatever system your organisation uses. For petty cash, there should be an authorised petty cash voucher. You will also need evidence that you know suitable methods of making a payment eg a bill for £1,000 should not be made out of petty cash or that a milk bill for £10 should be paid out of petty cash. You will need to show that you know how to record payments in the cash book and purchase ledger.

Finally

Remember that the portfolio is **your property** and **your responsibility**. Not only could it be presented to the external verifier before your award can be confirmed; it could be used when you are seeking **promotion** or applying for a more senior and better paid post elsewhere. How your portfolio is presented can say as much about you as the evidence inside.

> For further information about portfolios, BPP have produced a book *Building Your Portfolio*. It can be ordered using the order form at the back of this book or at *www.bpp.com/aat*.

INTRODUCTION

PART A

Accounting for sales and purchases

chapter 1

Sales invoicing and issuing credit notes

Contents

1 The problem
2 The solution
3 Documenting the supply of goods and services
4 The invoice
5 Methods of coding data
6 Discounts, rebates and allowances
7 VAT
8 Credit notes and debit notes
9 Customer credit limits
10 Generation of invoices and credit notes by computer

Performance criteria

1.1.A Accurately prepare invoices and credit notes in accordance with organisational requirements and check against source documents
1.1.B Ensure invoices and credit notes are correctly authorised before being sent to customers
1.1.C Ensure invoices and credit notes are correctly coded

Range statement

1.1.1 Invoices and credit notes: pricing; price extensions; discounts; VAT
1.1.2 Source documents: quotations; purchase orders; delivery notes; sales orders
1.1.3 Coded: manual systems; computerised systems

Knowledge and understanding

1 Types of business transactions and documents involved
4 General principles of VAT
5 Types of discounts
9 Credit limits
13 Methods of coding data
14 Operation of manual accounting systems
15 Operation of computerised accounting systems, including output
24 Organisational procedures for authorisation and coding of sales invoices

PART A   ACCOUNTING FOR SALES AND PURCHASES

Signpost
The topics covered in this chapter are relevant to **Unit 1**.

1 The problem

The local supermarket sells goods for immediate cash payment and so does not need to issue anything more than a receipt for the cash paid.

However, many businesses sell goods on credit. This means that the customer receives the goods now, but does not pay for them until, say, 30 days later.

These businesses need a method of keeping track of the sales they make.

- The correct goods are sent out to customers
- All goods sent out to customers are paid for
- If a customer returns goods, that the returns are in good condition and the customer receives a refund

Therefore the business needs a way of recording a customer's orders, to ensure that the customer is sent the correct goods. This will also act as a check if the customer disputes ordering the goods.

The business also needs to know what goods are sent out to a customer. If a customer returns goods, these need to be in good condition, so that they can be resold.

Finally, the business needs to make sure that the customer is sent a bill (**sales invoice**) for the goods sent out and that a refund (or **credit note**) is issued for all goods returned in good condition.

2 The solution

Many businesses solve the problem by having a sales department. This may be a separate unit or part of the accounts department.

A sales department works in the following way.

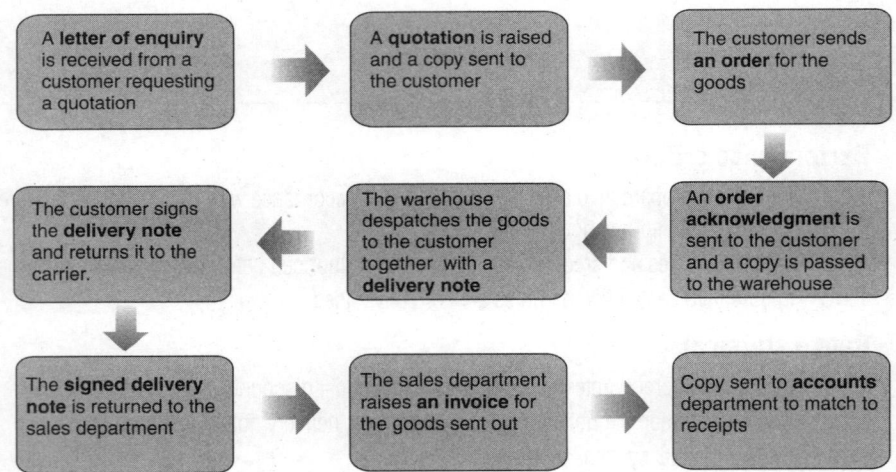

This represents an **ideal situation**. Businesses will vary on the amount of documents they produce. For example, an accountancy firm providing **services** will have no need for a delivery note.

1: SALES INVOICING AND ISSUING CREDITS

3 Documenting the supply of goods and services

3.1 The contract

Basic aspects of the **law of contract** are covered in Chapter 17. All you need to know now is that:

- A contract may be in **writing** or **spoken** (oral)
- It becomes legally binding when the two parties **agree**

For the purposes of this chapter, a sales contract is binding when the customer sends an order and the business accepts it, eg by sending an order acknowledgement.

3.2 The letter of enquiry and quotation

Someone who wants to buy goods may send a **letter of enquiry** to the seller to find out the cost.

 **ANYWHERE REMOVALS LIMITED**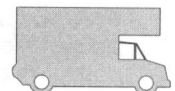

64 Luton Road, Dunford DN4 4PN

Telephone (01990) 42254 Fax (01990) 42401 VAT Reg No 943 441417

Pickett (Handling Equipment) Ltd
Unit 7
Western Industrial Estate
Dunford
DN2 7RJ

7 March 20X2

Dear Sirs

I shall be grateful if you will send me as soon as possible your quotation for the supply of the items listed below. Your quotation should indicate the delivery period.

6 x Medium weight sack trucks
2 x Low loading platform trucks

Yours faithfully

M Stephens

M Stephens (Mr)
General Manager

Registered office: 64 Luton Road, Dunford DN4 4PN   *Registered in England No 9482472*

The seller will send a **quotation** giving details of the goods and their cost.

PART A   ACCOUNTING FOR SALES AND PURCHASES

Pickett (Handling Equipment) Limited
Unit 7 Western Industrial Estate
Dunford DN2 7RJ
Tel: (01990) 72101 Fax: (01990) 72980 VAT Reg No 982 721349

11 March 20X2

Mr M Stephens
Anywhere Removals Ltd
64 Luton Road
Dunford DN4 4PN

Dear Mr Stephens   QUOTATION

Thank you for your letter dated 7 March 20X2. We are pleased to be able to provide a quotation as follows. This quotation is valid for a period of three months from the date of this letter, after which a new quotation will be supplied on request.

6 Medium weight sack trucks, Cat No ST 200 @ £52.50 each. 25mm 14 gauge steel tube. 30cm x 15cm toe plate. 98cm high x 48cm wide. 20cm cushion tyres. Available in blue or red.

2 Low loading platform trucks, Cat No PT 410 @ £117.00 each. 200kg capacity. Wheels 200mm x 50mm cushion tyres with roller bearings and two 125mm swivel castors. Timber platform. 107cm long x 61cm wide. Available in red only.

The above prices are subject to VAT at the standard rate of 17.5%.

Yours sincerely,

P Morley

P Morley
Sales Manager

Registered Office: 4 Arkwright Road, London E16 4PQ Registered in England No 2182417

The documents need not be in a letter format.

- The letter of enquiry may be a **standard printed form**.
- The quotation may be a **pre-printed price list** or catalogue giving details of product descriptions and prices.

The business may deal regularly with the seller and so already knows the current prices. There will be **no need for a quotation** and the buyer (purchaser) may start with a **purchase order**.

Activity 1.1

Kris owns a florist's shop, Aroma. As well as making cash sales in the shop, he also supplies potted plants to local offices and looks after the plants. He charges the offices monthly for this service.

He has received the following letter of enquiry

Dax Office Supplies Ltd

6 High Street
Market Town
MT5 2LH

Aroma
4 The Boulevard
Market Town
MT2 3AB

12 March 20X7

Dear Sir,

I am interested in your office plant service, as advertised in Yellow Pages.

Please could you let me have a quotation for the following.

1 Provision and care of 4 large evergreen shrubs in separate containers.
2 Provision and care of 6 small flowering plants in one container.

Yours faithfully

J Dax

J Dax
Office manager

Kris can supply the following:

	£
Large evergreen shrub in container, including maintenance	40 per month
Small evergreen shrub in container, including maintenance	25 per month
Large flowing shrubs in container, including maintenance	45 per month
Small flowing shrubs in container, including maintenance	30 per month
Planter containing 6 small flowering plants, including maintenance	75 per month

Prepare a quotation using the attached form. All prices exclude VAT. Today's date is 15 March 20X7. Leave the VAT and total lines blank for the moment.

PART A ACCOUNTING FOR SALES AND PURCHASES

Aroma

4 The Boulevard
Market Town
MT2 3AB

Quotation No 762

To:

Address:

Date:

DETAILS	PRICE EXCL VAT
	Sales
	VAT @ 17.5%
	Total

3.3 The order

If the customer finds the quotation satisfactory, he or she will send a **purchase order**.

ANYWHERE REMOVALS LIMITED

64 Luton Road Dunford DN4 4PN
Telephone (01990) 42254 Fax (01990) 42401 VAT Reg No 943 441417

Purchase order   NO: 9607

Pickett (Handling Equipment) Ltd
Unit 7
Western Industrial Estate
Dunford
DN2 7RJ

14 March 20X2

Quantity	Cat. No.	Description	Unit price £	Total price £
6	ST 200	Medium weight sack trucks (colour red)	52.50	315.00
2	PT 410	Low loading platform trucks	117.00	234.00
				549.00
		VAT @ 17.5%		96.07
		Total		645.07

Delivery to:
Anywhere Removals Ltd 64 Luton Road Dunford DN4 4PN

Delivery within 7 days, carriage paid

M Stephens

M Stephens
General Manager

3.3.1 Sellers' own order forms

A customer may use an **order form produced by the selling firm** and sent out with their catalogue or price list.

- Useful if the goods need detailed product codes
- Helps to ensure that the buyer **includes all the details required**
- Helps to **speed** the processing of orders by the use of a standard form
- Order can be matched with **delivery notes** and **invoices** of a similar format
- Computers may be able to read orders in a standard format

PART A ACCOUNTING FOR SALES AND PURCHASES

Even if a business receives a customer's own purchase order form, it may choose to transfer the details to its own internal **sales order form.** The corresponding customer purchase order should be filed with it.

This has the following additional advantages.

- The internal sales order shows that a customer's order is being **processed**
- **Prenumbering** the internal sales order forms helps to control sales orders eg which order came in first

3.4 Order acknowledgement

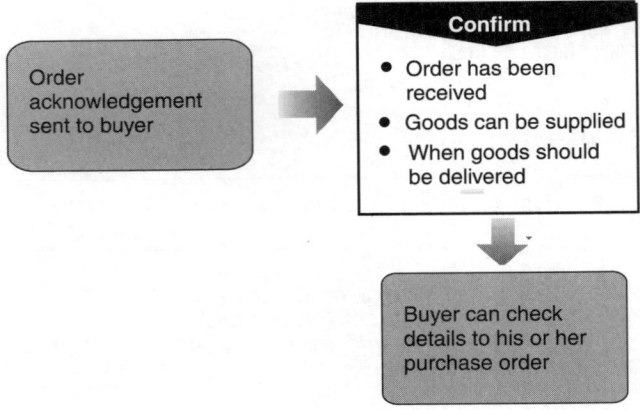

Activity 1.2

Dax Office Supplies Ltd have accepted the quotation prepared in Activity 1.1. Complete the following order acknowledgement. This will be Aroma's sales order no 543, today's date is 20 March 20X7 and the provision of plants will start on 1 April 20X7. Once again, ignore the VAT and total lines, for the time being.

1: SALES INVOICING AND ISSUING CREDITS

Aroma

4 The Boulevard
Market Town
MT2 3AB

ORDER ACKNOWLEDGEMENT 1724

To:

Address:

Date:

Sales order no:

DETAILS	PRICE EXCL VAT

Provision of plants to commence on

Sales

VAT @ 17.5%

Total

PART A   ACCOUNTING FOR SALES AND PURCHASES

3.5 Sales order set

An order acknowledgement may be produced as part of a **sales order set** which might be made up as follows.

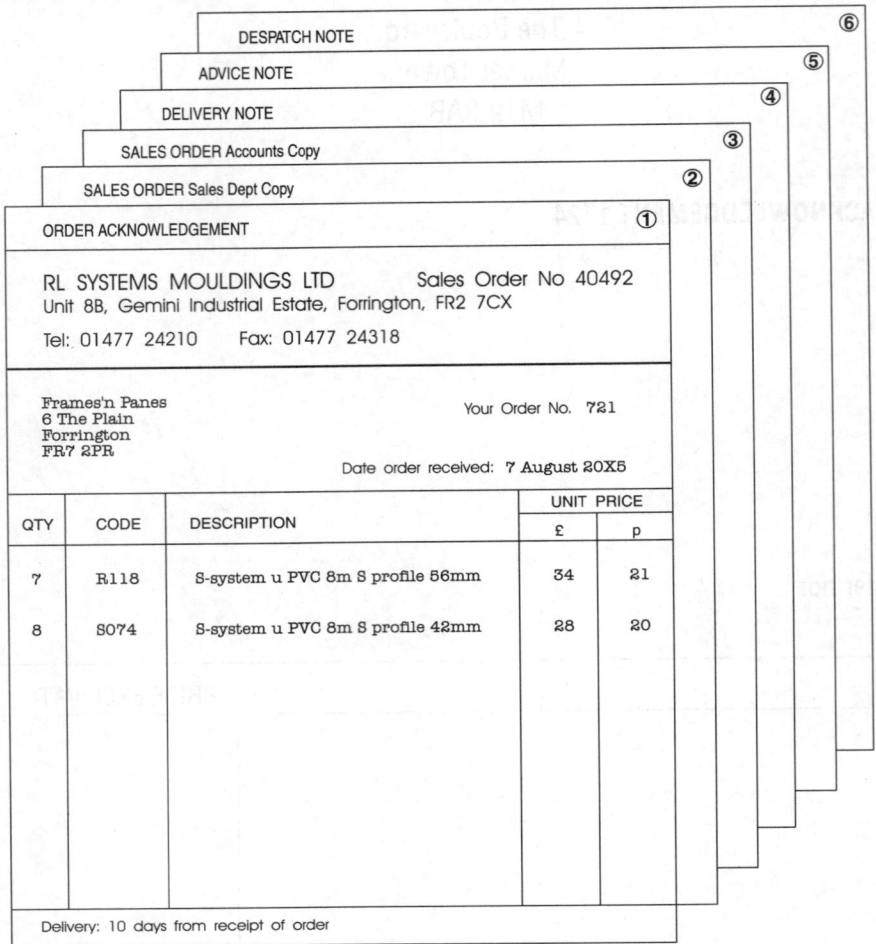

Key

1   Sent to the customer.

2   Sales order kept by the sales department to help deal with any queries. If the customer has sent in their own order form, this should be attached to it.

3   Copy sales order sent to accounts office. This will be filed to be matched with delivery note and invoice.

4   This is sent out with the goods. The purchaser signs the note as proof that the goods have been delivered. This is brought back to the supplier and matched to the sales order, so that an invoice can be raised.

5   This also goes out with the goods. However, it is left with the purchaser to enable him to check that the correct goods have been sent.

6   Warehouse copy. The storekeeper uses this copy to gather together the order. He enters the date of despatch and keeps this copy in case of query.

Remember that the sales department may be part of the accounts department, in which case there will be no need for separate copies 2 and 3.

4 The invoice

4.1 Invoice format

STUDENT SUPPLIES LIMITED
123 Factory Street Worktown London W19 4NB
Tel: 0181 123 4567 Fax: 0181 123 4589
(a)

INVOICE

Invoice Number: 1496 (l)
Your Order No: 3365 (m)

INVOICE TO:
Westshire County Council
46 Chamber Street
Camberwick Green
CG2 4SP
(b)

DELIVER TO:
Brilliant Primary School
School Road
Booktown
BK1 1AA
(c)

Date of Invoice/Taxpoint:
(d) 9 May 20X5

Date of Supply:
(e) 6 May 20X5

ITEM CODE	QUANTITY	DESCRIPTION	UNIT PRICE £	AMOUNT £
17004	450	12" Wooden rulers	0.12	54.00
	(f)	(g)	(h)	

SALES VALUE: 54.00
VAT AT 17.5%: 8.97
AMOUNT PAYABLE: 62.97

(i) (j) (k)
VAT No 245 8269 41   Terms: 5/7, n/30

PART A   ACCOUNTING FOR SALES AND PURCHASES

Key

(a)   The **name and address** of the **seller**

(b)   The **name and address** of the **purchaser**

(c)   **Delivery address** – Sometimes a purchaser wants the goods delivered to another address. In this example, the county council is paying for the goods but wants them delivered to the school who will be using them.

(d)   **Date** of the invoice and **tax point** – The tax point is the date of the sale for VAT purposes (usually the same as the invoice date)

(e)   Date of **supply** ie despatch date

(f)   **Quantity** of goods sold

(g)   **Description** of goods sold

(h)   **Price per unit** of goods sold, ie each ruler costs 12p

(i)   **VAT registration number** of the seller (only if the seller is registered for VAT)

(j)   **Terms of sale** eg '5/7' means 5% cash discount if paid within 7 days and 'n/30' means 'net 30 days' – net payment due 30 days after the invoice date

(k)   **Total amount** payable, including details and rate of VAT charged

(l)   **Invoice number,** the stationery is usually pre-numbered for control purposes

(m)   **Customer's reference** eg the customer's order number

Note: The VAT has been calculated on the gross amount less discount, which will be explained later in this chapter.

Other terms which you may come across on invoices include the following.

- **E & OE.** Usually printed at the bottom of an invoice, it means 'Errors and omissions excepted'. The seller reserves the right to correct any errors or any omissions at a later date (eg if there is an incorrect price on the invoice).

- **Carriage paid.** This means that the invoice price includes delivery of the goods to the buyer.

- **Ex works.** The invoice price does not include delivery, and the purchaser must therefore arrange transport.

- **Cash on delivery** or **COD.** The goods will have to be paid for in cash at the time of delivery to the buyer's premises.

- **FOB.** These letters stand for the words 'free on board' and may be found on import or export invoices. Prices exclude transport costs. 'FOB shipping point' means that the supplier pays all costs of carriage (shipping, insurance and freight for example) up to the point of shipping but the customer has to pay any carriage costs from that point on.

- **CIF.** In contrast to FOB, transport costs are included in prices. (The letters stand for 'cost, insurance, freight' or 'charged in full'.)

- **Proforma.** A proforma invoice includes all the details of a normal invoice but is not recorded in the accounting system. It is like a **dummy invoice**. A proforma is usually raised when cash must be received

before, or at the time of, delivery. Having a proforma allows the customer to prepare the necessary documentation to pay for the goods, but means that the seller does not record the sale until the cash is received.

Invoice forms of different businesses will be **designed in different ways**. However, they all show the same type of information.

4.2 Numbering of invoices

A business will **sequentially number the sales invoices** it issues, so that it can keep track of all the invoices it sends out.

A business needs to know that blank invoices are not misused by someone to obtain money dishonestly. There may be **security procedures** to ensure this, eg keeping blank invoices locked in a cupboard and maintaining registers of invoice forms. Any spoiled invoices should be kept, to prove that the form has not gone astray.

4.3 Checks over invoicing

A business will want to have **checking procedures** so that the invoices it sends out are correct.

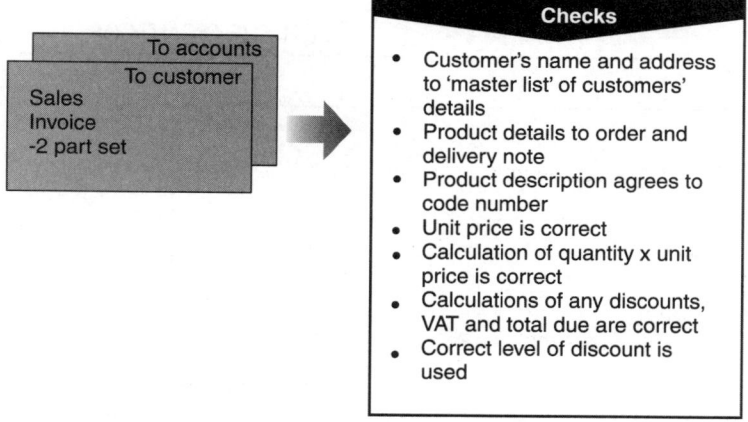

Ideally, there should be **segregation of duties.** The three areas of order acceptance, despatch of goods, and preparation of invoices should be carried out by different people.

PART A ACCOUNTING FOR SALES AND PURCHASES

Activity 1.3

Using the information in activities 1.1 and 1.2, complete the following invoice to Dax Office Supplies Ltd for the month of April 20X7. The invoice should be dated 1 May 20X1. Ignore VAT.

Aroma
4 The Boulevard
Market Town
MT2 3AB

SALES INVOICE NO 1762

To:

Address:

Date: FOR THE MONTH OF:

DETAILS	PRICE

Payment terms: 30 days   Sales

                                  VAT @ 17.5%

                                  Total

E & OE

5 Methods of coding data

5.1 Reasons for coding data

Each account in an accounting system has a **unique code**. If there were two customers called John Smith, you can tell their accounts apart by the different codes.

Coding saves time in copying out data because **codes are shorter** than 'longhand' descriptions. For this reason, and also to save storage space, computer systems make use of coded data.

In a sales system, the most obvious examples of codes are as follows.

- Customer account numbers
- Sales invoice numbers
- Product code numbers

These are all codes a business sets up and applies internally. External codes which affect the business include **bank account numbers** and **bank sort codes**.

Various coding systems (or combinations of them) may be used when designing codes. These are described below.

5.2 Sequence codes

Sequence codes make no attempt to classify the item to be coded. It is simply given the next available number in a rising sequence. New items can only be inserted at the end of the list and therefore the codes for similar items may be very different.

Sequence codes are rarely used when a large number of items are involved, except for document numbering (eg invoice numbers).

5.3 Block codes

Block codes provide a different sequence for each different group of items. For example for a particular firm, customers may be divided up according to area:

South East	code numbers 10,000-19,999
South West	code numbers 20,000-29,999
Wales	code numbers 30,000-39,999

The coding of customer accounts is then sequential within each block.

5.4 Significant digit codes

Significant digit codes incorporate some digit(s) which is (are) part of the descriptions of the item being coded. An example is:

5000	Electric light bulbs
5025	25 watt
5040	40 watt
5060	60 watt
5100	100 watt
etc	

5.5 Hierarchical codes

Hierarchical codes are allocated on the basis of a tree structure where the interrelationship between the items is of the paramount importance. A well known example is the Universal Decimal Code used by most libraries. For example:

5	Business
5 2	Finance
5 2 1	Cost accounting
5 2 1.4	Standard costing
5 2 1.4 7	Variance analysis
5 2 1.4 7 3	Fixed overhead variances

5.6 Faceted codes

Faceted codes are made up of a number of sections, each section of the code representing a different feature of the item. For example in a clothing store there might be a code based on the following facets.

Garment type	Customer type	Colour	Size	Style

If SU stood for suit, M for man and B for blue, a garment could be given the code SU M B 40 17. Similarly ND F W 14 23 could stand for a woman's white nightdress size 14, style 23. One of the great advantages of this system is that the type of item can be recognised from the code.

Faceted codes may be entirely numeric. For example, a large international company may allocate code numbers for each sales representative on the basis that:

Digit 1	Continent (eg America – 1, Europe – 2)
Digits 2/3	Country (eg England – 06)
Digit 4	Area (eg North – 3)
Digits 5/6	Representative's name (eg Mr J Walker – 14)

The code number may be expressed as 2/06/3/14.

5.7 Coding in the accounts ledger

An accounts general ledger will consist of a **large number of coded accounts**. For example, part of a general ledger might be as follows.

Account code	Account name
100200	Plant and machinery (cost)
100300	Motor vehicles (cost)
300000	Total debtors
400000	Total creditors
500130	Wages and salaries
500140	Rent and rates
500150	Advertising expenses
500160	Bank charges
500170	Motor expenses
500180	Telephone expenses
600000	Sales
700000	Cash

A business will choose its own codes for its general ledger accounts. The codes given in the above table are purely imaginary.

Activity 1.4

State what type of code is being used in section 5.7 above. Explain your answer.

6 Discounts, rebates and allowances

6.1 Types of discount

There are two types of discount.

Trade discount
- Offered to frequent customers or those buying in bulk
- Discount is deducted from the price of the goods at the time of sale
- It **reduces the cost** of the goods

Cash/settlement discount
- Offered for immediate payment
- Offered if customer pays the invoice within a specified time eg 7 days
- It **reduces the amount to be paid**

Example: Discounts

Martin trades widely in his district. In particular, he has three customers.

(a) Maurice is in the same business as Martin and receives 5% trade discount.

(b) Sol receives a trade discount of 7% once sales exceed £100.

(c) Tony receives a 10% cash discount for immediate payment or a 5% cash discount for all items paid for within 30 days of purchase.

In January 20X7, Martin makes sales of goods worth the following amounts before discounts have been deducted.

(a) To Maurice: £400
(b) To Sol: £700
(c) To Tony: £350 cash
£700 to be paid on 14.1.X7 for goods purchased on 3.1.X7

Calculate how much Martin has allowed as discounts in January. How much were trade and cash discounts?

Solution

		£	
Maurice	£400 × 5%	20	Trade
Sol	£700 × 7%	49	Trade
Tony	£350 × 10%	35	Cash: immediate
	£700 × 5%	35	Cash: prompt
		139	

Activity 1.5

Kris has an arrangement to supply flowers to Country Marquees. They need lots of cut flowers to decorate the inside of their tents and marquees. Therefore Kris has granted them the following discounts.

Discount of 5% on purchases over £100

Discount of 5% on settlement within 7 days and 2½% on settlement within 14 days. All invoices to be paid within 30 days of issue.

During March 20X7, Country Marquees have purchased flowers worth £2,000. Kris issued an invoice on 31 March 20X7 for the March sales. Calculate the trade and cash discounts available if Country Marquees pay £500 on 7 April, £1,000 on 14 April and £500 on 30 April. Ignore VAT.

6.2 Accounting for discounts

Trade Discount
A **reduction** in the amount of money demanded from a customer

- Deducted from the sales figure
- The sales figure on the invoice is shown **net** of the discount

Cash discount
An **optional** reduction in the amount due to be paid by the customer

- As the discount is optional, it is a matter of **financial**, not trading policy of the customer
- Encourages the customer to pay earlier
- As the taking of the discount is outside the control of the seller, the full sale price is recorded on the invoice
- If the discount is taken, it is recorded separately

PART A ACCOUNTING FOR SALES AND PURCHASES

Activity 1.6

Kris sells flowers to Country Marquees with a list price of £22,000. Kris offers a special deal of 10% trade discount, and a 2½% cash discount for payment within 20 days.

Tasks

Note. Ignore VAT.

(a) Calculate the amount Country Marquees will have to pay if it delays longer than 20 days before paying.

(b) Calculate the amount Country Marquees will pay if it pays within 20 days.

(c) Complete the blanks in the following table to show how the figures will appear on Kris' sales invoice.

Description		Price
Flowers	– list price	
	– less trade discount (…..%)	_____
	Sales	£____

Terms:

Net 30 days
Discount ………% if paid within ……….. days

6.3 Other types of discount

Businesses may offer other kinds of 'discounts' as incentives, to encourage buying in bulk or discourage buying from other businesses.

Rebates and **allowances** are very common and they are only mentioned briefly here.

A **rebate** is where the gas company (for example) will lower its overall tariff for customers who use over a certain number of units per year. The rebate is given in one of the following forms.

- A reduction in the bills for the following year
- A cheque for the calculated rebate amount

An **allowance** is giving a few extra units free of charge, if a certain number of units are ordered at one time. For instance, a video shop orders 50 videos and is sent another five **free of charge.**

7 VAT

7.1 General background

Many business transactions involve VAT (Value Added Tax), and most invoices show any VAT charged separately.

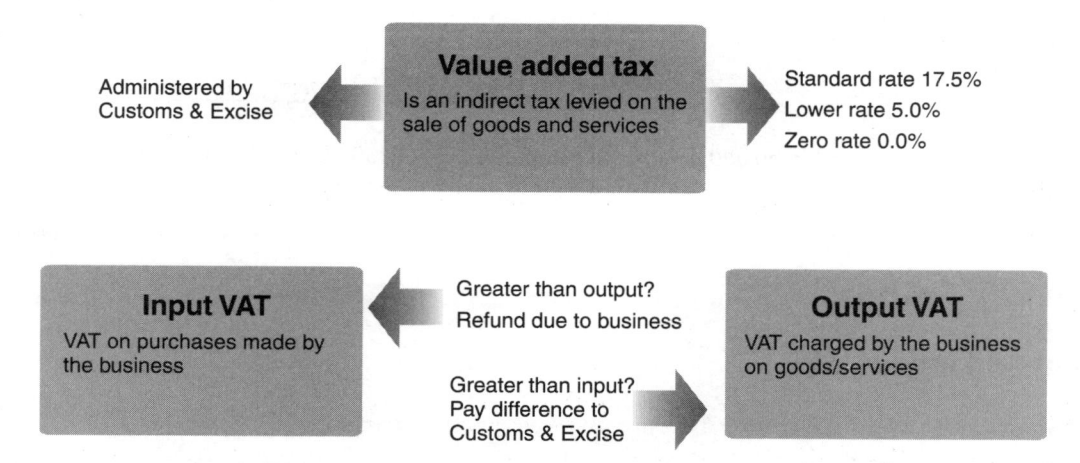

Value added tax is an indirect tax levied on the sale of goods and services.

- Administered by Customs & Excise
- Standard rate 17.5%
- Lower rate 5.0%
- Zero rate 0.0%

Input VAT: VAT on purchases made by the business

Output VAT: VAT charged by the business on goods/services

- Greater than output? Refund due to business
- Greater than input? Pay difference to Customs & Excise

VAT is charged by all members of the European Union (EU), though at different rates. Some countries, for example, charge 5% for some kinds of product and 10% on others.

Not all goods and services have VAT on them. **Exempt items** are not part of the VAT system.

7.2 Calculating VAT

If a standard rated product has a **net price** of £120, then the VAT is 17½% of £120.

VAT = £120 × 17.5/100
    = £21

The **gross price** of the product is therefore £120 + £21 = £141.

Gross price = Net price + VAT

	£
Purchaser pays gross price	141
Customs and Excise take VAT	(21)
Seller keeps net price	120

If the gross price of a standard rated product is £282, then you can work out the VAT which it includes by multiplying by 17.5/117.5 (or 7/47).

£282 × 17.5/117.5 = £42

Therefore the net price must be £282 − £42 = £240.

PART A ACCOUNTING FOR SALES AND PURCHASES

Where the calculation involves pence, then the rule is to round **down to the nearest penny**. For example

	£
Net price	25.75
VAT at 17½% (£25.75 ×17½% = £4.50625)	4.50
	30.25

Activity 1.7

The gross price of product A is £705.60 and the net price of product B is £480.95. What is the VAT @ 17.5% charged on each product?

7.3 Input and output VAT

Output tax received	Input tax paid	Total	Treatment
£1,000	£(900)	£100 received	Pay to C&E
£900	£(1,000)	£(100) paid	Refund from C&E

Example: Input and output tax

A company sells goods for £35,250 including VAT in a quarter (three months of a year). It buys goods for £32,900 including VAT. What amount will it pay to or receive from HM Customs & Excise for the quarter?

Solution

The **output tax** will be:

£35,250 × $\dfrac{17.5}{117.5}$ = £5,250

The **input tax** will be:

£32,900 × $\dfrac{17.5}{117.5}$ = £4,900

The tax **payable** is the output tax less the input tax = £350

1: SALES INVOICING AND ISSUING CREDITS

7.4 Some practical aspects of VAT

7.4.1 Registration

It would not be easy for HM Customs & Excise to administer and collect VAT if *all* businesses had to account for it. For this reason, **only businesses with at least a certain level of sales must register**.

7.4.2 Administrative time

VAT affects a large number of businesses. A business spends quite a lot of time administering VAT. There are several reasons for this.

- Working out the VAT position although there is a special scheme which allows accounting annually **every quarter**
- Recording all transactions involving VAT to show **separately** the net price, VAT and the gross price
- Failure to comply with all the VAT rules leads to **large penalties**

7.4.3 Discounts and VAT

If a **cash** discount is offered for prompt payment of the invoice, VAT is computed on the amount **after** deducting the discount (at the highest rate offered), **even if the discount is not taken**.

In Section 4.1 above, the VAT shown on the sample invoice was £8.97. The sales value was £54.00, but the terms included a 5% discount if paid within 7 days. **For VAT purposes**, it is assumed that the discount will be taken and so VAT is 17.5% × (54.00 − (5% × 54.00)): ie 17.5% of £51.30, which is £8.97.

PART A   ACCOUNTING FOR SALES AND PURCHASES

Activity 1.8

For Activity 1.6 above recalculate your answers for (a) and (b) if VAT was charged at the standard rate (ie 17.5%).

Activity 1.9

Given a VAT rate of 17½% and the information in activity 1.5, calculate the VAT due. Now complete the invoice below.

Aroma

4 The Boulevard
Market Town
MT2 3AB

SALES INVOICE NO: 1763

To: Country Marquees

Address: Crown Estate
           The Links
           Market Town
           MT5 6QQ

Date/Tax point:

DETAILS	PRICE

Terms and conditions:
   5% discount within 7 days   Sales
   2½% discount within 14 days   VAT @ 17.5%
   Net 30 days
                                        Total

E & OE

VAT Registration No: 987 6543 21

Activity 1.10

At the end of April 20X7, Kris is preparing the sales invoice for the month's sales to Country Marquees. Complete the sales invoice below using the following documents and information.

(a) Purchase order from Country Marquees
(b) Order acknowledgement
(c) Despatch note
(d) Delivery note
(e) Today's date is 30 April 20X7
(f) The terms are 10% trade discount and 2½% cash discount for payment within 20 days

(a) Purchase order

Country Marquees

Crown Estate
The Links
Market Town
MT5 6QQ

PURCHASE ORDER: 1293

Date: 3 April 20X7

Aroma
4 The Boulevard
Market Town
MT2 3AB

QUANTITY	DESCRIPTION	PRICE
5,000	Mixed carnations	£2,500
10,000	Red roses	£15,000
3,000	Yellow roses	£3,000
4,000	Mixed fern	£7,500

Delivery to our premises on 10 April 20X7

PART A   ACCOUNTING FOR SALES AND PURCHASES

(b)   Order acknowledgement

Aroma

4 The Boulevard
Market Town
MT2 3AB

ORDER ACKNOWLEDGEMENT NO: 1731

To: Country Marquees

Address: Crown Estate
          The Links
          Market Town
          MT5 6QQ

Date: 4 April 20X7

Sales order no: 1731

Your reference: order no 1293

DETAILS		PRICE EXCL VAT
5,000	Mixed carnations	2,500.00
10,000	Red roses	15,000.00
3,000	Yellow roses	3,000.00
4,000	Mixed fern	7,500.00
		28,000.00
Trade discount: 10%		(2,800.00)

This is not a VAT invoice:

Sales   25,200.00
VAT @ 17.5%

2½% discount within 20 days
30 days net

Total   _____

DELIVERY TO BE MADE TO THE ABOVE ADDRESS 10 APRIL 20X7

Note. This would usually include VAT, but this has been left blank for the purposes of this activity.

(c)   Despatch note

Aroma 🌸

4 The Boulevard
Market Town
MT2 3AB

DESPATCH NOTE NO: 1731

To:	Country Marquees
Address:	Crown Estate
	The Links
	Market Town
	MT5 6QQ
Date:	4 April 20X7

Sales order no: 1731

Your reference: order no 1293

DETAILS		PRICE EXCL VAT
5,000	Mixed carnations	2,500.00
10,000	Red roses	15,000.00
3,000	Yellow roses	3,000.00
4,000	Mixed fern	7,500.00
		28,000.00
Trade discount: 10%		(2,800.00)

Despatched 10 April 20X7

This is not a VAT invoice:

	Sales	25,200.00
	VAT @ 17.5%	
2½% discount within 20 days		
30 days net	Total	

DELIVERY TO BE MADE TO THE ABOVE ADDRESS 10 APRIL 20X7

PART A   ACCOUNTING FOR SALES AND PURCHASES

(d) Delivery note

Aroma
4 The Boulevard
Market Town
MT2 3AB

DELIVERY NOTE NO: 1731

To: Country Marquees

Address: Crown Estate
The Links
Market Town
MT5 6QQ

Date: 4 April 20X7

Sales order no: 1731

Your reference: order no 1293

DETAILS		PRICE EXCL VAT
5,000	Mixed carnations	2,500.00
10,000	Red roses	15,000.00
3,000	Yellow roses	3,000.00
4,000	Mixed fern	7,500.00
		28,000.00
Trade discount: 10%		(2,800.00)

This is not a VAT invoice:

Sales   25,200.00

VAT @ 17.5%

2½% discount within 20 days
30 days net

Total _____

DELIVERY TO BE MADE TO THE ABOVE ADDRESS 10 APRIL 20X7

Received in good condition:...... *J. Markowitz*

1: SALES INVOICING AND ISSUING CREDITS

Aroma

4 The Boulevard
Market Town
MT2 3AB

SALES INVOICE NO: 1775

To:

Address:

Date/Tax point:

DETAILS	PRICE

Terms and conditions:

2½% discount within 20 days
30 days net

Sales
VAT @ 17.5%

Total

E & OE

VAT Registration No: 987 6543 21

PART A ACCOUNTING FOR SALES AND PURCHASES

8 Credit notes and debit notes

8.1 The credit note

Using our earlier example in Section 4.1, suppose that Student Supplies sent out the invoice for a total of £162.97, instead of £62.97. The county council has been **overcharged** by £100. What is Student Supplies to do?

Or when the primary school received the rulers, 120 had been broken in the post and it was going to send these back. Although the County Council has received an invoice for £62.97, it has no intention of paying that amount because 120 were **useless**. Again, what is Student Supplies to do?

The answer is that the supplier (Student Supplies) sends out a **credit note**. A credit note reduces the amount due on an invoice (or invoices) already sent out.

STUDENT SUPPLIES LIMITED
123 Factory Street Worktown London W19 4NB
Tel: 0181 123 4567 Fax: 0181 123 4589

CREDIT NOTE

Credit Note No: 83
Re: Invoice No: 1496

CREDIT TO:
Westshire County Council
46 Chamber Street
Camberwick Green
CG2 4SP

Date of credit/Taxpoint:
10 May 20X7

ITEM CODE	QUANTITY	DESCRIPTION	UNIT PRICE £	AMOUNT £
17004	120	12" Wooden rulers	0.12	14.40
		VAT at 17.5%		2.39
		Total credit		16.79

Reason for credit
Goods damaged in transit. Original order no. 3365 (Brilliant Primary School).
Returns note number 42.
VAT No 245 8269 41 Terms:5/7, n/30

8.1.1 VAT and discounts on credit notes

Where a cash discount applied on the original invoice, **VAT is calculated** on credit notes on the **lowest amount** which the customer could have paid. In the example above, VAT is calculated as **£14.40 × 95% × 17.5% = £2.39**, because of the cash discount offered on the original invoice.

8.2 Checks over credit notes

Just as it is important to ensure that invoices are correct, it is important to have **checks on the credit notes** which are issued too.

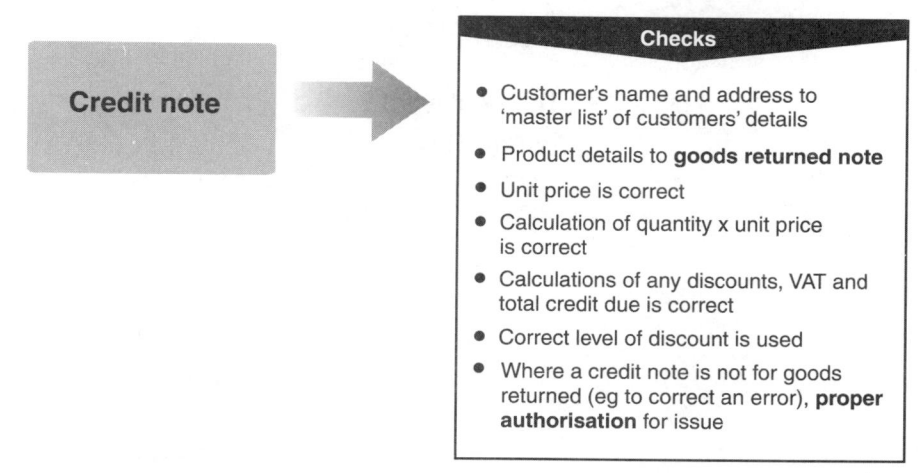

Credit note →

Checks
- Customer's name and address to 'master list' of customers' details
- Product details to **goods returned note**
- Unit price is correct
- Calculation of quantity × unit price is correct
- Calculations of any discounts, VAT and total credit due is correct
- Correct level of discount is used
- Where a credit note is not for goods returned (eg to correct an error), **proper authorisation** for issue

Notes. Since credit notes can be issued in cases not involving the return of goods, they should be authorised by a senior member of staff. When goods are returned, the warehouse staff should report full details of what has been returned and by whom on a **goods returned note**.

If an **incorrect invoice** is issued then a credit note may be issued for the **total amount** of that invoice. A new invoice can then be raised for the correct amount.

8.3 Reasons for issuing credit notes

- When a customer returns **faulty** or **damaged goods**
- When a customer returns perfect goods under a **sale or return agreement**
- When a **clerical error** is made so that the customer is overcharged
- When **fewer items have been delivered than have been invoiced**
- To **settle a dispute** with the customer
- To credit the customer for perfect returned goods when the supplier **has specifically agreed** to do so

8.4 The debit note

Supplier
- To **increase** an existing invoice eg price was too low
- Saves having to cancel and reissue an invoice

← **Debit note** →

Customer
- A means of formally requesting a credit note from a supplier
- Gives all the information needed in an easy form

PART A   ACCOUNTING FOR SALES AND PURCHASES

Activity 1.11

Kris received a call from Country Marquees concerning sales invoice no 1775 in activity 1.10. Although all the flowers were sent out, 1,000 red roses were found to be infested with greenfly and were returned by agreement with Kris. No replacements were sent out and Kris agrees that a credit note is due. Today is 5 May 20X7 and the number of the last credit note issued was C441. Complete the blank credit note below.

Aroma

4 The Boulevard
Market Town
MT2 3AB

CREDIT NOTE NO:

To:

Address:

Date/Tax point:

DETAILS	PRICE

Terms and conditions:

2½% discount within 20 days
30 days net

Sales
VAT @ 17.5%
Total

E & OE

VAT Registration No: 987 6543 21

9 Customer credit limits

9.1 What are customer credit limits?

When a business supplies goods or services on credit, **it is owed money**. There is a risk that the customer may not pay, eg if he goes bankrupt.

It makes sense to set a **credit limit**. This sets an **upper value** on the amount of goods or services that the business will supply on credit.

9.2 Setting a credit limit

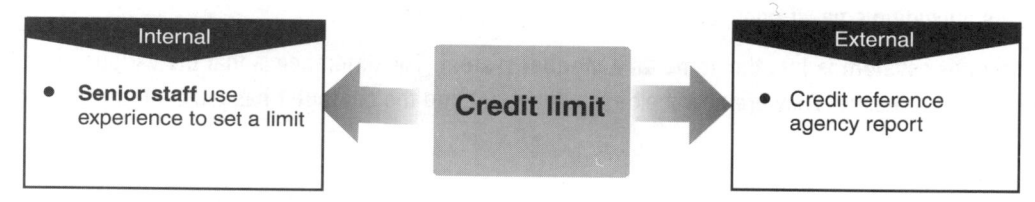

Internal
- **Senior staff** use experience to set a limit

→ Credit limit ←

External
- Credit reference agency report

Some businesses may use a combination of credit reference agency reports and personal experience.

9.3 Taking credit limits into account

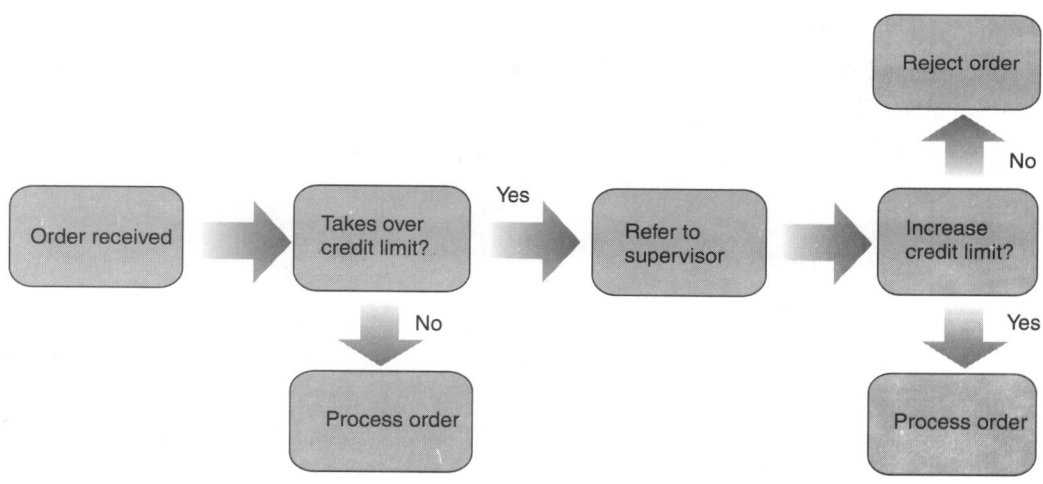

Order received → Takes over credit limit?
- No → Process order
- Yes → Refer to supervisor → Increase credit limit?
  - No → Reject order
  - Yes → Process order

If the order is rejected, most businesses will indicate to the customer how much needs to be paid off their account for the order to be accepted. This helps to keep customer goodwill.

PART A   ACCOUNTING FOR SALES AND PURCHASES

Activity 1.12

Kris has received an order from Country Marquees for £35,000 of flowers. Their credit limit is £40,000 and they have an outstanding invoice just issued for £28,000. Should Kris accept the order?

10 Generation of invoices and credit notes by computer

10.1 Working with computerised systems

Most businesses, including smaller ones, use computers for accounting.

In theory, a computer system is just the same as a manual system. The difference is that the various books of account have become invisible. They are now inside the computer and the computer has taken on the chores of entering and posting all the original data.

10.2 How are computers used in invoicing?

In computer terminology, a **file** is a collection of data having some common features. For example, a price list or a customer list may be held as a computer file.

An **invoicing program** operates by making use of two data files:

- The **customer file** (name, address, details of discounts agreed)
- The **product file** (descriptions, unit quantities and selling prices of each product)

These files are accessed by means of customer and product codes.

1: SALES INVOICING AND ISSUING CREDITS

Files
- Customer file
- Product file

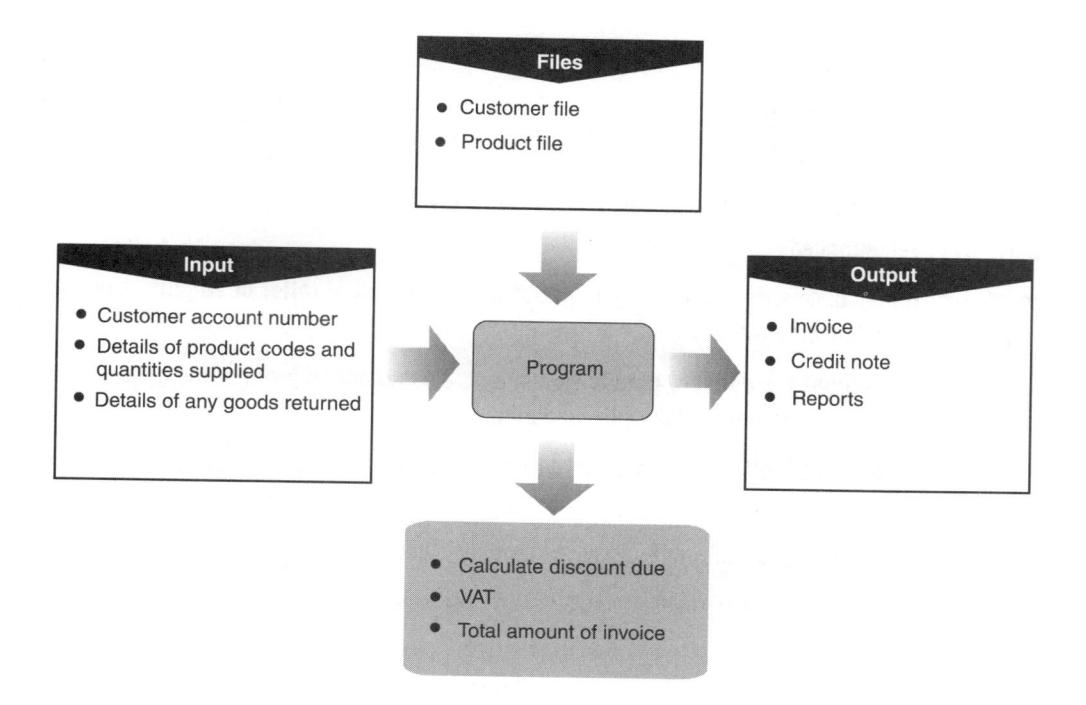

Input
- Customer account number
- Details of product codes and quantities supplied
- Details of any goods returned

Program
- Calculate discount due
- VAT
- Total amount of invoice

Output
- Invoice
- Credit note
- Reports

10.3 Reports produced

Reports can include some or all of the following.

- Details of goods sold (for stock ordering purposes)
- Sales of different products
- Sales to different customers
- Sales to customers by geographical areas
- Total net sales
- Total output VAT
- Total gross sales
- Total discounts allowed

PART A   ACCOUNTING FOR SALES AND PURCHASES

Key learning points

- ☑ A **credit transaction** takes place when the seller of goods or services does not expect to be paid until some time after they have been supplied.

- ☑ Documents which may be involved in a supply of goods include an **initial letter of enquiry**, a **quotation**, an **order** and an **order acknowledgement**.

- ☑ When the goods are supplied, a **delivery note** is signed by the customer as proof of the delivery and an **advice note** may be left with the customer for his or her records.

- ☑ **Multi-part stationery sets** are often used to provide many of these documents, and such sets may also include the invoice.

- ☑ The **invoice** is a demand for the customer to pay the amount owed, usually by a certain date.

- ☑ An invoice is usually numbered, and gives the seller's **VAT** registration number. A VAT registered business must charge VAT.

- ☑ Any **trade discount** will be subtracted from the price of goods before VAT is added.

- ☑ If a **cash discount** is offered, VAT is calculated on the price after deducting the maximum discount.

- ☑ **Invoice checks** include the following.
    - To orders
    - To despatch and delivery documents
    - To price lists
    - Calculations

- ☑ **Segregation of duties** helps to control sales. Separate people should be responsible for the three main areas.
    - Order acceptance
    - Control and despatch of goods
    - Invoice preparation

- ☑ A **credit note** will need to be issued if a customer has been charged too much or if goods have been returned.

- ☑ A business needs to place limits on the credit it allows to customers. Orders should not be accepted if they exceed customer **credit limits**.

- ☑ In a **computer-based system** invoices and credit notes may be produced using an invoicing program. The invoice or credit note will be created from:
    - Information in the customer file (accessed by customer code)
    - Information in the product file (accessed by product code)
    - Details keyed in by the computer operator

1: SALES INVOICING AND ISSUING CREDITS

Quick quiz

1. A credit transaction is a transaction in which the _____ does not pay for the goods or services until some time after they have been supplied. Complete the blank.

2. Name three documents which come before an invoice.

3. What is multi-part stationery?

4. What is meant by the 'tax point'?

   A   The date tax is payable to the Inland Revenue
   B   The date VAT is payable to Customs & Excise
   C   The date of the transaction for VAT purposes
   D   The date of the transaction for income tax purposes

5. 'Ex works' means that goods are delivered from the factory fully paid. True or false?

6. What is the rule about VAT and cash discounts?

7. What is a credit note?

8. What is a debit note?

Answers to quick quiz

1. A transaction in which the **buyer** does not pay for the goods or services until some time after they have been supplied.

2. (i)   A letter of enquiry
   (ii) A quotation
   (iii) A purchase order
   (iv) An acknowledgement
   (v)   A delivery note or advice note

3. Sets of stationery pre-printed with the type of document represented, eg invoice, acknowledgement. The details of the order are copied onto each part in the set.

4. C The date of the transaction for VAT purposes.

5. False. The invoice price does not include delivery.

6. The VAT is calculated on the amount net of the discount, regardless of whether the discount is taken.

7. A document subtracting an amount from an invoice already sent.

8. A document issued by a supplier to adjust an invoice already issued upwards or as a formal demand by a customer for a credit note.

PART A   ACCOUNTING FOR SALES AND PURCHASES

Activity checklist

This checklist shows which performance criteria, range statement or knowledge and understanding point is covered by each activity in this chapter. Tick off each activity as you complete it.

Activity		
1.1	☐	This activity deals with Range Statement 1.1.2: quotations
1.2	☐	This activity deals with Knowledge & Understanding point 1: types of business transactions and documents involved
1.3	☐	This activity deals with Performance Criteria: 1.1.A, 1.1.B and 1.1.C regarding the preparation of invoices
1.4	☐	This activity deals with Knowledge & Understanding point 13: methods of coding data
1.5	☐	This activity deals with Knowledge & Understanding point 5: types of discount
1.6	☐	This activity deals with Knowledge & Understanding point 5: types of discount
1.7	☐	This activity deals with Knowledge & Understanding point 4: general principles of VAT
1.8	☐	This activity deals with Range Statement: 1.1.1 Invoices and credit notes; discounts; VAT
1.9	☐	This activity deals with Performance Criteria 1.1.A regarding the preparation of invoices
1.10	☐	This activity covers Performance Criteria 1.1.A accurately prepare invoices in accordance with organisational requirements and check against source documents
1.11	☐	This activity deals with Performance Criteria 1.1.A, 1.1.B and 1.1.C regarding the preparation of a credit note
1.12	☐	This activity deals with Knowledge and Understanding point 24: organisational procedures for authorisation of sales invoices

chapter 2

Processing suppliers' invoices and credit notes

Contents

1 The problem
2 The solution
3 Purchase orders
4 Types of business purchase
5 Documenting goods and services received
6 Discounts received
7 VAT
8 Checking suppliers' invoices and credit notes
9 Action to deal with discrepancies

Performance criteria

2.1.A Check suppliers' invoices and credit notes against relevant documents for validity
2.1.B Check calculations on suppliers' invoices and credit notes for accuracy
2.1.C Identify and deduct available discounts
2.1.G Identify discrepancies and either resolve or refer to the appropriate person if outside own authority

Range statement

2.1.1 Documents: orders; suppliers' invoices; delivery notes; credit notes
2.1.2 Calculations: pricing, extensions and VAT
2.1.4 Discounts: settlement
2.1.7 Discrepancies: incorrect calculations; non-delivery of goods charged; duplicated invoices; incorrect discounts

PART A   ACCOUNTING FOR SALES AND PURCHASES

Knowledge and understanding

1   Types of business transactions and documents involved
4   General principles of VAT
5   Types of discounts
8   Different ordering systems: Internet, verbal and written
25 The nature of the organisation's business transactions
26 Organisational procedures for authorisation and coding of purchase invoices and payments

Signpost

The topics covered in this chapter are relevant to **Unit 2.**

1 The problem

When purchasing goods (or services), a business needs to be sure that:

- Only items needed for use in the business are ordered
- Payments are made only for items that have been ordered
- Payments are made only for items actually received and at the price agreed

Therefore the business needs a way of controlling who orders goods. If anyone can place an order, the business may end up paying for someone's personal computer.

The business also needs to know what goods and services have been received. If it does not keep records, the business can pay for goods that it never ordered or has not received.

Finally, a business needs to know what goods are still outstanding and what goods it has received but still needs to pay for.

2 The solution

Many businesses solve the problem by having a purchasing department. This may be a separate unit or part of the accounts department.

A purchasing department works in the following way.

2: PROCESSING INVOICES AND CREDIT NOTES

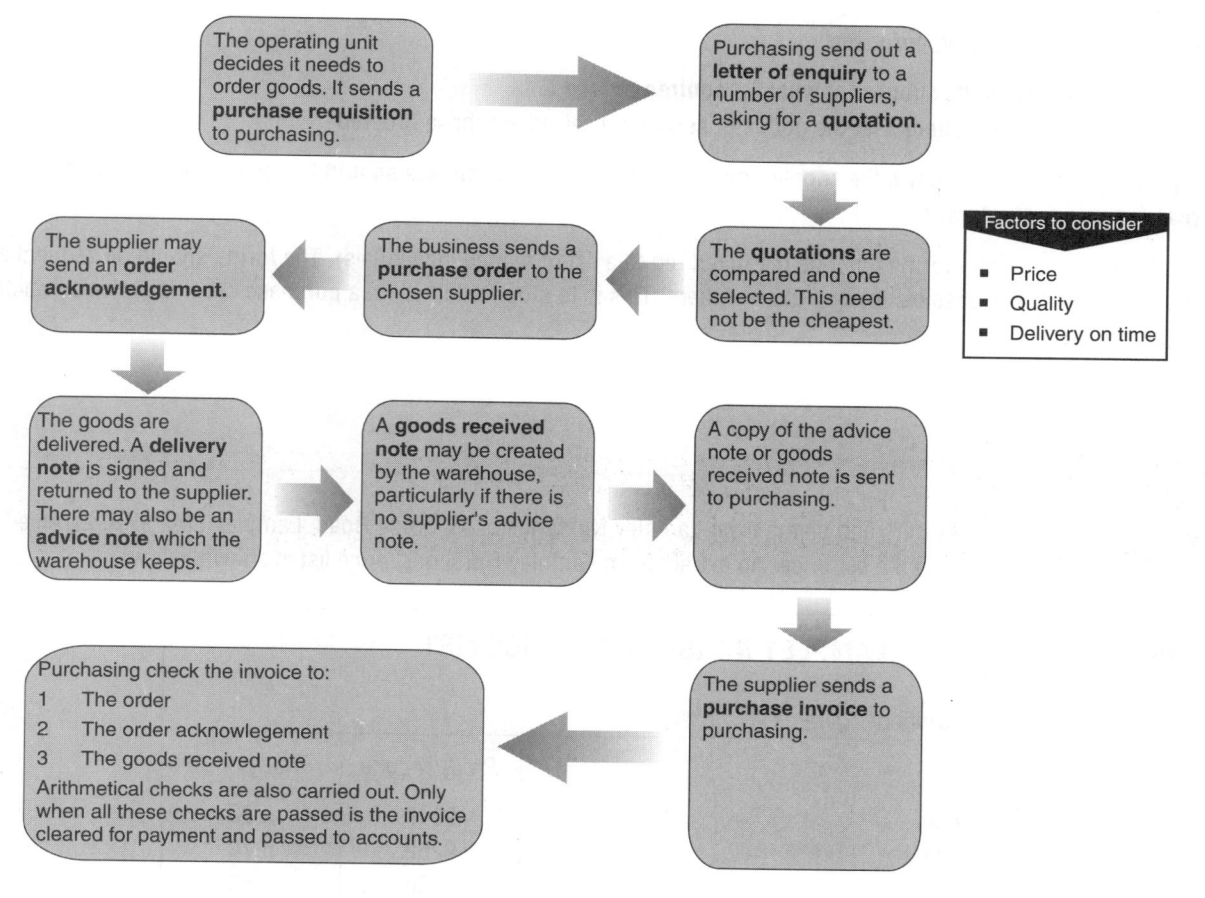

```
The operating unit          →    Purchasing send out a
decides it needs to              letter of enquiry to a
order goods. It sends a          number of suppliers,
purchase requisition             asking for a quotation.
to purchasing.
                                          ↓
The supplier may      ←    The business sends a    ←    The quotations are
send an order              purchase order to the        compared and one
acknowledgement.           chosen supplier.             selected. This need
                                                        not be the cheapest.
    ↓
The goods are             A goods received         →    A copy of the advice
delivered. A delivery     note may be created           note or goods
note is signed and        by the warehouse,             received note is sent
returned to the supplier. particularly if there is      to purchasing.
There may also be an      no supplier's advice
advice note which the     note.
warehouse keeps.
                                                              ↓
Purchasing check the invoice to:                         The supplier sends a
1   The order                      ←                     purchase invoice to
2   The order acknowlegement                             purchasing.
3   The goods received note
Arithmetical checks are also carried out. Only
when all these checks are passed is the invoice
cleared for payment and passed to accounts.
```

Factors to consider
- Price
- Quality
- Delivery on time

This represents the ideal situation. Smaller businesses may not have a separate purchasing department but they should ensure that all purchases are authorised by a **purchasing manager**, or other responsible individual.

3 Purchase orders

3.1 Types of purchaser

The purchaser can be a **company,** a **partnership**, or someone in business on their own (**'sole trader'**). Note that this refers to the **ownership** of the business, any of these can have employees.

The purchaser of goods (or services) enters into a **legally binding contract** with the supplier **when an agreement is made** eg when a purchase order is accepted.

3.2 The purchase order

A **purchase order** is sent to the chosen supplier, stating the product and quantity required. A formal purchase order is usually not required for relatively small purchases.

PART A   ACCOUNTING FOR SALES AND PURCHASES

The purchase order has two purposes.

- To notify the supplier of **what is required**
- To allow a **check** that the goods or services received are those ordered

A **signed purchase order** shows the supplier that the **order** is **valid. Suppliers should be instructed not to accept verbal or unsigned orders.**

Access to purchase order forms must be restricted (eg to a list of named individuals). The forms should be sequentially numbered, so that it is possible to keep track of them. This is to stop fraud, where a purchase order is stolen to validate a bogus invoice.

Activity 2.1

Aroma usually orders its flowers and plants from Lampley Nurseries of 47 Gorse Road, Lampley LM2 9PR. Lampley allow Kris a 10% discount on the list price. An extract from Lampley Nurseries' price list is shown below.

LAMPLEY NURSERIES – PRICE LIST

All prices are for units of 10 items

Product		Product code	Price per 10
Roses	– white	9248	5.20
	– yellow	9252	5.70
	– pink	9256	5.80
	– red	9259	5.90
Carnations	– white	0045	3.20
	– pink	0048	2.85
Ferns	– small	1041	4.00
	– large	1042	4.50
Freesias	– mixed, small blooms	7050	5.20
	– mixed, large blooms	7060	5.60

Kris needs to order the following items.

1,800	Freesias, mixed, small blooms
3,500	Roses, white
2,000	Roses, yellow
3,000	Carnations, pink

2: PROCESSING INVOICES AND CREDIT NOTES

Remember that the price list quotes for units of 10 items

Complete the following purchase order (no 1233), including details of the trade discount claimed and delivery details (by 13 April 20X7 at the latest). Today's date is 6 April 20X7.

Aroma

4 The Boulevard
Market Town
MT2 3AB

Purchase Order No:

To:

Address:

Date: VAT reg no: 987 6543 21

DESCRIPTION	CODE	NO OF UNITS	£

DELIVERY INSTRUCTIONS

Sub total
VAT @ 17.5%

Total

PART A   ACCOUNTING FOR SALES AND PURCHASES

3.3 Despatch of purchase orders

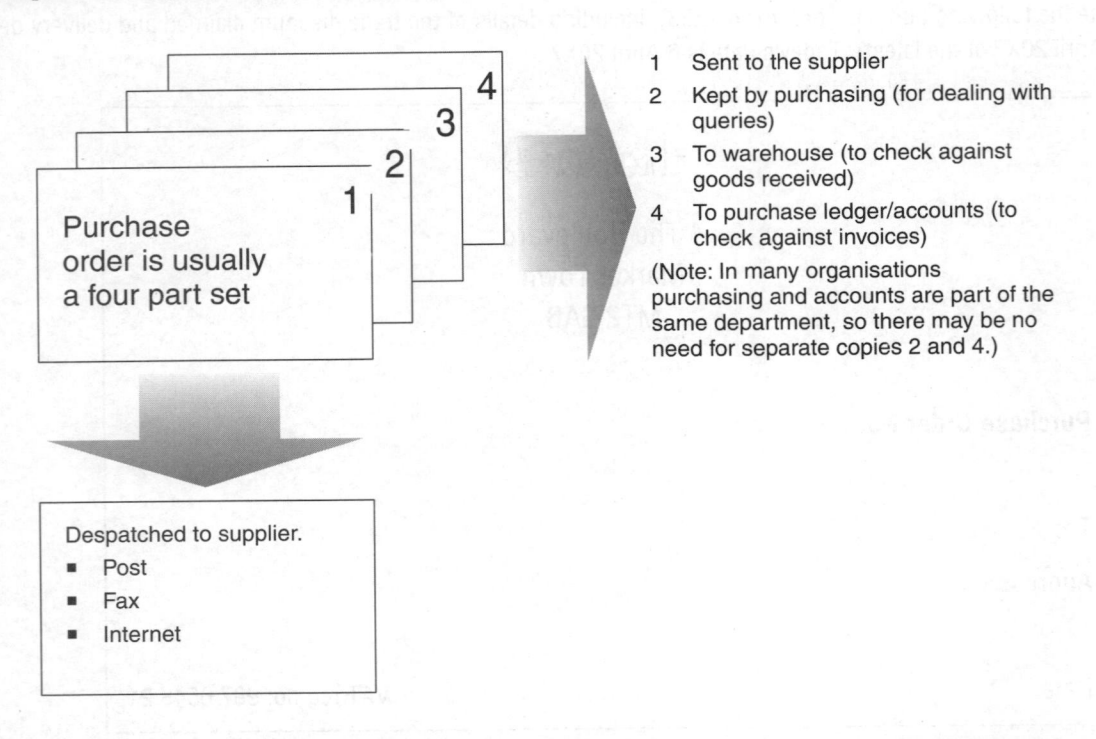

Purchase order is usually a four part set

1. Sent to the supplier
2. Kept by purchasing (for dealing with queries)
3. To warehouse (to check against goods received)
4. To purchase ledger/accounts (to check against invoices)

(Note: In many organisations purchasing and accounts are part of the same department, so there may be no need for separate copies 2 and 4.)

Despatched to supplier.
- Post
- Fax
- Internet

Orders sent by Internet cannot be 'signed' in the usual way. Therefore a purchase order must be completed and authorised in advance. Then the order number is quoted to the supplier. A copy of the Internet order must be printed off and attached to the relevant purchase order form for control purposes.

Orders are sometimes made by telephone in small organisations. However before the call is made, a purchase order must be completed and authorised. The order number should be quoted to the supplier.

Activity 2.2

Kris's business is rapidly expanding. He needs help, so he employs Chan as his bookkeeper and Ahmed to look after the stores of flowers and to make deliveries.

Kris is in a hurry and telephones an order to Lampley Nurseries without using a purchase order. He just scribbles a quick note on a pad. If he forgets to fill in a purchase order, what problems will this cause:

(a) for Chan
(b) for Ahmed

4 Types of business purchase

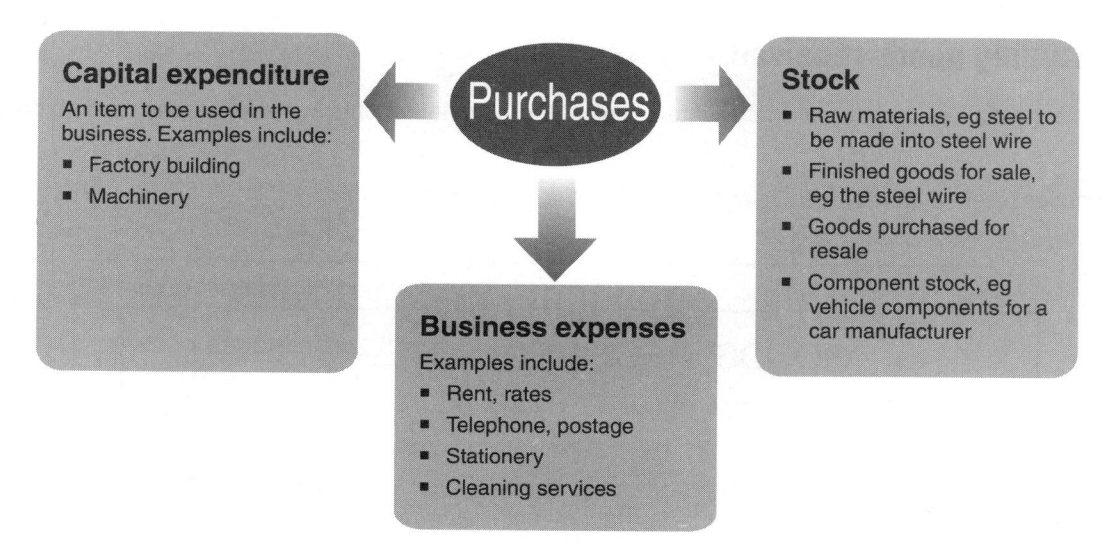

Capital expenditure
An item to be used in the business. Examples include:
- Factory building
- Machinery

Purchases

Stock
- Raw materials, eg steel to be made into steel wire
- Finished goods for sale, eg the steel wire
- Goods purchased for resale
- Component stock, eg vehicle components for a car manufacturer

Business expenses
Examples include:
- Rent, rates
- Telephone, postage
- Stationery
- Cleaning services

Activity 2.3

Kris has made some purchases. Classify them between stock, business expenses and capital, using the grid below

PURCHASE	CLASSIFICATION
Electricity for the shop	
Delivery van	
Red roses	
Gas supply for the shop	
Stamps	
Computer for processing purchase orders	
White carnations	
Shelving for displays in the shop	
Repairs to the shop windows	

5 Documenting goods and services received

5.1 Recording goods received

The details of goods received may be entered into a **book** or on **computer**, or onto a separate goods received note (GRN).

However goods received are recorded, they need to show the details below.

```
                                              ACCOUNTS COPY
         GOODS RECEIVED NOTE        WAREHOUSE COPY
                                              ①
   DATE:  7 March 20X7    TIME:  2.00 pm    NO  5565
   ORDER NO: 00917   ②
   SUPPLIER'S ADVICE NOTE NO:  202/739/X  ③   WAREHOUSE A

   QUANTITY      CAT NO      DESCRIPTION
   ④   16        SR 424      Granular salt, 25kg bags




   RECEIVED IN GOOD CONDITION:   F. P.  ⑤      (INITIALS)
```

Key

1   GRNs are **pre-numbered**, so checks can be made that all stock received has been invoiced.

2   This is the **purchase** order number. The warehouse staff take this from the copy purchase order held in the warehouse.

3   The supplier's advice note number allows any discrepancies to be followed up later.

4   Quantities and descriptions (including codes if known) are needed, **not** monetary values.

5   The person initialling the GRN is confirming the goods are in good condition.

One copy of the GRN is sent to the **purchasing or accounts department**, for checking to the supplier's invoice. The other copy is kept in the **warehouse**, so that a full record is available of all goods received.

Access to blank GRN forms must be strictly controlled. In particular, purchasing department staff should not have access to GRN forms. This stops staff from carrying out frauds involving the misuse of GRNs to validate bogus invoices.

Activity 2.4

Ahmed is in charge of the stores and keeps the blank GRNs. Chan asks him for a couple of blank GRNs, as she is setting up a file of sample documents for the auditors. Advise Ahmed about what he should do.

Activity 2.5

Lampley Nurseries have sent the flowers ordered in Activity 2.1. They are received on 10 April 20X7 at 10 am. All the flowers are correct, except that only 2,000 pink carnations are received. A further 1,000 will be sent tomorrow. Help Ahmed by completing the following GRN. The supplier's advice note number is 1746.

```
                                                    ACCOUNTS COPY
           GOODS RECEIVED NOTE          WAREHOUSE COPY
   DATE:                TIME:                 NO  5565
   ORDER NO:
   SUPPLIER'S ADVICE NOTE NO:                 WAREHOUSE A

   | QUANTITY | CAT NO | DESCRIPTION |

   RECEIVED IN GOOD CONDITION:                      (INITIALS)
```

5.2 Recording services received

A different form of recording is needed for services, (eg window cleaning, small repairs). The receptionist keeps a **service book** which all tradespeople sign when they begin and complete work.

PART A   ACCOUNTING FOR SALES AND PURCHASES

Example: Recording services received

R Handy, the local plumber, is asked to carry out a small repair by K Singh, the Office Manager at Greenfields Carparks Ltd. Handy arrives at the Greenfields offices at 9 am and signs in. Handy finishes the repair and signs out at 12 noon.

When the invoice arrives, it charges five hours' on-site labour. Mr Singh thinks this is excessive. A brief call to reception confirms that Handy was on site for three hours. This gives Mr Singh evidence to query the invoice with Mr Handy.

5.3 Other kinds of goods and services

In a large office there may be many people with the authority to purchase **small items of office equipment and stationery**. An invoice arrives for some plastic wallets and office staplers. However, no-one can remember having ordered them.

Can you think of some procedures which could help to avoid this situation?

- All office purchases are channelled through just **one or two people**.
- A **reference** is sent with all orders, eg the name of the person placing the order.

Activity 2.6

Chan keeps a service book which all service engineers sign on arrival and departure. She receives an invoice for plumbing repairs to the staff toilets. Write down the checks that you think Chan should carry out before paying the invoice.

5.4 Fraud

People will take fraudulent advantage of the **lack of control over payments for services** in some businesses.

Example: Fraud

Some firms were sent invoices for putting their name in a business directory, but this had not been requested by anyone in the firm. In some cases, the directory itself did not even exist. Payment was demanded immediately with serious consequences being threatened if payment was not made. Many businesses paid on demand and only realised their mistake too late. This is a **real life** example, it really happened.

The fraudsters hope that someone receiving the invoice will make a payment, because they cannot discover whether there is an approved order for the service.

Such frauds are often tried during **holiday periods**. There is a greater chance that the usual staff will be away and the stand-ins are less familiar with procedures.

6 Discounts received

6.1 Types of discount

As we saw in Chapter 1, there are two types of discount

Type of discount	Description	Timing	Status
Trade discount	A reduction in the **cost of goods** eg for buying goods in bulk.	Given on supplier's invoice	Permanent
Cash or settlement discount	A reduction in the **amount payable** for immediate or early payment in cash.	Given on payment	Withdrawn if payment not received within time period stated

Activity 2.7

Kris has three main suppliers, apart from Lampley Nurseries.

(a) Alfred offers a trade discount of 20%.
(b) Bertie gives a trade discount of 10%, and a cash discount of 5% if the invoice is paid immediately upon receipt.
(c) Charlie offers a 5% cash discount for immediate payment, or 2½% discount for payment within 10 days.

During the past month, Kris has ordered the following amounts before discounts.

(a) From Alfred: £2,000
(b) From Bertie: £6,000, of which £3,000 was paid immediately.
(c) From Charlie: £10,000, of which £2,000 was paid immediately, and £5,000 was paid within 10 days.

Chan wants to know how much was received as trade and cash discounts. Please advise her. Ignore VAT.

6.2 Recording trade and cash discounts

Trade discount → Invoice shows amount due **net** of the discount, ie only the amount demanded is recorded

Cash discounts ← Taking a discount is **optional**. The full amount of the goods is recorded. If the discount is taken, it is separately recorded in the books.

PART A   ACCOUNTING FOR SALES AND PURCHASES

Example: Prompt payment discounts received

A buys goods from B, on the understanding that A will be allowed a period of credit before having to pay for the goods. The terms of the transaction are as follows.

Date of sale: 1 July 20X7

Credit period allowed: 30 days

Invoice price of the goods (the invoice will be issued at this price when the goods are delivered): £2,000

Cash discount offered: 4% for immediate payment

A has the choice between:

(a) Holding on to the £2,000 for 30 days and then paying the full amount.
(b) Paying £2,000 less 4% (a total of £1,920) now.

This is a financing decision. Is it worthwhile for A to save £80 by paying her debts sooner? Or can she employ her cash more usefully for 30 days and pay the debt at the latest acceptable moment?

If A pays now, her bank account goes overdrawn for a month. The bank charges an overdraft fee of £50 together with interest of 1.4% per month (also charged on the overdraft fee). A currently has £150 in the bank (and an agreed overdraft facility). Assuming no other transactions, what should A do? Work it out before looking at the solution.

Solution

A pays now, so the bank account will be as follows.

		£
Funds		150.00
Less: payment		(1,920.00)
overdraft fee		(50.00)
Overdraft		(1,820.00)
Interest (1.4% × £1,820) added at end of the month		25.48

The discount is worth £80, but bank charges and interest of £50 + £25.48 will be incurred. However, the amount of the discount is still worth more than the bank charges by £4.52. A should therefore take advantage of the discount offered by B.

Activity 2.8

Aroma purchases goods with a list price of £30,000. The supplier offers a 7½% trade discount, and a 2½% cash discount for payment within 10 days.

Tasks

(a) Calculate the amount Aroma will pay if it delays longer than 10 days before paying.
(b) Calculate the amount the business will pay if it pays within 10 days.

Ignore VAT.

Businesses may be offered other kinds of 'discounts' as incentives, to encourage them to buy in bulk or to stop them buying goods from competitors. See Section 6.3 in Chapter 1 of this Text.

7 VAT

7.1 General introduction

Any business registered for VAT purposes must charge VAT. Therefore most purchase invoices show VAT charged.

Remember from Chapter 1:

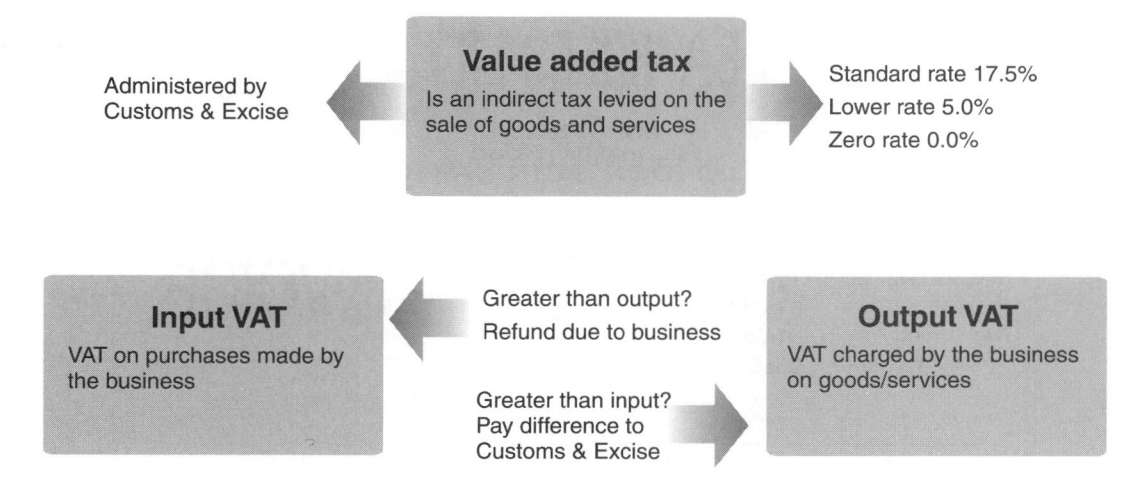

```
                                    Value added tax                    Standard rate 17.5%
         Administered by      ← Is an indirect tax levied on the →     Lower rate 5.0%
         Customs & Excise          sale of goods and services          Zero rate 0.0%


                                    Greater than output?
            Input VAT          ←    Refund due to business                  Output VAT
    VAT on purchases made by                                          VAT charged by the business
         the business                                                      on goods/services
                                    Greater than input?
                               →    Pay difference to
                                    Customs & Excise
```

Remember also that VAT is charged on the amount due after the highest rate of discount available, even if the discount is not taken.

Activity 2.9

Chan receives an invoice from Bertie for £7,000 before discounts and VAT. The invoice will be paid ten days after receipt. Given a VAT rate of 17.5% and the information in Activity 2.7, calculate the VAT due.

7.2 Input VAT

Input VAT is the amount paid by a business as its purchases. This can usually be recovered by offset against output tax received and any excess is reclaimed from Customs and Excise.

However, sometimes traders are *not* allowed to reclaim input VAT paid on their purchases.

PART A   ACCOUNTING FOR SALES AND PURCHASES

7.2.1 Non-deductible inputs

In such cases, the trader bears the cost of VAT and accounts for it as part of the cost of the purchase. The most important example of inputs being **non-deductible** are motor cars.

7.3 Documentation and VAT

There are special rules on the content of an invoice used as proof of purchase for reclaiming VAT – a **VAT invoice**.

```
                        BANGLES LTD
                          Jewel House
                         Richmans Road
                        LONDON SE1N 5AB


Invoice Number:  123456                              INVOICE
Date:            01/08/X7
Tax Point:       01/08/X7    (a)
Account Number:  3365


DELIVER TO        INVOICE TO:    Telephone Number 0171 123 4567
ABC Ltd                          VAT Registration Number 457 4635 19    (b)
112 Peters Square Same address   Northern Bank plc Code 20-25-42
Weyford                          Account Number 957023
Kent CR2 2TA


                                       Unit Price    Net Amount
Item Code   Description    Quantity         £             £

Your order number:  2490

13579A      Desks            30           250.00        7,500.00
            Delivery          1           100.00          100.00

                                     SALES VALUE:       7,600.00
                                  VAT AT 17.5%:  (c)    1,330.00
                                  AMOUNT PAYABLE:       8,930.00

E & OE
```

Key:

(a) **Tax point**. This determines when the transaction has taken place for VAT purposes, normally the invoice date. Note that, for cash transactions, the tax point is the date the transaction took place.

(b) **VAT registration number** of the supplier. This is to prove to HM Customs & Excise that the purchase was from a real supplier of standard rated goods. It should be in the form: GB 987 6543 21, although businesses that do not export goods and services may omit the 'GB'.

(c) **VAT rate**. The correct rate must be applied to each type of goods; if the goods are zero-rated then the rate would be shown as 0%.

8 Checking suppliers' invoices and credit notes

An **invoice** is a demand for payment. A **credit note** reduces or cancels the amount due on an invoice.

Suppliers often **post** invoices and credit notes. However, sometimes the invoice is delivered **with the goods themselves** by the carrier.

8.1 Checks

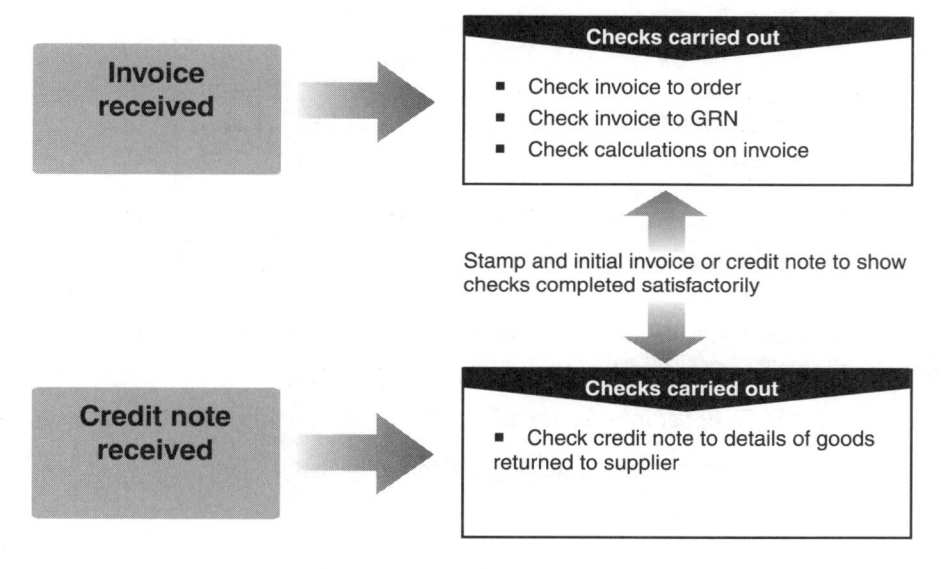

Invoice received → **Checks carried out**
- Check invoice to order
- Check invoice to GRN
- Check calculations on invoice

Stamp and initial invoice or credit note to show checks completed satisfactorily

Credit note received → **Checks carried out**
- Check credit note to details of goods returned to supplier

Once all the checks are carried out, it is important that the supporting evidence, such as purchase order and GRN, are stapled to the invoice before passing it on to accounts to be paid.

- Proves goods properly ordered and received
- Stops supporting evidence being used again to support a bogus invoice
- Immediately highlights a problem if same amounts are invoiced twice, as no supporting evidence to match with second invoice

PART A   ACCOUNTING FOR SALES AND PURCHASES

Example: Processing invoices received

Frank Okara works as a purchase ledger clerk for Ivory Carpets Ltd. The procedures of the company state that, on receipt of a supplier's invoice, a rubber stamp is entered on the front of the invoice. The stamp is set to show the date and looks like this.

```
RECEIVED

Checked to Purchase Order No:  [  ][  ][  ]
                       Prices  [  ]
                   Quantities  [  ]
         Checked to GRN No:    [  ][  ][  ]
                   Quantities  [  ]
             In good condition [  ]
   Supplier terms/discount agreed  [  ]
              VAT rate agreed      [  ]
   Calculations: Price extensions  [  ]
                       Additions   [  ]
                       Discount    [  ]
                       VAT         [  ]

Exceptions _____

Initials _____ Date _____

Payment authorised _____ Date _____
```

Key

(1) The term **price extensions** means the multiplying of prices by quantities to give a net total figure for that item (before discounts and VAT). For example:

230m^2 Twist pile carpet @ £7.42 per m^2 = £1,706.60.

(2) **Addition** is then necessary to add up the net total figures for all the items.

Solution

Frank processes some of the invoices which Ivory Carpets receives on 17 May 20X0.

The first invoice is a **telephone bill**, for which no purchase order or GRN applies. Frank carries out the other checks detailed on the stamp and completes it as shown below.

2: PROCESSING INVOICES AND CREDIT NOTES

RECEIVED	17 May 20X0
Checked to Purchase Order No:	N/A
Prices	
Quantities	
Checked to GRN No:	N/A
Quantities	
In good condition	
Supplier terms/discount agreed	✓
VAT rate agreed	✓
Calculations: Price extensions	✓
Additions	✓
Discount	N/A
VAT	✓
Exceptions _____	
Initials _____F.O._____ Date _17/5/X0_	
Payment authorised _____ Date _____	

The details on a second invoice, from Walter Wall Carpeting Supplies Ltd, agree with GRN number 240229. When he finds the purchase order (number 104299), Frank finds that the order states a price of £7.84 excluding VAT per box of brass threshold strips, while the invoice shows a price of £8.29 for these items. 200 boxes were delivered and invoiced. Frank finds no other discrepancies or errors, but he decides not to complete the calculation checks until the discrepancy has been clarified. Frank completes the invoice stamp as shown below.

RECEIVED	17 May 20X0
Checked to Purchase Order No:	104299
Prices	NO
Quantities	
Checked to GRN No:	240229
Quantities	✓
In good condition	✓
Supplier terms/discount agreed	✓
VAT rate agreed	✓
Calculations: Price extensions	
Additions	
Discount	
VAT	
Exceptions _Price does not agree with order_	
Initials _____ Date _____	
Payment authorised _____ Date _____	

PART A   ACCOUNTING FOR SALES AND PURCHASES

When he has finished checking all the invoices, Frank sorts them into two piles. One pile contains the invoices on which some further action must be taken. Frank keeps this pile and passes the other pile to Winston Peters, the Purchasing Manager, for authorisation. Winston will authorise all purchases of stocks, but will pass other items (eg the telephone bill) to other managers as appropriate. The authorised invoices will be entered in the accounting records (see Chapters 3 and 4) and then passed to the accounts department for payment.

Activity 2.10

Chan receives an invoice from Bertie, which shows the following information.

	£
Goods ordered	16,000
Trade discount	80
	15,920
VAT @ 17.5%	2,786
Net amount due:	13,134

Cash discount available if paid immediately upon receipt: £656.70.

(a) Chan finds GRNs totalling £15,500. How may errors are there on this invoice? Use the information given in activity 2.7 to help you.

(b) Assuming that Chan finds a further GRN for £600. Calculate the correct amount due and cash discount available.

9 Action to deal with discrepancies

9.1 Discrepancies and errors

Processing suppliers' invoices can bring to light discrepancies and apparent errors.

- **Prices** on the invoices are not those previously agreed with the supplier
- **Calculations** on invoices are incorrect
- An invoice for goods or services for which there is **no record of receipt**
- The same goods or services **invoiced twice** in error
- **Incorrect rate of discount or VAT** shown on an invoice

Some action is necessary to sort out the errors. Otherwise the supplier will continue to treat the invoices as outstanding and issue reminder notices. However do not send the invoice back or alter it.

Simple queries can be dealt with by a **telephone call** to the sales ledger department of the supplier. More complex queries, or queries involving large amounts, may need to be dealt with by **letter**.

Once an invoice has been received, it should **never be destroyed** or **forgotten** just because it contains an error. For many of the discrepancies which arise, the supplier needs to issue a **credit note** for the amount of the error.

# 2: PROCESSING INVOICES AND CREDIT NOTES

Example: Requesting a credit note

Frank Okara takes the following action regarding the discrepancies which he identified in the previous example.

Ivory Carpets received an invoice showing a price which disagreed with the price shown on the purchase order. Perhaps the purchase order is wrong. It could be based on an out of date quotation or price list and does not take account of a subsequent price rise.

Frank sees that the purchase order was signed by the Purchasing Manager. He telephones him and explains the query. The manager refers him to a quotation from Walter Wall Carpeting Supplies dated 27 February 20X0. The quotation gives a price of £7.84 for the items, as shown on the purchase order. Frank notes that the quotation states that the price quoted applies for a period of three months from the date of the quotation.

Frank drafts the letter below for the Purchasing Manager to sign.

IVORY CARPETS LIMITED

24 Greensea Avenue, Brighton BN4 7ER

Walter Wall Carpeting Supplies Ltd
72 Eckersley Road
London SW19 4PN

17 May 20X0

Dear Sirs

Re your invoice number 7242

Your quotation dated 27 February 20X0 stated a price of £7.84 for boxes of brass threshold strips (your reference X18), and indicated that this price applies until 26 May 20X0. Your invoice number 7242 shows a price of £8.29 for this item.

Please would you issue a credit note to us for the amount by which we have been overcharged.

Yours faithfully,

Winston Peters

Winston Peters
Purchasing Manager

PART A ACCOUNTING FOR SALES AND PURCHASES

Frank files the queried invoice with a copy of the above letter, in a lever arch file marked 'invoices awaiting credit'.

Many businesses **delay payment of a supplier's invoice on which a query is outstanding** until the query has been resolved. Delaying payment is, after all, likely to help to persuade the supplier to deal with the query promptly!

Activity 2.11

During April 20X7, a further two purchase orders are issued by Aroma to Lampley Nurseries (Activity 2.1), requesting the following goods for delivery by 30 April.

Purchase order no 1241 (14 April 20X7)

    1,000   Large ferns
    2,000   Mixed freesias, large blooms

Purchase order no 1274 (21 April 20X7)

    2,500   White roses
    1,500   Small ferns
    1,500   Large ferns

Goods inwards documentation up to 30 April 20X7 relating to goods received (including deliveries in response to purchase order no 1233) from Lampley Nurseries is set out below.

Two invoices received from Lampley nurseries are also shown.

Tasks

Check the supplier's invoices and the goods received documentation. You should also check whether all goods which have been ordered have been delivered during April.

Indicate clearly what checks you perform on the stamps below. Note any discrepancies or unusual features and indicate what action is to be taken in respect of them in the grid below.

Calculate the amount of any necessary adjustment arising from any pricing or calculation errors which you find on the invoices.

2: PROCESSING INVOICES AND CREDIT NOTES

```
┌─────────────────────────────────────┐
│                                     │
│   RECEIVED                          │
│                                     │
├─────────────────────────────────────┤
│   Checked to Purchase Order No: ☐☐☐☐│
│                         Prices    ☐ │
│                     Quantities    ☐ │
│         Checked to GRN No:  ☐☐☐☐    │
│                     Quantities    ☐ │
│                In good condition  ☐ │
│   Supplier terms/discount agreed  ☐ │
│                  VAT rate agreed  ☐ │
│   Calculations: Price extensions  ☐ │
│                       Additions   ☐ │
│                        Discount   ☐ │
│                             VAT   ☐ │
├─────────────────────────────────────┤
│   Exceptions _____  │
│                                     │
│   Initials _____ Date _____ │
│                                     │
│   Payment authorised _____ Date __ │
└─────────────────────────────────────┘
```

```
┌─────────────────────────────────────┐
│                                     │
│   RECEIVED                          │
│                                     │
├─────────────────────────────────────┤
│   Checked to Purchase Order No: ☐☐☐☐│
│                         Prices    ☐ │
│                     Quantities    ☐ │
│         Checked to GRN No:  ☐☐☐☐    │
│                     Quantities    ☐ │
│                In good condition  ☐ │
│   Supplier terms/discount agreed  ☐ │
│                  VAT rate agreed  ☐ │
│   Calculations: Price extensions  ☐ │
│                       Additions   ☐ │
│                        Discount   ☐ │
│                             VAT   ☐ │
├─────────────────────────────────────┤
│   Exceptions _____  │
│                                     │
│   Initials _____ Date _____ │
│                                     │
│   Payment authorised _____ Date __ │
└─────────────────────────────────────┘
```

PART A   ACCOUNTING FOR SALES AND PURCHASES

DISCREPANCY	SUGGESTED ACTION

AROMA GOODS RECEIVED NOTE			No: G924 Date: 14 April 20X7
Item	Code	Quantity	P.O. No.
Carnations, pink	0048	2,000	1233
Freesias, mixed, small blooms	7050	1,800	1233
Freesias, mixed, large blooms	7060	2,000	1241
Comments 50% of pink carnations (ie 1,000) damaged and unuseable.			

AROMA GOODS RECEIVED NOTE		No: G977 Date: 19 April 20X7	
Item	Code	Quantity	P.O. No.
Roses - white	9248	2,500	1233
Roses - yellow	9252	3,000	1233
Comments: Purchase order copy (1233) not found			

AROMA GOODS RECEIVED NOTE		No: H010 Date: April 20X7	
Item	Code	Quantity	P.O. No.
Ferns - large	1041	1,500	1274
Carnations - pink	0048	2,000	1233
Comments: Carnations - to complete PO 1233 and replace damaged goods			

LAMPLEY NURSERIES

47 GORSE ROAD, LAMPLEY LM2 9PR (Reg. office)

SALES INVOICE　　　　　　　　　　　　　　　　No. 7221

VAT No.: 742 4424 40　　　　　　Date/Taxpoint: 19 April 20X7

Item	Your ref.	Qty	Unit price £ p	Total £ p
0048 Carnations - pink	1233	200	2 . 85	570 . 00
9248 Roses - white	1233	250	5 . 70	1425 . 00
7050 Freesias, mixed, small blooms	1233	180	5 . 20	936 . 00
7060 Freesias, mixed, large blooms	1241	200	5 . 60	1120 . 00

Total	4051 . 00
Discount	40 . 51
	4010 . 49
VAT @ 17.5%	701 . 83
Amount due	4712 . 32

To: Purchase Ledger Dept.
　　Aroma
　　4, The Boulevard
　　Market town
　　MT2 4QQ

LAMPLEY NURSERIES
47 GORSE ROAD LAMPLEY LM2 9PR (Reg. office)

SALES INVOICE No. 7264

VAT No: 7 424 4244   Date/Taxpoint: 30 April 20X7

Item	Your ref.	Qty	Unit price £ p	Total £ p
0048 Carnations - pink	1233	200	2.85	570.00
1041 Ferns - small	1274	150	4.00	600.00
1042 Ferns - large	1274	150	4.50	675.00
9248 Roses - white	1274	250	5.70	1425.00
9252 Roses - yellow	1233	300	5.70	1710.00

	£ p
Total	4980.00
Discount	49.80
	4930.20
VAT @ 17.5%	862.78
Amount due	5792.98

To: Purchase Ledger Dept.
Aroma
4, The Boulevard
Market Town
Mt2 4QQ

PART A ACCOUNTING FOR SALES AND PURCHASES

Activity 2.12

Purchase order forms are produced in sequentially numbered 4-part sets. The first part (copy 1) is sent to the supplier; the second (copy 2) is retained in the purchasing department for their records; the third is sent to the goods inwards department; and the fourth is sent to the purchase ledger section of the accounts department.

Purchase invoices are checked to purchase orders and then to goods received notes. Other checks are also carried out before purchase invoices are approved.

The organisation has announced a suggestions scheme inviting employees to suggest improvements which might enhance efficiency in the organisation. A colleague of yours tells you that he is thinking of making a suggestion to the scheme about the processing of purchase invoices. He feels that four-part purchase invoices are an example of unnecessary 'red tape'. He intends to suggest that the third and fourth parts of the purchase order form be scrapped. Only copies 1 and 2 are needed, he says, as all purchase invoices are checked against goods received notes in any case.

Task

Write a memo to your colleague on this matter. Today's date is 7 April 20X7.

Will you support your colleague's suggestion? Are there any reasons for retaining the third and fourth parts of the purchase order form?

Activity 2.13

Chan receives a credit note from a supplier relating to goods worth £100, excluding VAT at 17½%.

(a) What is the significance of a credit note?

(b) List *three* situations which give rise to a supplier sending a credit note.

(c) Most of the following will assist Chan in checking a credit note. Say which, and why.

    (i) Purchase invoice received
    (ii) Goods received note
    (iii) Sales despatch note issued by Ahmed
    (iv) Goods returned note (drawn up by Ahmed)
    (v) Debit note (drawn up by Chan)
    (vi) Purchase order
    (vii) Supplier's price list
    (viii) A pocket calculator

Key learning points

- Businesses make **purchases** of different kinds.
  - **Raw materials** form part of the trading stock of the company.
  - There may also be other **business expenses**.
  - A purchase is called **'capital expenditure'** if it results in the acquisition of fixed assets or an improvement in the earning capacity of fixed assets.

- **Quotations** or **price lists** will be obtained before a purchase order is made.

- A copy of the **purchase order** will be kept for checking later with the invoice.

- **A business needs to keep track of the goods which it receives.** A warehouse will keep documents to record receipt of goods and any discrepancies or damaged goods.

- It may be **more difficult to keep a track of all the services** which a business receives, but this is important too for checking later with invoices.

- A goods received note (GRN) is a document recording what goods have been received in the purchaser's warehouse.

- **A discount is a reduction in the price of goods below the amount at which these goods are normally sold to the customers.**

- There are two kinds of **discount**.
  - **Trade discount:** a reduction in the cost of the goods
  - **Cash or settlement discount:** an optional reduction in the amount paid to the supplier

- VAT rules are complex. The main ones to remember here are:
  - **Output VAT** is charged on sales and **input VAT** is paid on purchases
  - **VAT invoices** must contain specific information to enable a purchaser to reclaim input VAT
  - VAT is **rounded down** to the nearest penny in calculations
  - If a cash discount is offered, the VAT is calculated on the amount **after taking** the discount

- **An invoice is a demand for payment.**

- **A credit note is used by a supplier to cancel all or part of a previously issued invoice.**

- **Procedures should exist to ensure that the business only pays what it should for goods and services received.** Suppliers' invoices and credit notes will be checked against order documentation and evidence that the goods or services invoiced have been received in good condition.

- **All calculations on suppliers' invoices and credit notes need to be checked for accuracy.** The calculations to be checked will include prices, price extensions, discounts and VAT calculations.

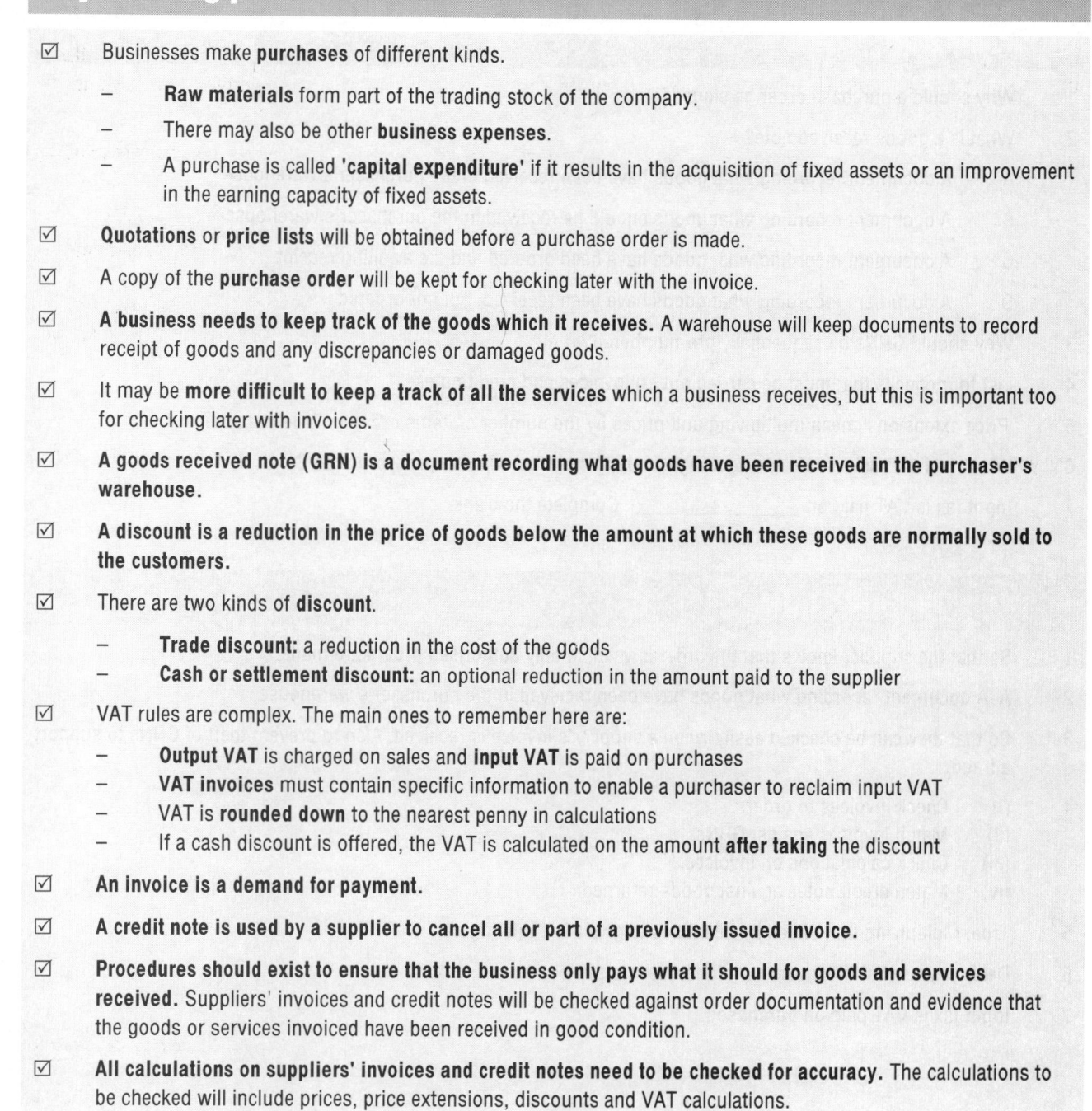

- Discrepancies and inaccuracies which may be found could include **incorrect calculations**, **goods invoiced** which have **not been received**, **duplicated invoices** or **incorrectly calculated VAT** or **discounts**.

PART A   ACCOUNTING FOR SALES AND PURCHASES

Quick quiz

1. Why should a purchase order be signed?
2. What is a goods received note?

   A A document recording what goods have been received in the purchaser's warehouse
   B A document recording what goods should be received in the purchaser's warehouse
   C A document recording what goods have been ordered and are awaiting receipt
   D A document recording what goods have been received, but not ordered

3. Why should GRNs be sequentially pre-numbered?
4. List four checks that must be carried out on invoices and credit notes.
5. 'Price extensions' mean multiplying unit prices by the number of items ordered. True or false?
6. What might a business do to encourage a supplier to deal with its query promptly?
7. Input tax is VAT paid on _____ . Complete the blank.

Answers to quick quiz

1. So that the supplier knows that the order is valid, ie only authorised orders are made.
2. **A** A document recording what goods have been received in the purchaser's warehouse.
3. So that they can be checked easily when a supplier's invoice is received. Also to prevent theft of GRNs to support a fraud.
4. (i)   Check invoices to orders.
   (ii) Match invoices against GRNs.
   (iii) Check calculations on invoices.
   (iv) Match credit notes against goods returned.
5. True. Multiplying unit prices by quantities to give a net total figure.
6. Delay payment of the invoice until the query is settled.
7. Input tax is VAT paid on **purchases**.

Activity checklist

This checklist shows which performance criteria, range statement or knowledge and understanding point is covered by each activity in this chapter. Tick off each activity as you complete it.

Activity

2.1	☐	This activity deals with Range Statement 2.1.1 documents: orders
2.2	☐	This activity deals with Range Statement 2.1.1 documents: orders and 2.1.7 discrepancies
2.3	☐	This activity deals with Knowledge and Understanding 26: the nature of the organisation's business transactions
2.4	☐	This activity deals with Knowledge and Understanding 1: types of business transactions and the documents involved
2.5	☐	This activity deals with Range Statement 2.1.7 discrepancies: non-delivery of goods
2.6	☐	This activity deals with Performance Criteria 2.1.A: check suppliers' invoices and credit note against relevant documents for validity
2.7	☐	This activity deals with Performance Criteria 2.1.C: identity and deduct available discounts
2.8	☐	This activity deals with Performance Criteria 2.1.C: identity and deduct available discounts
2.9	☐	This activity deals with Range Statement 2.1.2: calculations: VAT
2.10	☐	This activity deals with Performance Criteria 2.1.A: check suppliers' invoices against relevant documents for validity and Performance Criteria 2.1.B: check calculations on suppliers' invoices for accuracy
2.11	☐	This activity deals with Performance Criteria 2.1.A, 2.1.B and 2.1.G
2.12	☐	This activity deals with Range Statement 2.1.1 documents: orders
2.13	☐	This activity deals with Performance Criteria 2.1.A: check suppliers' credit notes against relevant documents for accuracy

PART A ACCOUNTING FOR SALES AND PURCHASES

chapter 3

Sales and sales returns day books

Contents

1. The problem
2. The solution
3. What is the sales day book?
4. What is the sales returns day book?
5. Analysing sales transactions in the day books
6. Posting the day book totals

Performance criteria

1.1.C Ensure invoices and credit notes are correctly coded
1.1.D Enter invoices and credit notes into books of prime entry according to organisational procedures
1.1.E Enter invoices and credit notes in the appropriate ledgers

Range statement

1.1.3 Coded: manual systems; computerised systems
1.1.4 Books of prime entry: manual sales day book; manual sales returns day book; relevant computerised records
1.1.5 Ledgers: manual main ledger; manual subsidiary ledger; computerised ledgers

Knowledge and understanding

18 Relationship between accounting system and the ledger
24 Organisational procedures for authorisation and coding of sales invoices
25 Organisational procedures for filing source documents

PART A   ACCOUNTING FOR SALES AND PURCHASES

> **Signpost**
> The topics covered in this chapter are relevant to **Unit 1**.

1 The problem

In Chapter 1, we looked at how credit sales are invoiced.

We now need to consider how these invoices (and any credit notes) are recorded in the books of the business.

Invoices and credit notes need to be recorded for the following reasons.

- **Total sales** figure
- **Who** owes the business money
- **When** the business should ask for money

A business needs to know how well it is doing and so it needs a record of the total sales made.

The business also needs to make sure that it receives the money due for all the sales it has made. Therefore it needs a record of who owes it money and when these amounts are due to be paid.

2 The solution

If every invoice and credit note were to be recorded directly in the accounts, it would be very time consuming and the records would soon be unwieldy.

Therefore the invoices and credit notes are initially recorded in **day books**. A summary of these day books is then posted to the accounts.

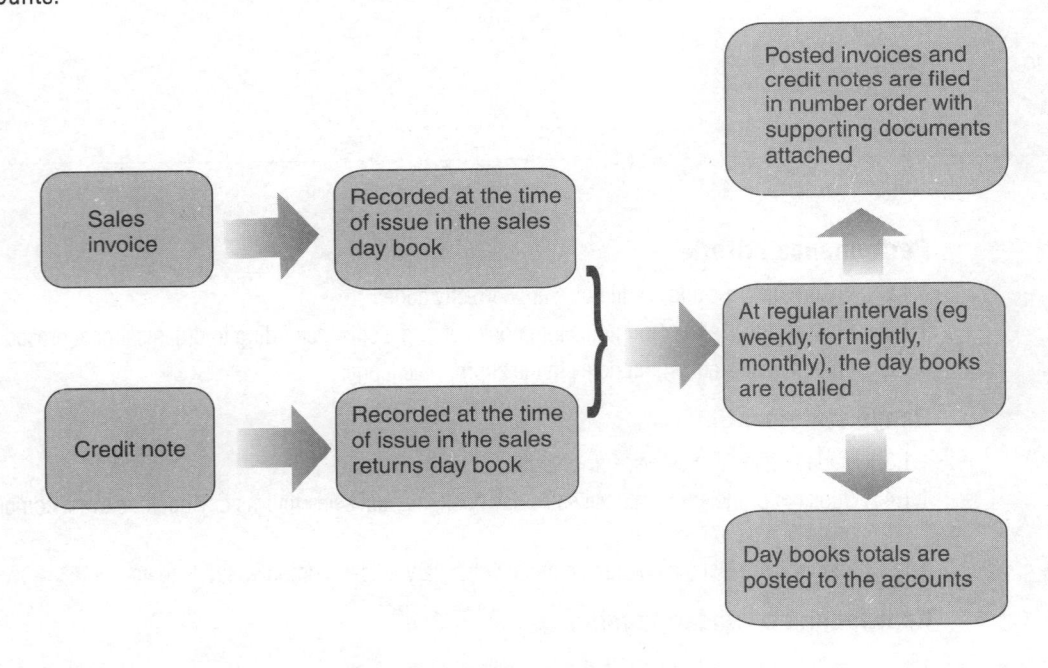

```
Sales invoice  →  Recorded at the time of issue in the sales day book  ⎫
                                                                       ⎬ → At regular intervals (eg weekly, fortnightly, monthly), the day books are totalled
Credit note    →  Recorded at the time of issue in the sales returns day book ⎭

                → Posted invoices and credit notes are filed in number order with supporting documents attached

                → Day books totals are posted to the accounts
```

72

The frequency of the posting will depend on the number of sales. For example, a business sending out 50 invoices a month will probably do a monthly posting; while a business with 50 invoices a day will probably do weekly postings.

3 What is the sales day book?

3.1 The need for the sales day book

A business needs a way of **recording** and **summarising** the contents of the invoices and credit notes it sends out, which are called 'source documents'.

The **sales day book** is a list of all the sales invoices sent out each day.

3.2 The function of the sales day book

A transaction is recorded in the sales day book before being recorded elsewhere, so the sales day book is a **'book of prime entry'** or a **'primary record'**.

The term 'book' is misleading, books of prime entry are often not actual books, but are files hidden in the memory of a computer. **Nevertheless, the principles of how transactions are recorded remain the same whether the records used are computerised or manual.**

Example: sales day book

An extract from the sales day book of Boot and Shoe Supplies appears as follows.

Date	Invoice number	Customer	Net total £	VAT £	Gross total £
10.1.X5	20247	S Jones	172.00	30.10	202.10
	20248	Abbey Supplies Ltd	84.50	14.78	99.28
	20249	Cook & Co	292.70	51.22	343.92
	20250	Texas Ltd	172.00	30.10	202.10
	20251	Dinham Shoes	74.75	13.08	87.83
	20252	Mentor Ltd	272.05	47.60	319.65
		Totals	1,068.00	186.88	1,254.88

- The items are listed in the day book in **unbroken numerical sequence**, of invoice number.

- So the numbers of **spoiled invoices** are entered too, with blanks in the 'amounts' columns and/or a note as cancelled under 'customer', so that it is clearly recorded that no invoice with that number has been raised.

PART A ACCOUNTING FOR SALES AND PURCHASES

Activity 3.1

Aroma has issued the following sales invoices on 16.3.X7. Record them in the sales day book below. VAT is to be calculated at 17.5%.

Invoice	I 2058	To: Country Marquees	Total sales (excl. VAT)	£15,000.00
Invoice	I 2059	To: ABC Catering	Total sales (excl. VAT)	£2,500.00
Invoice	I 2060	To: Country Marquees	Total sales (excl. VAT)	£10,250.00

Extract from Aroma's sales day book

Date	Invoice no	Customer	Net sales	VAT	Gross

3.3 Analysis of sales

Some businesses need a split of their net sales figure between the main products sold eg between boots and shoes in the above example. This is solved by providing additional columns for analysis.

Example: Analysed sales

Date	Invoice number	Customer	Sales of boots	Sales of shoes	VAT	Gross total
101.X5	20247	S Jones	150.00	22.00	30.10	202.10
	20248	Abbey Supplies Ltd	–	84.50	14.78	99.28
	20249	Cook & Co	202.70	90.00	51.22	343.92
	20250	Texas Ltd	172.00	–	30.10	202.10
	20251	Dinham Shoes	–	74.75	13.08	87.83
	20252	Mentor Ltd	72.05	200.00	47.60	319.65
		Totals	596.75	471.25	186.88	1,254.88

Activity 3.2

Task

Complete and total the sales day book of Aroma on Page 77 in respect of the following transactions. Sales are analysed into the following categories.

A   Flower sprays
B   Bouquets
C   Catering displays
D   Hire of office plants

The customer's name follows the invoice number.

17/3/X7   Invoice I2060 – Kirby Catering

Product description	Amount (inc VAT) £
Flower sprays	68.15
Bouquets	72.85
	141.00

17/3/X7   Invoice I2061 – Boddington Kitchens Ltd

Product description	Amount (inc VAT) £
Catering displays	42.03
Catering displays	30.92
Bouquets	65.00
Hire of office plants	13.67
	151.62

17/3/X7   Invoice I2062 – Invoice form spoiled

17/3/X7   Invoice I2063 – Placesetters Ltd

Product description	Amount (inc VAT) £
Catering displays	30.92
Bouquets	40.50
Hire of office plants	32.69
	104.11

PART A ACCOUNTING FOR SALES AND PURCHASES

18/3/X7   Invoice I2064 – Anston Mayne

Product description   *Amount (inc VAT)*
                                                £
Bouquets   141.00

18/3/X7   Invoice I2065 – Nye & Co

Product description   *Amount (inc VAT)*
                                                £
Flower sprays   48.62
Flower sprays   10.45
                                                59.07

18/3/X7   Invoice I2066 – Dindins Ltd

Product description   *Amount (inc VAT)*
                                                £
Catering displays   37.10
Hire of office plants   8.88
                                                45.98

18/3/X7   Invoice I2067 – Major John Design

Product description   *Amount (inc VAT)*
                                                £
Flower sprays   45.30
Bouquets   45.30
                                                90.60

Further information

Customer account numbers are as follows.

Anston Mayne	A01
Boddington Kitchens Ltd	B09
Dindins Ltd	D06
Fuller Crockery	F03
Kirby Catering	K02
Major John Design	M09
Nye & Co	N04
Placesetters Ltd	P11

Note. VAT is charged at 17.5%.

AROMA - SALES DAY BOOK

Date	Invoice No.	Customer No.	Gross total	A	B	C	D	VAT
			TOTAL					

4 What is the sales returns day book?

The **sales returns day book** lists credit notes issued in date and number order.

An entry from the sales returns day book of Boot and Shoe Supplies looks like this.

Date	Credit note number	Customer	Net total £	VAT £	Gross total £
10.1.X7	C2214	Pediform Ltd	29.40	5.14	34.54

Some sales returns day books may have an extra column headed 'goods returned', for entering a **description of the goods returned**. Alternatively the net total may be analysed between products as for the sales day book.

Businesses with a small number of returns, may enter credit notes as **figures in brackets in the sales day book** instead.

5 Analysing sales transactions in the day books

- In a **manual system of accounting**, the sales day book will have the details of each invoice – each transaction – written out by hand. The details of credit notes are similarly written directly into the sales returns day book, as we have already seen in Sections 3 and 4 above.

- In a **computerised sales system**, transaction details will probably be entered onto the system using a keyboard and VDU (visual display unit).

5.1 Analysing sales by computer

An analysis can be prepared using a **computer spreadsheet**.

You may already be familiar with spreadsheets. The use of spreadsheets is covered in more detail in Unit 4. Here we illustrate a **simple use of spreadsheets**, and some introductory details are given in case you are unfamiliar with them.

A spreadsheet is illustrated below.

The shaded square is called a **cell** and is referred to as F5 (ie where the column and row meet).

Information is inserted into a cell using a keyboard.

Spreadsheets can be used to perform mathematical tasks automatically for example, cell F5 may be set to add together any numbers entered in cells F1 to F4 above it.

Example: Analysed sales day book using a spreadsheet

Suppose that we wanted to analyse our sales transactions (at sales value excluding VAT) into the following types:

GB	Gents' boots
LB	Ladies' boots
GS	Gents' shoes
LS	Ladies' shoes
A	Shoe polish/accessories

Once we have keyed in the information on each invoice, our sales day book spreadsheet model might look like this. Note that the totals of columns F to J come to the total of column C (the sales net of VAT), not column E.

	A	B	C	D	E	F	G	H	I	J	K
1	Boot and Shoe Supplies					Credit sales			Date:	10101X1	
2	Invoice	Cust	Net	VAT	Gross	GB	LB	GS	LS	A	
3	No	No	£	£	£						
4	20247	J042	172.00	30.10	202.10		95.45		76.55		
5	20248	A009	84.50	14.78	99.28					84.50	
6	20249	C124	292.70	51.22	343.92				292.70		
7	20250	T172	172.00	30.10	202.10			172.00			
8	20251	D249	74.75	13.08	87.83	74.75					
9	20252	M201	272.05	47.60	319.65	94.20		72.42	105.43		
10											
11											
:											
24	Total		1,068.00	186.88	1,254.88	168.95	95.45	244.42	474.68	84.50	

Spreadsheets can be very useful. However, if it has been **set up incorrectly**, or if data has been **entered incorrectly** without any check being made on its accuracy, then the **spreadsheet may contain errors**. Just because a spreadsheet has been produced by a computer, it does not follow that it is free of errors.

5.2 Computerised sales packages

As with a manual sales day book, a sales day book spreadsheet can be updated by each individual invoice being entered by somebody. Many businesses operate computerised accounting packages, however, with one part dealing with sales transactions (generally called a 'sales ledger package').

PART A   ACCOUNTING FOR SALES AND PURCHASES

5.2.1 Basic system

Sales invoice produced manually → Details keyed into computer → Computer produces sales and sales returns day books

5.2.2 Invoicing package

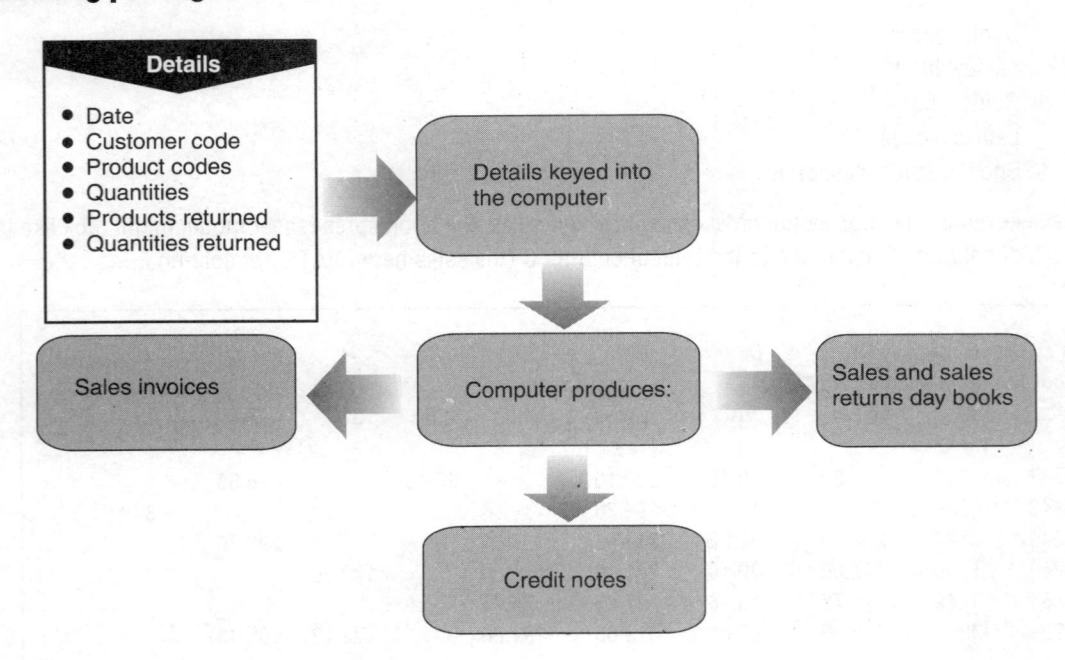

Details
- Date
- Customer code
- Product codes
- Quantities
- Products returned
- Quantities returned

→ Details keyed into the computer → Computer produces:
- Sales invoices
- Sales and sales returns day books
- Credit notes

5.2.3 Integrated system

The whole sales system is recorded by computer.

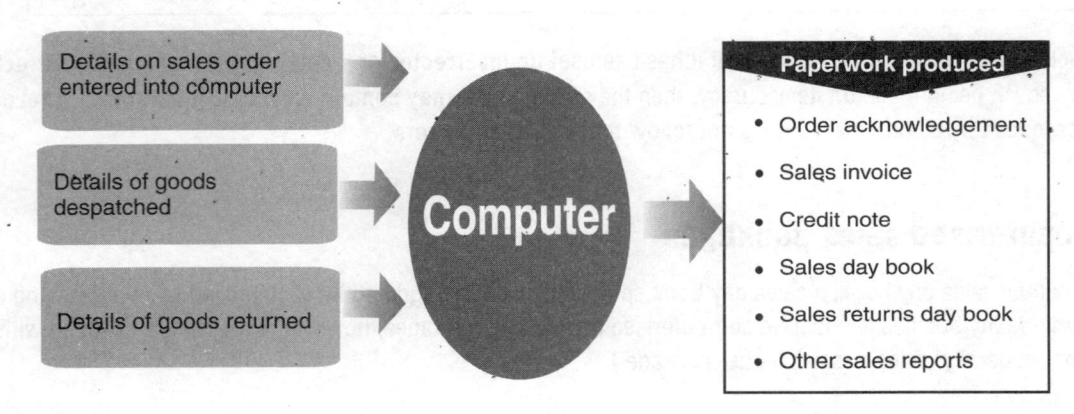

Inputs to Computer:
- Details on sales order entered into computer
- Details of goods despatched
- Details of goods returned

Paperwork produced
- Order acknowledgement
- Sales invoice
- Credit note
- Sales day book
- Sales returns day book
- Other sales reports

6 Posting the day book totals

6.1 Personal accounts for debtors

A business needs records to show when and from whom it should ask for the money due following a credit sale. Can the sales day book achieve that objective on its own?

The answer is no. A listing of sales transactions in chronological order, as in the sales day book, does not meet these needs.

- For many businesses, the sales day book includes very large numbers of invoices.
- The same customer can appear in different places in the sales day book.
- At any point in time, a customer may owe money on several unpaid invoices.

We need a way of showing **who** owes **what** amount to the business and **when**.

This need is met by keeping **'personal accounts'** for each individual customer (debtor) in the **sales ledger (**see Chapter 6).

Each individual sales transaction is entered in the sales day book and needs to be recorded in the personal sales ledger account of the customer.

Personal accounts are sometimes called 'memorandum accounts' because the recording of transactions in these accounts is **not** part of the double entry. The **general ledger** accounts to which the double entry postings are made are sometimes called 'impersonal accounts'.

6.2 Recording the double entry

The transactions entered in the sales day book need to be recorded in the 'double entry' system of bookkeeping.

We will deal with double entry bookkeeping in Chapter 5.

PART A ACCOUNTING FOR SALES AND PURCHASES

Key learning points

- ☑ The **sales day book** lists the invoices raised by a business when it supplies goods or services on credit.
- ☑ The **sales returns day book** lists the credit notes raised when goods are returned.
- ☑ The sales day book and the sales returns day book are **'books of prime entry'**: transactions are recorded in them before being recorded elsewhere.
- ☑ **How transactions are entered in the books of prime entry depends upon the accounting system used**.
  - Details will be entered from invoices in some systems.
  - In others, information about orders and goods despatched will be entered and the invoices and primary records of sales will be generated by computer.
- ☑ **Sales may be analysed** into different categories.
- ☑ A **spreadsheet** can be used to analyse the day book.
- ☑ The day book totals for sales and returns are posted to the **double entry accounts.**
- ☑ The amounts owed by individual debtors are entered in the **sales ledger personal accounts** (**memorandum accounts**).

Quick quiz

1 What is the purpose of the sales day book?
2 What is the purpose of the sales returns day book?
3 Why do businesses maintain personal accounts in the sales ledger?

    A   To backup the information in the sales day book
    B   To ensure that the sales figure is correct
    C   To show who owes what at any given time
    D   As a double check on the sales returns day book

4 A cash sale will be shown in the sales ledger. True or false?

Answers to quick quiz

1 To record credit sales on a daily basis.
2 To record returns of credit sales on a daily basis.
3 **C** To show who owes what to the business at any given time. This information is not in the sales day book or the sales returns day book.
4 False. The sales ledger only records credit sales.

PART A ACCOUNTING FOR SALES AND PURCHASES

Activity checklist

This checklist shows which performance criteria, range statement or knowledge and understanding point is covered by each activity in this chapter. Tick off each activity as you complete it.

Activity

3.1 ☐ This activity deals with Performance Criteria 1.1.D enter invoices and credit notes into books of prime entry according to organisational procedures

3.2 ☐ This activity deals with Performance Criteria 1.1.D enter invoices and credit notes into books of prime entry according to organisational procedures

chapter 4

Purchase and purchase returns day books

Contents

1 The problem
2 The solution
3 What is the purchase day book?
4 What is the purchase returns day book?
5 Entering purchase transactions in the day books
6 Posting the day book totals
7 Manual and computerised accounting systems
8 Batch processing and control totals

Performance criteria

2.1.D Correctly code invoices and credit notes
2.1.E Correctly enter invoices and credit notes into books of prime entry according to organisational procedures

Range statement

2.1.3 Code: manual system; computerised systems
2.1.5 Books prime entry: manual purchases day book; manual purchases returns day books; relevant computerised records

Knowledge and understanding

14 Methods of coding data
15 Operation of manual accounting systems
16 Operation of computerised accounting systems, including output
18 Batch control

PART A   ACCOUNTING FOR SALES AND PURCHASES

> **Signpost**
> The topics covered in this chapter are relevant to **Unit 2**.

1 The problem

A business needs to keep track of all its purchases.

- To provide a record of **total purchases**
- To make a **single payment** covering a number of invoices from one supplier
- To take advantage of **credit periods** and **discounts allowed**

A record of total purchases is needed for each accounting period (eg each month, quarter, year). This helps the business to know if its sales exceed purchases (ie it is making a profit) each period.

A business receives many invoices, and maybe some credit notes, each month. It is time consuming to pay each invoice separately. Therefore the business needs to know **how much** it owes to each supplier which can be settled by a single payment.

Most suppliers allow a business a **credit period** in which to pay (eg 30 days, 60 days). It makes sense to take advantage of this by paying towards the end of the credit period.

Taking advantage of the credit terms, helps the 'cash flow' of a business by keeping money in the bank longer.

- It earns more interest on a positive bank balance
- It pays less interest on an overdraft (negative bank balance)

2 The solution

As we saw in the previous chapter on sales the solution is to record the invoices and credit notes in day books.

Invoices are recorded in the purchase day book and credit notes received in the purchase returns day book.

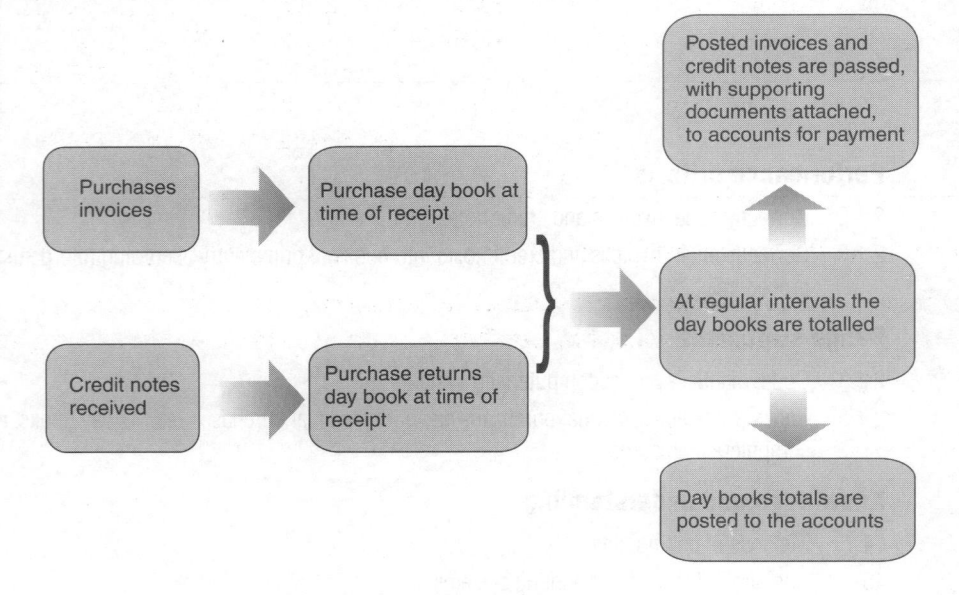

```
Purchases invoices  →  Purchase day book at time of receipt
                                                              ⎫
                                                              ⎬ →  At regular intervals the day books are totalled
                                                              ⎭
Credit notes received  →  Purchase returns day book at time of receipt

At regular intervals the day books are totalled
    ↑                                ↓
Posted invoices and credit    Day books totals are
notes are passed, with        posted to the accounts
supporting documents
attached, to accounts
for payment
```

3 What is the purchase day book?

The **source documents** – the suppliers' invoices – are recorded in the **purchase day book**.

A purchase day book is a detailed list of all the invoices received from suppliers of goods and services. It is a **book of prime entry**.

Activity 4.1

Which one of the following would you expect to see in a purchase day book?

- (a) Cash payments
- (b) Invoices received from suppliers
- (c) Cash purchases
- (d) Personal accounts
- (e) Purchase ledger control accounts

Example: Purchase day book

An extract from a purchase day book for Doppel Printers Ltd is shown below.

Date	Ref	Supplier name	Supplier a/c no	Total before VAT £	VAT £	Invoice total £
10.1.X1	1423	V Princely	4009	152.00	26.60	178.60
	1424	Grantcroft Ltd	5020	28.00	4.90	32.90
	1425	Midnorth Electric plc	4010	116.80	20.44	137.24
	1426	Hartley & Co	5008	100.00	17.50	117.50
	1427	Cardright Ltd	3972	278.00	48.65	326.65
				674.80	118.09	792.89

The purchase invoices will be from many different suppliers and, therefore, they are not sequentially numbered.

Some organisations assign **sequential numbers to purchase invoices** (using a stamp or a sticker), as Doppel Printers Ltd has (1423 – 1427). This is an example of **coding** (see Chapter 1) and helps to ensure that all purchase invoices are included in the records.

PART A   ACCOUNTING FOR SALES AND PURCHASES

Activity 4.2

Aroma has received the following invoices on 16.3.X7. The last purchase invoice entered in the purchase day book was 1763. Complete the extract from the purchase day book below.

Lampley Nurseries	£2,000 + VAT £350.00
Alfred	£500 + VAT £87.50
Bertie	£1,000 + VAT £175.00
Charlie	£200 + VAT £35.00

Lampley Nurseries is supplier L01, Alfred is A07, Bertie is B02, and Charlie is C05. (*Note:* These are further examples of coding.)

Date	Reference	Supplier	Supplier a/c no	Net	VAT	Gross

Purchase day books are almost always analysed to show the different types of purchases (see Section 5 of this chapter).

4 What is the purchase returns day book?

A business may return goods to suppliers and will expect a credit note.

The **purchase returns day book** lists credit notes received in date order.

Columns in the purchase returns day book will record similar details to those in the purchase day book illustrated in Section 3 above. There may be an extra column to record the details of the goods returned.

Goods may be returned to the supplier in the following cases.

- Goods that are **faulty** or **damaged** and a credit note requested
- Goods purchased on a **'sale or return'** basis if they cannot be sold
- Goods in good condition but **surplus to requirements** at the supplier's discretion

A business does not have to keep a separate purchase returns day book. Many businesses record credit notes as a negative entry in the purchase day book.

Activity 4.3

Which of the following cases would you classify as a purchase return? (*Helping hand:* there may be more than one right answer.)

(a) Goods purchased by a customer and returned to you.

(b) You have been billed twice, by accident, for a single amount of goods, and you return the duplicate purchase invoice.

(c) You have received some goods which are faulty and you send them back. You have posted the invoice received in respect of the goods.

(d) A customer sends back some sub-standard goods to you.

(e) A supplier sends back some goods to you which you have delivered there by mistake, thinking the supplier was in fact a customer.

(f) An item of stock is damaged in a fire at your warehouse and you have to go back to the original supplier to order a replacement.

(g) You question an invoice because you have been billed for items which you have not ordered, and which you have not received.

(h) You have been delivered a quantity of goods in excess of your requirements. The supplier agrees that you can return them.

5 Entering purchase transactions in the day books

5.1 Writing up the day books

- In a **manual system**, invoice details will be entered by hand in the purchase day book and credit note details in the purchase returns day book
- In a **computerised purchase system**, purchase invoice and credit note details will be entered directly into the computer records

5.2 Analysis of purchases

Many purchase day books have further columns which split the purchases into different categories.

PART A ACCOUNTING FOR SALES AND PURCHASES

Example: Analysing purchases

Doppel Printers Ltd makes purchases of raw materials for stock which include paper, card and ink. The company wants to analyse its other purchases into 'electricity' and 'other' categories. The purchases made on 10 January 20X1 consisted of the following.

Ref	Supplier name	Supplier a/c no	Details
1423	V Princeley	4009	Paper
1424	Grantcroft Ltd	5020	Ink
1425	Midnorth Electric plc	4010	Electricity
1426	Hartley & Co	5008	Desk fans for administrative office
1427	Cardright Ltd	3972	Card

The invoices can be analysed in the purchase day book as follows (we have omitted the column for supplier name, which can be identified from the supplier account number).

PURCHASE DAY BOOK

Date: 10.1.X1

Ref	Supplier	Net total £	VAT £	Gross total £	Paper £	Card £	Ink £	Electricity £	Other £
1423	4009	152.00	26.60	178.60	152.00				
1424	5020	28.00	4.90	32.90			28.00		
1425	4010	116.80	20.44	137.24				116.80	
1426	5008	100.00	17.50	117.50					100.00
1427	3972	278.00	48.65	326.65		278.00			
		674.80	118.09	792.89	152.00	278.00	28.00	116.80	100.00

Note that the analysis columns show amounts *exclusive* of VAT.

Activity 4.4

The invoice reference numbers and supplier codes in the above example illustrate the coding of data. If necessary, refer to Section 5 of Chapter 1, then complete the matrix below.

Code	Type of code
Invoice reference numbers	
Supplier code numbers	

Activity 4.5

Using the information in Activity 4.2 and below, complete the extract of Aroma's analysed purchase day book. Kris wants to analyse his purchases between roses, carnations and potted plants. All other items are put into the sundry column.

Lampley Nurseries: Roses £1,000, potted plants £500, carnations £300, ferns £200
Alfred: £500 carnations
Bertie: £500 carnations, £500 ferns
Charlie: £200 freesias

Aroma purchase day book

Date	Reference	Supplier Ref no	Net	VAT	Gross	Roses	Carnations	Potted plants	Sundry

How a purchase is analysed will depend upon the nature of the business. In a television and hi-fi shop, purchases of paper are likely to be analysed as stationery or office expenses.

Some businesses keep separate day books for stock purchases (the purchase day book) and for expenses (the **expenses day book**).

A spreadsheet can be used to analyse the information in the purchase day book in a similar way as shown for the sales day book in Section 5 of Chapter 3. Alternatively, an analysed purchase day book might be available in a computerised accounting package.

6 Posting the day book totals

As for sales, the totals of the purchase and purchase returns day books need to be **posted** to the accounts.

6.1 Recording transactions in personal accounts for creditors

A business needs to know **what it owes to each supplier** (creditor).

Why do the day books not meet this need? The answer is because they provide only a **chronological** listing of purchase transactions.

This could involve large numbers of purchase invoices and credit notes each day or each week. It is not practical to work out from the day books alone how much is owed to a particular supplier.

As each invoice or credit note is recorded in the day books, it is also entered in the personal purchase ledger account of the supplier. The personal accounts in the purchase ledger are **memorandum** accounts, not part of the double entry system.

The purchases also need to be recorded using double entry bookkeeping. This will be dealt with in Chapter 5.

7 Manual and computerised accounting systems

It is important to realise that all of the books of prime entry (and the ledgers) may be either hand-written books or computer records. Most businesses use computers in some way.

All computer activity can be divided into three processes.

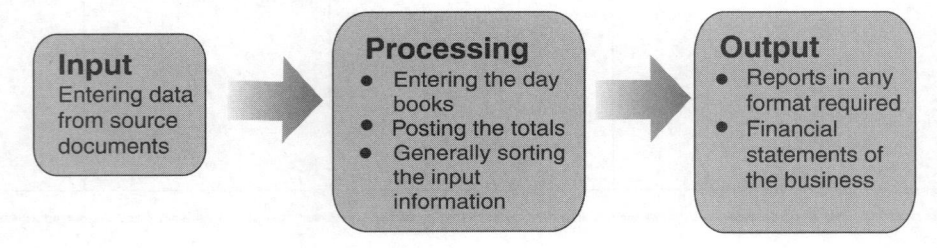

Input
Entering data from source documents

→

Processing
- Entering the day books
- Posting the totals
- Generally sorting the input information

→

Output
- Reports in any format required
- Financial statements of the business

Activity 4.6

Kris's friend Ivan Issue believes that computerised accounting systems are more trouble than they are worth because 'you never know what is going on inside that funny box'.

Task

Explain briefly why computers might be useful in accounting.

8 Batch processing and control totals

8.1 Batch processing

Batch processing is where similar transactions are gathered into batches, and then each batch is sorted and processed by the computer.

Inputting individual invoices into a computer for processing can be time consuming and expensive. Instead invoices can be gathered into a **batch** and **input and processed all together**.

Batches can vary in size, depending on the type and volume of transactions, and on any limit imposed by the system on batch sizes.

This type of processing is less time consuming than **transaction processing,** where transactions are processed individually as they arise.

8.2 Control totals

If a batch of documents is input, it is important to know that there are no errors. A **control total** is used to calculate the value of the documents and this can then be checked to the value of the batch on the computer.

Example: Control total

A batch of 30 purchase invoices has a manually calculated total value of £42,378.47. When the batch is input, the computer adds up the total value of the invoices input and produces a total of £42,378.47. The control totals agree and so no further action is required. If they were different, the operator would need to find the error eg an invoice has not been entered on the computer or the manual total was incorrect.

PART A   ACCOUNTING FOR SALES AND PURCHASES

Key learning points

- The **purchase day book** lists the invoices received from credit suppliers.
- The **purchase returns day book** lists the credit notes received when goods are returned to suppliers.
- The purchase day book and the purchase returns day book are **books of prime entry:** transactions are recorded in them before being recorded elsewhere.
- Usually, all purchases of goods and services are recorded in one day book. However, an **expenses day book** may be kept to record expenses, as distinct from purchases for stock.
- **Purchases and expenses may be analysed into different categories** in the day books. A **computer spreadsheet** might be used to produce the analysis.
- The **day book totals** for purchases and purchase returns are **posted to the accounts.**
- The **amounts owed to individual suppliers (creditors)** are **entered in the purchase ledger personal accounts (memorandum accounts).**

Quick quiz

1   What is the purchase day book used for?
2   What does the purchase returns day book do?

Answers to quick quiz

1   To keep a list of all the invoices received from suppliers of goods or services to the business.
2   It lists credit notes received in respect of purchase returns in chronological order.

PART A ACCOUNTING FOR SALES AND PURCHASES

Activity checklist

This checklist shows which performance criteria, range statement or knowledge and understanding point is covered by each activity in this chapter. Tick off each activity as you complete it.

Activity

4.1	☐	This activity deals with Range Statement 2.1.5 primary records: manual purchases day book
4.2	☐	This activity deals with Performance Criteria 2.1.E correctly enter invoices as primary records according to organisational procedures
4.3	☐	This activity deals with Range Statement 2.1.5 primary records: purchase returns day book
4.4	☐	This activity deals with Performance Criteria 2.1.D correctly code invoices and credit notes
4.5	☐	This activity deals with Performance Criteria 2.1.E correctly enter invoices as primary records according to organisational procedure
4.6	☐	This activity deals with Knowledge and Understanding 17: operation of computerised accounting systems including output

chapter 5

Double entry bookkeeping

Contents

1. The problem
2. The solution
3. Business basics
4. Assets and liabilities
5. The accounting equation
6. The business equation
7. Creditors and debtors
8. Double entry bookkeeping
9. Posting the sales day books
10. Posting the purchase day books

Performance criteria

- 1.1.D Enter invoices and credit notes into books of prime entry according to organisational procedures
- 1.1.E Enter invoices and credit notes in the appropriate ledgers
- 2.1.E Correctly enter invoices and credit notes into books of prime entry according to organisational procedures
- 2.1.F Enter invoices and credit notes in the appropriate ledgers

Knowledge and understanding

- 1.11 & 2.11 Double entry bookkeeping
- 1.22 & 2.24 Relevant understanding of the organisation's accounting systems and administrative systems and procedures
- 1.23 & 2.25 The nature of the organisation's business transactions

Signpost
The topics covered in this chapter are relevant to both **Units 1 and 2.**

PART A   ACCOUNTING FOR SALES AND PURCHASES

1 The problem

As we have seen in Chapters 3 and 4, it is easy to summarise invoices and credit notes in the day books. However we now need a way of transferring this information into the books of account.

Any method of writing up the books (bookkeeping), needs to satisfy the following.

- Reflect the commercial reality of the transaction
- Be recorded accurately
- Any errors can be spotted relatively easily

2 The solution

The solution is called **double entry bookkeeping.**

Double entry bookkeeping was invented to help medieval Italian bankers keep records of the people who gave them money to invest and those who borrowed from the banks.

The bankers realised that each transaction had a two-fold effect on the business.

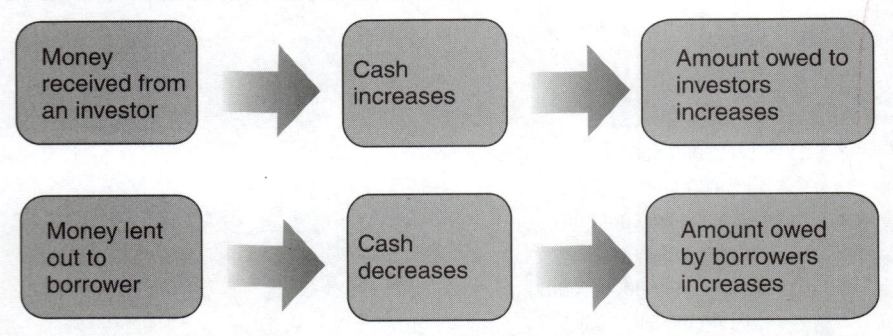

Money received from an investor → Cash increases → Amount owed to investors increases

Money lent out to borrower → Cash decreases → Amount owed by borrowers increases

Double entry bookkeeping reflects this two-fold effect by requiring two entries in the books for every transaction.

The two entries are called **debits** and **credits**. For every debit entry, there must be an equal credit entry. So when all transactions have been entered:

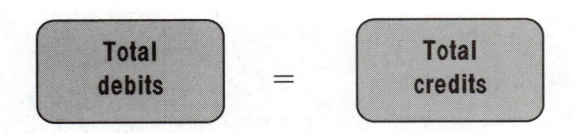

Total debits = Total credits

If total debits do not equal total credits, then an error has been made.

3 Business basics

3.1 What is a business?

Before looking at the mechanics of double entry, what do we mean by a **business**?

- A business manufactures, sells or supplies **goods and services**.
- A business uses **economic resources** to create goods or services which customers will buy.
- A business is an organisation **providing jobs** for people to work in.
- A business invests money to make even **more money for its owners.**

This last definition – investing money to make money – introduces the key idea of **profit**.

3.2 Profit

Businesses vary in character, size and complexity. They range from small businesses (the local shopkeeper or plumber) to very large ones (ICI or BP). However they all want to **earn a profit**.

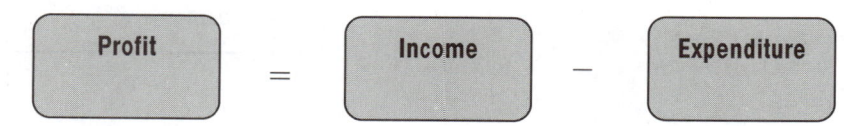

$$\boxed{\text{Profit}} = \boxed{\text{Income}} - \boxed{\text{Expenditure}}$$

If expenditure exceeds income, then a **loss** is made.

Double entry bookkeeping records income and expenditure in order to be able to calculate profit. However, double entry bookkeeping goes further than this, it also records what a business **owns** (assets) and what it **owes** (liabilities).

PART A   ACCOUNTING FOR SALES AND PURCHASES

4 Assets and liabilities

4.1 Assets

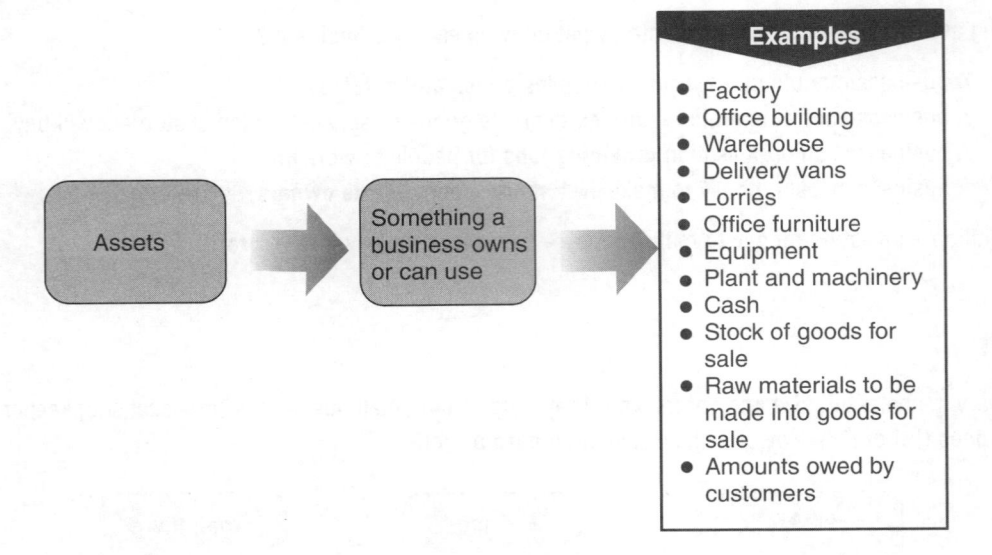

Assets → Something a business owns or can use →

Examples
- Factory
- Office building
- Warehouse
- Delivery vans
- Lorries
- Office furniture
- Equipment
- Plant and machinery
- Cash
- Stock of goods for sale
- Raw materials to be made into goods for sale
- Amounts owed by customers

4.2 Fixed assets

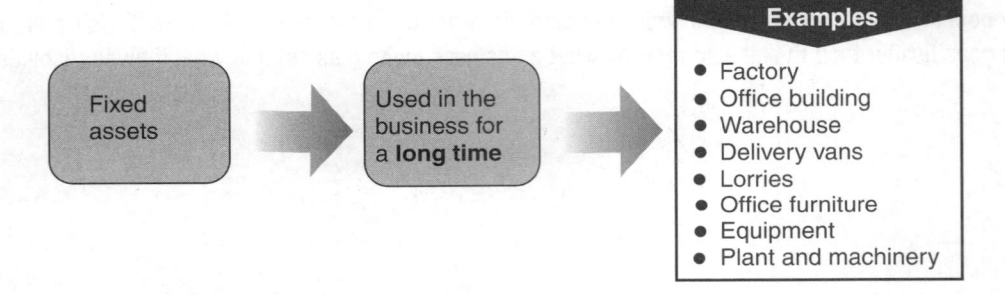

Fixed assets → Used in the business for a **long time** →

Examples
- Factory
- Office building
- Warehouse
- Delivery vans
- Lorries
- Office furniture
- Equipment
- Plant and machinery

4.3 Current assets

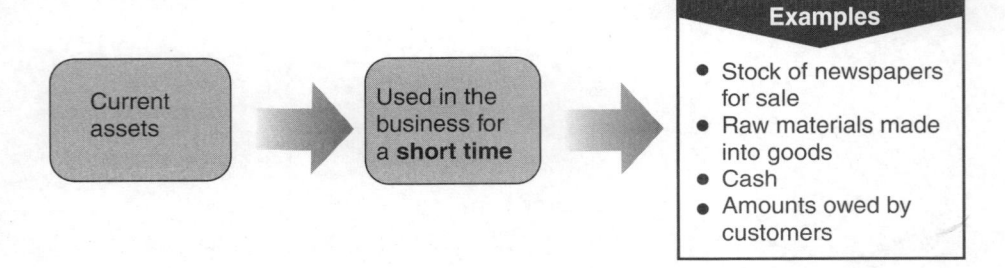

Current assets → Used in the business for a **short time** →

Examples
- Stock of newspapers for sale
- Raw materials made into goods
- Cash
- Amounts owed by customers

4.4 Liabilities

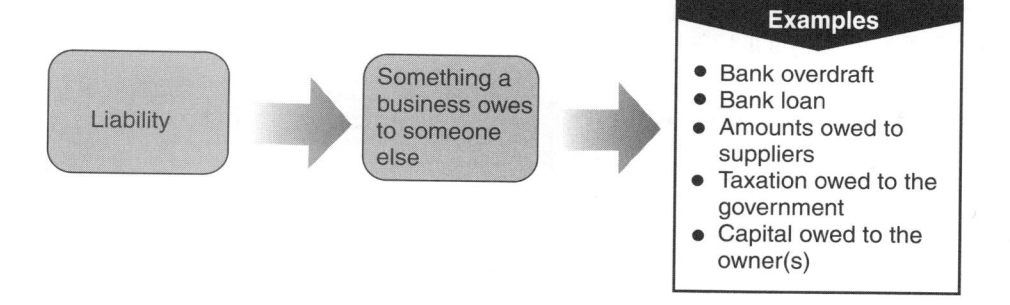

Liability → Something a business owes to someone else →

Examples
- Bank overdraft
- Bank loan
- Amounts owed to suppliers
- Taxation owed to the government
- Capital owed to the owner(s)

4.5 Capital

Examples: Ownership

(a) **Limited company**

A limited company is owned by its shareholders. In **law**, the company is separate from the shareholders. The company can make contracts in its own name, hold assets and owe liabilities. The shareholders are not responsible for the company's liabilities. The shareholders' liability is **limited** to the amount they pay for their shares.

(b) **Partnership**

A partnership is owned by two or more people. A, B and C may trade as ABC Building Supplies. However, because ABC Building Supplies is not a limited company, A, B and C are legally responsible for all the amounts owed by the partnership.

(c) **Sole trader**

A sole trader, Sonia, may trade as Sonia's Hair Salon. However, legally Sonia and her hair salon are one and the same.

In the above examples, **the law** sees no difference between a business run by a sole trader or partnership and the owner(s). However, for **accounts purposes**, the business is always treated as a separate entity from its owners.

When an owner puts money into a business, for accounts purposes this is treated as a liability of the business, and it is called **capital**.

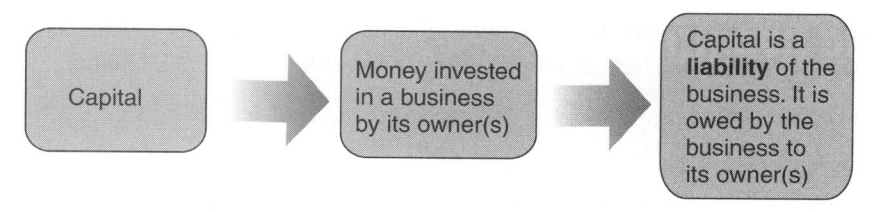

Capital → Money invested in a business by its owner(s) → Capital is a **liability** of the business. It is owed by the business to its owner(s)

PART A   ACCOUNTING FOR SALES AND PURCHASES

Activity 5.1

Complete the grid below, by ticking the appropriate column for each item.

	Asset	Liability	Capital
Bank overdraft			
Factory			
Money paid into a business by the owner			
Bank account			
Plant and machinery			
Amounts due from customers			
Amounts due from suppliers			
Stock of goods for sale			

5 The accounting equation

The **accounting equation** states that the **assets** and **liabilities** of a business must always be **equal**.

$$Assets = Liabilities$$

However, as we saw in Section 4.5 above, **capital** is a form of liability, so we can restate the accounting equation.

$$Assets = Liabilities + Capital$$

Example: Accounting equation

On 1 July 20X7, Petula opens a market stall selling perfume. She puts £2,500 from her savings into the business. From an accountant's viewpoint, the business has cash of £2,500 but owes Petula capital of £2,500.

Assets	=	Liabilities	+	Capital
Cash £2,500	=	£0	+	£2,500

As a business trades, there will be changes in the assets and liabilities. However, the accounting equation will always apply.

Example: Trading and profit

On 2 July 20X7, Petula buys 100 bottles of perfume for £1,000 and sells all of them on her market stall for £1,500 cash. How do these transactions affect the accounting equation?

(a) **Purchase of perfume**

	Assets	=	Liabilities	+	Capital
Perfume	1,000				
Cash	1,500				
(2,500 – 1,000)					
	£2,500		£0		£2,500

(b) **Sale of perfume**

Petula has sold all her perfume for £1,500 but it only cost her £1,000. Remember profit = income – expenditure.

Profit = 1,500 – 1,000
= £500

Profit is earned by the business, but how is this reflected in the accounts? Profit is owed to the owner of the business and so is added to capital.

	Assets	=	Liabilities	+		Capital
Perfume (1,000 – 1,000)	0				Capital	2,500
Cash	3,000				Profit	500
(1,500 + 1,500)					(1,500 – 1,000)	
	£3,000		£0			£3,000

So far we have only considered cash transactions. What happens to the accounting equation if credit transactions occur?

Also what happens if an owner takes money out of the business? For accounting purposes, the money an owner takes out of a business is called drawings.

Example: Credit and drawings

On 3 July 20X7, Petula buys 200 bottles of perfume for £2,000. However she agrees with the supplier that she will pay for the perfume in 7 days' time.

In the market that day Petula sells all the perfume for £3,000. She then takes out £500 for her personal use.

(a) **Purchase of perfume on credit**

	Assets	=	Liabilities		+	Capital	
Perfume	2,000		Owed to supplier	2,000		Capital b/f	3,000
Cash	3,000						
	£5,000			£2,000			£3,000

PART A ACCOUNTING FOR SALES AND PURCHASES

(b) **Sales of perfume**

Petula has sold all her perfume

Profit = income − expenditure
= 3,000 − 2,000
= £1,000

	Assets	=	Liabilities	+		Capital
Perfume (2,000 − 2,000)	0		Owed to supplier	2,000	Capital b/f	3,000
Cash (3,000 + 3,000)	6,000				Profit (3,000 − 2,000)	1,000
	£6,000			£2,000		£4,000

(c) **Drawings**

	Assets	=	Liabilities	+		Capital
Perfume	0		Owed to supplier	2,000	Capital b/f	3,000
Cash (6,000 − 500)	5,500				Profit Drawings	1,000 (500)
	£5,500			£2,000		£3,500

From the above examples, we can see

Capital = Capital introduced + Profit − Drawings

Activity 5.2

Joanne has purchased goods totalling £25,000. She paid cash of £10,000 and the rest has been bought on credit. She has only just started trading and put £20,000 cash into the business from her savings. Use the grid below to calculate the accounting equation.

Assets = Liabilities + Capital

Activity 5.3

Joanne has sold all her goods for £50,000. She withdraws £5,000 for her own use. Using the information from Activity 5.2 above, complete the grid below.

Assets   =   Liabilities   +   Capital

---

6 The business equation

As we saw above:

Assets = Liabilities + Capital

Capital = Capital introduced + Profit − Drawings

So the accounting equation can be restated as:

Assets = Liabilities + Capital introduced + Profit − Drawings

If you think about it, capital can be introduced in any period. Also profit is earned in different periods.

Assets = Liabilities + Capital introduced in current period + Capital introduced in previous periods + Profit earned in current period + Profit earned in previous periods − Drawings

The business equation is a way of calculating the profit earned in a period.

Profit earned in the current period (P) = Assets − Liabilities + Drawings in current period (D) − Capital introduced in the current period (C)

Assets less liabilities are also known as net assets. So if I is the increase in net assets in the current period:

P = I + D − C

PART A   ACCOUNTING FOR SALES AND PURCHASES

Activity 5.4

Joanne has now been in business for a year. At the beginning she introduced capital of £20,000. At the end of the year, her net assets were £50,000 and her drawings totalled £5,000. What was her profit for the year? Use the grid below.

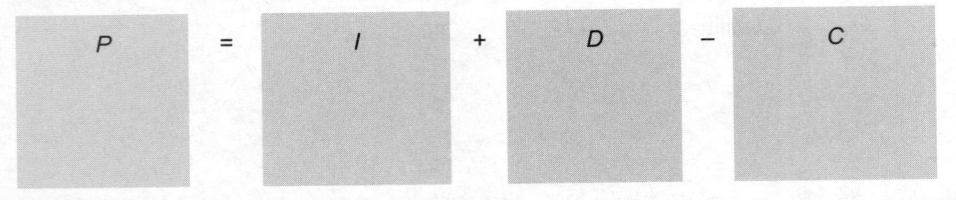

P	=	I	+	D	−	C

7 Creditors and debtors

We have already looked at sales on credit and purchases on credit in the earlier chapters of this book.

7.1 Sale on credit

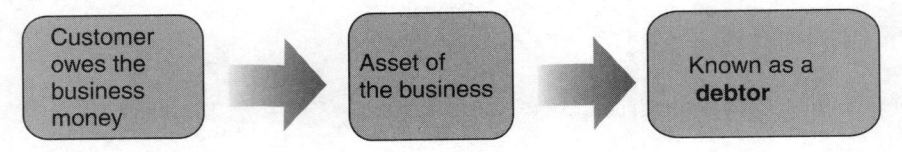

Customer owes the business money → Asset of the business → Known as a **debtor**

7.2 Purchase on credit

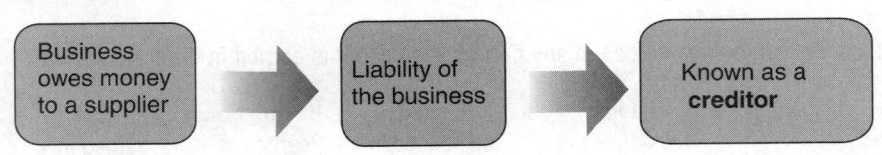

Business owes money to a supplier → Liability of the business → Known as a **creditor**

Activity 5.5

(a) Kris of Aroma buys good totalling £75,000. He pays cash of £15,000. How much does he owe his creditors?

(b) Kris has sold goods totalling £150,000. If £50,000 of this was a cash sale, how much is owed by his debtors?

8 Double entry bookkeeping

8.1 Introduction

We are now in a position to look at the bookkeeping entries of the business.

A **debit** is used to record increases in **assets**.

A **credit** is used to record increases in **liabilities** or **capital**

From Section 5, the accounting equation states:

| Assets | = | Liabilities | + | Capital |

So, from the two-fold nature of transactions:

| Total debits | = | Total credits |

8.2 Double entry bookkeeping

Transactions are usually recorded in a 'T' account, with debits on the left hand side and credits on the right.

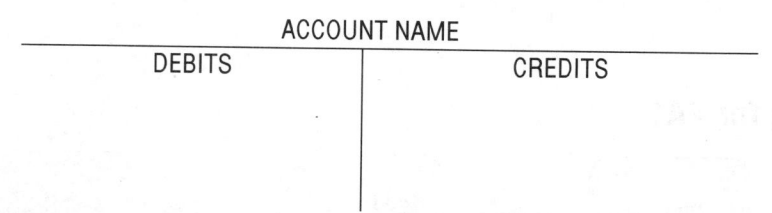

```
                    ACCOUNT NAME
         DEBITS          |         CREDITS
                         |
                         |
```

The two sides of the 'T' represent the two sides of the accounting equation.

```
                    ACCOUNT NAME
         DEBITS          |         CREDITS
         Assets          |         Liabilities
                         |         Capital
                         |
```

So a debit will **increase** an asset and a credit will **decrease** an asset. Similarly a credit will **increase** a liability and a debit will decrease it.

Remember that:

| Capital | = | Capital introduced | + | Profit | − | Drawings |

As profit increases capital, profit will be a **credit** entry in the accounts. However drawings decrease capital and so drawings will be a **debit** entry.

PART A ACCOUNTING FOR SALES AND PURCHASES

Profit can be stated as:

Profit = Income − Expenditure

Income increases profit and so is a **credit** entry, while expenditure decreases profit and so is a **debit** entry.

8.2.1 Summary:

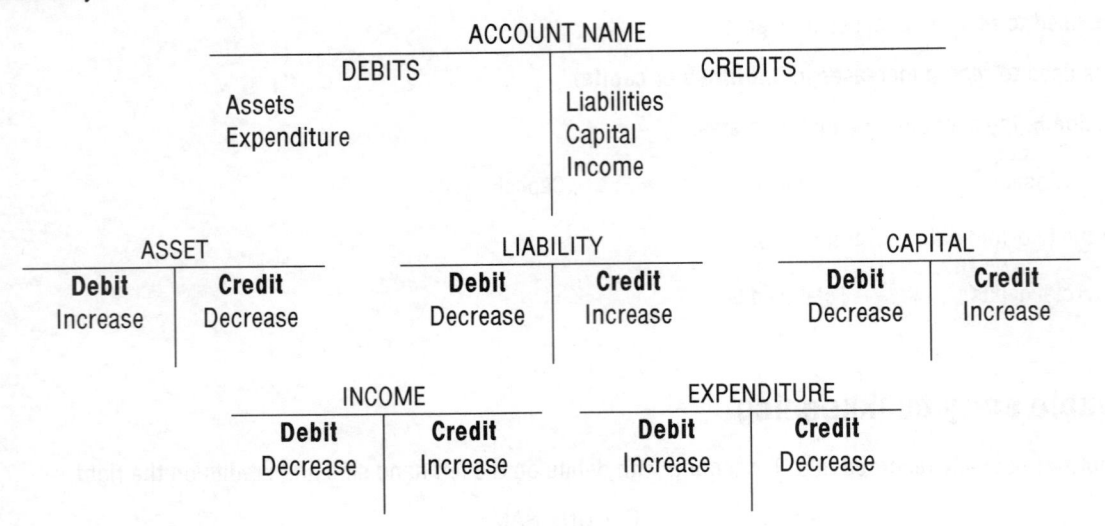

ACCOUNT NAME	
DEBITS	**CREDITS**
Assets	Liabilities
Expenditure	Capital
	Income

ASSET			LIABILITY			CAPITAL	
Debit	**Credit**		**Debit**	**Credit**		**Debit**	**Credit**
Increase	Decrease		Decrease	Increase		Decrease	Increase

INCOME			EXPENDITURE	
Debit	**Credit**		**Debit**	**Credit**
Decrease	Increase		Increase	Decrease

8.3 Accounting for VAT

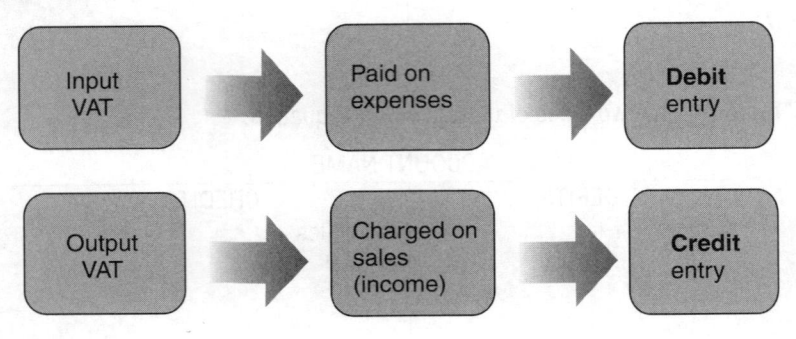

Input VAT → Paid on expenses → **Debit** entry

Output VAT → Charged on sales (income) → **Credit** entry

Therefore the VAT account is

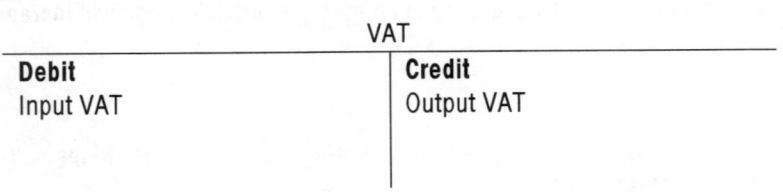

VAT	
Debit	**Credit**
Input VAT	Output VAT

Example: Double entry

Consider the position of Petula at the end of 3 July 20X7. What transactions have been carried out since she started business on 1 July 20X7 and what is the double entry?

(a) **1 July 20X7**

		Debit	*Credit*
(i)	Introduction of cash – increases asset of cash and increases capital owed to Petula	Cash: £2,500	Capital: £2,500

(b) **2 July 20X7**

		Debit	*Credit*
(i)	Purchase of perfume – increases expenditure on purchases and decreases asset of cash	Purchases: £1,000	Cash: £1,000
(ii)	Sale of perfume – cash increased by £1,500, and income (sales) increased by £1,500	Cash: £1,500	Sales: £1,500

(c) **3 July 20X7**

		Debit	*Credit*
(i)	**Purchase on credit** Purchases of perfume increased and creditors increased	Purchases: £2,000	Creditors: £2,000
(ii)	**Sale of perfume** Sales increased by £3,000, and cash increased by £3,000	Cash: £3,000	Sales: £3,000
(iii)	**Drawings** Cash decreased and drawings increased	Drawings: £500	Cash: £500

Tutorial note. It is usual to post total income received to sales and to work out the total profit figure at the end of a period, rather than on each transaction.

Example: Entries in the accounts

If we post the entries to the 'T' accounts, we get the following position.

CASH

		£			£
1.7.X7	Capital	2,500	2.7.X7	Purchases	1,000
2.7.X7	Sales	1,500	3.7.X7	Drawings	500
3.7.X7	Sales	3,000			

CAPITAL

		£			£
3.7.X7	Cash (drawings)	500	1.7.X7	Cash	2,500

PURCHASES

		£		£
2.7.X7	Cash	1,000		
3.7.X7	Creditors	2,000		

PART A ACCOUNTING FOR SALES AND PURCHASES

	SALES		
£			£
	2.7.X7	Cash	1,500
	3.7.X7	Cash	3,000

	CREDITORS		
£			£
	3.7.X7	Purchases	2,000

Activity 5.6

Complete the grid below to reflect the double entry for the following transactions.

                                              Debit   *Credit*

(a) Loan of £5,000 received from the bank
(b) A payment of £800 cash for purchases
(c) The owner takes £50 cash to buy a birthday present for her husband
(d) The business sells goods costing £300 for £450 cash
(e) The business sells goods costing £300 for £450 on credit

Activity 5.7

Now post the transactions in Activity 5.6 to the 'T' accounts.

	CASH			BANK LOAN	
£		£	£		£

	PURCHASES			DRAWINGS	
£		£	£		£

	SALES			DEBTORS	
£		£	£		£

9 Posting the sales day books

The transactions entered in the sales day book need to be recorded in the accounts by 'double entry'.

Before we can record the double entry, the sales day book must be **totalled** and **ruled off**, to include all transactions since the book was last ruled off. In our examples in Chapter 3, the day books have already been ruled off and totalled.

A business will have a **cash account** as part of its double entry in which receipts of cash are recorded.

Clearly no entries can be made in the cash account when a credit transaction first takes place, because initially no cash has been received. Where then are the details of the transaction entered?

The solution is to use a sales ledger control account, also called a sales control account, a debtors' control account or a total debtors' account. This shows the total amount owing from debtors at any time.

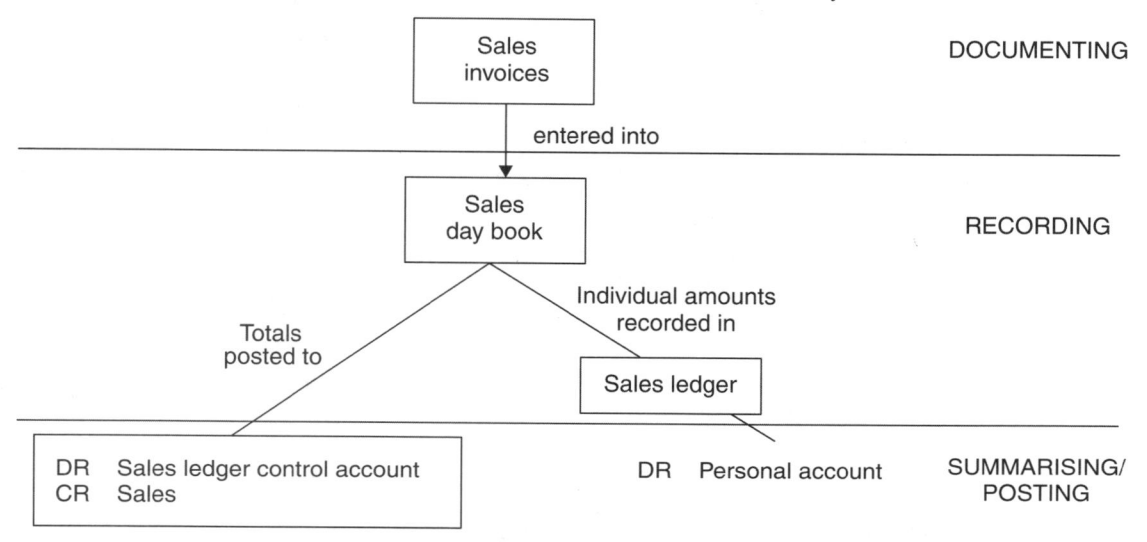

```
                     ┌─────────────┐
                     │    Sales    │                    DOCUMENTING
                     │  invoices   │
                     └──────┬──────┘
                        entered into
─────────────────────────────┼──────────────────────────────────────
                     ┌──────▼──────┐
                     │    Sales    │                    RECORDING
                     │  day book   │
                     └──┬───────┬──┘
                        │       │  Individual amounts
              Totals    │       │     recorded in
             posted to  │       │
                        │    ┌──▼────────┐
                        │    │Sales ledger│
                        │    └─────┬─────┘
─────────────────────────┼──────────┼────────────────────────────────
     ┌──────────────────▼──────┐   │
     │ DR  Sales ledger control │   │  DR  Personal account   SUMMARISING/
     │     account              │   │                          POSTING
     │ CR  Sales                │   │
     └──────────────────────────┘
```

We will look at the sales ledger in detail in Chapter 6.

9.1 The double entry

The sales summarised in the sales day book have two aspects:

- An increase in an **asset** (debtors) – a debit entry
- An increase in **income** (sales) – a credit entry

For sales made to credit customers the entries made will be:

		£	£
DEBIT	Debtors (Sales ledger control account)	X	
CREDIT	Sales account		X

We do not need to record each sales transaction separately in the ledger. We use the day book totals to summarise the transactions.

PART A   ACCOUNTING FOR SALES AND PURCHASES

9.1.1 VAT

Looking back at the transactions in Chapter 3, VAT is charged on the sales. The business must account to HM Customs & Excise for the output VAT it collects.

In order to keep track of the amount it owes to or is owed by Customs and Excise, the business keeps a Value Added Tax Account (perhaps called a VAT Control Account).

The VAT which customers owe to the business is included in the overall amount owed (debtors), but the other side of the entry for the output VAT is an **increase in the liability of the business to pay over VAT to HM Customs & Excise**. The double entry will have this form.

		£	£
DEBIT	Sales ledger control account (gross)	X	
CREDIT	VAT account		X
	Sales account (net)		X

9.1.2 Sales returns day book

When goods are returned, we want to decrease sales. The double entry will take the following form.

		£	£
DEBIT	VAT account	X	
	Returns account (or sales account) (net)	X	
CREDIT	Sales ledger control account (gross)		X

9.1.3 Sales analysis

Sales can be analysed into different categories in the sales day book. Rather than maintaining a single account for sales, a business may split the sales into a number of accounts.

Example: Double entry recording of sales

Using the example in Chapter 3, Section 5, the double entry for Boot and Shoe Supplies would look like this:

		£	£
DEBIT	Sales ledger control account	1,254.88	
CREDIT	VAT control account		186.88
	Sales – gents' boots account		168.95
	Sales – ladies' boots account		95.45
	Sales – gents' shoes account		244.42
	Sales – ladies' shoes account		474.68
	Sales – shoe polish/accessories account		84.50

The total amount posted to the debit side equals the total amount posted to the credit side (check this).

9.2 The posting summary

The entries from Boot and Shoe Supplies' sales day book and sales return day book in Chapter 3, can be summarised in a **posting summary**.

Example: Posting summary

BOOT AND SHOE SUPPLIES
Posting summary

Account name	Account code	Dr £	Dr p	Cr £	Cr p
Sales ledger control a/c	60400	1,254	88	34	54
Sales - GB	01010			168	95
Sales - LB	01020			95	45
Sales - GS	01030			244	42
Sales - LS	01040			474	68
Sales - A	01050			84	50
Returns - GB	01110	29	40		
VAT	70700	5	14	186	88
TOTALS		**1,289**	**42**	**1,289**	**42**

Posted by ......C.F............   Date ......10/1/X7............

The total of the **debits** and **credits** posted must be equal. If these two columns do not add to the same figures, there is an error. The error must be found before postings are made.

Debit is abbreviated to Dr and credit to Cr.

Once a posting summary has been entered in the books, it is **filed** for future reference

PART A ACCOUNTING FOR SALES AND PURCHASES

Activity 5.8

Task

Complete the posting summary form below with the double entry required to record the sales on 17 and 18 March 20X7 as detailed in Activity 3.2 in Chapter 3.

AROMA			No:	
Posting summary				
Date .... Prepared by .... Authorised by				
Account		Code	DR £ p	CR £ p
Totals				

5: DOUBLE ENTRY BOOKKEEPING

Further information

The last postings form was numbered 120.

The following is a list of account codes, for use in Activities 5.8 and 5.9.

Sales A	2010
Sales B	2020
Sales C	2030
Sales D	2040
Sales returns A	2310
Sales returns B	2320
Sales returns C	2330
Sales returns D	2340
VAT control account	4000
Purchase ledger control account	0310
Sales ledger control account	0210

Activity 5.9

On 24 March 20X7, the sales returns day book of Aroma records the fact that credit notes were issued to Anston Mayne and Major John Design in respect of all the purchases they made on 18 March 20X7 (as recorded in Activity 3.2).

Task

Using the account codes given in Activity 5.8, complete the posting summary form below (to be numbered 132) with the double entry required to record the issue of these credit notes.

PART A ACCOUNTING FOR SALES AND PURCHASES

AROMA			No:	
Posting summary				
Date .... Prepared by .... Authorised by				
Account	Code	DR £ p		CR £ p
Totals				

Activity 5.10

(a) The closing balance at the end of an accounting period for Aroma's VAT control account is £12,572.50 CR.

    (i) This means that £12,572.50 is owed by .... to .... (complete the blanks).

    (ii) Does the balance represent an asset or a liability?

        Asset / Liability   (circle the correct answer)

(b) The closing balances on the accounts below are credit or debit balances, as indicated. Indicate by circling the correct answer whether the balances represent an asset to the business, a liability of the business, an expense item or income earned (revenue).

Account	Credit or debit balance				
Sales	CREDIT	Asset	Liability	Expense	Revenue
Sales returns	DEBIT	Asset	Liability	Expense	Revenue
Sales ledger control account	DEBIT	Asset	Liability	Expense	Revenue
Discounts allowed	DEBIT	Asset	Liability	Expense	Revenue
Cash	CREDIT	Asset	Liability	Expense	Revenue

9.3 Cash sales

A cash sale does **not pass through the sales ledger** nor the **sales ledger control account**. The double entry can be completed in the form:

		£	£
DEBIT	Cash account (gross)	X	
CREDIT	VAT account		X
	Sales (net)		X

10 Posting the purchase day books

We will now look at **posting** the purchases information in the accounts of the business.

10.1 Double entry recording of purchases

There is a **purchase ledger control account** (or 'creditors control account'). This records **in total** the amounts owing to creditors.

PART A ACCOUNTING FOR SALES AND PURCHASES

Purchases can be of **capital** or **revenue** items.

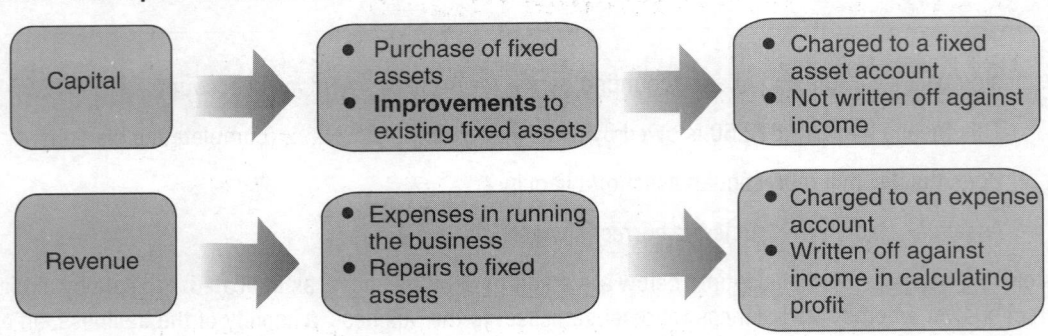

```
Capital  ⟹  • Purchase of fixed assets        ⟹  • Charged to a fixed asset account
              • Improvements to existing            • Not written off against income
                fixed assets

Revenue  ⟹  • Expenses in running the business ⟹  • Charged to an expense account
              • Repairs to fixed assets             • Written off against income in
                                                      calculating profit
```

When a business purchases something on credit from a supplier, the double entry will be:

(a) a **credit** to the purchase ledger control account

(b) a **debit** to either:

   (i) purchases (a purchase for resale) or expenses (eg office stationery, electricity, rent)

   or

   (ii) fixed assets (if the item is capital expenditure)

We can show the basic double entry as follows.

		£	£
DEBIT	Purchases/expenses/fixed asset account	X	
CREDIT	Purchase ledger control account		X

Usually purchases are all posted to one purchases account. However, expenses are posted to different accounts for each type of expense eg rent account, electricity account, etc. Similarly fixed assets are usually posted to separate accounts for factory, plant and machinery, office equipment etc.

10.1.1 VAT and purchases

In most businesses part of the amount due to the creditors is input VAT. The other side of the double entry for VAT is a **decrease** in the liability to HM Customs & Excise. So this is a **debit** to the VAT (control) account in the main ledger.

The double entry for **VAT and purchases** will therefore be as follows.

		£	£
DEBIT	Purchases/expenses account (net)	X	
	VAT account	X	
CREDIT	Purchase ledger control account (gross)		X

The double entry for **purchase returns including VAT** (credit notes received) will be as follows.

		£	£
DEBIT	Purchase ledger control account (gross)	X	
CREDIT	VAT account		X
	Purchases/expenses account (net)		X

Example: Posting purchases and returns

The double entry needs to be posted for the purchases made in Section 5 of Chapter 4. The following credit note (in respect of damaged paper) is shown in the purchase returns day book of Doppel Printers Ltd for 10 January 20X7.

				RDB07
Ref	Supplier a/c no.	Net total £	VAT £	Gross total £
C014	4009	30.00	5.25	35.25

First show the posting summary for the purchases. Check that you can see how the necessary information is derived from the analysed day book.

		£	£
DEBIT	Paper account	152.00	
	Card account	278.00	
	Ink account	28.00	
	Electricity account	116.80	
	Other expenses account	100.00	
	VAT account	118.09	
CREDIT	Purchase ledger control account		792.89
		792.89	792.89

And now the purchase return.

		£	£
DEBIT	Purchase ledger control account	35.25	
CREDIT	VAT account		5.25
	Paper account		30.00
		35.25	35.25

Doppel Printers Ltd might use a posting summary like the one below.

PART A ACCOUNTING FOR SALES AND PURCHASES

DOPPEL PRINTERS LIMITED
Postings sheet

Account name	Account code	Nominal ledger Dr £ p	Nominal ledger Cr £ p
Purchase ledger control account	70100	35 25	792 89
Paper	02400	152 00	
Electricity	03215	116 80	
Other expenses	03428	100 00	
Paper returns	02401		30 00
VAT	70200	118 09	5 25
Card	02500	278 00	
Ink	02600	28 00	
TOTALS		828 14	828 14

Posted by .......A.B............ Date ....10/1/X7..........

Activity 5.11

You work for Bodgett DIY. You receive the following invoices from suppliers on the morning of 23 November 20X7. Each invoice has already been given a reference for Bodgett DIY's own accounting system.

Tasks

(a) Post the invoices to the purchase day book, using the sheet provided on Page 125.

(b) Set out the *double entry* for these transactions. Use the *account postings* form provided on Page 126.

5: DOUBLE ENTRY BOOKKEEPING

Supplier account codes
Macin	1310
Payper, Overr, Crackes	1510
Pitiso Tools	1550
Throne Bathware	2010

Main ledger account codes
VAT	0694
Purchase ledger control account	0730
Tool purchases	4000
Painting and decorating purchases	5000
Bathroom items purchases	6000

To: Purchase ledger
Bodgett's DIY
Broad Street
Stornaway
ORKNEY

PITISO TOOLS
Zhivago House
Lawrence Street, Edinburgh
Phone: 01939 72101

SALES INVOICE
No: 21379
Date: 21/11/X7
Tax point: 21/11/X7

Stock code	Item	Quantity	£ p	£ p
0105	Hammer drills	20	70.00	1,400.00
0210	Hacksaw	10	5.00	50.00
0340	Electric screwdriver	15	7.00	105.00
0560	Hammers (10 in)	7	1.50	10.50
0791	Vices - metal	4	3.95	15.80
				1,581.30
		VAT 17 ½%		276.72
		TOTAL PAYABLE		1,858.02

Delivery
- as above

Bodgett's reference number 712

Pitiso Tools Ltd Registered Office: Zhivago House, Lawrence Street, Edinburgh
Reg No: 322 1014   VAT: 875 2121 91

PART A ACCOUNTING FOR SALES AND PURCHASES

MACIN	
Macin (UK) Ltd Northern Region Convention Street GLASGOW (Phone 01838 89414) VAT reg 389 4121 05	To: Purchase Ledger Bodgett's DIY Superstore Broad Street STORNAWAY
Invoice No: 84/Q	Customer No: BODG 1
Date/tax point: 21/11/X7	Terms: 28 days

Items ordered	Quantity	Unit price £ p	Total £ p
Paint stripper PYB75 White gloss paint DUL10 Primer SX91 Wallpaper paste 'STICKO-2000'	200 tins 400 x 1 litre 800 x 0.5 litre 500 packets	4.00 12.00 5.00 3.50	800.00 4,800.00 4,000.00 1,750.00
Total			11,350.00
VAT @ 17 ½%			1,986.25
Total payable		⟶	13,336.25
Reg office: Water Street, Rainham, Essex Reg no: 528 1000			

Bodgett's reference number: 713

THRONE Bathware

Habsburg Street
Windsor
BERKS
01421 374911

VAT reg 413 9721 08

SALES INVOICE

No: 4963
Date/tax point: 21/11/x7

Purchase Ledger
Bodgett's DIY Superstore
Broad Street
STORNAWAY

Description	£ p	Quantity	£ p
Wash basin 12 x 15	25.90	2	51.80
Kitchen sink 'Excelsior'	31.20	3	93.60
Steel taps	7.40	7	51.80
Gold plated taps	60.50	6	363.00
Baths	200.20	4	800.80
Micro-whirlpool bath	250.10	1	250.10
'Luxor' shower units	70.30	5	351.50
'Standard' shower units	50.30	4	201.20
Total			2,163.80
VAT @ 17 ½%			378.66
Total including VAT			2,542.46

Bodgett's reference number: 714

Reg office: Habsburg Street, Windsor, Berks
Reg no: 7000

PART A ACCOUNTING FOR SALES AND PURCHASES

Bodgett DIY
Broad Street
Stornaway
ORKNEY

Delivery if different

PAPER, OVERR, CRACKES HOME FURNISHINGS

Plastery House, Rachman Street, Inverness
Phone: (01563) 810372

SALES INVOICE: 0711

DATE/TAX POINT: 21/11/X7

Item	Code	Quantity	£ p	£ p
Towel rails for bathroom	B121	1	16.90	16.90
Wallpaper 4 x 20 metres	H272	10	8.50	85.00
Wallpaper 4 X 40 metres	H274	15	16.25	243.75
Curtain rails 'A'	H351	10	20.00	200.00
Curtain rails 'B'	H352	12	35.00	420.00
				965.65
Value Added Tax				17½ %
				168.98
Total payable				1,134.63

Bodgett's reference number: 715

VAT registration no: 434 5567 89

Bodgett Purchase day book analysis

Page 41

	A	B	C	D	E	F	G	H	I	J	K	L	M
1													
2	Date	Ref	Supplier	Supplier account	Total	VAT	Purchase cost	Tools	Painting & decorating	Bathroom items			
3													
4	23/11/97												
5													
6													
7													
8													
9													
10													
11													
12													
13													
14	Total for 23/11/97												

PART A   ACCOUNTING FOR SALES AND PURCHASES

ACCOUNT POSTINGS			DR	CR
Account code	Ref		£　p	£　p
DATE				
Posted by				

Activity 5.12

Tasks

(a) Enter the details supplied below into the *purchase returns day book* of Bodgett DIY for 23 November 20X7, using the sheet provided on page 128.

(b) Write the necessary double entry on the account postings form provided on page 129.

Items to be entered to purchase returns day book

1. A consignment of bathroom units from Dothelot DIY was found to be infested with woodworm. It was billed on invoice 7912, and the purchase day book reference is 613. The amount is valued at £176.25 inclusive of VAT.

2. Some paint stripper bought from C and R Builders Merchants Wholesalers plc had to be returned because it did not comply with the safety standards specified by Bodgett's DIY a while before. The amount was £221 excluding VAT. This was on supplier invoice 794, purchase day book reference 612.

3. Some items of bathroom equipment from The House Foundation had to be returned as they were leaking. The value of the goods returned, excluding VAT, was £959.59. This was found on supplier invoice 91113, purchase day book reference 627.

Dothelot, C and R, and The House Foundation will be sent debit notes number 64, 65 and 66 respectively dealing with these items.

Account numbers in Bodgett's accounting system are as follows.

Purchase ledger account codes
C and R	7211
Dothelot	8523
The House Foundation	6644

Main ledger account codes
Purchases returns (bathware)	6050
Purchases returns (painting and decorating)	5050
Purchases returns (tools)	4050
VAT	0694
Purchase ledger control account	0730

PART A ACCOUNTING FOR SALES AND PURCHASES

	A	B	C	D	E	F	G	H	I	J	K	L	M
1	Bodgett	Purchase returns day book										Page 5	
2	Date	Debit note ref	Supplier	Supplier account	Total	VAT	Purchase return total	Tools	Painting & decorating	Bathroom items	Purchase ref		
3													
4													
5	23/11/X7												
6													
7													
8													
9													
10													
11													
12													
13													
14	Total for 23/11/X7												

ACCOUNT POSTINGS

Account code	Ref		DR £ p	CR £ p

DATE

Posted by ....

PART A ACCOUNTING FOR SALES AND PURCHASES

Key learning points

- ☑ In order to achieve competence in the skills test for Units 1 and 2 it is vital that you acquire a thorough understanding of the **principles of double entry bookkeeping.**
- ☑ A **business** may be defined in various ways. Its purpose is to make a **profit** for its owner(s).
- ☑ **Profit** is the excess of income over expenditure.
- ☑ A business **owns assets** and **owes liabilities**.
- ☑ For accounting purposes it is important to keep business assets and liabilities **separate** from the personal assets and liabilities of the owners.
- ☑ **Assets** are items belonging to a business and used in the running of the business. They may be **fixed** (such as machinery or office premises), or **current** (such as stock, debtors and cash).
- ☑ **Liabilities** are sums of money owed by a business to outsiders such as a bank or a trade creditor.
- ☑ **Assets = Capital + Liabilities** (the accounting equation).
- ☑ **P = I + D − C** (the business equation).
- ☑ Double entry book-keeping requires that every transaction has two accounting entries, a **debit** and a **credit.**
- ☑ The sales day book totals are posted as follows.

  - DEBIT: Sales ledger control account (gross) £X
  - CREDIT: VAT account £X
  - Sales account (net) £X

- ☑ The amounts owed by individual debtors are posted to the sales ledger **personal** (memorandum) accounts.
- ☑ The purchase day book totals are posted as follows.

  - DEBIT: Purchases/expenses/fixed assets (net) £X
  - VAT account £X
  - CREDIT: Purchase ledger control account (gross) £X

- ☑ The amounts owed to individual creditors are posted to the purchase ledger **personal** (memorandum) accounts.

Quick quiz

1. *Complete the blank.* A business's prime objective is earning a _____.
2. Define profit.
3. Which of the following is an asset?

    A Bank overdraft

    B Stock for resale

    C Creditor

    D Bank loan

4. Which of the following is a liability?

    A Factory

    B Plant and equipment

    C Capital

    D Debtor

5. How does the accounting view of the relationship between a business and its owner differ from the strictly legal view?
6. State the basic accounting equation.
7. What does the business equation attempt to show?
8. What is the main difference between a cash and a credit transaction?
9. Define double entry book-keeping.
10. What is the double entry for a credit purchase?

DEBIT	CREDIT

11. What is the double entry where a credit sale includes VAT?

DEBIT	CREDIT

PART A   ACCOUNTING FOR SALES AND PURCHASES

Answers to quick quiz

1 A business's prime objective is earning a **profit**.

2 Profit is the excess of income over expenditure.

3 **B** Stock for resale. The rest are liabilities.

4 **C** Capital is owed to the owner(s) and is a liability. The rest are assets.

5 In accounting a business is always treated as a separate entity from its owners, even though in law there is not always a distinction (eg a sole trader and a partnership).

6 Assets = Capital + Liabilities.

7 The business equation describes the relationship between a business's increase in net assets in a period, the profit earned, drawings taken and capital introduced.

8 The main difference between a cash and a credit transaction is simply a matter of time - cash changes hands immediately in a cash transaction, whereas in a credit one it changes hands some time after the initial sale/purchase takes place.

9 Double entry book-keeping is a system of accounting which reflects the fact that every financial transaction gives rise to two equal accounting entries, a debit and a credit.

10

DEBIT	CREDIT
Purchases	Creditors (purchase ledger control account)

11

DEBIT	CREDIT
	Sales (net)
Debtors (sales ledger control account) (gross)	VAT

5: DOUBLE ENTRY BOOKKEEPING

Activity checklist

This checklist shows which performance criteria, range statement or knowledge and understanding point is covered by each activity in this chapter. Tick off each activity as you complete it.

Activity

5.1	☐	This activity deals with Knowledge and Understanding points 1.23 and 2.25: the nature of the organisation's business transactions.
5.2	☐	This activity deals with Knowledge and Understanding points 1.23 and 2.25: the nature of the organisation's business transactions.
5.3	☐	This activity deals with Knowledge and Understanding points 1.23 and 2.25: the nature of the organisation's business transactions.
5.4	☐	This activity deals with Knowledge and Understanding points 1.23 and 2.25: the nature of the organisation's business transactions.
5.5	☐	This activity deals with Knowledge and Understanding points 1.23 and 2.25: the nature of the organisation's business transactions.
5.6	☐	This activity deals with Knowledge and Understanding points 1.11 and 2.11: double entry bookkeeping.
5.7	☐	This activity deals with Knowledge and Understanding points 1.11 and 2.11: double entry bookkeeping.
5.8	☐	This activity deals with Knowledge and Understanding points 1.11 and 2.11: double entry bookkeeping.
5.9	☐	This activity deals with Knowledge and Understanding points 1.11 and 2.11: double entry bookkeeping.
5.10	☐	This activity deals with Knowledge and Understanding points 1.11 and 2.11: double entry bookkeeping.
5.11	☐	This activity deals with Performance Criteria 2.1.E and 2.1.F regarding purchases invoices.
5.12	☐	This activity deals with Performance Criteria 2.1.E and 2.1.F regarding purchase credit notes.

PART A ACCOUNTING FOR SALES AND PURCHASES

chapter 6

The sales ledger

Contents

1. The problem
2. The solution
3. Personal accounts for credit customers
4. Maintaining customer records
5. Recording transactions in the sales ledger
6. Matching cash received

Performance criteria
1.1.E Enter invoices and credit notes in the appropriate ledgers

Range statement
1.1.5 Ledger: manual main ledger; manual subsidiary ledger; computerised ledgers

Knowledge and understanding
11 Double entry bookkeeping, including balancing accounts
18 Relationship between the accounting system and the ledger
22 Relevant understanding of the organisation's accounting systems and administrative systems and procedures

Signpost
The topics covered in this chapter are relevant to **Unit 1.**

PART A   ACCOUNTING FOR SALES AND PURCHASES

1 The problem

A business needs to know what each individual customer owes to the business.

- A customer may **query** his account balance
- A business usually sends out **monthly statements** to each customer
- Managers need to check the **credit position** of each customer and ensure that they do not exceed their **credit limit**
- A business needs to **match** payments received to individual invoices

The sales day book does not fulfil these needs, as it is simply a chronological listing of invoices issued.

2 The solution

The solution is to have **personal** accounts for each customer, showing the balance owing to the business. The ledger containing all of these personal accounts is called the **sales ledger**.

2.1 Sales ledger postings

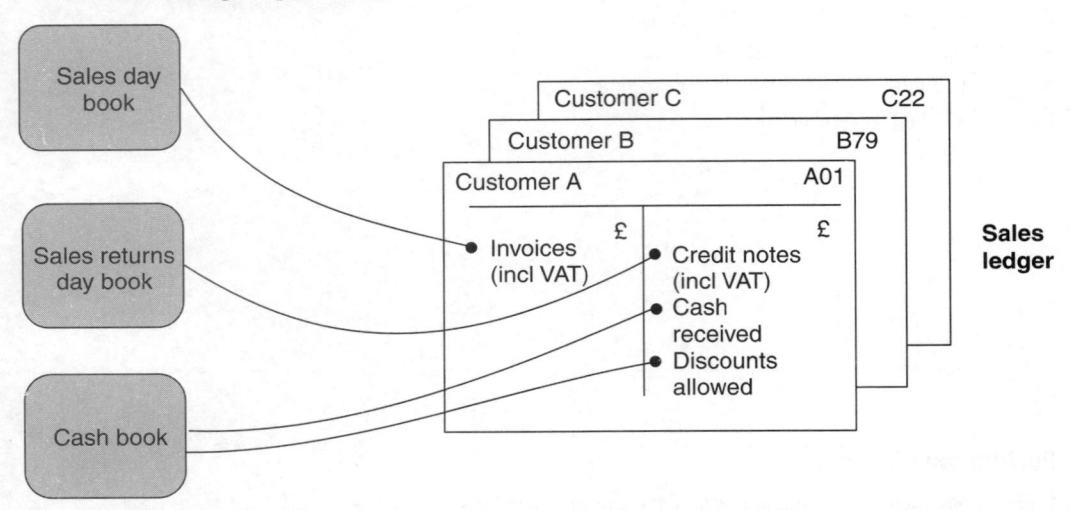

Sales day book → Invoices (incl VAT)

Sales returns day book → Credit notes (incl VAT)

Cash book → Cash received, Discounts allowed

Customer A A01
Customer B B79
Customer C C22

Sales ledger

The sales ledger records amounts owing from customers. These are **debtors** and so the sales ledger is an **asset account.**

SALES LEDGER

DEBIT	CREDIT
INCREASE	**DECREASE**

Invoices increase the amount owing and so are **debits**. Credit notes, discounts allowed and amounts received from customers reduce the amount owing and so are **credits**.

3 Personal accounts for credit customers

3.1 Balancing accounts

Each customer account is given a reference or code number (A01, B79, C22 above). This reference (sometimes called the 'sales ledger folio') can be used in the sales day book instead of, or in addition to, the customer name.

Here is an example of how a sales ledger account can be laid out.

CHEF & CO   A/c no: C124

Date	Details	£	Date	Details	£
1.1.X7	Balance b/d	250.00			
10.1.X7	Sales - SDB 48		10.1.X7	Cash	250.00
	(invoice 0249)	343.92	11.1.X7	Balance c/d	343.92
		593.92			593.92
11.1.X7	Balance b/d	343.92			

Notice how the debit and credit sides have been **balanced off** at 11.1.X7 to show the same total (£593.92). As debits exceed credits by £343.92, the account has a **debit balance**. This is carried forward to the next period by crediting £343.92 as balance **carried down** (c/d) in this period and debiting £343.92 as balance **brought down** (b/d) in the next period.

The opening balance owed by Chef & Co on 11 January 20X7 is now £343.92 instead of £593.92, because of the £250 receipt which came in on 10 January 20X7.

3.2 Personal accounts as memorandum accounts

In manual systems of accounting and in **some** computerised accounting systems, the personal accounts of customers **do not form part of the double entry system of bookkeeping**.

This is because the personal accounts include details of transactions which have already been summarised in day books and posted to ledger accounts in the **main ledger**.

For example, sales invoices are recorded in the sales account, VAT account and sales ledger control account. **The personal accounts of customers do not then form part of the double entry system: if they did, transactions would be recorded twice over.** Therefore the sales ledger is known as a **subsidiary ledger**.

3.3 Computerised sales ledger

However, in some computerised systems, **the sales ledger is 'integrated' with the main ledger**.

PART A   ACCOUNTING FOR SALES AND PURCHASES

Usually, in a manual system, the memorandum accounts reflect the various individual customer balances, making up the sales ledger control account. In an integrated system, individual customers' accounts **do** form part of the double entry system and there is **no separate sales ledger control account.** The computer system just adds up all the individual balances to produce the sales ledger control account total.

This means that the main ledger posting summary and the sales ledger postings could be combined as follows.

BOOT AND SHOE SUPPLIES   Posting summary

Account name	Account code	Ref	Dr £	p	Cr £	p
Abbey S	A009	20248	99	28		
Cook & Co	C124	20249	343	92		
Dinham	D249	20251	87	83		
S Jones	J042	20247	202	10		
Mentor	M201	20252	319	65		
Pediform	P041	C2214			34	54
Texas Ltd	T172	20250	202	10		
Sales GB	O1010				168	95
Sales LB	O1020				95	45
Sales GS	O1030				244	42
Sales LS	O1040				474	68
Sales A	O1050				84	50
Returns GB	O1110		29	40		
VAT	70700				181	74
TOTALS			1284	28	1284	28

Posted by ...... *C.F* ......   Date ...... *10/1/X7* ......

It is unlikely that you will be assessed on integrated ledger systems in your skills test.

3.4 Businesses not needing a sales ledger

Surely all but the very smallest businesses will need to maintain a sales ledger? **No, even some very large businesses have no credit sales at all.**

- Chains of supermarkets making sales by cash, cheque or credit card.
- Other businesses selling only to one or two customers eg a defence contractor selling only to a government.

4 Maintaining customer records

A business will keep a **personal account for each of its regular customers**.

4.1 Opening a new customer account

If an order is received from someone who does not hold a credit account with the business, an account needs to be opened for the new customer.

However, the new account must be **properly authorised**, in accordance with the procedures of the business.

Supplying goods and services on credit involves the **risk that the customer may be unable to pay**.

4.1.1 Credit check

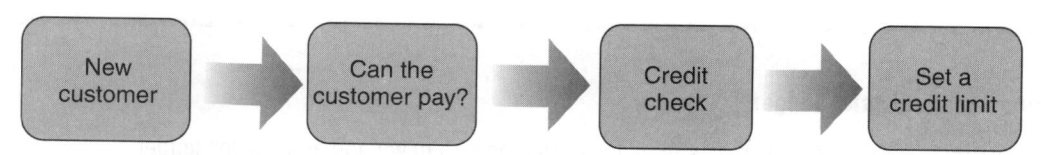

New customer → Can the customer pay? → Credit check → Set a credit limit

This credit limit will usually be set by a manager or senior employee.

4.1.2 Credit limit

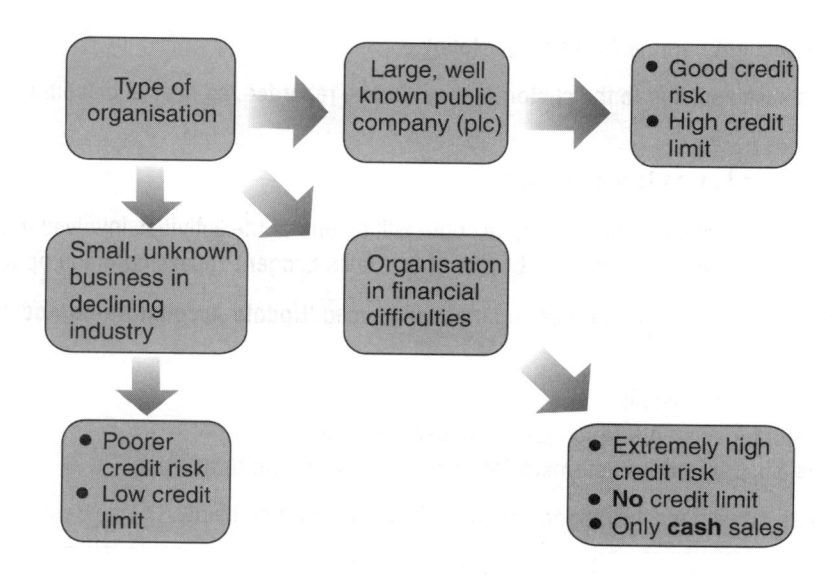

- Type of organisation
  - Large, well known public company (plc) → Good credit risk; High credit limit
  - Small, unknown business in declining industry → Poorer credit risk; Low credit limit
  - Organisation in financial difficulties → Extremely high credit risk; **No** credit limit; Only **cash** sales

Activity 6.1

Aroma has three new customers. Chan has carried out a preliminary credit check and needs to report back to Kris. Given the results of the credit checks shown below, complete the grid to show whether you recommend that Kris give a high, medium or low credit limit or extends no credit at all.

Swansong Ltd — old established river cruises company, with good credit record.

Helping Hands Agency — newly established cleaning staff agency. Owner has a poor payment record.

Bear and Stag Investments — a new investment brokers. Owned by a former City analyst, who is the chief adviser. Excellent credit rating.

PART A   ACCOUNTING FOR SALES AND PURCHASES

| Customer | Credit limit ||| No credit |
	High	Medium	Low	

4.1.3 Opening a manual sales ledger

In a **manual system**, customer details may simply be written on to a new page in the sales ledger.

- Customer name and address
- Credit limit
- Customer account number (sales ledger folio)

Any special terms of business applying to the customer may also be recorded, eg special discounts, credit period, sale or return basis and so on.

4.1.4 Opening a computerised sales ledger account

In a **computerised sales ledger system**, opening an account will be one of the activities involved in maintaining customer records. In a menu-driven system it will be one of the Sales Ledger Processing menu options.

For example, option 1 of the Sales Ledger Processing menu is headed **'Update Account Name/Address'**. Using this option, we can do the following.

- Enter new customer details
- Delete customer accounts which are no longer required
- Amend details of existing customers (eg change of credit limit or address)

The layout of the computer screen for this option can look like the illustration below.

SALES LEDGER SYSTEM: CUSTOMER DETAILS

ACCOUNT CODE: (1)   I 024   CUSTOMER NAME: Ivory Carpets Ltd (2)

CONTACT NAME: Frank Ward   CUSTOMER ADDRESS:
                                23 Switchback Rd
SALES REPRESENTATIVE: S Morley   Headingly   (3)
                                Leeds
                                LS3 4PS

CREDIT LIMIT: (4)   £2,000

CREDIT PERIOD: 30 days   LAST TRANSACTION DATE: 07.02.X4

                                CURRENT BALANCE: £1,424.67

Key

1 **Account code** – a unique code for each customer. To open a new customer account, enter a new customer code and complete the remaining details.

2 **Customer name**.

3 **Customer address** – ensure the full postal address, including post code, is entered. In a fully computerised system, this address will appear on invoices, statements etc. If there is a separate **delivery** address, eg a warehouse away from the main offices, this needs careful noting.

4 **Credit limit** – a computer system will usually **warn the operator** if an invoice will take the customer over the credit limit and allow the option of **cancelling the transaction**. If goods have already been delivered, then a stop can be put on the account, until the customer pays off some of the outstanding balance. Sometimes a manager may need to review the account to see if the credit limit needs to be **increased** eg if the customer is a good credit risk, but is simply ordering more from the business due to an increase in its trade.

4.2 Existing customer accounts

Some customers may only make occasional purchases from the business, so that most of the time they do not owe anything to the business.

Once a customer has an account, it makes sense to keep it open even if the customer has not made a purchase recently. If the customer wants to make another purchase, the customer's account is still 'active'.

There may be dormant accounts, where there have been no transactions for some considerable time. If they are unlikely to be used again, consider closing these accounts. This tidies the ledger and stops old and unnecessary data being produced.

A computerised sales ledger package may include an optional facility for the automatic deletion of zero balances from the sales ledger at the end of a period.

For deleting zero balances	Against deleting zero balances
Save time by deleting 'one-off' sales.	'Zero' accounts may become active again so it is useful to keep them open.
	Avoids having to re-open accounts for customers who return after trying another supplier.
	Keeping all previous customers on the ledger provides a useful customer listing for marketing purposes.

The decision to opt for a facility to delete all zero accounts will depend on the nature of the business.

PART A ACCOUNTING FOR SALES AND PURCHASES

Activity 6.2

Chan has been reviewing the sales ledger. She finds that two accounts have zero balances. One is for a customer who usually pays cash (in advance). The other is for a customer that clears his account at the end of each month. Should either of these accounts be deleted? Why?

Customer	Delete (Y/N)	Reason

5 Recording transactions in the sales ledger

5.1 Manual recording

In a manual system, the sales ledger is usually written up at the same time as entries are made in the sales day book or cash book.

5.2 Computerised recording

In a computerised system, transactions may be input directly to customer accounts in the sales ledger ('transaction processing') or alternatively stored as a transaction file to form a part of the next updating run.

Example: Sales ledger transactions

Marlon & Co started trading at the beginning of April. During April, the sales day book and the sales returns day book showed the following transactions.

Sales day book

Date	Name	Invoice ref	Net total £ p	VAT £ p	Gross total £ p
2 April	Turing Machinery Ltd	2512	250.00	43.75	293.75
4 April	G Wright	2513	300.00	52.50	352.50
9 April	G Wright	2514	725.00	126.87	851.87
9 April	Turing Machinery Ltd	2515	620.00	108.50	728.50
10 April	Simpsons Ltd	2516	85.00	14.87	99.87
24 April	Simpsons Ltd	2517	1,440.00	252.00	1,692.00
25 April	Simpsons Ltd	2518	242.00	42.35	284.35
25 April	G Wright	2519	1,248.00	218.40	1,466.40
30 April	Totals		4,910.00	859.24	5,769.24

Sales returns day book

Date	Name	Credit note	Net total £ p	VAT £ p	Gross total £ p
23 April	G Wright	0084	220.00	38.50	258.50
25 April	Turing Machinery Ltd	0085	250.00	43.75	293.75
30 April	Totals		470.00	82.25	552.25

During May, the following payments for goods sold on credit were received.

Payments received

		£ p
7 May	Turing Machinery Ltd	728.50
14 May	G Wright	352.50
14 May	Simpsons Ltd	99.87

We need to show the entries as they would appear in the individual sales ledger accounts.

Sales ledger

TURING MACHINERY LTD

Date	Details	£ p	Date	Details	£ p
2 April	Invoice 2512	293.75	25 April	Credit note 0085	293.75
9 April	Invoice 2515	728.50	7 May	Cash book	728.50
		1,022.25			1,022.25

G WRIGHT

Date	Details	£ p	Date	Details	£ p
4 April	Invoice 2513	352.50	23 April	Credit note 0084	258.50
9 April	Invoice 2514	851.87	14 May	Cash book	352.50
25 April	Invoice 2519	1,466.40	31 May	Balance c/d	2,059.77
		2,670.77			2,670.77
21 May	Balance b/d	2,059.77			

SIMPSONS LTD

Date	Details	£ p	Date	Details	£ p
10 April	Invoice 2516	99.87	14 May	Cash book	99.87
24 April	Invoice 2517	1,692.00	31 May	Balance c/d	1,976.35
25 April	Invoice 2518	284.35			
		2,076.22			2,076.22
31 May	Balance b/d	1,976.35			

Many computerised accounting systems use a three-column format, with debit items in the left hand column, credit items in the middle column and the balance in the right hand column.

For example, the entries in G Wright's account in the sales ledger might appear as follows in a three-column format.

Sales ledger	A/c name: G Wright	Debit	Credit	Balance
4 April	2513	352.50		352.50
9 April	2514	851.87		1,204.37
23 April	0084		258.50	945.87
25 April	2519	1,466.40		2,412.27
14 May	Cash book		352.50	2,059.77

PART A   ACCOUNTING FOR SALES AND PURCHASES

Marlon and Co's transactions have been recorded in the sales ledger memorandum accounts, but not in the double entry system.

We dealt with the double entry postings in the previous chapter. The following example acts as revision.

Example: Posting transactions

The payments received will be posted as debits in the cash account. (The cash account is an asset account and payments received increase the cash balance.)

CASH ACCOUNT

Date	Details	£ p			£ p
7 May	Turing Mach. Ltd	728.50			
14 May	G Wright	352.50			
14 May	Simpsons Ltd	99.87			

Sales income excluding VAT will be **credits** in the **sales account**.

SALES ACCOUNT

		£ p	Date	Details	£ p
			30 April	Sales day book	4,910.00

Sales returns excluding VAT will be **debits** in the **sales returns account**.

SALES RETURNS ACCOUNT

Date	Details	£ p			£ p
30 April	Sales returns day book	470.00			

VAT on sales and **sales returns** will be **credits** and **debits** respectively in the **VAT account**.

VAT ACCOUNT

Date	Details	£ p	Date	Details	£ p
30 April	Sales returns day book	82.25	30 April	Sales day book	859.24

To complete the double entry, we need to post the **total amounts owed** and the **payments received** to the **debit** and **credit** side respectively of the sales ledger control account.

SALES LEDGER CONTROL ACCOUNT

Date	Details	£ p	Date	Details	£ p
30 April	Sales day book total	5,769.24	30 April	Sales returns day book total	552.25
			7 May	Cash book	728.50
			14 May	Cash book	452.37
			31 May	Balance c/d	4,036.12
		5,769.24			5,769.24
31 May	Balance b/d	4,036.12			

Note that in this case the two amounts of cash received on 14 May have been added together to give the daily total posted to the total debtors account. Notice that the balance on the sales ledger control account is the same as the total of the individual accounts in the sales ledger (£0 + £2,059.77 + £1,976.35 = £4,036.12).

5.3 Posting summary

Double entry	Source	Debit (Dr)	Credit (Cr)
Total invoices (incl VAT)	SDB	Sales ledger control a/c	
Net invoices (excl VAT)	SDB		Sales a/c
VAT	SDB		VAT a/c
Total returns (incl VAT)	SRDB		Sales ledger control a/c
Net returns (excl VAT)	SRDB	Sales a/c	
VAT	SRDB	VAT a/c	
Cash received	CB	Cash a/c	Sales ledger control a/c
Memorandum	Source	Debit (Dr)	Credit (Cr)
Each invoice (incl VAT)	SDB	Individual sales ledger a/c	
Each return (incl VAT)	SRDB		Individual sales ledger a/c
Cash received	CB		Individual sales ledger a/c

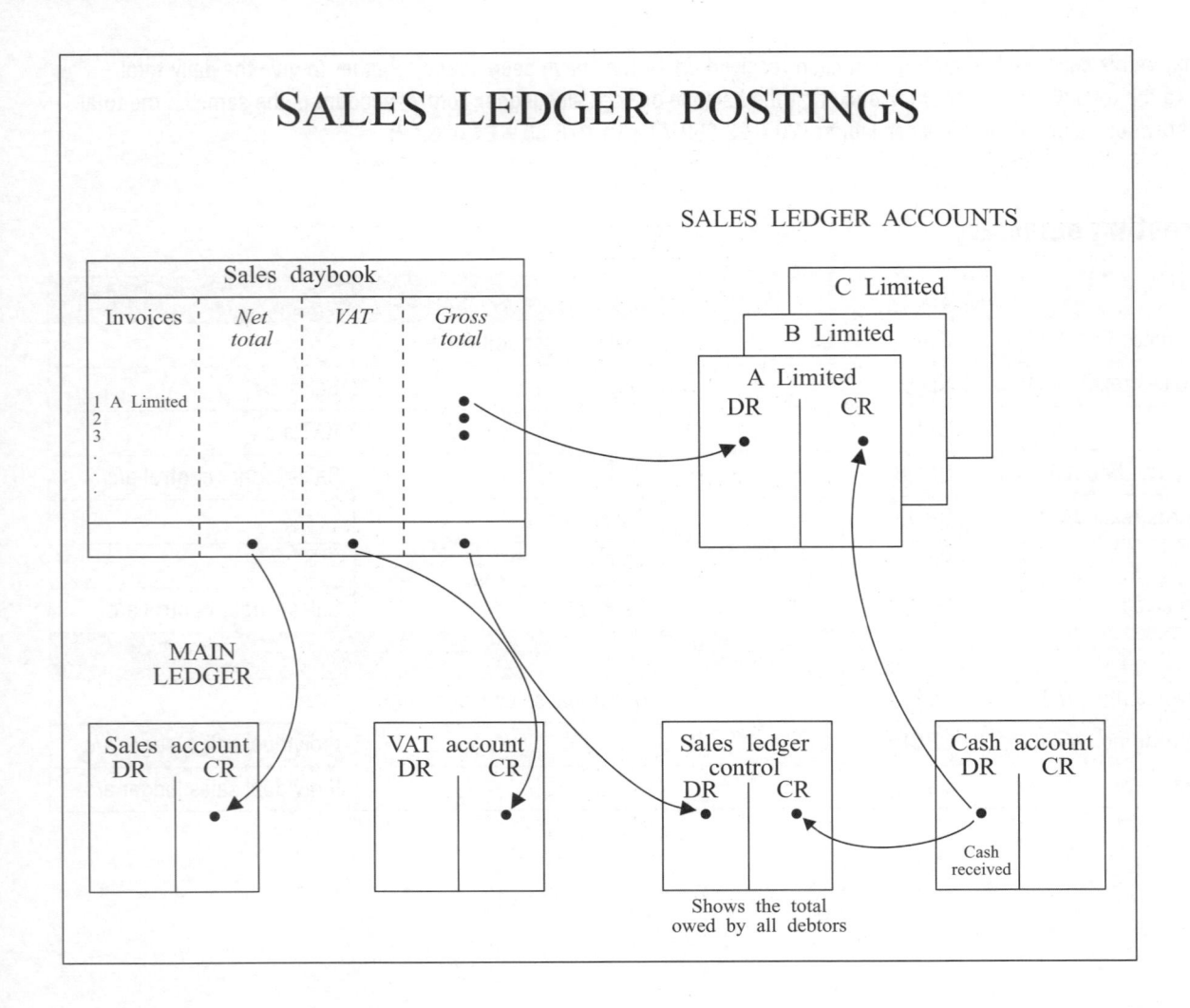

PART A   ACCOUNTING FOR SALES AND PURCHASES

SALES LEDGER POSTINGS

[Diagram showing flow from Sales daybook (with columns: Invoices, Net total, VAT, Gross total) to Sales Ledger Accounts (A Limited, B Limited, C Limited) and to the Main Ledger containing Sales account, VAT account, Sales ledger control account (Shows the total owed by all debtors), and Cash account. Cash received flows from Cash account to Sales ledger control and to the individual sales ledger accounts.]

5.4 Checking the sales ledger recording: reconciling individual totals to sales ledger control account

From the above diagram, it should be obvious that:

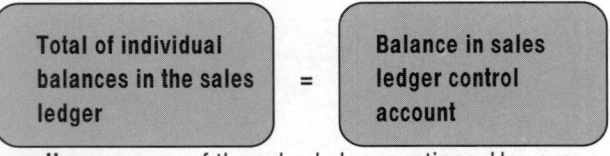

> **Total of individual balances in the sales ledger** = **Balance in sales ledger control account**

This provides a **check on the accuracy** of the sales ledger postings. However, you will not be learning how to do this until Unit 3.

Activity 6.3

You are presented with the following transactions from Aroma's sales day book and sales returns day book for 1 January 20X7.

SALES DAY BOOK FOLIO 82						
Date	Customer account	Invoice number	Goods value £.00	VAT (17½%) £.00	Total £.00
1/1/X7	001	100	72.34	12.66	85.00
1/1/X7	030	101	83.53	14.62	98.15
1/1/X7	001	102	14.46	2.53	16.99
1/1/X7	132	103	17.20	3.01	20.21
1/1/X7	075	104	104.77	18.33	123.10
1/1/X7	099	105	30.40	5.32	35.72
1/1/X7	001	106	64.97	11.37	76.34
Total 1/1/X7			387.67	67.84	455.51

SALES RETURNS DAY BOOK FOLIO 73						
Date	Customer account	Credit note	Invoice reference	Goods value £.00	VAT (17½%) £.00	Total £.00
1/1/X7	099	C44	89	301.03	52.68	353.71

Tasks

(a) Post the transactions to the sales ledger accounts provided below.

(b) Set out the double entry for the transactions shown.

(c) Comment on any unusual items resulting from your work in (a) and itemise any additional procedures which you consider necessary. Is there anything which should be brought to your supervisor's attention?

PART A ACCOUNTING FOR SALES AND PURCHASES

CUSTOMER NAME: Arturo Aski

ACCOUNT 001

ADDRESS: 94 Old Comedy Street, Vaudeville, 1BR, W. Meds

CREDIT LIMIT: £2,200

Date	Description	Transaction Ref	DR £	DR p	CR £	CR p	Balance £	Balance p
Brought forward 1/1/X7							2,050	37

CUSTOMER NAME: Maye West

ACCOUNT 030

ADDRESS: 1 Vamping Parade, Holywood, Beds, HW1

CREDIT LIMIT: £1,000

Date	Description	Transaction Ref	DR £	DR p	CR £	CR p	Balance £	Balance p
Brought forward 1/1/X7							69	33

6: THE SALES LEDGER

| CUSTOMER NAME: | Naguib Mahfouz | ACCOUNT 075 |

ADDRESS: 10 Palace Walk, London NE9

CREDIT LIMIT: £1,500

Date	Description	Transaction Ref	DR		CR		Balance	
			£	p	£	p	£	p
Brought forward 1/1/X7							--------	------

| CUSTOMER NAME: | Josef Sveik | ACCOUNT 099 |

ADDRESS: 99 Balkan Row, Aldershot

CREDIT LIMIT: £700

Date	Description	Transaction Ref	DR		CR		Balance	
			£	p	£	p	£	p
Brought forward 1/1/X7							353	71

149

PART A   ACCOUNTING FOR SALES AND PURCHASES

				ACCOUNT
CUSTOMER NAME:	*Grace Chang*			132
ADDRESS:	*Red Dragon Street, Cardiff, CA4*			
CREDIT LIMIT:	£1,200			

Date	Description	Transaction Ref	DR		CR		Balance	
			£	p	£	p	£	p
	Brought forward 1/1/X7						1,175	80

6 Matching cash received

6.1 What is the customer's sales ledger balance made up of?

The **balance** on a sales ledger account shows **how much that customer owes** at any particular time.

Where a customer only makes **occasional purchases**, it is easy to see which invoices are unpaid and so make up the account balance at any particular time.

Example: Sales ledger account

The computer printout below shows all entries in Martlesham Ltd's account in the sales ledger of Domma Ltd, since Martlesham became a customer of Domma in June 20X3.

DOMMA LIMITED A/C NAME: MARTLESHAM LTD		SALES LEDGER SYSTEM A/C NO: M024 DATE: 22.1.X4		
		Debit	*Credit*	*Balance*
30.6.X3	Invoice 7214	*472.25*		*472.25*
28.7. X3	Cash received		472.25	0.00
3.8. X3	Invoice 7298	282.00		282.00
21.8. X3	Invoice 7342	424.70		706.70
7.9. X3	Credit note 0141		74.50	632.20
17.9. X3	Cash received		632.20	0.00
10.12. X3	Invoice 7621	845.25		845.25
24.12. X3	Invoice 7710	92.24		937.49
7.1.X4	Cash received		842.25	92.24
20.1.X4	Invoice 7794	192.21		284.45
	Balance			284.45

It should be fairly easy to see that the balance at 22 January 20X4 of £284.45 consists of the amounts due on invoices 7710 and 7794.

A business may have regular customers receiving hundreds of invoices each year.

- Some invoices may be **queried** by the customer and payment withheld until a credit note is issued.
- Payments received from the customer may be in the order that the invoices are **approved** for payment by the customer and not the order in which the invoices are issued.

Clearly, for this customer, it is not so easy to see what invoices remain unpaid at any time.

Why do we need to know exactly which items make up a customer's sales ledger balance?

- **Allocated credit terms**, any invoices not paid within this period must be chased up
- Settle any **disagreement** with the customer

There are two ways of keeping track of the customer's account.

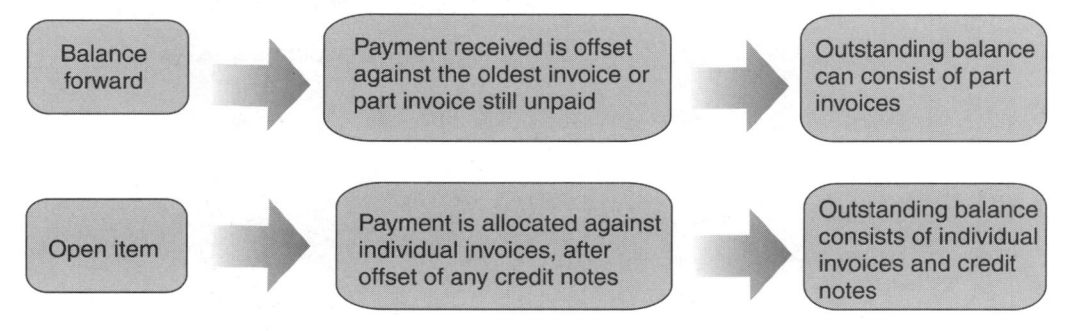

Balance forward → Payment received is offset against the oldest invoice or part invoice still unpaid → Outstanding balance can consist of part invoices

Open item → Payment is allocated against individual invoices, after offset of any credit notes → Outstanding balance consists of individual invoices and credit notes

6.2 Matching cash received with invoices and credit notes: open item

Open item method

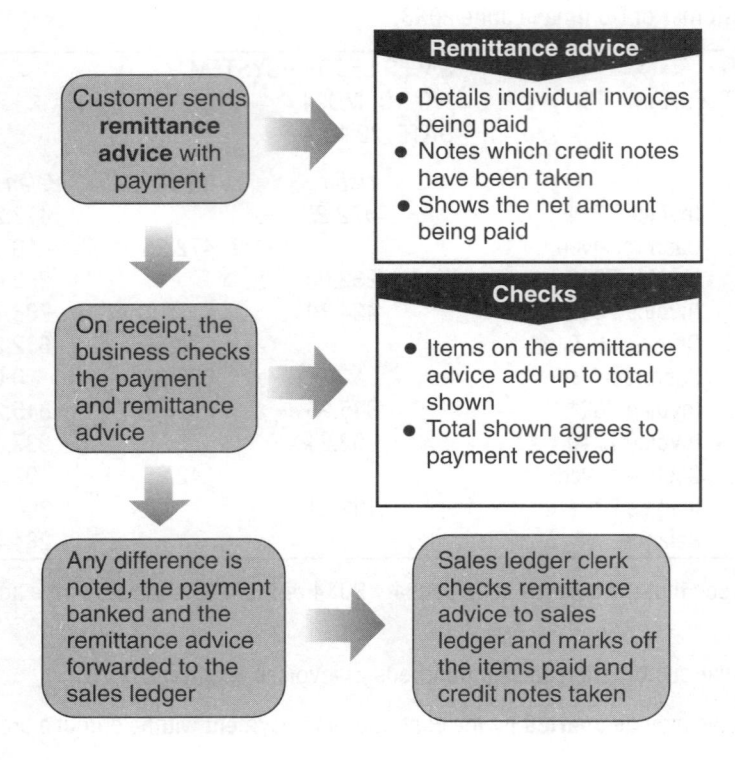

```
Customer sends remittance advice with payment  →  Remittance advice
                                                   • Details individual invoices being paid
                                                   • Notes which credit notes have been taken
                                                   • Shows the net amount being paid

On receipt, the business checks the payment and remittance advice  →  Checks
                                                                       • Items on the remittance advice add up to total shown
                                                                       • Total shown agrees to payment received

Any difference is noted, the payment banked and the remittance advice forwarded to the sales ledger  →  Sales ledger clerk checks remittance advice to sales ledger and marks off the items paid and credit notes taken
```

Example: Matching cash received in open item systems

Continuing the above example, Martlesham Ltd sent with their payment of 17 September 20X3 a remittance advice as shown below.

Remittance advice

Heath Ltd
The Green
Menton PR2 4NR

Martlesham Ltd
24 Heath Road
Menton PR7 4XJ

17 September 20X3

Date	Details	Amount/£
3.08.X3	Invoice 7298	+282.00
21.08.X3	Invoice 7342	+424.70
07.09.X3	Credit note 0141	−74.50
	PAYMENT ENCLOSED	632.20

In the sales ledger account below,
DR = debit
CR = credit
* = matched receipt

```
DOMMA LIMITED                                    SALES LEDGER SYSTEM
A/C NAME: MARTLESHAM LTD                              A/C NO: M024
                                                      DATE: 22.1.X4
                                Dr        Cr      Balance
30.6.X3     Invoice 7214      472.25               472.25    PAID
28.7.X3     Cash received               472.25       0.00      *
3.8.X3      Invoice 7298      282.00               282.00    PAID
21.8.X3     Invoice 7342      424.70               706.70    PAID
7.9.X3      Credit note 0141            74.50      632.20    PAID
17.9.X3     Cash received              632.20        0.00      *
10.12.X3    Invoice 7621      845.25               845.25    PAID
24.12.X3    Invoice 7710       92.24               937.49
7.1.X4      Cash received              845.25       92.24      *
20.1.X4     Invoice 7794      192.21               284.45
            Balance                                284.45
```

To find out the make-up of a customer's balance, it will be cumbersome and unnecessary to keep printing out details of all transactions even after they have been paid. A computer report may be produced showing only those items which remain unpaid (open items). In the case of Martlesham Ltd, this appears as follows on 22 January 20X4.

```
DOMMA LIMITED                                    SALES LEDGER SYSTEM
A/C NAME: MARTLESHAM LTD                              A/C NO: M024
                                                      DATE: 22.1.X4
                                Dr        Cr      Balance
24.12.X3    Invoice 7710       92.24                92.24
20.1.X4     Invoice 7794      192.21               248.45
            Balance                                284.45
```

However, the system **must** continue to keep full records of all transactions.

6.3 Unmatched cash in an open item system

Sometimes it is not possible to match cash receipts exactly to outstanding times. This is called **unmatched cash.**

There are different reasons why a receipt may remain unmatched.

- The clerk may **omit to match the cash in error**.
- There may be an **error on the customer's remittance advice** which means that the cash cannot be fully matched.

PART A ACCOUNTING FOR SALES AND PURCHASES

- The payment may have been **sent without a remittance advice**.
- The customer may have sent a **'round sum' amount** or payment on account (eg exactly £1,000, or 25% of balance) to pay off part of their balance without specifying to which items the amounts relate.

A customer may make round sum payments or payments on account, in accordance with a **schedule of payments** agreed with the customer. Such an agreement may be made if the customer is in **financial difficulties**.

In such a case, it may be better to match receipts with the oldest part of the debt by the **'balance forward'** method, rather than recording it as 'unmatched cash'.

A round sum payment will always result in an amount of cash **remaining unmatched** because it is insufficient to match with the next invoice on the ledger.

Example: Round sum payments or payments on account

Domma Ltd has a customer Hampstead Ltd (Account number H002) with which it has agreed a schedule of payments whereby Hampstead Ltd pays £1,000 at the beginning of each month to clear its remaining debt. £1,000 was paid under this agreement on 2 January 20X4.

At 31 January 20X4, the items remaining unpaid by Hampstead Ltd appeared in Domma Ltd's sales ledger as shown below.

DOMMA LIMITED				SALES LEDGER SYSTEM
A/C NAME: HAMPSTEAD LTD				A/C NO: H002
				DATE: 31.1.X4
		Dr	Cr	Balance
10.9.X3	Invoice 7468	649.45		649.45
24.9.X3	Invoice 7513	424.91		1,074.36
14.10.X3	Invoice 7581	342.72		1,417.08
15.11.X3	Invoice 7604	724.24		2,141.32
2.1.X4	Unmatched cash		322.90	1,818.42
	Balance			1,818.42

We need to show how £1,000 cash received from Hampstead Ltd on 1 February 20X4 will be recorded in the ledger.

The cash available for matching, and the items with which it is matched, are shown below.

	£	£
2.1.X4 payment - unmatched part		322.90
1.2.X4 payment		1,000.00
Cash to be matched		1,322.90
Items to be matched		
Invoice 7468	649.45	
Invoice 7513	424.91	
		(1,074.36)
Cash remaining unmatched		248.54

The remainder of the January payment has now been matched, as has part of the February payment. The balance remaining after invoices 7468 and 7513 have been matched is £248.54, which is not sufficient to match fully with invoice number 7581 for £342.72.

After matching the cash received on 1 February, the ledger shows the account balance as follows.

```
DOMMA LIMITED                                    SALES LEDGER SYSTEM
A/C NAME: HAMPSTEAD LTD                                  A/C NO: H002
                                                          DATE: 2.2.X4

                                        Dr          Cr       Balance
14.10.X3        Invoice 7581          342.72                  342.72
15.11.X3        Invoice 7604          724.24                1,066.96
1.2.X4          Unmatched cash                    248.54      818.42
                Balance                                       818.42
```

6.4 Balance forward system

Some sales ledger systems may allow an invoice to be shown as 'part-paid'. In this case, it should be made clear whether an invoice amount shown on a listing is a **part-paid** amount or whether it is instead the full amount of the invoice. This is how a **'balance forward' system**, as opposed to the open item system, works.

Activity 6.4

A long-established customer of Aroma is called Mr Ranjit Singh, of 19 Amber Road, St Mary Cray. His account number is 1124.

Mr Singh's business is a seasonal one but he still requires a steady supply of plants throughout the year.

Mr Singh pays in two different ways. Some invoices he pays off in full. At other times he sends in a payment 'on account' to cover amounts outstanding, but these are not allocated directly to any particular invoice. They are deemed to apply to the earliest uncleared invoices outstanding, unless there is a dispute, or the invoice has had a specific payment made to it.

A computer virus has caused irrecoverable damage to the computer system.

You have to 'reconstruct' the sales ledger for the past few months to discover what Mr Singh owes, as he has requested a statement.

You unearth the following transactions.

PART A ACCOUNTING FOR SALES AND PURCHASES

Cash receipts (from cash book)

Date	Cash book reference	£
15/2/X7	004	1,066.05 (Note)
25/3/X7	006	500.00
15/4/X7	007	500.00
15/5/X7	031	500.00
20/5/X7	038	500.00
20/6/X7	039	500.00
22/6/X7	042	923.91
Total receipts		4,489.96

Note. This covers invoices 236 and 315.

Invoices	Date	Value (inc VAT) £
236	1 January 20X7	405.33
315	2 February 20X7	660.72
317	3 February 20X7	13.90
320	5 February 20X7	17.15
379	21 February 20X7	872.93
443	31 March 20X7	213.50
502	1 May 20X7	624.30
514	15 May 20X7	494.65
521	19 May 20X7	923.91
538	22 May 20X7	110.00
618	1 July 20X7	312.17
619	2 July 20X7	560.73
Total		5,209.29

Credit notes
C32 (against invoice 538)	8 July 20X7	110.00

Tasks

(a) Post all the transactions to a reconstructed sales ledger. Assume that there was a nil balance at the beginning of the year. Head up the columns: *Date; Transaction reference; Debit; Credit;* and *Balance*.

(b) Give a breakdown of Mr Singh's balance, stating which invoices are still outstanding.

6: THE SALES LEDGER

Key learning points

- ☑ The sales ledger contains the personal accounts of credit customers of the business.

- ☑ An account must be kept for each customer so that the business always has a full record of how much each customer owes and what items make up the balance.

- ☑ A customer's account in the sales ledger will normally show a debit balance: the customer owes money to the business and is therefore a debtor of the business.

- ☑ Usually customers' personal accounts are maintained separately from the main ledger, as 'memorandum' accounts in the subsidiary ledger. Sales ledger postings then do not form part of the double entry in the system of bookkeeping.

- ☑ Instead, a sales ledger control or total debtors' account is maintained in the main ledger to keep track of the total of the amounts which make up the entries in the individual personal accounts.

- ☑ Opening a new sales ledger account requires authorisation by a senior official. The amount of credit allowed to each individual customer should be kept within acceptable limits of risk.

- ☑ Cash received from the customer is matched with invoices in order to show which items remain unpaid. The customer indicates on the remittance advice which items are being paid.

PART A   ACCOUNTING FOR SALES AND PURCHASES

Quick quiz

1   What does the sales ledger contain?
2   In manual accounting systems the personal accounts of customers do not form part of the double entry system. True or false?
3   What factors determine the credit limit allocated to a particular customer?
4   How might you check the accuracy of the amounts recorded in the sales ledger?
5   What is the 'open item' method of keeping track of a customer's account?
6   In the 'balance forward' method, any payment received is simply allocated to the _____ items or _____ items which remain unpaid. *Complete the blanks.*

Answers to quick quiz

1   The personal accounts of customers.
2   True.
3   (i)   The payment record of the customer
    (ii)   The industry in which he operates
    (iii) The size of the customer
4   Work out the total of the balances on the individual sales ledger accounts and compare this with the total balance on the total debtors account.
5   A method which keeps track of individual items which remain unpaid or get paid.
6   Any payment received is simply allocated to the **oldest** items or **part** items which remain unpaid.

Activity checklist

This checklist shows which performance criteria, range statement or knowledge and understanding point is covered by each activity in this chapter. Tick off each activity as you complete it.

Activity

6.1	☐	This activity deals with Knowledge and Understanding point 22: relevant understanding of the organisation's accounting systems and administrative systems and procedures.
6.2	☐	This activity deals with Knowledge and Understanding point 22: relevant understanding of the organisation's accounting systems and administrative systems and procedures.
6.3	☐	This activity deals with Performance Criteria 1.1.E.
6.4	☐	This activity deals with Performance Criteria 1.1.E.

PART A ACCOUNTING FOR SALES AND PURCHASES

chapter 7

The purchase ledger

Contents

1 The problem
2 The solution
3 Personal accounts for suppliers
4 Maintaining supplier records
5 Recording transactions in the purchase ledger
6 Payments to suppliers
7 The age analysis of creditors and other reports
8 Contra entries with the sales ledger

Performance criteria
2.1.F Enter invoices and credit notes in the appropriate ledgers

Range statement
2.1.4 Discounts: settlement
2.1.6 Ledgers: manual main ledger: manual subsidiary ledger; computerised ledgers

Knowledge and understanding
11 Double entry bookkeeping, including balancing accounts
15 Operation of manual accounting systems
16 Operation of computerised accounting systems, including output
19 Relationship between the accounting system and ledger
25 The nature of the organisation's business transactions

Signpost
The topics covered in this chapter are relevant to **Unit 2.**

PART A   ACCOUNTING FOR SALES AND PURCHASES

1 The problem

The purchase day books provide a chronological record of the invoices and credit notes received by a business from all credit suppliers.

However this will not answer all needs.

- If a supplier requests **payment of the full balance due to him**
- To check that the monthly supplier's **statement of account** is correct
- To maintain a **complete record** of the items making up the balance owed to each supplier, so that **appropriate payments** can be made
- To make **monthly payments** covering a number of invoices, rather than each invoice separately

2 The solution

The answer is to keep individual supplier personal accounts in the **purchase ledger**.

Each personal account shows the amount owed to each supplier.

2.1 Purchase ledger postings

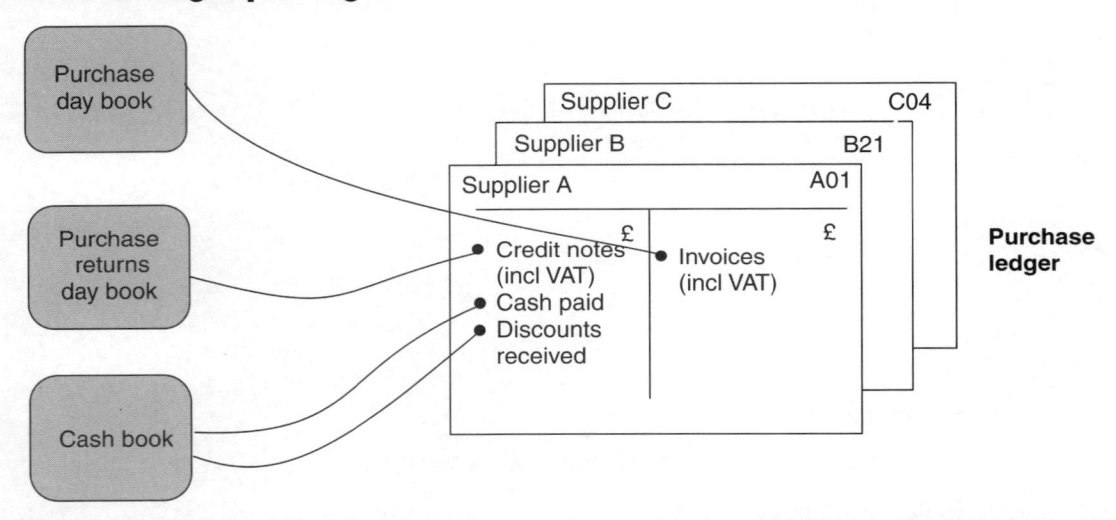

```
Purchase day book ──────────┐
                            │
                            ▼
Purchase returns day book ──→ Supplier A / B / C
                            • Credit notes (incl VAT)   • Invoices (incl VAT)
                            • Cash paid
                            • Discounts received
                            
Cash book ──────────────────┘
```

Purchase ledger

The purchase ledger records amounts due to suppliers. These are **creditors** and so the purchase ledger is a **liability account**.

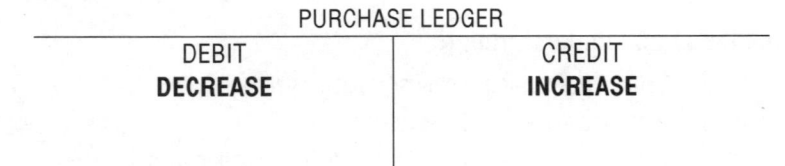

PURCHASE LEDGER	
DEBIT	CREDIT
DECREASE	**INCREASE**

Invoices increase the amount owing and so are **credits**. Credit notes, discounts received and cash paid reduce the liability and so are **debits.**

2.2 Terminology

- Subsidiary ledger (purchase ledger or sales ledger)
- Main ledger (the main double entry records, may be called the general or nominal ledger)
- Integrated ledger (where the subsidiary ledgers form part of the double entry eg in a **computerised system**)

For the purposes of the Units 1 and 2 Skills Test, integrated ledgers are unlikely to be assessed.

3 Personal accounts for suppliers

3.1 Balancing accounts

An example of a purchase ledger account is shown below.

COOK & CO   PL32

Date 20X2	Details	£	Date 20X2	Detail	£
15 March	Purchase returns PRDB 21	50.00	15 March	Balance b/d	200.00
15 March	Cash CB 44	135.00	15 March	Invoice rec'd PDB 37	315.00
15 March	Discount rec'd CB 44	15.00			
16 March	Balance c/d	315.00			
		515.00			515.00
			16 March	Balance b/d	315.00

At the end of a period, accounts are **balanced off**. The debits and credits are each totalled. If the debits exceed the credits, then there is a **debit balance**. If the credits exceed the debits, there is a **credit balance**.

In the account for Cook & Co, the debits total £200.00, while the credits total £515.00. The credits exceed the debits by £315.00 so there is a credit balance of £315.00.

This balance is recorded by debiting **balance c/d** (carried down) with £315.00 and crediting balance b/d (brought down) with £315.00. The balance b/d means that the business owes Cook & Co £315.00.

3.2 Debit balances in the purchase ledger

If we pay more than £315 to Cook & Co, we will be left with a net debit balance on Cook & Co's personal account. For instance, if we pay £375, there will be a net debit balance of £60. This indicates that the creditor owes us £60.

PART A   ACCOUNTING FOR SALES AND PURCHASES

Debit balances in the purchase ledger are unusual, but they can sometimes arise.

- **Deposit** paid in advance of receipt of the goods
- **Overpayment** of the creditor's balance made in error
- **Credit note** received after full payment has been made of the balance

If debit balances are arising on purchase ledger accounts frequently, some **investigation** may be needed. The occurrence of debit balances could indicate that procedures in the purchase ledger department need to be improved.

3.3 Organisations not needing a purchase ledger

Maintaining a separate purchase ledger is a waste of time for businesses with very few credit purchases. Examples include small shops, clubs and associations. Any credit purchases will be posted direct to the **main ledger accounts**.

3.4 Trade creditors

The purchase ledger contains the personal accounts of creditors for the supply of both goods and services. It will normally cover only the **trade creditors** of the business.

Trade creditors

Trade creditors = Liabilities arising from the **trade** of the business

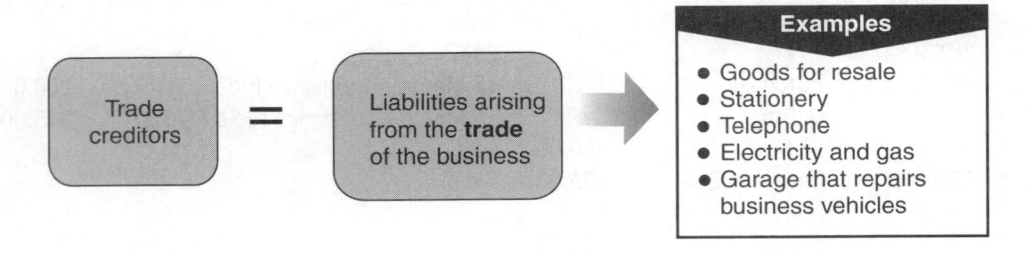

Examples
- Goods for resale
- Stationery
- Telephone
- Electricity and gas
- Garage that repairs business vehicles

3.5 Other creditors

Other creditors are recorded directly in main ledger accounts. Examples of 'other creditors' include the following.

- **Liabilities to pay wages and salaries**
- **Taxes** (eg PAYE) and other amounts (eg VAT) which are collected by the business on behalf of third parties
- Amounts payable *not* directly related to the main trade of the business, eg purchase of fixed assets

Some items of **overhead expenditure** (eg rent and rates) are treated as trade creditors in some businesses, while others treat them as other creditors.

Activity 7.1

(a) What is the status of a trade creditor in the accounts of a business?

    (i) An asset
    (ii) A liability
    (iii) An expense
    (iv) An item of revenue

(b) Which of the following accounts are normally found in a purchase ledger (ie which are *trade* creditors)?

Accounts		Purchase ledger (Y/N)
(i)	Personal accounts for suppliers of subcomponents	
(ii)	Inland Revenue	
(iii)	Customs & Excise for VAT	
(iv)	Suppliers of raw materials stocks	
(v)	Bank overdraft	
(vi)	Long-term bank loan	
(vii)	Telephone expenses	
(viii)	Drawings	
(ix)	Proprietor's capital	

4 Maintaining supplier records

4.1 Opening a new ledger account for a supplier

Opening a ledger account for a new supplier must be **authorised**. The procedures of a business should specify in detail who can authorise opening a new supplier account.

This is important because frauds sometimes involve putting transactions through a dummy supplier account.

In a manual system, an account will be opened showing the following details.

- Supplier's name and address
- Supplier's account number (the supplier's own reference)
- Account number (in the purchase ledger)
- Credit limit
- Special terms, eg discounts, credit period etc

A computerised purchase ledger system needs to be able to create, delete and amend suppliers' details on the **supplier master file**.

PART A ACCOUNTING FOR SALES AND PURCHASES

In a menu-driven purchase ledger system, an option on the purchase ledger system might produce the following menu.

1. Update account name/address
2. Ledger postings
3. Enquiries
4. Dispute/release
5. Creditors total

Option 1 will enable the user to do the following.

- Enter new supplier details, together with discount and trading terms
- Delete supplier accounts which are no longer required
- Amend details of existing suppliers, eg change of address

Each supplier has a **unique account number** chosen by the purchasing business. This means that any particular supplier can be identified by just the account number.

There may be good reasons for maintaining **more than one account** for a particular supplier, eg he supplies different categories of goods and services.

A printing company might order its raw materials (paper and ink) from the same company which provides office stationery.

The different types of purchases are posted to different accounts in the main ledger (eg the **paper and ink** and **stationery accounts**). So operating different accounts may avoid confusion.

The purchase ledger system should have a facility for recording **suppliers' credit limits**. This warns the user if the total outstanding exceeds the credit limit. Payments to the supplier are needed before more orders are placed.

4.2 Deleting and amending existing accounts

Any supplier record no longer required should be **deleted**. It may be possible to specify that a supplier account is automatically deleted if the balance falls to zero.

However, there are good reasons why you should not make use of such a facility.

- Retain supplier records on the ledger for future reference
- Avoid having to create a new supplier record when you start trading again with a supplier whose balance has fallen to zero

However, if a business makes numerous 'one-off' purchases, the facility may help reduce the size of the supplier files and to make the ledger more manageable.

To **amend the supplier record,** enter the account number and alter the particular 'fields' of data concerned. Appropriate authorisation will be necessary in order to avoid fraud.

4.3 'Open item' and 'balance forward'

In a computerised purchase ledger package, and in most manual systems, the account may be either an **'open item'** or a **'balance forward'** type account.

- By the **open item method**, cash paid is matched directly against outstanding invoices. At the end of the period (say a month), any invoices remaining unpaid are carried forward to the next period. Most purchase ledger systems are of this type.

- By the **balance forward method**, cash paid is matched against the oldest outstanding invoices. At the end of the period, a balance is carried forward to the next period. A problem of this method is that parts of invoices will be carried forward.

4.4 Dividing the ledger

The purchase ledger may be **divided up into parts**, for administrative convenience. This may reduce the risk of fraud by having different clerks post different parts of the ledger. For example, there might be three purchase ledgers.

Purchase ledger 1, for suppliers with names beginning A-J
Purchase ledger 2, for suppliers with names beginning K-O
Purchase ledger 3, for suppliers with names beginning P-Z

Alternatively, the ledger might be divided by geographical region. The sales ledger may be divided in the same ways.

Activity 7.2

Aroma operates a computerised purchases ledger system. Chan is offered the following menu.

1	Account name and address update
2	Postings
3	Enquiries
4	Dispute
5	Creditors total

(a) Briefly describe Option 1.

(b) What sort of transactions would you post in Option 2?

PART A ACCOUNTING FOR SALES AND PURCHASES

Activity 7.3

Chan has posted the following transactions to a purchase ledger account.

Date	Narrative	Trans ref	Debit £ p	Credit £ p	Balance £ p
Balance at 31/8/X7					NIL
2/9/X7		P901		453.10	453.10
3/9/X7		P902		462.50	915.60
4/9/X7	Cash	C9901	462.50		453.10
5/9/X7		P903		705.90	1,159.00
7/9/X7		P904		25.50	1,184.50
12/9/X7	Cash	C9902	705.90		478.60
15/9/X7		P905		914.30	1,392.90
17/9/X7		P906		692.53	2,085.43
19/9/X7	Cash	C9903	692.53		1,392.90
21/9/X7		P907		805.39	2,198.29
22/9/X7		C9904	914.30		1,283.99
25/9/X7		P908		478.60	1,762.59
28/9/X7	Cash	C9905	805.39		957.20
29/9/X7	Cash	C9906	478.60		478.60
30/9/X7		P909		92.70	571.30
Balance at 30/9/X7					£571.30

Tasks

At close of business on 30 September 20X7, identify which invoices are outstanding, applying:

(a) the open item method

(b) the balance forward method

5 Recording transactions in the purchase ledger

In a computer system, accounts can be updated directly (**transaction processing**) or stored on a **transaction file** for a later updating run. Similarly a manual system may be posted daily, weekly or monthly.

5.1 Recording purchases and cash paid

The chart below shows how entries are made in purchase ledger accounts.

7: THE PURCHASE LEDGER

PURCHASE LEDGER POSTINGS

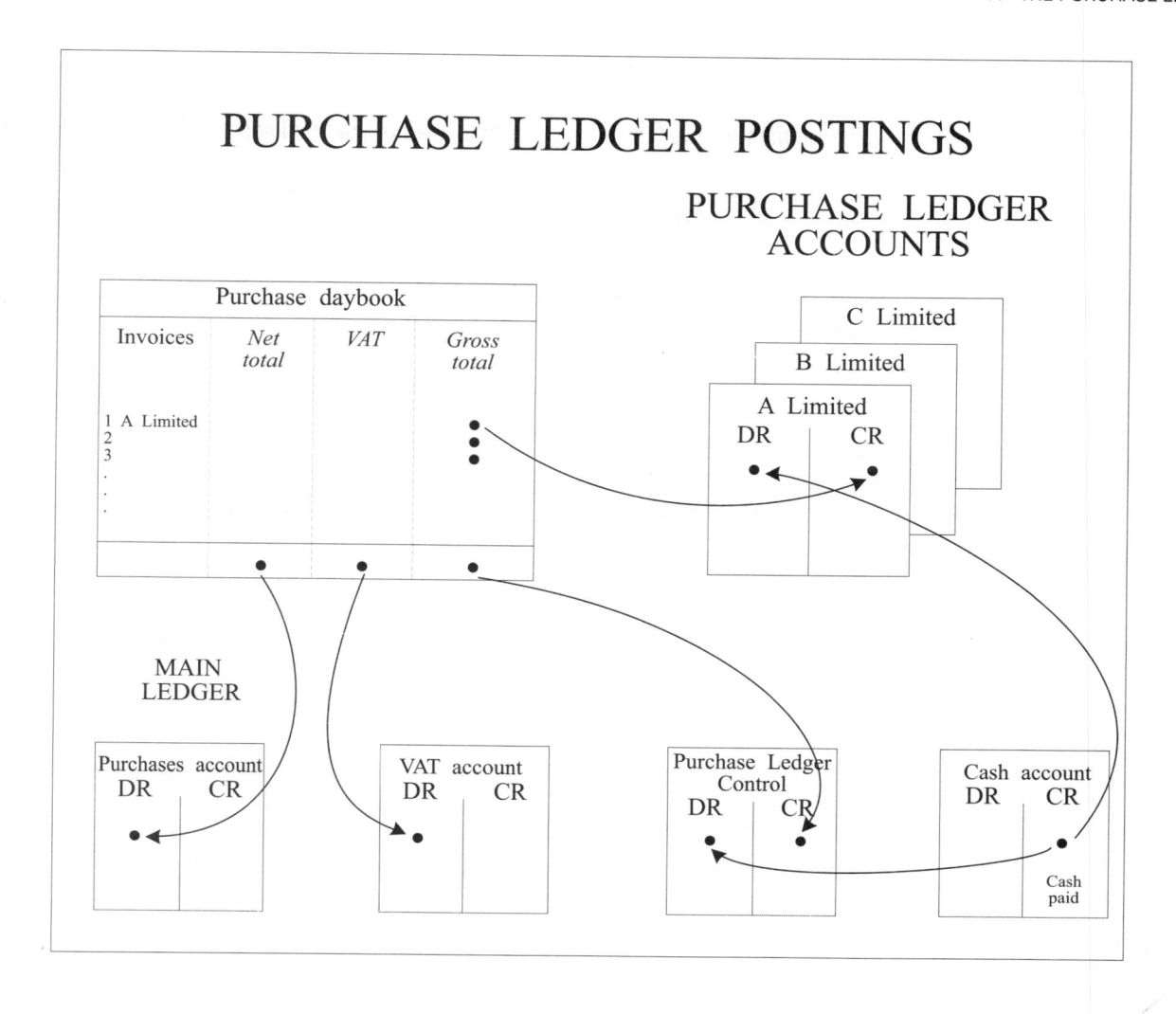

5.1.1 Posting summary

Double entry:		Debit (DR)	Credit (CR)
Total invoices (incl VAT)	PDB		Purchase ledger control a/c
Net invoices (excl VAT)	PDB	Purchases or expense a/c	
VAT	PDB	VAT a/c	
Cash paid	CB	Purchase ledger control a/c	Cash account

Memorandum:
Each invoice (incl VAT) — Individual purchase ledger a/c (CR)
Each cash payment — Individual purchase ledger a/c (DR)

5.2 Posting purchase returns

Remember purchase returns **reduce** purchases. Postings of credit notes received are made to the **debit** of the purchase ledger accounts. In the main ledger, the double entry postings are **debit purchase ledger control account** and **credit purchases**.

PART A ACCOUNTING FOR SALES AND PURCHASES

5.3 Discounts received

Some businesses account for cash discounts received from suppliers by a 'memorandum' discounts received column in the cash book (see Chapter 14).

Discounts received **reduce** purchases and so are **debits** to the individual creditors' accounts. The appropriate double entry main ledger entries follow.

		£	£
DEBIT	Purchase ledger control account	X	
CREDIT	Discounts received		X

5.4 Retention of records

All purchase invoices and credit notes should be retained and filed after processing in case of query (from the supplier, the management or the auditors).

Where VAT is involved, invoices and credit notes must be retained for six years.

Filing will be dealt with in Chapter 9.

Activity 7.4

Aroma's purchase day book includes the following entries.

	Gross	VAT	Net	Purchases	Gas	Stationery
Alfred	1,175.00	175.00	1,000.00	1,000.00		
N. Gas Co	822.50	122.50	700.00		700.00	
Bertie	587.50	87.50	500.00	500.00		
Stanner supplies	705.00	105.00	600.00			600.00

Kris made a return to Alfred and the following credit note is in the purchase returns day book.

	Gross	VAT	Net	Purchases	Gas	Stationery
Alfred	293.75	43.75	250.00	250.00		

Tasks

(a) Complete the memorandum purchase ledger accounts, using the 'T' accounts below.

(b) Complete the double entry, using the 'T' accounts below.

ALFRED		BERTIE	
£	£	£	£

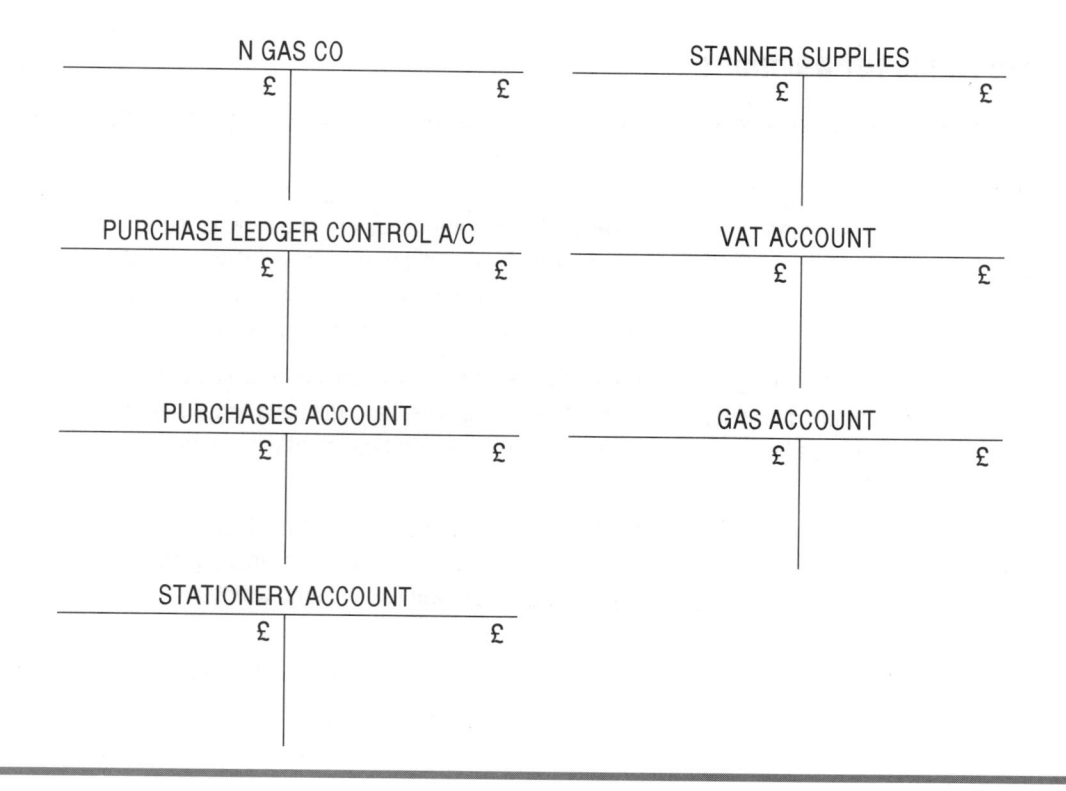

7: THE PURCHASE LEDGER

```
            N GAS CO                              STANNER SUPPLIES
       £              £                          £                £
       |              |                          |                |
       |              |                          |                |


   PURCHASE LEDGER CONTROL A/C                      VAT ACCOUNT
       £              £                          £                £
       |              |                          |                |
       |              |                          |                |


         PURCHASES ACCOUNT                          GAS ACCOUNT
       £              £                          £                £
       |              |                          |                |
       |              |                          |                |


        STATIONERY ACCOUNT
       £              £
       |              |
       |              |
```

6 Payments to suppliers

Payments to suppliers are best made on a regular basis, say monthly, as a matter of efficiency.

6.1 Methods of payment

Different methods of payment to suppliers are available.

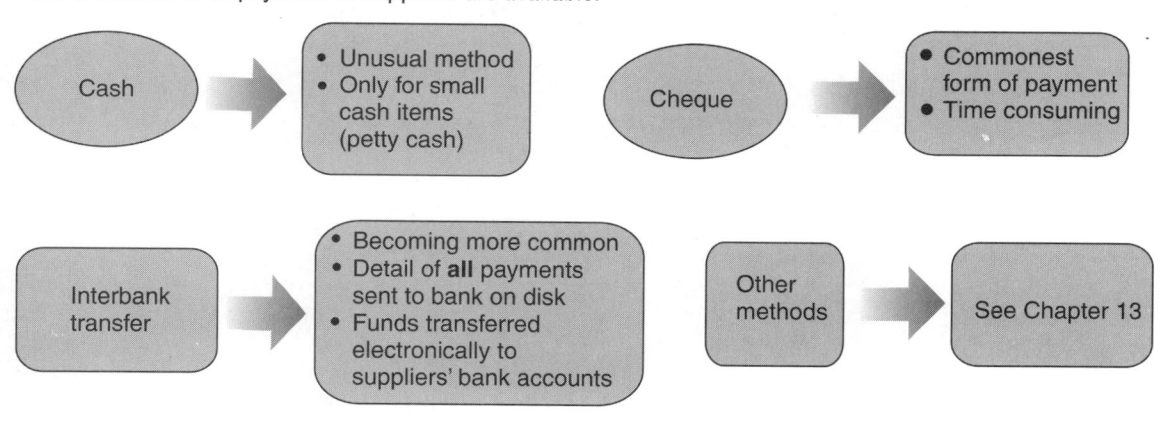

- Cash → • Unusual method
  • Only for small cash items (petty cash)

- Cheque → • Commonest form of payment
  • Time consuming

- Interbank transfer → • Becoming more common
  • Detail of **all** payments sent to bank on disk
  • Funds transferred electronically to suppliers' bank accounts

- Other methods → See Chapter 13

6.2 Selecting items for payment

Deciding when and who to pay is a key function of a business's management and only a senior person should decide.

All systems	Computerised purchase ledger system
The items for payment may be selected manually.	A **'suggested payments'** listing shows what should be paid to whom, based on settlement days and discounts offered. This needs to be checked manually in case there are any reasons to make a different payment from that 'suggested'.
If **queries** on any invoices are outstanding the invoice should not be paid until the query has been settled. (The invoice should be kept in a separate 'queried invoices' file.)	There may be a facility to 'flag' items which should not be paid for the time being. The 'flag' will need to be 'released' when the dispute is settled, so that payment can be made.
It may be desirable to take the full period of credit from each supplier.	The number of days before settlement can be recorded for each supplier. There may be an option of making automatic payments and this will list all items which are now due to be paid. This list will *exclude*: • Items which have not yet reached their settlement date • Items which are 'in dispute'

6.3 Computer cheques and remittance advices

A computerised purchase ledger system may offer the option of **printing cheques for payments to suppliers.** Special cheque stationery is needed.

A **remittance advice** is normally sent with each payment to tell the supplier what the payment is for. This too may be produced by a computerised purchase ledger system.

7: THE PURCHASE LEDGER

```
                        REMITTANCE ADVICE

KT Electronics                    R&B Sound Services Ltd
4 Reform Road                     Belton Estate
Wokingham                         Peterborough
Berkshire                         PE4 4DE


                                  30/06/X3
Account number: 427424            Your ref: RBS/2011

Date        Details                         Amount/£
08/05/X3    Invoice  202481                 624.60
21/05/X3    Invoice  202574                  78.40
24/05/X3    Credit note C40041              (62.20)

            Payment enclosed for            640.80
```

6.4 Checks over payments

It is important for a business to have **procedures to ensure that only valid payments are made** - ie only the payments which *should* be made by the business.

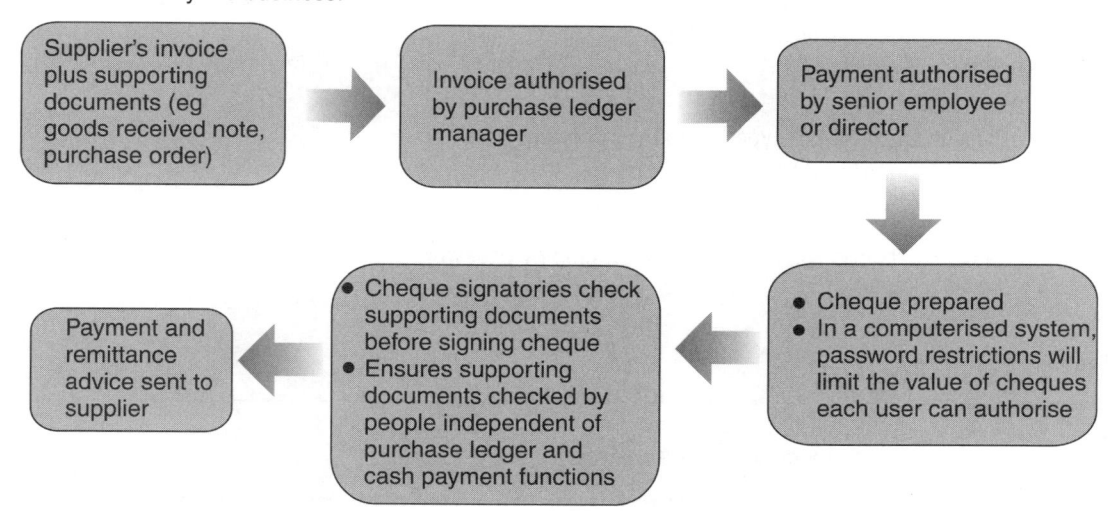

```
┌─────────────────┐     ┌─────────────────┐     ┌─────────────────┐
│ Supplier's      │     │                 │     │ Payment         │
│ invoice         │     │ Invoice         │     │ authorised      │
│ plus supporting │ ──▶ │ authorised      │ ──▶ │ by senior       │
│ documents (eg   │     │ by purchase     │     │ employee        │
│ goods received  │     │ ledger manager  │     │ or director     │
│ note, purchase  │     │                 │     │                 │
│ order)          │     │                 │     │                 │
└─────────────────┘     └─────────────────┘     └─────────────────┘
                                                        │
                                                        ▼
┌──────────────┐   ┌──────────────────────────┐   ┌─────────────────────┐
│ Payment and  │   │ • Cheque signatories     │   │ • Cheque prepared   │
│ remittance   │   │   check supporting       │   │ • In a computerised │
│ advice sent  │◀──│   documents before       │◀──│   system, password  │
│ to supplier  │   │   signing cheque         │   │   restrictions will │
│              │   │ • Ensures supporting     │   │   limit the value   │
└──────────────┘   │   documents checked by   │   │   of cheques each   │
                   │   people independent of  │   │   user can authorise│
                   │   purchase ledger and    │   │                     │
                   │   cash payment functions │   │                     │
                   └──────────────────────────┘   └─────────────────────┘
```

PART A   ACCOUNTING FOR SALES AND PURCHASES

Automatic payment methods in a large organisation may include **mechanical signature of payments by computer**. If such a system is used, there is not the same check on individual payments and there will have to be strong checks over whether purchase ledger balances are correct to ensure that wrong payments are not made.

If automated electronic payments methods (such as **BACS**) are used, there will need to be special procedures to ensure that all payments included on the tape submitted to BACS are properly authorised.

Sometimes, the usual payment method may need to be bypassed. For example, a special **manual payment** may be needed if the credit limit is exceeded. Proper checks will be needed in such cases and high level authorisation obtained.

7 The age analysis of creditors and other reports

7.1 The age analysis of creditors

An **age analysis of creditors** is a listing showing how old the creditor balances are.

It highlights any supplier accounts which are **long overdue**, for whatever reason.

The totals of the age analysis indicate the **age 'profile'** of creditors' accounts. This profile is used by business managers to check whether the business would be better off paying creditors a little later in order to improve its cash flow position.

7.2 Other reports

- Purchase day book listings
- Purchase returns day book listings
- Purchase ledger balances by supplier
- Supplier statements
- VAT analysis
- Purchases analysis – by type of product, different sites, etc
- List of supplier accounts
- Mailing list of suppliers' names and addresses

Access to purchase ledger reports will normally be restricted by **password**.

Activity 7.5

What, briefly, is the significance of a *creditors'* age analysis?

8 Contra entries with the sales ledger

Sometimes, a business **purchases goods from** and **sells goods to** the same person on credit.

- **Purchase** invoices will be entered in the **purchase day book** and recorded in the supplier's individual account in the purchase ledger
- **Credit sales** invoices are entered in the **sales day book** and subsequently recorded in the customer's individual account in the sales ledger

Even though the supplier and the customer are the same person, he will have a **separate account in each ledger**. If A owes B £200 for purchases and B owes A £350 for credit sales, the net effect is that B owes A £150. However, in the books of A, there will be the following entries.

- A creditor in the purchase ledger - B - for £200
- A debtor in the sales ledger - B - for £350

If A and B decide to settle their accounts by **netting off** their respective debts (and getting B to write a single cheque for the balance of £150), settlement would be made **by a contra entry**.

The contra entries in the accounts of A would be to set off the smaller amount (£200 owed *to* B) against the larger amount (£350 owed *by* B).

(a) In the *sales ledger and purchase ledger:*

DEBIT	Creditor's account (B) purchase ledger - to clear	£200	
CREDIT	Debtor's account (B) sales ledger - leaving balance of £150		£200

(b) In the *main ledger.*

DEBIT	Purchase ledger control account	£200	
CREDIT	Sales ledger control account		£200

The contra entries must be made in both the personal accounts for B and also in the purchase ledger and sales ledger control accounts in the main ledger.

PART A ACCOUNTING FOR SALES AND PURCHASES

Activity 7.6

You are the purchase ledger clerk for Aroma, and the date is 28 August 20X7. The company operates a non-integrated purchase ledger system.

The purchase ledger account for a supplier called Kernels Ltd shows the following.

		(Debit)/Credit £	Balance £
01.08.X7	Balance b/f		76.05
01.08.X7	Invoice 20624	42.84	118.89
07.08.X7	Cash	(76.05)	42.84
16.08.X7	Invoice 20642	64.17	107.01
16.08.X7	Invoice 20643	120.72	227.73
16.08.X7	Invoice 20642	64.17	291.90
21.08.X7	Cash	(400.00)	(108.10)
22.08.X7	Invoice 20798	522.18	414.08
24.08.X7	C91004	42.84	456.92
27.08.X7	Invoice 21114	144.50	601.42
27.08.X7	Invoice 21229	42.84	644.26

The following facts came to light.

(a) Kernels Ltd's invoice 21201 for £97.40, dated 23 August 20X7, was misposted to the account of MPV Ltd in the purchase ledger.

(b) The cash payment of £400.00 made on 21 August 20X7 relates to another creditor, ASR Ltd.

(c) Item C91004 dated 24 August 20X7 is in fact a credit note.

(d) Invoice 20642 has been posted to the account twice.

(e) Kernels Ltd has a balance of £37.50 in the sales ledger, which is to be set off against its balance in the purchase ledger.

Tasks

Set out the postings for the above items and write up the Kernels Ltd's account accordingly, posting these entries to the account.

Distinguish between main ledger adjustments and memorandum account adjustments. Balance off the Kernels Ltd account and show the balance b/d to the next period.

Tutorial note. If you are in doubt about the debits and credits, remember that a purchase ledger account is a **liability**. Therefore debits **reduce** the account and credits **increase** the balance owing.

Key learning points

- ☑ The purchase ledger contains the personal accounts of suppliers (trade creditors) of the business.

- ☑ The suppliers' personal accounts provide the business with a full record of how much it owes to each supplier and the make up of the balance.

- ☑ A supplier's account in the purchase ledger will normally show a credit balance: the supplier is owed money by the business and is therefore a creditor of the business.

- ☑ Other creditors which a business may have include the tax authorities, banks and employees (for any wages and salaries due).

- ☑ Opening a new purchase ledger account or amending an existing record will require the authorisation of a senior official.

- ☑ A computerised system may use a 'menu' system through which supplier records may be added, deleted or amended. Authorisation may be by way of a password known only to authorised employees.

- ☑ Payments to suppliers should be organised according to the periodic procedures of the business. Checks and authorisation are necessary in order to ensure that only valid payments are made.

- ☑ Payment methods vary, and the checks necessary will differ according to the payment methods used. This will be dealt with in detail in Chapter 13.

- ☑ The age analysis of creditors shows the age 'profile' of creditors' balances on the purchase ledger. It indicates how quickly the business is paying off its liabilities.

- ☑ A computerised purchase ledger will also allow a number of other reports to be printed out as necessary.

- ☑ Contra entries 'net off' amounts due to and from the same parties in the purchase ledger and sales ledger respectively.

PART A   ACCOUNTING FOR SALES AND PURCHASES

Quick quiz

1   What does the purchase ledger contain?
2   *Complete the blank.* Trade creditors are _____ relating to the trade of the business.
3   Give two examples of 'other creditors'.
4   What does the age analysis of creditors do?
5   What does settlement 'in contra' mean?

   A   Set off two balances in the purchase ledger
   B   Set off two balances in the sale ledger
   C   Set off a balance in the purchase ledger against a balance in the sales ledger for the same person or business
   D   Set off an Invoice and a credit note in the purchase ledger

Answers to quick quiz

1   The personal accounts showing how much is owed to each credit supplier of the business.
2   Trade creditors are **liabilities** relating to the trade of the business.
3   (i)   Wages and salaries
    (ii) VAT
4   Lists creditors' balances analysed between different 'ages' of debt, eg one month old, two months old etc.
5   C   An amount due from a customer in the sales ledger is set off against an amount owed to the same person in the purchase ledger, and *vice versa.*

7: THE PURCHASE LEDGER

Activity checklist

This checklist shows which performance criteria, range statement or knowledge and understanding point is covered by each activity in this chapter. Tick off each activity as you complete it.

Activity

7.1	☐	This activity deals with Knowledge and Understanding point 25: the nature of the organisation's business transaction.
7.2	☐	This activity deals with Knowledge and Understanding point 16: the operation of computerised accounting systems.
7.3	☐	This activity deals with Knowledge and Understanding points 15 and 16.
7.4	☐	This activity deals with Performance Criteria 2.1.F.
7.5	☐	This activity deals with Knowledge and Understanding points 15 and 16.
7.6	☐	This activity deals with Performance Criteria 2.1.F, Range Statement 2.1.6 regarding main and subsidiary ledgers, and Knowledge and Understanding point 11: double entry bookkeeping, including balancing accounts.

PART A ACCOUNTING FOR SALES AND PURCHASES

chapter 8

Communications with debtors

Contents

1 The problem
2 The solution
3 The statement of account
4 The age analysis of debtors and other reports
5 Dealing with debtor's queries
6 Demand for payment
7 Credit control

Performance criteria
1.1.F Produce statements of account for despatch to debtors
1.1.G Communicate politely and effectively with customers regarding accounts using the relevant information from the aged debtors analysis

Range statement
1.1.6 Statements: manual; computerised
1.1.7 Communicate: respond to queries; chase payments

Knowledge and understanding
22 Relevant understanding of the organisation's accounting systems and administrative systems and procedures
26 House style for correspondence

Signpost
The topics covered in this chapter are relevant to **Unit 1.**

PART A   ACCOUNTING FOR SALES AND PURCHASES

1 The problem

A business sends out invoices to its customers. However, how can it be sure that the customer receives them all?

A customer makes payments to the business. How can the business be sure that it has recorded all receipts from customers? Are receipts being posted to the wrong customer? Are receipts being stolen?

2 The solution

There needs to be **communication** between the customer (debtor) and the business.

This usually takes the form of a **statement of account**. The statement lists the following.

- Balance brought forward from previous period
- Invoices sent out during the period
- Credit notes sent out during the period
- Payments received during the period
- Balance carried forward (still owing to the business) at the end of the period
- Statement of terms eg payment due date

Statements are usually sent out monthly.

The business expects that the customer will check the statement and raise **queries**.

- Invoices listed but not received by the customer
- Disputed invoices for which the customer has still not received a credit note
- Payments made by the customer that are not on the statement

3 The statement of account

3.1 Statements of account

There will be a steady flow of invoices sent out to customers. Some customers may be sent a handful of sales invoices each month; others may be sent a lot more (depending on the nature of the business).

If a business expected its customers to pay **separately** for each individual sales invoice that it sent, the customer would have to prepare **several cheques** each month. This is wasteful in administrative time and resources. Instead, the seller sends out to the customer, in addition to separate invoices, a **statement of account.**

The statement of account is usually produced by a **computer**, though it may be **typed out by hand**.

3.1.1 Example of a statement of account

STATEMENT OF ACCOUNT

Pickett (Handling Equipment) Limited
Unit 7, Western Industrial Estate
Dunford DN2 7RJ

Tel: (01990) 72101   Fax: (01990) 72980   VAT Reg No 982 721 349

Accounts Department
Finstar Ltd
67 Laker Avenue
Dunford DN4 5PS

Date: 31 May 20X2

A/c No: F023

Date	Details	Debit £ p	Credit £ p	Balance £ p
30/4/X2	Balance brought forward from previous statement ①			492 22
3/5/X2	Invoice no. 34207 ②	129 40		621 62
4/5/X2	Invoice no. 34242 ②	22 72		644 34
5/5/X2	Payment received - thank you ④		412 17	232 17
17/5/X2	Invoice no. 34327 ②	394 95		627 12
18/5/X2	Credit note no. 00192 ③		64 40	562 72
21/5/X2	Invoice no. 34392 ②	392 78		955 50
28/5/X2	Credit note no. 00199 ③		107 64	847 86
	Amount now due		⑤ £	847 86

Terms: 30 days net, 1% discount for payment in 7 days. E & OE ⑥

Registered office: 4 Arkwright Road, London E16 4PQ   Registered in England No 2182417

Key

1 Balance brought forward
2 New invoices sent out
3 Credit notes sent out
4 Payments received
5 Balance now outstanding
6 Terms

You can see from this statement that as at 31 May 20X2 Finstar Ltd owes a total of £847.86 to Pickett.

PART A   ACCOUNTING FOR SALES AND PURCHASES

Activity 8.1

Can you say how much of this balance is made up of invoices or credit notes from before May 20X2?

3.2 Statements of account with remittance advice forms

A statement may be produced with a remittance advice form attached. The customer can tear off the remittance advice and send it with the payment to indicate the invoices (less any credit notes) to which the payment relates. An example is set out below.

STATEMENT

Los Ninjos & Co
Belton Estate
Peterborough

TO: ABC & Co
4 The Mews
Middlesborough

A/C REF: 12379
DATE: 010497
PAGE: 1

DATE	DETAILS		DEBIT	CREDIT
020297	Invoice	20381	96.27	
050297	Invoice	20414	113.44	
110297	Invoice	20522	84.95	
210297	C/note	C9410		22.00
010397	Cash received			272.66
120397	Invoice	20529	212.11	
150397	Invoice	20611	106.07	
290397	Invoice	22100	78.90	
300397	C/note	C9422		23.48

CURRENT	30 DAY	60 DAY	90 DAY	120+ DAY
373.60	0	0	0	0

AMOUNT DUE

£373.60

REMITTANCE ADVICE

Los Ninjos & Co
Belton Estate
Peterborough

FROM: ABC & Co
4 The Mews
Middlesborough

A/C REF: 12379
DATE: 010497
PAGE: 1

DATE	DETAILS		DEBIT	CREDIT
020297	Invoice	20381	96.27	
050297	Invoice	20414	113.44	
110297	Invoice	20522	84.95	
210297	C/note	C9410		22.00
010397	Cash received			272.66
120397	Invoice	20529	212.11	
150397	Invoice	20611	106.07	
290397	Invoice	22100	78.90	
300397	C/note	C9422		23.48

OUR TERMS 30 DAYS. YOUR PROMPT
SETTLEMENT WOULD BE APPRECIATED.
THANK YOU.

AMOUNT DUE

£373.60

If the amount being paid is not the full amount due per the statement, then the customer can indicate on the remittance advice why there is a difference, as shown below.

PART A   ACCOUNTING FOR SALES AND PURCHASES

REMITTANCE ADVICE

Los Ninjos & Co
Belton Estate
Peterborough

FROM: ABC & Co
4 The Mews
Middlesborough

A/C REF: 12379
DATE: 010497
PAGE: 1

DATE	DETAILS		DEBIT	CREDIT
020297	Invoice	20381	96.27	
050297	Invoice	20414	113.44	
110297	Invoice	20522	84.95	
210297	C/note	C9410		22.00
010397	Cash received			272.66
120397	Invoice	20529	212.11 ✓	
150397	Invoice	20611	106.07 ✓	
290397	Invoice	22100*	78.90	
300397	C/note	C9422		23.48 ✓

Credit due – ref. our letter 31/3/97

OUR TERMS 30 DAYS. YOUR PROMPT
SETTLEMENT WOULD BE APPRECIATED.
THANK YOU.

AMOUNT DUE

£294.70   ~~£373.60~~

However, be aware that debtors may prefer to send an internally-generated remittance advice which indicates how the payment is made up.

Activity 8.2

You work for Muzak Ltd in the sales ledger department. A new assistant, Boris Thug, has recently been taken on to help you. He is keen, but as he is so inexperienced you have made it a policy to review his work.

You were ill for a couple of days, at the time you normally send out reminder letters to late paying debtors. To help you out, Boris has drafted some for you.

One such letter refers to a customer, J L Baudrillard plc, who has *two* accounts with you. On your sales ledger, these appear as:

- J L Baudrillard plc Head Office (A/c no BA01)
- J L Baudrillard plc Robotics (A/c No BB01)

J L Baudrillard plc is an old and valued customer, and has done increasing amounts of business with Muzak Ltd over the years. J L Baudrillard plc has recently appointed a new finance director, Mr Martin Jacques.

Muzak Ltd's sales ledger is computerised.

Tasks

(a) Review Boris's letter to J L Baudrillard plc in the light of:

  (i) The most recent statement on *each* J L Baudrillard plc account

  (ii) Your own Screen Enquiry of the Customer Reference file and sales ledger accounts

  (iii) The notes Boris himself made on September 7 regarding the balances on the J L Baudrillard plc accounts at that date

  (iv) Your own common sense

  Note down *anything* and *everything* in Boris's draft which you regard as incorrect or inappropriate. Boris regards his letter as ready for posting.

(b) State any matters which need to be raised about your accounts with J L Baudrillard plc and what action you would take as a consequence.

PART A ACCOUNTING FOR SALES AND PURCHASES

Boris's draft letter to J L Baudrillard plc

Finance Director
Baudrilard
Charles House
Postmodern Industrial Estate
Frontage, Wilts

14/9/X7

Dear Mr Baudrilard

We've got problems with your account which you will see from the statement I sent you two weeks ago. Your always going overdrawn and this month you don't seem to have paid us. Please do something about it, or I might have to call in a soliciter or debt collector.

I remain, sir, your obedient servant,

Boris Thug, Assistant

Boris's screen enquiry 7/9/X7

Boris has also noted down the following details from an enquiry he made of the system on 7 September 20X7.

SALES LEDGER BALANCE ENQUIRY NOTE

Amount outstanding

	£
BA01 Baudrillard PLC Head Office	35,752.62
BB01 Baudrillard PLC Robotics	25,978.41

DATE 7/9/X7

Statements of account

MUZAK LTD

99 Bleak Street, London N3
Phone: 0151 234 5678 Fax: 0151 234 5679
VAT reg: 231 1423

STATEMENT OF ACCOUNT

J L BAUDRILLARD PLC ROBOTICS
SIMULACRA HOUSE,
CYBERNETIC STREET,
STEPFORD,
LINCS

Account: BB01
Date: 31/8/X7

Date	Item	£ p	£ p	£ p
1/8/X7	BALANCE FROM STATEMENT 31/7/X7			25,011.92
3/8/X7	CREDIT NOTE 975		7,121.07	17,890.85
4/8/X7	CREDIT NOTE 977		985.72	16,905.13
10/8/X7	PAYMENT RECEIVED - THANK YOU		7,429.49	9,475.64
25/8/X7	INVOICE 9491	11,071.32		20,546.96
31/8/X7	BALANCE			20,546.96

Reg office: 99 Bleak Street, London N3 Reg no: 231 1423

PART A ACCOUNTING FOR SALES AND PURCHASES

MU2AK LTD

99 Bleak Street, London N3
Phone: 0151 234 5678 Fax: 0151 234 5679
VAT reg: 231 1423

STATEMENT OF ACCOUNT

J L BAUDRILLARD PLC HEAD OFFICE
CHARLES HOUSE
POSTMODERN INDUSTRIAL ESTATE
FRONTAGE
WILTS

Account: BA01
Date: 31/8/X7

Date	Item	£ p	£ p	£ p
1/8/X7	BALANCE FROM STATEMENT 31/7/X7			25,553.01
4/8/X7	INVOICE 0483	7,121.07		32,674.08
9/8/X7	INVOICE 3448	985.72		33,659.80
14/8/X7	PAYMENT RECEIVED - THANK YOU		17,639.56	16,020.24
25/8/X7	INVOICE 9372	8,131.41		24,151.65
31/8/X7	**BALANCE**			24,151.65

Reg office: 99 Bleak Street, London N3 Reg no: 231 1423

Details from screen enquiry 14/9/X7

Customer:	J L Baudrillard plc Robotics BB01		
	Simulacra House		
	Cybernetic St		
	Stepford		
	Lincs		
Phone	01941 821010		
Fax	01941 821013		
Credit Limit	£20,000		Last reviewed 1/1/20X2

Customer:	J L Baudrillard plc Head Office	BA01	
	Charles House		
	Postmodern Industrial Estate		
	Frontage		
	Wilts		
Phone	01711 468246		
Fax	01711 468247		
Credit Limit	£50,000		Last reviewed 1/1/20X6

PART A ACCOUNTING FOR SALES AND PURCHASES

SALES LEDGER RUN — 31/8/X7

CUSTOMER:	J L BAUDRILLARD PLC ROBOTICS DIVISION	ACCOUNT NO:
ADDRESS:	SIMULACRA HOUSE, CYBERNETIC STREET, STEPFORD, LINCS	BB01
PHONE:	01473 979149	

Date	Trans ref	DR £ p	CR £ p	Balance £ p
30/6/X7				19,215.68
9/7/X7	Invoice 3448	985.72		20,201.40
10/7/X7	Invoice 3492	7,429.49		27,630.89
15/7/X7	Cash book 15/7		9,740.04	17,890.85
31/7/X7	Invoice 0483	7,121.07		25,011.92
3/8/X7	Credit note 975		7,121.07	17,890.85
4/8/X7	Credit note 977		985.72	16,905.13
10/8/X7	Cash book 10/8		7,429.49	9,475.64
25/8/X7	Invoice 9491	11,071.32		20,546.96
		26,607.60	25,276.32	

8: COMMUNICATIONS WITH DEBTORS

SALES LEDGER RUN				31/8/X7
CUSTOMER: J L BAUDRILLARD PLC HEAD OFFICE			ACCOUNT NO:	
ADDRESS: CHARLES HOUSE, POSTMODERN INDUSTRIAL ESTATE, FRONTAGE, WILTS			BA01	
PHONE: 01711 468246				

Date	Trans ref	DR £ p	CR £ p	Balance £ p
30/6/X7				15,504.66
8/7/X7	Invoice 0107	8,312.50		23,817.16
14/7/X7	Cash book 17/4		19,372.50	4,444.66
21/7/X7	Invoice 0252	17,639.56		22,084.22
28/7/X7	Invoice 0371	3,468.79		25,553.01
4/8/X7	Invoice 0483	7,121.07		32,674.08
9/8/X7	Invoice 3448	985.72		33,659.80
14/8/X7	Cash book 14/8		17,639.56	16,020.24
25/8/X7	Invoice 9372	8,131.41		24,151.65
		45,659.05	37,012.06	

4 The age analysis of debtors and other reports

4.1 The age analysis of debtors

A business needs a way of knowing whether some of the invoices are **long overdue,** so that those invoices can be followed up with the customer.

If a sales ledger consists of a large number of accounts, it is a long and time-consuming task to go through the details of each account to look for old items.

A lot of time can be saved by summarising the 'age' of the items in the various sales ledger accounts in a single schedule. This is achieved by what is called an **age analysis of debtors**.

PART A ACCOUNTING FOR SALES AND PURCHASES

An **age analysis of debtors** breaks down the individual balances on the sales ledger according to how long they have been outstanding.

4.2 What does the age analysis look like?

The age is calculated according to the **date of the transaction.**

Account number	Customer name	Balance	Up to 30 days	Up to 60 days	Up to 90 days	Over 90 days
\ DOMMA LIMITED						
AGE ANALYSIS OF DEBTORS AS AT 31.1.X4						
B004	Brilliant Ltd	804.95	649.90	121.00	0.00	34.05
E008	Easimat Ltd	272.10	192.90	72.40	6.80	0.00
H002	Hampstead Ltd	1,818.42	0.00	0.00	724.24	1,094.18
M024	Martlesham Ltd	284.45	192.21	92.24	0.00	0.00
N030	Nyfen Ltd	1,217.54	1,008.24	124.50	0.00	84.80
T002	Todmorden College	914.50	842.00	0.00	72.50	0.00
Totals		5,311.96	2,885.25	410.14	803.54	1,213.03
Percentage		100%	54.4%	7.7%	15.1%	22.8%

Note. Up to 60 days means older than 30 days but less than 60 days, etc.

An age analysis of debtors can be prepared manually or by computer. **Computerisation does make the job a lot easier.**

Activity 8.3

Prepare an aged debtors analysis for the following debtors, ie Tricorn Ltd, Volux Ltd and Yardsley Smith Ltd.

Tricorn Ltd T004		£
Balance b/f	30.6.X3	94.80
Balance c/f	31.1.X4	94.80
Volux Ltd V010		£
15.11.X3	Invoice	500.00
17.11 X3	Invoice	241.25
5.12.X3	Cash received	(500.00)
6 12. X3	Invoice	342.15
23.1.X4	Invoice	413.66
Balance c/f	31.1.X4	997.06
Yardsley Smith & Co Y020		£
1.12.X3	Invoice	520.60
8.12.X3	Invoice	712.30
31.12.X3	Cash received	(1,212.30)
4.1.X4	Invoice	321.17
Balance c/f	31.1.X4	341.77

4.3 How is the age analysis used?

The age analysis is used to **help decide what action to take about older debts**. Going down each column in turn starting from the column furthest to the right and working across, we can see that there are some rather old debts which ought to be investigated.

- **Correspondence** may already exist in relation to some of these items.
- Perhaps some older invoices are still **in dispute**.
- Maybe some debtors are in **financial difficulties**.

From the above age analysis of Domma Ltd's debtors, the relatively high proportion of debts over 90 days (22.8%) is largely due from Hampstead Ltd. Other customers with debts of this age are Brilliant Ltd and Nyfen Ltd.

The age analysis is also used to give a broader picture of the total debtors. If there seems to be a high percentage of older debts, we may question whether the **credit control department**, who chase up slow payers, is performing its role properly.

Sometimes, a column listing **customer credit limits** will appear on the age analysis of debtors. This will make it easy to see which customers (if any) have exceeded or are close to exceeding their current credit limit.

4.4 Other computerised reports

Computerisation of sales ledger processing also allows a number of other reports to be printed out from the information held on the ledger. Access to sales ledger reports may be restricted to authorised staff members, whose password will allow them access.

Other reports

- Sales day book listings
- Statements of account
- VAT analysis
- Sales analysis – by type of product, area, sale representative etc
- List of customer accounts
- Customer mailing lists

A VAT analysis can be useful if the business has sales at different VAT rates. Also if the business **imports or exports goods**, the analysis can be used to prepare the **EU Intrastat** report (showing how much VAT-able supplies were made to other EU countries).

5 Dealing with debtors' queries

5.1 General communications

Sending out statements of account is a **regular routine**.

PART A   ACCOUNTING FOR SALES AND PURCHASES

Other communications with debtors arise on a less regular basis, depending upon which discrepancies, unusual features or queries occur. Such communications may involve **telephone calls** as well as **written forms of communication**.

Example: Business letter

An example of a business letter involving a debtor is set out below. Britton Trading Co plc has received a complaint from one of the firm's regular customers, UK Freight plc. UK Freight have received a statement indicating that payment of their account is overdue and that settlement must be made immediately. The amount stated to be outstanding is £2,340.20. UK Freight plc says that a cheque for this amount was paid on 23 August 20X3 but no acknowledgement of receipt was received.

Investigations have revealed that an incorrect ledger entry was made on 26 August 20X3. Payment of £2,340.20 was actually credited to the account of UK Carriage plc. August was a month in which there were staff changes in the office.

BRITTON TRADING CO PLC
WOLVERHAMPTON
WEST MIDLANDS

UK Freight plc
Tingeley Street
MANCHESTER
M12 4RS

22 September 20X3

Ref: YN/87/33

Dear Sirs

PAYMENT OF ACCOUNT: £2,340.20 [1]

I was sorry to learn of your complaint regarding a statement received from us indicating that payment of your account is overdue[2].

Having investigated the matter[3], I confirm that we did receive a cheque for £2,340.20[4] from you on the 26 August. I regret that this payment was incorrectly credited as a result of unforeseen pressures on our accounting procedures at that time[5]. I am pleased to report that the error has been rectified: your account is fully paid up and I have taken steps to ensure that its creditworthiness is not impaired by this incident[6].

Please accept my sincere apologies for the concern caused to you[7]. I do not anticipate any recurrence of this problem, but if I can be of any further assistance please do not hesitate to contact me directly[8].

Yours faithfully

R Coe

R Coe
Senior Accounts Clerk
Extension 3320

Note the following features in the above letter, which should be borne in mind whenever a business letter is sent.

Letter feature	Comments
1 Letter title	Always be as clear as possible about the matter covered in the letter - a brief letter title is ideal.
2 Tone	This letter is polite and appropriately apologetic, without being grovelling, defensive or impertinent.
3 Action taken	Always state what action has been taken when investigating a customer complaint.
4 Amounts and dates	Stating the exact amounts and the dates of disputed transactions is vital for the customer to understand what you are saying.
5 Cause of error	It is not strictly necessary to give an explanation for why something went wrong (in theory, the customer is simply concerned that it has been corrected) but it lets the customers see that you have control of the overall situation, even if mistakes are made occasionally.
6 Future action	Consider what effect an error might have on a customer in the future, and reassure them.
7 Apologise	It is polite and reassuring to the customer for you to apologise for the mistake, and to reassure them.
8 Further contact	Reassure the customer that any further queries on the matter will be readily dealt with; make sure your name, and preferably your extension number, are clear on the letter.

Example: Short informal report

The complaint from UK Freight plc was received by Mr Case who asks for a short informal report on the matter.

REPORT ON CUSTOMER COMPLAINT: UK Freight plc payment of £2,340.20

TO: Mr Case   Ref: IRC/85/20
FROM: R Coe   Date: 21 September

1   Background

    I have investigated the situation with regard to this complaint. I have consulted all ledger entries relevant to this account, and to accounts of similar names, at the time of the claimed payment. The last week in August was a time of extraordinary staff turnover and therefore unusual stress in the office.

2   Findings

    A cheque for £2,340.20 was indeed received from UK Freight plc on 26 August. This amount was credited in error to the account of UK Carriage plc. and an acknowledgement of receipt issued to them. The incorrect entry may have been made by temporary staff.

PART A   ACCOUNTING FOR SALES AND PURCHASES

> 3   Action taken
>
> I have corrected the ledger entries for UK Freight plc and UK Carriage plc, and ensured that the creditworthiness of the former account is not affected. I have written a letter of apology and explanation to UK Freight plc (copy attached), and I have issued a warning to the accounts clerks about the ease with which such an error can be made. I have also explained the erroneous receipt to UK Carriage plc and apologised for the mistake.
>
> R Coe, Senior Accounts Clerk

5.2 Debtors' queries

The sales ledger department may be in **regular contact** with the purchase ledger department of a customer. The customer's purchase ledger department processes the seller's invoices and so will receive and take action on the seller's statements.

There will be various queries which need to be sorted out between the two departments.

Much of this contact will be by telephone, perhaps with later confirmation in writing. Fax machines are particularly useful to send a copy document eg an invoice which cannot easily be read out over the telephone.

Major matters, and matters where some formal confirmation is necessary, will probably need to be dealt with by letter.

However a query is received, it should be dealt with promptly and courteously. This is good business sense and helps to ensure that good relations are maintained with customers.

Examples of debtors' queries

In the following paragraphs, we consider a number of different enquiries and the appropriate responses. In each of these examples, the situations described are set in the **sales ledger department of Pickett (Handling Equipment) Ltd** and involve other departments of that company, as appropriate. Highlight what you consider to be the key areas of each situation, and check that they are included in the solution.

Situation 1: opening a customer account

The Buying Manager of Cash Factories plc has held meetings with Pickett's Sales Manager Paul Morley with a view to becoming a regular customer of Pickett. The first orders have already been placed, and the Sales Manager has asked for a **credit account to be set up for this new customer**.

You obtain a credit reference agency report on Cash Factories plc which indicates that the company is financially sound and recommends a credit limit of up to £100,000. Paul Morley considers that the maximum balance of the new account is unlikely to exceed £20,000 at any one time and requests that the credit limit for Cash Factories plc be set at £50,000. The Financial Director authorises this proposed limit.

Draft a letter dated 2 June 20X2 to R Staite, the Buying Manager of Cash Factories plc, at 630 Atlantic Avenue, Dunford DN9 9TB, confirming the opening of the new account and the credit limit allocated, and the standard credit terms (30 days net, a discount of 1% for payment within 7 days, statements of account issued monthly).

8: COMMUNICATIONS WITH DEBTORS

Pickett (Handling Equipment) Limited
Unit 7, Western Industrial Estate
Dunford DN2 7RJ

Tel: (01990) 72101   Fax: (01990) 72980   VAT Reg No 982 721 349

R Staite Esq
Buying Manager
Cash Factories plc
630 Atlantic Avenue
Dunford DN9 9TB

2 June 20X2

Dear Mr Staite

Following your recent meetings with our Sales Manager Paul Morley, I confirm that a sales account has been opened for your company.

The reference number for the account is C024 and the credit limit applying to the account is initially £50,000.

Our terms are 30 days net, and a discount of 1% is given for payment within 7 days. Statements of account are issued monthly.

Yours sincerely

N Norman

N Norman
Financial Controller

Situation 2: prospective customer with financial difficulties

On 7 June 20X2, Tryiton Ltd submitted a purchase order for goods to be supplied on credit to the value of £2,400 approximately. Tryiton Ltd does not currently have a sales ledger account with Pickett and is unable to provide any references. A report obtained from a credit reference agency suggests that Tryiton Ltd may be in financial difficulties and declines to recommend any credit limit.

Draft a letter to Tryiton Ltd, of 124 Luton Avenue, Dunford DN10 6RB, explaining that credit cannot be extended.

PART A ACCOUNTING FOR SALES AND PURCHASES

Pickett (Handling Equipment) Limited
Unit 7, Western Industrial Estate
Dunford DN27 7RJ

Tel: (01990) 72101   Fax: (01990) 72980   VAT Reg No 982 721 349

Tryiton Limited
124 Luton Avenue
Dunford DN10 6RB

7 June 20X2

Dear Sirs

Thank you for your purchase order No P9093.

I regret that we are unable to extend credit to your company, although we would be able to supply the goods you require if you make payment in advance. Should you wish to trade with us on this basis, please contact our Sales Manager, Paul Morley.

We look forward to hearing from you.

Yours faithfully

N Norman

N Norman
Financial Controller

Situation 3: payment not received

An Accounts Assistant at Finstar Ltd telephones on 1 June 20X2, thanking you for the Statement of Account for May 20X2 (see Paragraph 3.5). The Assistant says that the statement is incorrect, as it does not show the payment of £117.77 made on 28 May 20X2 which she says cleared invoices 34207, 34242, credit note 00192 and all amounts relating to periods earlier than May 20X2.

The points to be made in replying include the following.

- The payment made on 28 May is not shown in the statement dated 31 May because the payment was either in the post or waiting to be processed by the sales ledger department when the statement was prepared.

- Assuming that the payment is received, it will be reflected in the next statement of account issued at the end of June.

- A payment of £117.77 does not completely clear the items which you specify.

		£
Invoice	34207	129.40
	34242	22.72
Credit note	00192	(64.40)
Balance brought forward		492.22
Payment received		(412.17)
		167.77
Payment sent		117.77
Amount remaining unpaid		50.00

5.3 Requests for credit notes

Many communications with debtors involve requests by customers for credit notes against goods or services already invoiced.

- Goods have been damaged in transit
- The amount delivered is less than the amount invoiced.

Until a credit note is issued, the statement will simply show the full amount invoiced.

Many businesses will, therefore, wait until any credit notes claimed are issued before paying a specific invoice. This encourages the seller to issue credit notes quickly to minimise any delay in payment being received.

Activity 8.4

You work for Tune Ltd. The company sells a variety of products, including Divas (two models - the Callas and the Sutherland) and Super Conductors. Divas are made to order, and it takes about four weeks to produce them. One of your customers is Beethoven plc. Beethoven plc's purchase ledger clerk, Herbert V Karajan, has rung you with a query regarding an invoice.

He is questioning invoice number 4321. He says he only received one Diva, not the two as he was billed on that invoice. Karajan also says that he's owed a 10% trade discount.

You dig out file copies of invoice 4321 and the corresponding delivery note.

Task

Address the following questions.

(a) What would you do to find out more about Karajan's claim? What has gone wrong?

(b) How would you deal with Karajan's query? What documentation is involved? Draft a written reply to him covering the discrepancy and the discount.

PART A ACCOUNTING FOR SALES AND PURCHASES

INVOICE

&TUNE LTD
Discord Street, Crochety, Sussex

Date/tax point: 1/7/X7
Invoice no: 4321

Please quote number 379

Beethoven plc
Symphony Promenade
Quavertree, Essex

	List price per unit £ p	Trade discount	Invoice £ p	VAT 17½% £ p	Total £ p
1 super conductor	705.99		705.99	123.54	829.53
2 'Callas' divas	211.88		423.76	74.15	497.91
Total			1,129.75	197.69	1,327.44
Comments *Delivery note ref 4321*					

Reg office: Discord Street, Crochety, Sussex   Reg no: 451 059
VAT reg no: 678 9012

8: COMMUNICATIONS WITH DEBTORS

```
┌─────────────────────────────────────────────────────────────────────┐
│ 4321                                              DELIVERY NOTE     │
│                                                                     │
│                      &TUNE LTD                                      │
│                                                                     │
│  Date/tax point: 1/7/X7                                             │
├─────────────────────────────────────────────────────────────────────┤
│                                                                     │
│  Beethoven plc                                                      │
│  Symphony Promenade                                                 │
│  Quavertree, Essex                                                  │
│                                                                     │
├──────┬──────────────────┬─────────┬─────────────────────────────────┤
│ Qty  │ Item             │ Order   │ Signature (checked and accepted)│
├──────┼──────────────────┼─────────┼─────────────────────────────────┤
│  1   │ super conductor  │  897    │ H V Karajan for Beethoven plc   │
│  2   │ 'Callas' divas   │  897    │ H V Karajan for Beethoven plc   │
│      │                  │         │                                 │
│      │                  │         │ 1 diva returned because         │
│      │                  │         │ not a Callas diva, but          │
│      │                  │         │ a Sutherland diva               │
├──────┴──────────────────┴─────────┴─────────────────────────────────┤
│ Date delivered                       Driver                         │
├─────────────────────────────────────────────────────────────────────┤
│ Reg office: Discord Street, Crochety, Sussex  Reg no: 451 059       │
│ VAT reg no: 678 9012                                                │
├────────────────────────┬──────────────────────────┬─────────────────┤
│ Yellow copy to customer│ Pink copy to the warehouse│ Blue copy to accounts │
└────────────────────────┴──────────────────────────┴─────────────────┘
```

6 Demands for payment

Not all customers pay on or before the due date for payment!

- The mildest letter about an overdue account is a **'request for payment'**, and is likely to be sent out at a specific period after the failure to pay a debt.

PART A ACCOUNTING FOR SALES AND PURCHASES

- As a debt becomes longer overdue, **more strongly worded reminders** and demands may be called for in an attempt to secure payment.

A credit sale is a legally binding contract, and accordingly the creditor can sue the debtor for payment if it is not made under the terms of the contract.

For simple reminders or further demands for payment, it may be simplest for a business to use **standard letters**.

Some computerised accounting packages can print off standard letters for sending out to overdue debtors and these will be sent at certain specified times after invoicing, eg when the debt has been overdue 2 weeks, 1 month, 5 weeks and so on.

Personal contact with the customer concerned may be important in obtaining payment.

While standardised letters cost little in staff time to send out, the lack of the **'personal touch'** may result in customers simply ignoring them.

For **'key account' customers** (see Section 7), or for customers whose debt is long overdue, a more personal approach may be necessary.

An individually written debt collection letter will have the following features.

- **Statement of amount due**
- Other relevant details (account no, date)
- Reference to previous reminders sent, if account is long overdue

⬇

- Reminder of **terms agreed for payment**
- Other relevant information: where/ how to pay, discounts for quick payment etc
- Other information depending on whether this is a first, second or final request

⬇

- **Request for payment**
- Action to be taken if payment not forthcoming
- The tone should be firm but not aggressive
- Each warning should be courteous

Standard forms of collection letter used by a business might look similar to those below.

Letter 1

Dear Customer

I write to inform you that the balance on your account of £xxx.xx has not been settled for over 30 days. As a result of this, I have to inform you that we cannot offer a discount on this occasion.

I look forward to receiving payment and hope you will take advantage of our cash discount arrangements in the future.

Yours faithfully

Letter 2

Dear Customer

It has come to our attention that settlement of your account now exceeds 60 days but still it has not been paid. I take this opportunity to remind you that we now require a payment of £xxxx.xx in settlement of your account.

If you have any queries regarding this account, then please contact us as soon as possible to resolve any possible problems.

I must inform you that if payment is not forthcoming, then we will find it necessary to take action on this matter.

Yours faithfully

7 Credit control

7.1 Basics of credit control

Credit control ensures that payments are received from debtors on time and that late payers are followed up promptly.

Larger businesses will have special **credit control departments**, whose work is often very important in maintaining the cash flow of the business.

Customers gain some **cash flow advantage** from paying as late as they can. Some customers will seek to exploit this advantage, however unfair this may seem.

In many businesses, some customers become known as habitually **late payers** and the credit control department is likely to spend a lot of time dealing with them.

The **telephone** and the **letter** will both be important methods of communication in credit control.

A good credit controller will be persistent as well as persuasive. The new credit controller will soon learn that one often cannot take 'the cheque's in the post' for an answer!

7.2 Objectives of credit control

Credit control may be described as the **management of debtors**.

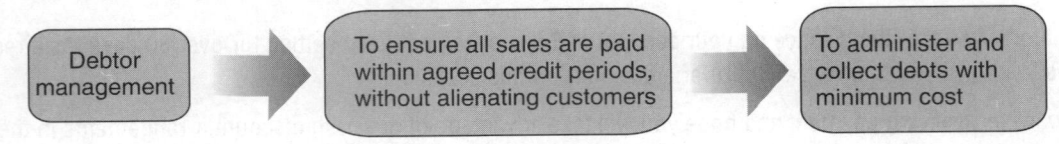

Debtor management → To ensure all sales are paid within agreed credit periods, without alienating customers → To administer and collect debts with minimum cost

7.3 Setting out customer terms

It is important that **credit terms are stated clearly**, as well as the conditions for any cash discounts.

Credit terms and cash discount terms should be set out in documentation.

- When the customer **order is acknowledged**
- When the customer is **invoiced**
- When the customer is sent a **statement of account**

Abbreviated phrases such as '2% 14 days' are more open to misinterpretation, than the words '2% cash discount may be deducted if payment is received within 14 days of the invoice date'.

A policy of credit terms and cash discounts will need to be **enforced properly**.

Customers may try to take the discount whether or not they pay on time. If widely accepted, this practice makes the cash discount 'policy' rather pointless.

7.4 Credit rating and credit limits

A business which simply supplies goods on credit to any customer in any quantity without applying any **credit limit** is at considerable risk, because some customers may not pay in the end.

However, it is important to balance that risk against the need to allow **sufficient credit to allow the business to prosper**.

If a business sets very low customer credit limits, it may avoid any bad debts. However, the business may suffer if it has made much lower sales than it could.

It is good practice for a business to set credit limits for all customer accounts. Credit limits will be based on the business's assessment of the customer's ability to pay. How can this be assessed?

- For major customers, by obtaining copies of the **annual accounts**.
- Using a **credit rating agency** (for example Dunn & Bradstreet).
- Obtain **trade and bankers' references,** eg a new customer may be asked to provide the names of referees. Like all references, references on customers are often more significant for what they do *not* say than for what they do say!
- **Exchange information** on **customer credit risks**.
- Require **personal guarantees** from a company's directors.

Activity 8.5

Stravinsky Products Ltd, is a company with whom Aroma have had no prior business relationship. It wishes to set up an account. Stravinsky is promising a lot of business, and wants a large credit limit to match.

Tasks

(a) Set out what information about the prospective customer is needed to open the account. What further measures would you undertake to ensure that the credit limit asked for is appropriate?

(b) Explain what you would do to set up the account.

7.5 'Key account' customers

In a typical business, 20% of the customers account for 80% of the sales and therefore for 80% of the debts. Such customers will often receive special treatment in the sales effort. In managing the debts of these **key account** customers, special treatment also needs to be given.

Managers need to establish a **good working relationship** with whoever makes the **payment decisions** in the customer organisation.

For large debts, it may be a good idea to telephone well before the due date so that any problems can be resolved and a promise of payment obtained.

The credit manager will then ring back on the due date, if payment is not received, so confronting the customer with the fact that the promise has been broken.

7.6 Putting an account on stop

Letters of demand should be sent at specific intervals. When payment becomes very long overdue, **deliveries to the non-paying customer should be stopped**.

In stopping deliveries, it is important for the **credit control department to liaise with the sales management team**. 'Insensitive' credit control procedures could damage relations with customers.

7.7 Solicitor's letter

There will be some point at which a business will seek **outside help** to collect an overdue debt. It is likely that plenty of warning will have already been given to the customer that this next step is about to be taken.

The best known form of outside help is probably **legal help from a solicitor**. However, other organisations who can help include **trade organisations** in certain industries, and **debt collection agencies**.

Bringing in outside help costs money. The work of collecting overdue debts involves staff time, which also has a cost. At some point, staff time and outside agency fees may exceed the value of the debt itself.

PART A   ACCOUNTING FOR SALES AND PURCHASES

Key learning points

- ☑ A **statement of account** is sent periodically (usually monthly) to the credit customers of a business. It summarises the business which has taken place in the month with that customer and shows the total amount due from the customer.

- ☑ The **age analysis of debtors** is useful for deciding which debts need to be chased up. The analysis also provides a general guide on whether debts are being collected quickly enough.

- ☑ Various other useful reports may be printed out from a **computerised sales ledger package**.

- ☑ **Dealing with queries** from customers **involves the use of different communication media**, including written communication, telephone and fax.

- ☑ The medium used should be appropriate to the task involved.

- ☑ The **response to customers' queries** should always be **prompt** and should always be **courteous**.

- ☑ The **credit control function** in an organisation has to ensure that all sales are paid for within the agreed credit period while maintaining customer relations. The **credit controller** has to administer and collect debts at minimum cost.

- ☑ Major debtors may receive particularly careful treatment as **'key account' customers**.

- ☑ **Credit limits** are set on the basis of the customer's ability to pay. To make this assessment, the business may refer to the customer's annual accounts, to credit rating agencies, or to other sources of information from their own business or the industry.

- ☑ If **debts become long overdue**, eventually the **legal process** or other **outside agencies** may need to be brought in. If a **customer goes into liquidation**, the **business is unlikely to recover more than a small proportion of its debt**.

Quick quiz

1. What is the purpose of a statement of account?
2. What is a remittance advice for?
3. What is a debtors' age analysis?
   - **A** An alternative to credit control procedures
   - **B** A check on the sales ledger
   - **C** A means of controlling debtors
   - **D** A breakdown of debtor balances into different periods of outstanding debt
4. If the supplier makes a mistake, why might he give the customer an explanation as to why things went wrong?
5. A credit sale is a legally binding contract. True or false?
6. What is credit control?
7. An account is put 'on stop' when payments are long _____. *Complete the blank.*

Answers to quick quiz

1. It summarises the transactions entered into by a customer over a given period and shows the amount currently due.
2. A customer returns a remittance advice with his payment to indicate the invoices (less credit notes) to which the payment relates.
3. **D**
4. It shows that the supplier is in control and knows about his own system. This will be reassuring to the customer.
5. True.
6. Credit control is the task of ensuring that payments are received from debtors on a timely basis.
7. An account is put 'on stop' when payments are long **overdue**. (Senior authority is required.)

PART A   ACCOUNTING FOR SALES AND PURCHASES

Activity checklist

This checklist shows which performance criteria, range statement or knowledge and understanding point is covered by each activity in this chapter. Tick off each activity as you complete it.

Activity

8.1		This activity deals with Performance Criteria 1.1.F and Range Statement 1.1.6: statements: manual, computerised.
8.2		This activity deals with Performance Criteria 1.1.G, concerning communication with debtors, and Knowledge and Understanding point 26: house style for correspondence.
8.3		This activity deals with Performance Criteria 1.1.G concerning the preparation of an age analysis of debtors.
8.4		This activity deals with Performance Criteria 1.1.G concerning communications with debtors.
8.5		This activity deals with Knowledge and Understanding point 22: relevant understanding of the organisation's accounting systems and administrative systems and procedures.

chapter 9

Communications with creditors

Contents

1. The problem
2. The solution
3. Suppliers' statements of account
4. Dealing with creditors' queries
5. Management of creditors
6. Retaining files

Performance criteria

2.1.G Identify discrepancies and either resolve or refer to the appropriate person if outside own authority
2.1.H Communicate appropriately with suppliers regarding accounts

Range statement

2.1.7 Discrepancies: incorrect calculations; non-delivery of goods charged; duplicated invoices; incorrect discounts
2.1.8 Communicate: orally; in writing

Knowledge and understanding

1. Types of business transactions and the documents involved
3. Document retention policies
24. Relevant understanding of the organisation's accounting systems and administrative systems and procedures
25. The nature of the organisation's business transactions
27. House style for correspondence
28. Organisational procedures for filing source information

PART A   ACCOUNTING FOR SALES AND PURCHASES

> **Signpost**
> The topics covered in this chapter are relevant to **Unit 2**.

1 The problem

Maintaining good relations with suppliers are essential for the smooth running of a business.

Late payment can lead to a refusal to supply any more goods, or to do so on a cash in advance basis.

2 The solution

As with all business dealings, **good communications** are essential.

If a business is not paying its bills because there is a problem with an invoice, then the supplier needs to know about it.

This chapter deals with communications with suppliers (creditors) in general and with queries in particular.

3 Suppliers' statements of account

3.1 Suppliers' statements

It is usual for a supplier to send a **monthly statement of account** to each of its credit customers. The monthly statement will show the following.

- **Any balance brought forward** from the previous month's statement
- The **business transactions** during the month
    - The amounts of **invoices** issued
    - Any **credit notes** issued
    - Any **payments** received
- The amount due for payment
- Any balance carried forward

    These are often called **'supplier statements'**.

These supplier's statements are the same statements of account that we looked at in the previous chapter. In Chapter 8, we were dealing with the statement from the point of view of the sender. In this chapter, we will look at the statement from the recipient's viewpoint.

A business may not receive statements of account from all of its suppliers.

- A supplier may not send a statement for a **single purchase** or to a customer who makes **irregular purchases**.
- Small suppliers (who issue few invoices) may not send out **any** statements of account.

Suppliers whose **credit terms** require payment within a certain period (commonly 30 days) of the statement date, must send statements to **all of their customers**.

Each supplier's statement should be stamped with the **date of receipt** for future reference. Some suppliers' credit terms require payment within a certain period of the **receipt** of the statement. Therefore a record of that date is needed for dealing with suppliers' queries.

The supplier's statement will have been prepared from the information held on the supplier's sales ledger. A statement of account is reproduced below.

STATEMENT OF ACCOUNT

Pickett (Handling Equipment) Limited
Unit 7, Western Industrial Estate
Dunford   DN2 7RJ

Tel: (01990) 72101   Fax: (01990) 72980   VAT Reg No 982 7213 49

Accounts Department
Finstar Ltd
67 Laker Avenue
Dunford   DN4 5PS

RECEIVED 1 JUN X1

Date: 31 May 20X1

A/c No: F023

Date	Details	Debit £ p	Credit £ p	Balance £ p
30/4/X1	Balance brought forward from previous statement			492 22
3/5/X1	Invoice no. 34207	129 40 ✓		621 62
4/5/X1	Invoice no. 34242	22 72 ✓		644 34
5/5/X1	Payment received - thank you		412 17 ✓	232 17
17/5/X1	Invoice no. 34327	394 95 ✓		627 12
18/5/X1	Credit note no. 00192		64 40 ✓	562 72
21/5/X1	Invoice no. 34392	392 78		955 50
28/5/X1	Credit note no. 00199		107 64 ✓	847 86
	Amount now due		£	847 86

Terms: 30 days net, 1% discount for payment in 7 days. E & OE

Registered office: 4 Arkwright Road, London E16 4PQ   Registered in England No 2182417

The statement is received on 1 June 20X1 and is passed to Linda Kelly who is the purchase ledger clerk at Finstar Ltd. Linda obtains a printout of the transactions with Pickett (Handling Equipment) Ltd from Finstar's purchase ledger system. (The reason why Linda has made ticks on the statement and on the printout which follows will be explained below.)

PART A   ACCOUNTING FOR SALES AND PURCHASES

FINSTAR LIMITED		PURCHASE LEDGER
ACCOUNT NAME:	PICKETT (HANDLING EQUIPMENT) LIMITED	
ACCOUNT REF:	P042	
DATE OF REPORT:	1 JUNE 20X1	
Date	Transaction	(Debit)/Credit £
16.03.X1	Invoice 33004	350.70
20.03.X1	Invoice 33060	61.47
06.04.X1	Invoice 34114	80.05
03.05.X1	Invoice 34207	129.40 ✓
04.05.X1	Payment	(412.17) ✓
06.05.X1	Invoice 34242	22.72 ✓
19.05.X1	Invoice 34327	394.95 ✓
19.05.X1	Credit note 00192	(64.40) ✓
28.05.X1	Payment	(117.77)
30.05.X1	Credit note 00199	(107.64) ✓
	Balance	337.31

The purchase ledger of Finstar shows a balance due to Pickett of £337.31, while Pickett's statement shows a balance due of £847.86.

3.2 Supplier statement reconciliations

Linda wants to be sure that her purchase ledger record for Pickett is correct and so she prepares a **supplier statement reconciliation**.

These are the steps to follow.

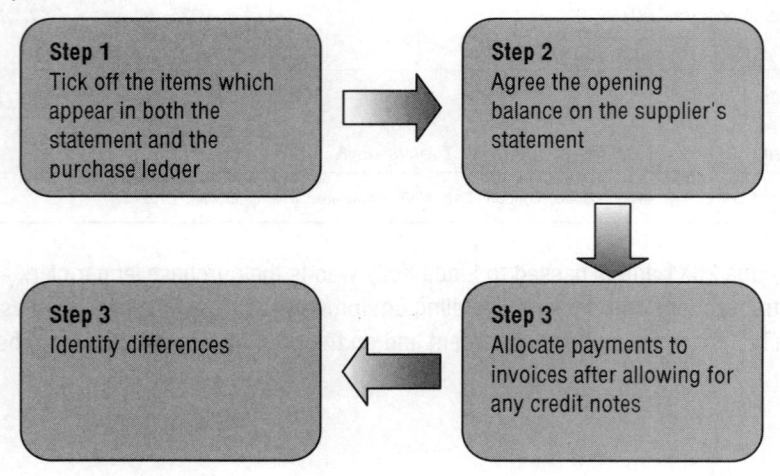

Step 1 Tick off the items which appear in both the statement and the purchase ledger

Step 2 Agree the opening balance on the supplier's statement

Step 3 Allocate payments to invoices after allowing for any credit notes

Step 3 Identify differences

Example: Supplier reconciliation

Linda applies the above steps to Pickett's statement.

Step 1 The common items have been ticked off on the statement and purchase ledger above.

Step 2 The balance brought forward at 30.4.X1 consists of three invoices.

	£
33004	350.70
33060	61.47
34114	80.05
	492.22

Step 3 Invoices 33004 and 33060 were paid on 4 May and 34114 was part of the payment on 28 May.

Step 4 Pickett's statement does not show the payment of £117.77 made on 28 May. However this is reasonable, as the cheque was probably still in the post. The statement also shows an invoice 34392 dated 21 May, which is not in the purchase ledger. This is surprising. Finstar needs to check if the invoice has been received (using the purchase day book), if so has it been posted to the wrong account? If it has not been received, Linda will need to contact Pickett and ask for a duplicate.

SUPPLIER STATEMENT RECONCILIATION
ACCOUNT: PICKETT (HANDLING EQUIPMENT) LTD (P042)

	£
Balance per supplier's statement	847.86
Less: Payment (28 May) not on statement	(117.77)
Invoice (supplier no 34392) on statement, not on purchase ledger	(392.78)
Balance per purchase ledger	337.31

3.3 The reasons for reconciling items

Reconciling items may occur as a result of the following items.

Reconciling item	Effect	Status
Payments in transit	A payment will go in the purchase ledger when the cheque is issued or when a bank transfer instruction is made. There will be delay (postal, processing) before this payment is entered in the records of the supplier. Any statement of account received by post will also be out of date by the length of time taken to deliver it.	Timing difference
Omitted invoices and credit notes	Invoices or credit notes may appear in the ledger of one business but not in that of the other due to error or omission. However, the most common reason will be a timing difference in recording the items in the different ledgers.	Error or omission or timing difference

Reconciling item	Effect	Status
Other errors	Addition errors can occur, particularly if a statement of account is prepared manually. Invoice, credit note or payment amounts can be misposted. Regular reconciliation of supplier statements will minimise the possibility of missing such errors.	Error

3.4 Frequency of reconciling supplier statements

Ideally, **all** supplier statements should be reconciled **monthly**.

In practice, many businesses cannot do this and prepare reconciliations for **major supplier's statements only**. These are not necessarily the largest credit balances in the purchase ledger. They are the accounts where it is most likely that significant errors will occur because of the volume or high value of purchases made.

It is a good idea to cover all suppliers' accounts periodically by adopting a **rotational system of reconciliations**. Major suppliers' accounts are all reconciled monthly. Some other accounts are reconciled each month so that each is reconciled at least once every three months.

Activity 9.1

(a) What is the point of obtaining a statement from a supplier on a regular basis?

(b) If you have accounts with a hundred different creditors what would be the point of checking, say, 10% of their balances?

3.5 Filing and retention of suppliers' statements

Suppliers' statements should be **filed for future reference**. Each month's statements are usually filed by alphabetical order of supplier name. Lever arch files are commonly used for this purpose.

Filing is dealt with in more detail in Section 6 of this chapter.

4 Dealing with creditors' queries

A purchase ledger department will deal with **requests or demands for payment**, as well as discrepancies and errors. These may be dealt with by letter or telephone.

It makes good business sense for all queries to be dealt with using high standards of **promptness and courtesy**.

9: COMMUNICATIONS WITH CREDITORS

We looked at some of the rules and principles of written communication in Chapter 8. In the following paragraphs we look at a situation involving an exchange of letters between a company and its supplier.

Pay attention to the **style of the language** used in the examples below. Also note the **format of the letters** and the **problem which is being addressed**.

Example: Being chased for payment

You are Ms Mai Ling, Senior Accounts Clerk of Tradewell Office Products and Services Ltd, of Easy Street Manchester M12 7SL. It is 22 June.

Your firm has an account (No: 33521) with Britline Carriers plc, who transports many of your products for you. You have just received a statement from Britline, accompanied by the following letter.

BRITLINE CARRIERS PLC
Sutton Lane, Liverpool LW6 9BC
Telephone: 0151 – 324 7345/6

Directors:
D Smith (Managing)
P Patel
C Wilkes

Registered office:
Sutton Lane Liverpool LW6 9BC
Reg. No 34567
Reg. in England

Ref: NC/nn TO 16

21 June 20X0

Accounts Department
Tradewell Office Products & Services Ltd
Easy St
MANCHESTER M12 7SL

Dear Sir

OVERDUE ACCOUNT: 33521

Further to the statement sent to you on 16 May 20X0 it appears that your account for April 20X0 totalling £1,402.70 remains outstanding. Please find enclosed a copy statement.

The terms of credit extended to your company were agreed as 30 days from receipt of statement.

We should appreciate settlement of the above account at your earliest convenience.

Yours faithfully

N Competant

N Competant
Accounts Department

enc

You check your files. A cheque for the outstanding amount was sent to Britline on 6 June, but no acknowledgement was received. You also wonder if you have forfeited your usual 5% prompt payment discount because of the error.

PART A   ACCOUNTING FOR SALES AND PURCHASES

You need to write an appropriate letter of complaint and query.

TRADEWELL OFFICE PRODUCTS & SERVICES LTD
Easy Street, Manchester, M12 7SL

22 June 20X0

Our ref: ML/db
Your ref: NC/nn TO 16

Mr N Competant,
Accounts Department,
Britline Carriers plc.,
Sutton Lane,
LIVERPOOL LW6 9BC

Dear Mr Competant,

ACCOUNT NUMBER 33521

I am concerned by the contents of your letter of 21 June, requesting payment of £1,402.70 outstanding on the above account for April 20X0.

Our files indicate that a cheque payment was made by us on 6 June, within 30 days of the statement dated 16 May. No acknowledgement of payment was received from you.

It would appear there has been an error of some kind, and I would be grateful if you would kindly consult your records.

I am also rather concerned that we may not have been credited with the usual 5% prompt payment discount in these circumstances. Perhaps you can reassure me on this point.

Yours sincerely,

Mai Ling

Mai Ling (Ms)
Senior Accounts Clerk

Notes

1   'Your ref' picks up the reference given on Britline's collection letter.

2   The tone is formal and 'civilised' throughout: the cheque may have been lost in the post - being abusive is of little value.

3   The letter starts by referring to Britline's communication, with relevant details. It then states the nature of your concern, and the actions you expect Britline to take.

Example: Dealing with a complaint

You are Mr M Barrast, Accounts Manager of Britline Carriers plc. TOPS' complaint has been referred to you and you discover that a cheque was indeed received from them on 7 June. Unfortunately, Britline lost two of its ledger clerks that week due to illness, and it appears that the temporary replacement credited £1,402.70 to another firm's account by mistake.

You need to write an appropriate letter of apology and explanation to Ms Ling at TOPS.

BRITLINE CARRIERS PLC

Sutton Lane, Liverpool LW6 9BC
Telephone: 0151 - 324 7345/6

Directors:
D Smith (Managing)
P Patel
C Wilkes

Registered office:
Sutton Lane
Liverpool LW6 9BC
Reg. No 34567
Reg. in England

Our ref: ML/nn TO 17
Your ref: ML/db

27 June 20X0

Ms M Ling
Senior Accounts Clerk
Tradewell Office Products & Services Ltd
Easy St
MANCHESTER M12 7SL

Dear Ms Ling

PAYMENT OF ACCOUNT: 33521

I was sorry to learn of your complaint of 22 June regarding the statement we sent you indicating that payment of your account was overdue.

Having checked our records, I discovered that we did indeed receive your cheque for £1,402.70 on 7 June. Due to unfortunate circumstances affecting our accounts department at that time, the payment was regrettably credited to another customer account. I am pleased to report that the error has been rectified and that your prompt payment discount has not been affected.

Please accept my sincere apologies for the concern caused to you in this matter. We anticipate no recurrence of our departmental problems, but if I can be of assistance in any other way, do not hesitate to contact me.

Yours sincerely

M Barrast

M Barrast
Accounts Manager

PART A ACCOUNTING FOR SALES AND PURCHASES

Notes

1. The reference picks up Ms Ling's last letter.
2. The tone is apologetic, but positive. Emphasis is on investigation and rectification of the mistake - not shame and guilt.
3. Again, the context is laid out first, followed by an explanation and summary. Note that the details of the clerk's illness etc were irrelevant.
4. Mr Barrast apologises for the 'concern' caused - not the 'inconvenience', which is an over-used cliché.

Activity 9.2

It is your first day at work on the purchase ledger at D E Fences Ltd.

Your boss, the Chief Accountant, has given you a pile of correspondence to sort through. He is a busy person, and believes in starting off new employees 'at the deep end'. He requires you to make suggestions about dealing with problems raised.

The first letter is from Reginald Gray, Financial Controller of Jack Use Ltd.

>   **Jack Use Ltd**
>   **Unit 3**
>   **Pleading Business Park**
>   **Pleading**
>   **Lines**
>
> To Purchase Ledger
>   DE Fences Ltd
>   Chancery Courtyard
>   Dock Green
>   Putney
>
> To whom it may concern
>
> Dear Sir/Madam
>
> I attach our statement, and must demand immediate payment by return of post of the overdue balance thereon of £7,424.15. This is the third time we have written to you. Any further delay will result in us putting the matter in the hands of our solicitors.
>
> Yours sincerely
>
> *Reginald Gray*
>
> Regional Gray
> Financial Controller

What should you do first of all? Choose one of the options below.

(1) Pay up without further ado.

(2) Ignore the letter on principle, as its tone is threatening.

(3) Phone up and say 'the cheque's in the post', to keep them off your back, and then check the statement.

(4) Send the letter to the Managing Director of D E Fences Ltd, Roseanne Barrister.

(5) Look up a firm of solicitors in the 'Yellow Pages' or local business guide, and fax them a copy of the letter with a note from you asking them to help out.

(6) Interrupt your boss and show him the letter.

(7) Look in the file for any previous correspondence and tackle it on your own.

Activity 9.3

You are A Technician, Senior Accounts Assistant of Paywell Services Ltd of 24 Maidstone Road, Taunton TA4 4RP. The date is 24 February 20X7.

Your firm has an account number P942 with Recycle Ltd, a company with which you have traded for many months. Recycle Ltd offers a settlement discount of 2½% for payment within the credit terms. You have recently received a letter from Recycle as shown below.

PART A   ACCOUNTING FOR SALES AND PURCHASES

RECYCLE LIMITED
Jarvis Lane Maidenhead Berkshire SL6 4RS Tel: 01628 722722

Accounts Department
Paywell Services Ltd
24 Maidstone Road   20 February 20X7
Taunton TA4 4RP
Our ref: DW/SB 42

Dear Sir or Madam

OVERDUE ACCOUNT No. P942

I enclose a copy statement of account showing that £2,642.50 remains outstanding on your above account. The original statement was sent to you on 10 January 20X7, and the amount shown on this statement was payable within 30 days of the date of the statement.

We would appreciate immediate settlement of the above account.

Yours faithfully

D Waite

D Waite (Ms)
Accounts Department

On reviewing your files, you find that the outstanding balance was paid by BACS transfer (the usual method of payment to this creditor) on 31 January 20X7. In August and October 20X6, there had been correspondence between Paywell and Recycle Ltd due to Recycle's failure to credit BACS payments to the correct account.

Task

Write an appropriate letter to the creditor.

5 Management of creditors

It may seem advantageous to pay suppliers (creditors) as **late as possible**. However, you can easily appreciate how such a policy might alienate suppliers.

A business will need to take a broader view of its approach to **managing its liabilities to suppliers.**

5.1 Objective of creditor management

The objective of creditor management is **to maximise credit periods taken whilst not jeopardising relationships with suppliers.**

5.2 Creditor management policies and procedures

An awareness of the objective of creditor management will help **members of staff** to understand why queries should be dealt with in a particular manner.

A business should **negotiate the terms of credit** with its major suppliers and should set guidelines as to when payments should be made.

In reaching this decision on its policies, a business will need to consider various factors.

Factor	Effect
Dependence on supplier	Businesses vary in the extent of their **dependence on particular suppliers.** Some large companies may have small suppliers which are highly dependent on *them*, so that the business can dictate terms to the supplier.
Flexibility of creditors on payment	HM Customs & Excise and the Inland Revenue are extremely **inflexible** with regard to payments of VAT and PAYE respectively. **Late payments incur penalties**.
Long-term importance of the supplier	The supplier may be unique in what it provides or the need for the supplier may increase in future. It will be important to ensure that relationships are kept as positive as possible.

5.3 Discounts and early payment

There may be benefits in paying a supplier early in order to take up **cash discounts** offered. However, it may not be advantageous to take cash discounts if the cost of **financing the early payment is greater than the discount.**

Example: Discounts

A Ltd owes B Ltd £1,000 at 1 April. B Ltd's credit terms allow A to pay the full amount on 31 May or to take a cash discount of 1% if it pays one month early (ie by 1 May). If A Ltd pays early, it must finance the payment from its bank overdraft, on which it pays monthly interest of 1.5% per annum. Should A Ltd take up the discount?

A Ltd has two alternatives.

(a) **Pay on 31 May**

   A Ltd will pay £1,000.00.

(b) **Pay on 30 April**

   A Ltd will pay £1,000 less 1% = £990.00.

PART A ACCOUNTING FOR SALES AND PURCHASES

This will increase A Ltd's bank overdraft by £990 for one month, for which A Ltd *have* to pay interest of £990.00 × 1.5% = £14.85.

The total cost of paying on 30 April is therefore £990.00 + £14.85 = £1,004.85.

The early payment option (b) is more expensive by £4.85 (£1,004.85 – £1,000.00). Therefore, other things being equal, A Ltd should delay payment until 31 May and not take up the cash discount.

5.4 Practical tips in creditor management

Suppliers may accept **extended credit terms** if they are sure that they will receive payment on certain predecided dates. If payment is late, but the supplier does not know how much later it is going to be, the relationship may suffer. Therefore keep suppliers **informed**.

Regular formal and informal meetings may be arranged with suppliers. These meetings will help to clarify payment terms and dates with the parties involved.

There may be some advantage in a business **sharing information on suppliers** with other customers of that supplier.

A supplier is likely to have negotiated payment terms separately with different customers, particularly with its largest customers. Finding out about the terms and discounts given to other customers may provide some useful 'ammunition' in negotiations.

If a business does run into **cash flow problems**, it may make sense for it to settle its small accounts first. This will enable it to benefit from maintaining a reliable supply from those suppliers at a relatively low cost. The 'credit management' effort can then be concentrated on large creditor balances.

The **payment method used** may have implications for relationships with suppliers. Although direct transfers by BACS save staff time and costs incurred in handling cheques, **cheque payments do have certain other advantages.**

A cheque has a cash flow advantage
- There is a time lapse between the creditor receiving the cheque and when it is cleared through the bank account.
- BACS transfers take place immediately

A cheque has a psychological advantage
- Suppliers are more aware of cheques because they see cheques.
- Bank transfers occur 'out of sight' and are only appreciated when the supplier receives his bank statement

6 Retaining files

6.1 Preparing documents for filing

When documents have been received, acknowledged, acted upon or have otherwise fulfilled their immediate purpose, they are ready to be filed.

(a) The document is **indicated as being ready for filing** – eg a box initialled by the recipient or supervisor. This means that the filing clerk can file it.

(b) **Paper clips and binders are removed** leaving flat sheets for filing, and holes punched appropriate to the storage method so that documents can be inserted.

(c) Documents are placed at **random in a filing tray**, or kept in rough order in a **concertina file**.

(d) If the document is an internally generated one it may have a **file reference** on it already ('Our reference ....' at the head of letters). If not, a **reference number** will have to be determined.

(e) The **reference number**, or **name** or **subject** of the file into which the document is to be inserted should be shown on the document.

(f) Batches of documents can then be **sorted** (by name, subject and so on) and put into the appropriate filing sequence (chronological, numerical or whatever).

(g) Documents are **inserted in the appropriate place** in appropriate files. This process should be carried out daily to avoid pile-ups and disorganisation.

6.2 Opening a new file

If there is no existing file for a document, a **new file** will be opened. This will involve the following.

(a) In a centralised filing system, a **request** and **authorisation** for a new file to be opened. This is to check for duplication or misnaming of files.

(b) **Appropriate housing** for the document - a **folder** or **binder**, noting size, colour and so on as necessary. An extra pocket may have to be inserted in sequence for suspended files.

(c) **Identification**. Writing the number or name on files or suspension pockets or on a suitable tag or label. Colour coding may also be used.

(d) **Adding** the new file name/number to the index, file list, and cross-referencing system.

The procedure will be much the same as when a file cannot hold any more documents, and a **continuation file** is needed. Simply mark the cover of the original file 'Volume 1' and add the range of dates its subject matter covers. Then open a new file marked 'Volume 2'.

Activity 9.4

What matters should you take account of when you are considering opening a new file for some documents in your possession?

PART A   ACCOUNTING FOR SALES AND PURCHASES

Activity 9.5

The following is an extract from your organisation's permanent file on customer number 476/23/3.

Company:	Folworth Ltd
Address:	47 Bracewell Gardens London EC2
Directors:	Robin Folworth Margaret Foster Laurence Oldfield
Purchasing manager:	John Thornhill

You have just had a letter from this company which is shown on the next page.

Your task is to update the permanent file as necessary. Use the grid below to record any new information

Company:	
Address:	
Directors:	
Purchasing Manager:	

FOLWORTH (Business Services) Ltd
Crichton Buildings
97 Lower Larkin Street   London   EC4A 8QT

GETTING THINGS DONE

D. Ashford
Sales Department
Bosley Products Ltd
Ducannon House
4-6 West Brook Road
LONDON W12 7LY

8 August 20X6

Dear Mr Ashford

Account No. 476/23/3

I should be grateful for a reply to my letter of 30 July regarding the above account.

Yours sincerely

D Simmonds

D. Simmonds
Purchasing Manager

Folworth (Business Services) Ltd, Registered Office:
Crichton Buildings, 97 Lower Larkin Street, London, EC4A 8QT
Registered in England, number 9987654
Directors:
R. Folworth, BA ACA; J. Crichton; M. Foster; L. Oldfield MA; T. Scott; J. Thornhill BSc

6.3 Retaining information

When information in the files is no longer needed on a daily basis, it is not automatically thrown away. It is generally dealt with in one of the following ways.

(a) **Microfilmed or microfiched** for long-term storage.
(b) Retained in its original form and stored elsewhere (**archiving**) for a certain period of time.
(c) **Securely destroyed**.

Imagine how distressed you would be if you needed a legal document and you found that it had been destroyed during the latest office spring-clean! (Alternatively, imagine trying to find an urgently needed current file, with *all* the paperwork of the organisation's history still in the active filing system!)

Information which is no longer current, but which may be needed in future, should be given a revised **status**. Examples include no longer active, but semi-active; no longer semi-active, but non-active - a prime candidate for the **archive**!

A **retention policy** is the amounts of time decided on for the holding of various types of information.

Retention periods vary. Documents concerned with the legal establishment of the organisation will have to be kept permanently, as will the annual accounts. Simple legal contracts will have to be kept for six years, and more important sealed ones for twelve. Other documents may be kept at the organisation's discretion but the principle overall is: if you think you might need it - keep it!

Some recommended retention periods include the following.

Document	Years
Agreements	12
Balance sheets	30
Bank statements	6
Cheque counterfoils	1
Correspondence files	6
Credit notes	6
Customs and Excise VAT records	6
Delivery notes	1
Directors' reports	30
Expense claims	1
Insurance claims forms	6
Leases, expired	12
Licences for patents	30
Medical certificates	1
Patents, expired	12
Paying-in books	1
Powers of attorney	30
Prospectuses	30
Purchase orders	6
Quotations, out	6
Royalty ledgers	30
Sales invoices	6
Share applications	12
Specifications, product	6
Tax records	6

Try to find out what your organisation's policy is for the retention of documentation.

6.4 Archiving information

Even non-active files may need to be kept for future reference.

In most organisations, office space is scarce and filing space is limited.

Information that needs to be retained is often stored away in boxes in storage spaces such as storehouses, spare cupboards and inaccessible places. Such storage of files is known as **archiving.**

Activity 9.6

Dribble Ltd, a very small company, file their correspondence as follows.

(a) All incoming mail is placed on a 'current' file initially. It is usually actioned within a week after which the correspondence is filed permanently.

(b) Business customers each have their own separate correspondence file.

PART A   ACCOUNTING FOR SALES AND PURCHASES

(c) Correspondence with domestic customers is placed on a single file; only one file has been needed per year since the business started in 1944.

(d) Letters relevant to the latest year's accounts are filed in a file entitled 'Auditors'.

(e) There is also an extremely thick file entitled 'Miscellaneous 1959 –'.

This is the theory, and Derek Dribble, who founded the business, was an enthusiastic filer. His son, Dominic, however, sees himself as a dynamic entrepreneur and cannot be bothered with it. The current file has not been reviewed for several years and presently includes the following documents.

1   Letter from Miskimin Ltd dated 9.9.04 returning goods.

2   Undated letter from Jacksnares School concerning jumble sale.

3   Letter from London Borough of Greenwich dated 31.12.05 concerning Business Rates.

4   Letter dated 21.7.98 from Dribble Ltd to Mr T N Clipper requesting payment in advance. This has 'Pending - 28.7.98' written across it in red ink.

5   Letter dated 4.3.06 from A J Butterworth Esq requesting '2 × green spats (pair), 1 × red spats (pair)'.

6   Letter from Landlord notifying rent increase as from 1.9.02

7   Letter dated 26.5.96 from Hardman and Free Shoes Ltd ordering '20 pairs spats'.

8   Memo to 'all staff including secretaries' concerning the staff Christmas lunch. This is dated 3.12.03.

9   Letter from Jacksnares School dated 7.5.06 thanking Dribble Ltd for their 'generous donation but unfortunately returning goods unsold'.

10 Letter from Dudley Theatre Company dated 14.4.06 ordering '7 pairs of spats in white'.

11 Letter dated 14.2.06 from Major John Cummings asking for a brochure.

12 Letter dated 14.3.06 from Major John Cummings ordering '1 pair in a conservative colour'.

13 Letter from Miskimin Ltd dated 24.8.04 ordering '2 dozen pairs in white'.

14 Letter from Mr Howard P Wisebacker dated 17.2.00 congratulating Dribble Ltd on 'keeping up a fine old tradition'.

15 Letter dated 17.11.05 from Period Costumiers Ltd ordering '50 pairs, 10 in each colour'.

16 Letter from London Borough of Greenwich notifying dates of refuse collection as from 3.12.05.

17 Letter from Period Costumiers Ltd dated 12.1.06 ordering '50 pairs, 10 in each colour'.

18 Letter dated 15.3.06 from Mrs A J Butterworth returning goods.

19 Letter regarding insurance claim dated 19.4.99.

20 Memo to 'all staff' about summer outing in July 2006.

Task

It is November 2006. Which of these documents would you remove from the current file and where would you place them?

Do you have any suggestions for improving the system?

6.5 Deleting or destroying information

Once information becomes **out-of-date**, it may be **deleted or destroyed**.

Be aware that screwing up a piece of paper and throwing it in the bin is not destroying it. Even if information (particularly financial information) is out-of-date it may still be damaging if it falls into the wrong hands. Waste paper bins are the first place that the wrong eyes will look!

Many organisations have **shredding devices** or a system of disposal which involves **special confidential waste bags**. Find out what your organisation's system is and be sure to use it.

PART A ACCOUNTING FOR SALES AND PURCHASES

Key learning points

- A business will probably receive a **statement of account** monthly from most or all of its credit suppliers. The date of receipt of suppliers' statements should be noted.

- The supplier's statement of account shows, at the date of the statement, the **supplier's records of the transactions** between the purchasing business and the supplier. This may differ from the records held on the purchase ledger of the purchasing business because of errors or timing differences.

- A **supplier statement reconciliation** shows the items accounting for these differences between the supplier's statement of account and the purchase ledger of the purchasing business.

- Reconciling supplier statements is an **important way of clearing up discrepancies**. If all supplier statements are not reconciled monthly, at least those of major suppliers and a selection of other accounts ought to be.

- **Creditors' queries** should be dealt with promptly and courteously on all occasions.

- **Management of creditors** is not usually given as much emphasis by businesses as the management of debtors through the credit control function. Nevertheless, it is important to ensure that policies and procedures on making payments to creditors are consistent with keeping reasonable levels of stock, maintaining cash flows and keeping good relationships with suppliers.

- **Adding new information** to an information storage system involves the following.
    - Indicating that the information is ready for filing
    - Removing any paperclips or binders
    - Placing information in a filing tray or concertina file
    - Allocating a reference number if there is not already a file reference
    - Sorting batches of documents containing information
    - Inserting the documents into the appropriate place in appropriate files

- Information is usually **destroyed** by using shredding devices or by placing in confidential wastebags.

- In general, when information is no longer needed on a daily basis, it is retained in its original form and stored elsewhere; this is known as **archiving**.

- A **retention policy** is the amount of time decided on by an organisation for the holding of various types of information.

- Material containing information **must be kept in good condition** and stored in an appropriate location.

Quick quiz

1. Why might a business *not* receive a statement of account from a supplier?
2. Why would a supplier statement reconciliation be performed?
3. Give three examples of reconciling items.
4. Suppliers' statements (ideally) should be reconciled .... to purchase ledger records. *Complete the blank.*
5. What is the objective of creditor management?

    A To maximise the credit period taken
    B To maximise the credit period taken without jeopardising relationship with suppliers
    C To maximise the credit period given
    D To maximise discounts taken

6. It is always advantageous to take advantage of a cash discount. True/false?
7. How is information that is no longer needed on a regular basis dealt with?

Answers to quick quiz

1. A statement might not be sent by a small supplier, or to a business which has only made a 'one off' purchase.
2. A business will want to check that its purchase ledger records are correct.
3. (i)   Payments in transit
   (ii) Omitted invoices and credit notes
   (iii) Errors
4. Suppliers' statements (ideally) should be reconciled **monthly** to purchase ledger records.
5. **B**. To maximise the credit period taken without jeopardising relationships with suppliers.
6. False. If the cost of financing the early payment (eg bank overdraft interest) is more than the discount, it should not be taken.
7. - Microfilmed or microfiched
   - Archived
   - Destroyed

PART A   ACCOUNTING FOR SALES AND PURCHASES

Activity checklist

This checklist shows which performance criteria, range statement or knowledge and understanding point is covered by each activity in this chapter. Tick off each activity as you complete it.

Activity

9.1	☐	This activity deals with Knowledge and Understanding point 1: types of business transactions and the documents involved.
9.2	☐	This activity deals with Performance Criteria 2.1.G.
9.3	☐	This activity deals with Performance Criteria 2.1.H.
9.4	☐	This activity deals with Knowledge and Understanding point 28: organisational procedures for filing source information.
9.5	☐	This activity deals with Knowledge and Understanding point 28: organisational procedures for filing source information.
9.6	☐	This activity deals with Knowledge and Understanding point 28: organisational procedures for filing source information.

PART B

Accounting for receipts

chapter 10

Receiving and checking money

Contents

1. The problem
2. The solution
3. Remittance advices
4. Documents given to customers
5. Types and timing of money received from customers
6. Cash: physical security
7. Cheques: legal considerations
8. Receipt of cheque payments
9. Receipt of card payments
10. EFTPOS
11. Other receipts

Performance criteria
1.2.A Check receipts against relevant supporting information
1.2.D Identify unusual features and either resolve or refer to the appropriate person

Range statement
1.2.1 Receipts: cash; cheques; an automated payment
1.2.3 Unusual features: wrongly completed cheques; out of date cheques; credit and debit card limits exceeded; disagreement with supporting documentation

Knowledge and understanding
6. Cheques, including crossings and endorsements
7. The use of banking documentation
8. Automated payments
19. Credit card procedures
20. Methods of handling and storing money, including the security aspects

PART B   ACCOUNTING FOR RECEIPTS

> **Signpost**
> The topics covered in this chapter are relevant to **Unit 1**.

1 The problem

Any business needs to have **good control** over cash flow.

A business can not make payments, if it has no **receipts**. Therefore it must exercise **control** over **receipts**.

2 The solution

Systems must be designed to ensure the following.

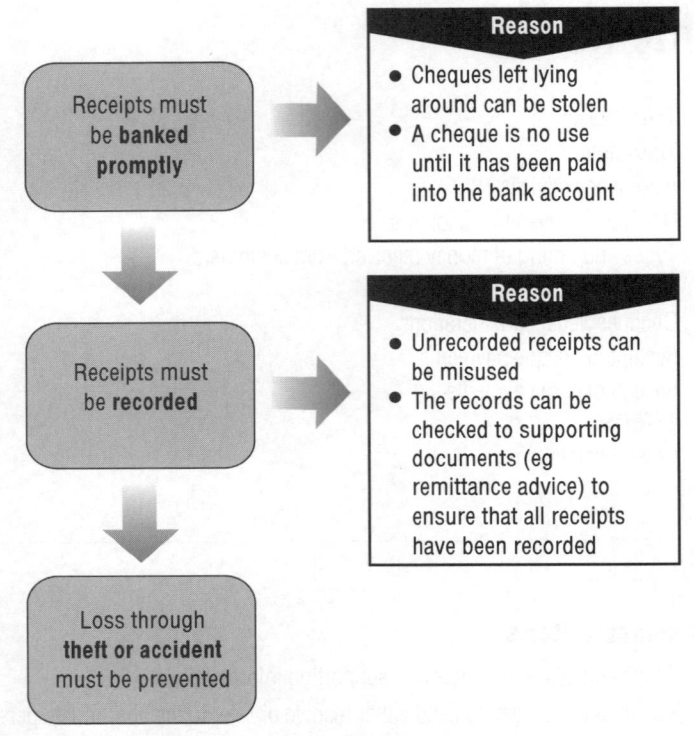

Receipts must be banked promptly

Reason
- Cheques left lying around can be stolen
- A cheque is no use until it has been paid into the bank account

Receipts must be recorded

Reason
- Unrecorded receipts can be misused
- The records can be checked to supporting documents (eg remittance advice) to ensure that all receipts have been recorded

Loss through theft or accident must be prevented

One way of preventing loss through accident or theft, is to **segregate duties**. This means that one person banks the receipts, but a separate person records them.

3 Remittance advices

3.1 Remittance advice

When a cheque arrives, it is usually accompanied by a **remittance advice**. This document shows which invoices a payment covers.

It is common for a supplier to send a statement which has a **detachable remittance advice** as shown here.

PART B ACCOUNTING FOR RECEIPTS

STATEMENT

Los Ninjos & Co
Belton Estate
Peterborough

TO: ABC & Co
4 The Mews
Middlesborough

A/C REF: 12379
DATE: 0104X7
PAGE: 1

DATE	DETAILS		DEBIT	CREDIT
0202X7	Invoice	017220	96.27	
0502X7	Invoice	017496	113.44	
1102X7	Invoice	017649	84.95	
2102X7	C/note	024173		22.00
0103X7	Cash received	C100		272.66
1203X7	Invoice	017780	212.11 ✓	
1503X7	Invoice	017821	106.07 ✓	
2903X7	Invoice	017944	78.90 ✓	
3003X7	C/note	025327		23.48 ✓

CURRENT	30 DAY	60 DAY	90 DAY	120+ DAY
373.60	0	0	0	0

AMOUNT DUE

£373.60

REMITTANCE ADVICE

Los Ninjos & Co
Belton Estate
Peterborough

FROM: ABC & Co
4 The Mews
Middlesborough

A/C REF: 12379
DATE: 0104X7
PAGE: 1

DATE	DETAILS		DEBIT	CREDIT
0202X7	Invoice	017220	96.27	
0502X7	Invoice	017496	113.44	
1102X7	Invoice	017649	84.95	
2102X7	C/note	024173		22.00
0103X7	Cash received	C100		272.66
1203X7	Invoice	011780	212.11 ✓	
1503X7	Invoice	017821	106.07 ✓	
2903X7	Invoice	017944	78.90 ✓	
3003X7	C/note	025327		23.48 ✓

OUR TERMS 30 DAYS. YOUR PROMPT SETTLEMENT WOULD BE APPRECIATED. THANK YOU.

AMOUNT DUE

£373.60

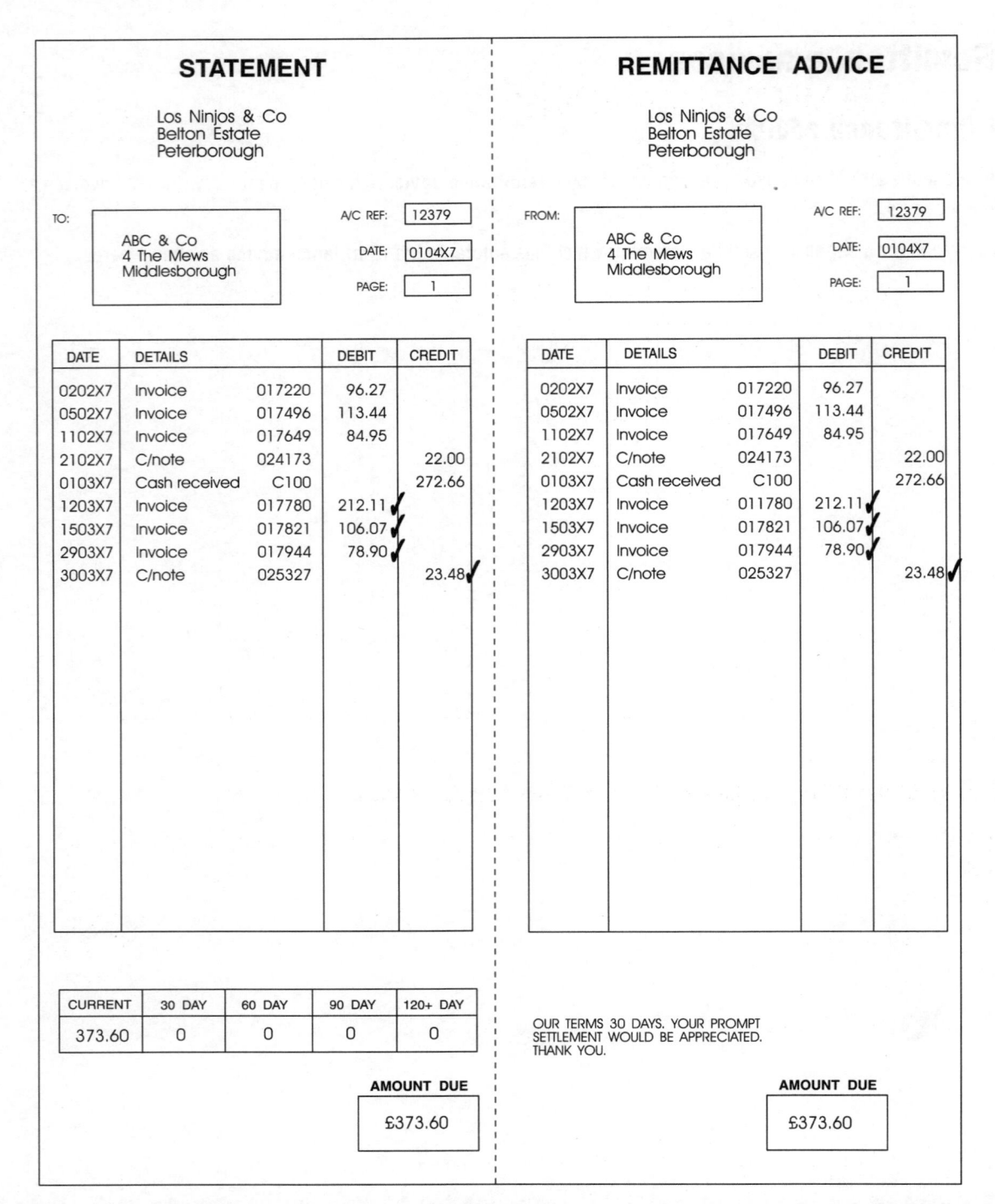

The customer will mark off those invoices which are covered by the particular payment. This tear-off advice will then be returned with the payment, although it may send its own remittance advice instead or as well (see next page).

10: RECEIVING AND CHECKING MONEY

```
┌─────────────────────────────────────────────────────────────────┐
│                                                                 │
│   REMITTANCE ADVICE                         ABC & Co            │
│   TO:   Los Ninjos & Co                     4 The Mews          │
│         Belton Estate                       Middlesborough      │
│         Peterborough                                            │
│                                                                 │
├─────────────────────────────────────────────────────────────────┤
│   Account Ref  [01NIN]   Date [0504X7]    Page  [1]             │
├─────────────┬──────────────────────┬─────────┬────────┬─────────┤
│    DATE     │      DETAILS         │INVOICES │ CREDIT │ PAYMENT │
│             │                      │         │ NOTES  │ AMOUNT  │
│  12.3.X7    │ Invoice       017780 │ 212.11  │        │ 212.11  │
│  15.3.X7    │ Invoice       017821 │ 106.07  │        │ 106.07  │
│  29.3.X7    │ Invoice       017944 │  78.90  │        │  78.90  │
│  30.3.X7    │ Credit note   025327 │         │ 23.48  │ - 23.48 │
│             │                      │         │        │         │
│             │                      │ 397.08  │ 23.48  │ 373.60  │
└─────────────┴──────────────────────┴─────────┴────────┴─────────┘
```

3.2 Procedures to compare receipt with remittance advice

The member of staff who records the receipt should compare it with the remittance advice, using the following procedures.

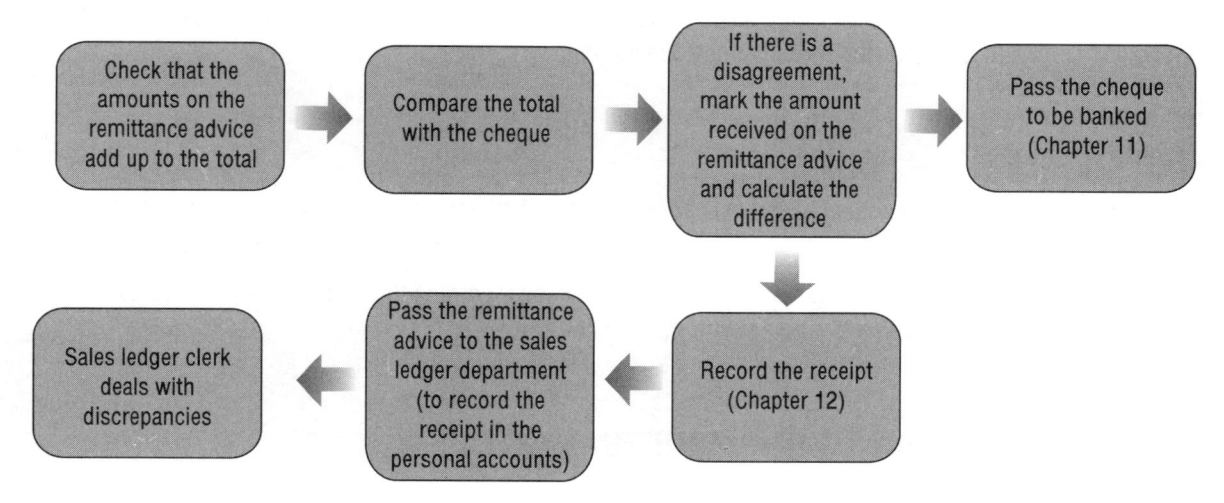

Check that the amounts on the remittance advice add up to the total → Compare the total with the cheque → If there is a disagreement, mark the amount received on the remittance advice and calculate the difference → Pass the cheque to be banked (Chapter 11)

↓

Sales ledger clerk deals with discrepancies ← Pass the remittance advice to the sales ledger department (to record the receipt in the personal accounts) ← Record the receipt (Chapter 12)

PART B ACCOUNTING FOR RECEIPTS

3.3 Other forms of supporting documentation for a receipt

A remittance advice is the most likely documentation to accompany a receipt from a **credit customer**.

However, in the course of business **other kinds of receipt** may occur, which will have different kinds of supporting documentation.

3.3.1 Completion statement

Suppose your business owns a building. It is not being used and so a decision is made to sell it. When it is sold a cheque is received from the solicitor together with a **completion statement**.

		£	£
MESSRS R DRY & CO **SOLICITORS**			
To: ABC & Co			
Completion Statement for sale of 3 Orchard Road to XYZ & Co			
Sale price agreed			530,000.00
Less: Disbursements			
Stamp duty @ 2%		10,600.00	
Agent's fees @ 1½% (invoice attached)		7,950.00	
Solicitors' fees (invoice attached)		892.45	
			19,442.45
Remittance enclosed			510,557.55

This has the same effect and purpose as a remittance advice.

Businesses will receive very few completion statements, unless they **buy and sell property all the time** as part of their trade as, perhaps, property developers.

The sale of other assets, such as motor vehicles used by staff, will be more frequent and will be supported by documentation similar to invoices, rather than remittance advices.

3.3.2 Retail receipts

Payments (using cash, cheques and card vouchers) by **shop or retail customers** do not have any supporting documentation written by the customer.

The business selling the goods creates its own 'remittance advice' by recording the receipt on a cash register or on a manually written receipt voucher (see the next section).

4 Documents given to customers

A **receipt** is a document given by the seller to the buyer when goods change hands in exchange for payment. It may be a till receipt, a written receipt or some other form of receipt.

4.1 Till receipts

Cash registers or **'tills'** are used mainly in retail shops, where the money is handed over directly by the customer when the transaction takes place.

Most shops have electronic cash registers, often registering the details of items sold using bar code readers, which operate as follows.

- Record the value of the sale of each item
- Calculate the total value of the sale if more than one item is sold
- Calculate the required change to give to a customer once the operator has keyed in how much money has been handed over
- Issue a till receipt showing the entire transaction
- Sum up the transactions at the end of the day

The cash register is acting as part of the **control over calculating and giving change** to customers. There are a number of potential errors in giving change, each of which will affect the customer directly and the business indirectly.

Potential error in giving change	Effect	Controlled by
Calculating and giving **too little change**	Customer annoyance - loss of goodwill	Cash register
Calculating and giving **too much change**	Loss of money by business	Cash register
Physically taking **incorrect amount** from till	Either of the above	Making sure staff are careful, well trained and have reasonable mathematical ability

Activity 10.1

You are operating the cash till at Aroma's shop. The following sales are made on 4 April.

Customer	Amount of sale £	Notes and/or coin tendered
1	7.42	£10 note
2	29.21	Three £10 notes
3	7.98	£10 note
4	44.44	Two £20 notes and five £1 coins
5	39.25	Four £10 notes
6	57.20	Five £10 notes, £5 note, four 50p coins and four 5p coins
7	9.46	£10 note, two 20p coins and three 2p coins
8	10.17	£10 note and 50p coin
9	59.62	Three £20 notes, 10p coin and 2p coin
10	12.93	£20 note

PART B ACCOUNTING FOR RECEIPTS

Tasks

Assuming that, at the start of the day, there are all the notes and coins which will be needed:

(a) State the amount of change which is due to each customer.

(b) State the notes and/or coin which will be given to each customer, using the minimum possible number of notes and/or coin.

Use the grid below to record your answers.

Customer	Change due	Notes/coins given to customer as change
1		
2		
3		
4		
5		
6		
7		
8		
9		
10		

Do not use a calculator for this activity - it is a good test of mental arithmetic.

Here is an example of a till receipt from a restaurant.

```
        YOUR RECEIPT
         THANK YOU
        *** ARNIE'S ***
                  (a)
       VAT NO  423 4895 26  (g)

   15-08-X7 (b)    K. SMITH 123456 (h)
      12:19                  (i) 33

   TABLE NO              123
   ROAST CHICKEN (c)   £9.50
   SOUP          (c)   £3.25
   SALAD         (c)   £3.00
   ORANGE        (c)   £3.75
   COFFEE        (c)   £1.20
          5N8
   TOTAL       (d)   £20.70
   CASH        (e)   £25.00

   CHANGE      (f)    £4.30
```

Key:

(a) The name of the selling company or business
(b) The date/tax point (and possibly the time) of the transaction
(c) The price of each of the goods purchased (including VAT)
(d) The total value of goods purchased (including VAT)
(e) The amount tendered (given) by the customer
(f) The amount of change given to the customer
(g) The VAT number (if applicable) of the selling company or business
(h) The name of the assistant and/or cashier
(i) The till number

The first four items are those which normally **must** be shown in order to give sufficient information. The others are optional, but most businesses find that the more information on each receipt, the easier it is to sort out queries. The VAT number will often be shown because it is useful for customers who are VAT-registered; for normal retail customers it is irrelevant. Sometimes the amount and rate of VAT will be shown separately at the bottom of the receipt.

4.1.1 The legal standing of a till receipt

A till receipt is **not conclusive evidence of a payment**.

However, it is modern practice for many retail shops to refuse to exchange goods or refund money unless the original till receipt is produced.

This does not apply to all shops; it depends on whether the goods are easy to recognise as their own brand, or the ease with which the shops themselves can return the goods to the manufacturer.

PART B   ACCOUNTING FOR RECEIPTS

To be safe, customers should keep till receipts until they are sure the goods are satisfactory.

4.2 Written receipts

Where a cash register is not used then a **written or typed receipt** may be required.

Some goods sold have a **unique registration or code number** to make them identifiable. Unique code numbers are used for goods sold under guarantee (the supplier will repair or replace the goods for free within the time period specified in the guarantee).

The code number is used by the supplier to make sure that the correct goods are being repaired or replaced, and not something that was bought elsewhere. Examples are electrical goods and cameras.

The shop will usually keep a copy of the receipt by using carbon paper to copy through onto another piece of paper.

Clarence's Cameras Ltd 14 The View Brighton VAT no 721 9903 47	Date/tax point: 17.7.X7		**No. 78**
	List Price	VAT rate	Total
1 × Pencos 38 SL Camera ref: 34782938	372.00	17½%	372.00
1 × 35mm lens Pencos ref: 4983297	89.00	17½%	89.00
VAT @ 17½% Total	461.00		461.00 80.67 £ 541.67

4.3 Evidence of payment other than in cash

Method of payment	Evidence of payment
Credit card	A copy of the **signed credit card voucher**. There will be a record of the transaction on the **customer's monthly credit card statement** (important when a credit card has been used to buy things over the telephone, so there is no voucher).
Debit card	As with credit cards, a copy of the signed **debit card voucher** and a record will appear on the **customer's bank statement**.
Cheque	The customer should keep a record on the cheque stub. The payment will appear on the **customer's bank statement**.
Banker's draft, postal orders etc	The **issuing bank or post office** will hold records of the items issued.

5 Types and timing of money received from customers

5.1 Types of receipt from customers

In the last section, when we mentioned a 'receipt', we were referring to the document given **to the purchaser by the seller** when goods changed hands. In this section we use the term receipt in a different sense.

A **receipt** also means the **payment received** for goods or services supplied.

In this chapter we will look at the most common forms of receipt.

- Cash (Section 6)
- Cheque (Sections 7 and 8)
- Plastic cards (Sections 9 and 10)

There are other less usual forms of receipt (depending on the type of business).

- Standing order
- Direct debit
- CHAPS
- BACS

These will be dealt with in Section 11.

5.2 Timing of money received from customers

The **timing of the receipts of a business** will depend on a variety of factors.

- The type of business
- The type of sales (credit/cash or both)
- Seasonal and economic trends

5.2.1 Type of business

Let us look at three different kinds of business and the receipts they would expect on an average day.

Newsagent	Clothes shop	Building contractor
500 receipts at an average of £1 each	20 receipts at an average of £200 each	3 receipts at an average of £150,000 each
Total = £500	Total = £4,000	Total = £450,000

PART B ACCOUNTING FOR RECEIPTS

Compare the transactions; it is not just **total receipts** that are different.

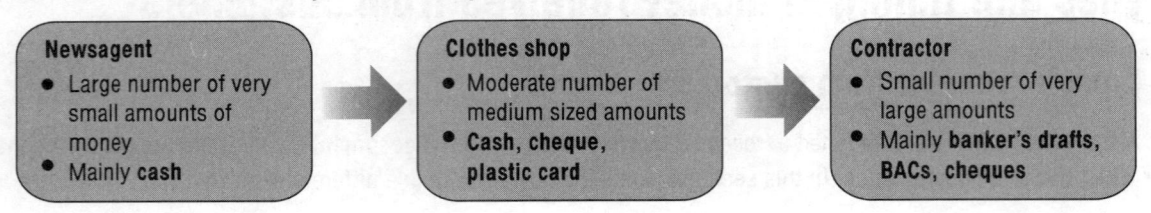

Newsagent
- Large number of very small amounts of money
- Mainly **cash**

→

Clothes shop
- Moderate number of medium sized amounts
- **Cash, cheque, plastic card**

→

Contractor
- Small number of very large amounts
- Mainly **banker's drafts, BACs, cheques**

5.2.2 Credit/cash sales

Some kinds of businesses make the bulk of their sales to customers on **credit**. Others deal only with **cash sales**, ie customers must pay for the goods on taking them, the actual payment can be cash, cheque or card.

Type of sale	Typical business	Typical customer	Examples
Cash sale	Retailers	General public	Supermarkets Newsagents Chemists
Credit sale	Trading businesses	Other trading or retail businesses, who *ultimately* sell to general public as final consumer	Manufacturers of steel, gas, plumbing equipment, providers of training

Ignoring seasonal trends, the pattern of receipts experienced by these two types of business will be completely different.

- A retail business will get a fairly steady flow of receipts.
- A trading business gets the bulk of its receipts on the date credit customers are due to pay, often the end of the month.

5.2.3 Seasonal trends

The effect of the seasons on various types of business is fairly obvious. These are some examples, but you should be able to think of many more.

- Sales receipts will increase dramatically for many **retail shops** and **manufacturers of consumer goods** in the period up to **Christmas**.
- **Easter egg manufacturers** will get nearly all their receipts in the few months around **Easter**.
- Makers of **swimming costumes** will get far more in sales receipts in **summer** than in winter.

It is worth remembering that manufacturers, and to some extent shops, will make and sell lots of different things in order to get a **more even cash flow during the year**.

5.2.4 Economic trends

When the economy of the country is doing well (a time of **boom**), then many businesses will increase their sales volume and so the money they receive.

When the economy is doing badly (a time of **recession**), then **total sales volume will often fall**, producing a lower level of receipts. Receipts from sales will also be affected if a **customer goes bankrupt** before he has paid his bill; this can happen quite often in a recession.

Cash flow becomes very important in a recession because, if a company cannot pay the money it owes people when it is due, then it has become **insolvent**. The law says that an insolvent company must stop trading and close down.

6 Cash: physical security

6.1 Legal tender

We all know what **money** looks like but what is it? It is the notes and coins that are the legal tender of a country.

The Coinage Acts specify what must be accepted as **legal tender** in the UK.

Form	Made of	Denomination	Maximum tendered	Comments
Coins	Bronze	1p, 2o	20p	Known as copper
Coins	Cupro-nickel	5p, 10p	£5	Known as silver
Coins	Cupro-nickel	20p, 25p (commemorative crowns), 50p	£10	Known as silver
Coins	Cupro-nickel	£1, £2	Any amount	Known as silver
Bank of England	Paper	£5, £10, £20 £50	Any amount	Bank of Scotland notes are legal tender in Scotland, **not** in England, Wales and N Ireland, though they are generally accepted

We will spend the rest of this section looking at the problems of **security** (mainly forgery, theft and accidental loss) which trouble organisations dealing with large amounts of cash.

Cash is the most insecure form of receipt. There are many aspects to security and some will only apply to businesses of a certain size.

6.2 Forgery

There are frequent cases of **forgery** of larger denomination notes (£50, £20 and £10). It is advisable to examine all notes carefully before they are accepted; the metal thread incorporated into all these notes is difficult to duplicate.

Special marker pens and ultra-violet light detection equipment can now be used to check **bank notes**.

Even **small denomination notes and coins are forged**. London Underground was at one time forced to stop accepting 50 pence coins in ticket machines as some people were using 10 pence pieces wrapped in foil to fool the machines.

PART B　ACCOUNTING FOR RECEIPTS

6.3 Theft

Theft by staff is a risk which many businesses have to take. This risk can be reduced by checking employee references carefully and monitoring them closely for their first few months of work.

Larger companies may take out **fidelity insurance** to cover staff who deal with cash and other forms of money. The company can reclaim stolen money from the insurer when a member of their staff has been proved to be dishonest.

Some of the security precautions discussed below are helpful in preventing staff theft as well as customer theft.

6.3.1 Cash register security

The **cash register should be secure**, with keys needed to operate it. Staff should be trained in the importance of keeping their keys safe and of not leaving the cash register open.

Cash registers which are activated by different keys unique to each member of staff can give a **breakdown of sales by staff member**. This is another aid to preventing staff theft because it will indicate staff who are not entering sales and pocketing the customer's money.

At the end of the day, a reconciliation should be carried out to check that total sales recorded agrees to cash received.

Activity 10.2

Suppose that the cash held in the till at the start of business on 4 April in Activity 10.1 is £36.40.

Calculate the amount of money which you would expect to find in the till at the end of the day.

Present your answer in the following form.

£

　　Cash float at start of the day
　　Sales in the day
　　Cash held at the end of the day

6.3.2 Safes

If possible, cash should be removed from the till regularly (leaving only a relatively small amount) and stored in a safer place. However, the cash removed should be placed in a container identifying the till, so that till checks can be carried out at the end of the day. Obviously, the ideal place would be a **safe**.

Safes come in several varieties.

- Stand-alone safes
- Wall safes
- Floor safes

Whatever kind of safe is used it should be in a place out of view of the customer.

For convenience a chute may be incorporated into the safe, to allow money to be put into the safe in a container without opening the safe door.

The number of **safe keys** should be kept to a minimum and access to the keys restricted.

6.3.3 Protective glass

Some businesses use **protective glass** (called a 'bandit screen') between the customer and the cashier to protect against theft *and* to ensure the safety of the cashiers.

This measure is used in banks and building society branches, and also at petrol stations and many off licences after dark.

6.3.4 Strong box

Many retail outlets use a **strong box** at each cash register.

When the cashier receives a large bank note, he or she will not place it in the cash register, but will put it down a chute or slot which leads to a strong box.

The strong box is built into the counter under the cash register. The cashier can put money in but cannot take any out and of course customers cannot get into it.

The money in the strong box can be removed at the end of the day when all the customers have gone home.

6.3.5 Security guards and collections

Larger organisations will employ their own **in-house security staff**. As well as watching cashiers to check for theft, these security guards will accompany the staff who collect cash from the tills regularly during the day.

External security firms may be employed to collect money from the business premises and take it directly to the bank. This kind of firm uses trained staff and secured transport and is liable for the goods or money it carries.

6.3.6 Night safes

Where a business finds it impossible to bank money during normal banking hours, most banks will provide a key to their **night safe**.

When it is unlocked and the lid is opened, it exposes only a small space in which the cash is deposited. Once the lid is closed the cash drops into a larger storage area within the bank.

The bank issues boxes or wallets in which to put money and a press to mark the tags which close the boxes. Each press has a unique number on it which is allocated to one customer.

In this way each box can be identified by the bank before it is opened and customers' deposits cannot be mixed up.

6.3.7 Frequent banking

In general, cash should be taken to the bank on a **regular and fairly frequent basis**; this minimises the amount of money on the business premises. This may be particularly important if the amount of money the business can hold is limited under its insurance policy.

It is not a good idea to let the same person go to the bank every day at the same time; for security reasons it is better to **vary the member of staff** who takes the money to the bank and the **time of day it is taken**.

6.4 Accidental loss

Cash should never be sent by post; if it is lost or stolen there is no way to trace or recover it.

6.5 Security of other receipts

Cheques and **card vouchers** are less valuable to a thief but they are as important to a business as the cash it receives. Consequently, the same security procedures should be maintained for cheques and card vouchers as for cash.

A cheque may be sent through the post, although it should be properly prepared (as discussed later).

Other forms of receipt are rarer in nature and are likely to be banked immediately (for instance, a bankers' draft).

There are receipts (standing orders, direct debits, BACS transfers and so on) which will be **transferred automatically** into the business's bank account and physical security procedures are therefore unnecessary.

7 Cheques: legal considerations

Cheques are the commonest receipt most businesses handle.

7.1 Legal aspects of cheques

A **cheque** is 'an unconditional order in writing addressed by a person to a bank, signed by the person giving it, requiring the bank to pay on demand a sum certain in money to or to the order of a specified person or bearer'.

This formal definition can be explained more easily if we look at a specimen cheque.

10: RECEIVING AND CHECKING MONEY

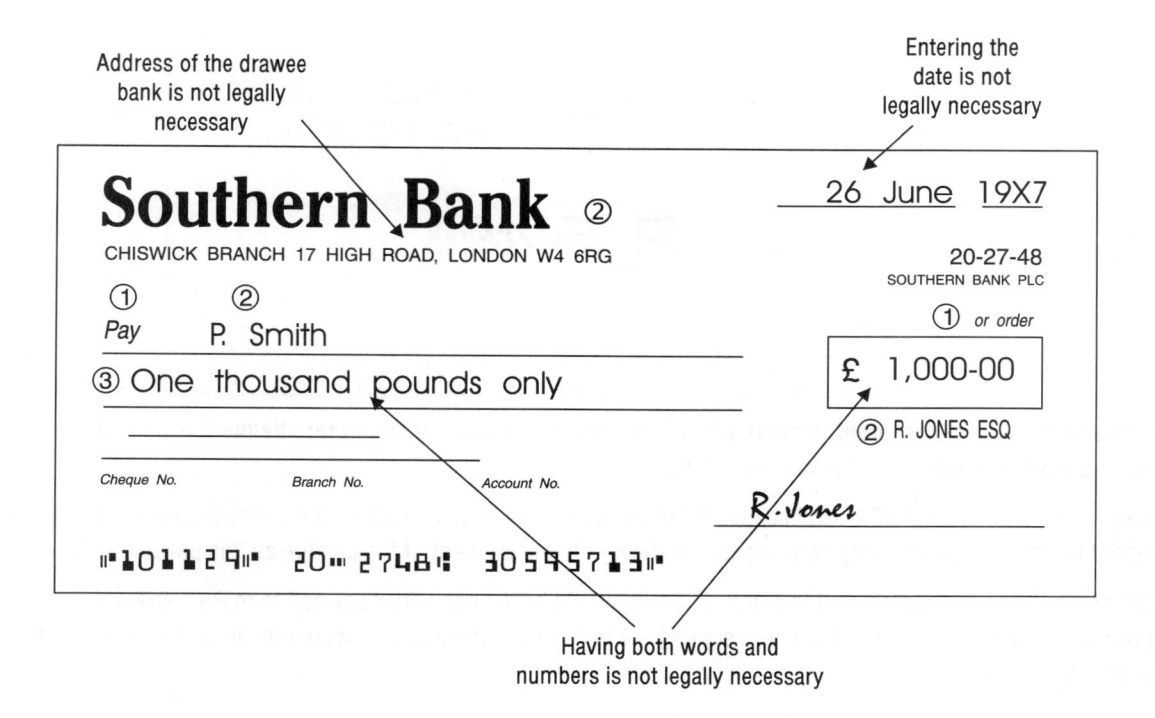

```
Address of the drawee                                Entering the
bank is not legally                                  date is not
necessary                                            legally necessary

┌─────────────────────────────────────────────────────────────────────┐
│                                                                     │
│     Southern Bank  ②                    26 June  19X7               │
│     CHISWICK BRANCH 17 HIGH ROAD, LONDON W4 6RG                     │
│                                                    20-27-48         │
│      ①        ②                                    SOUTHERN BANK PLC│
│     Pay     P. Smith                               ①  or order      │
│                                                 ┌──────────────┐    │
│     ③ One thousand pounds only                  │ £  1,000-00  │    │
│                                                 └──────────────┘    │
│                                                    ② R. JONES ESQ   │
│     Cheque No.   Branch No.   Account No.                           │
│                                                    R. Jones         │
│     ⑈101129⑈  20⑈2748⑊  30595713⑈                                   │
└─────────────────────────────────────────────────────────────────────┘

                        Having both words and
                        numbers is not legally necessary
```

Key

1 **An unconditional order in writing.** The cheque must specify who to pay ('to the order of a specified person') or be to 'bearer. The words on the cheque state 'pay' .... 'or order'. This means that the person you make the cheque payable to can **endorse it** (see later in this section). A cheque can be written on anything, the cheques produced by banks, etc, are merely for convenience. It must be unconditional in the sense that you cannot write a cheque to BT, **conditional** that they will give you a new phone.

2 **Addressed by a person to a bank, signed by the person giving it, ... to the order of a specified person or bearer.** Note that three parties are required for a cheque to be valid.

   (a) **The payee:** the people to whom payment is ordered to be made (P Smith)
   (b) **The payer (or drawer):** the customer who issues the cheque and who must sign it (R Jones)
   (c) **The drawee:** the bank on which the cheque is drawn (Southern Bank)

3 **To pay on demand a certain sum of money.** Obviously the cheque must show the amount of money being paid. The amount does **not** legally have to be stated in both words and numbers. If it is and they do not agree, then the **amount in words** is assumed to be correct.

If the cheque is payable to 'bearer', anyone in possession of the cheque can demand payment.

7.2 Endorsement

It is not necessary for the **payee** to sign a cheque. However, if he wishes to transfer the rights to someone else, he must **sign the back of the cheque to endorse it.**

Using the cheque shown above, if the payee P Smith wanted to give the cheque to ABC & Co to settle a debt, then he would sign the reverse of the cheque and send it to ABC & Co.

PART B ACCOUNTING FOR RECEIPTS

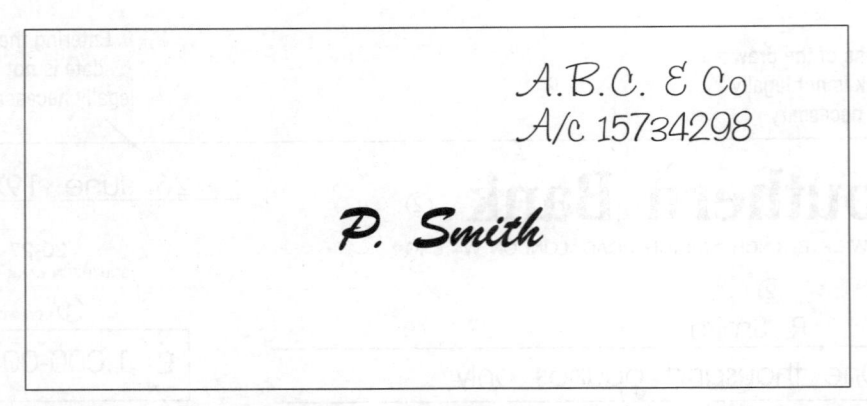

> A.B.C. & Co
> A/c 15734298
>
> *P. Smith*

P Smith has made an **endorsement in blank** which converts the cheque from an **order cheque** (payable to a specific person) to a **bearer cheque** (payable to the holder).

The cheque now belongs to ABC & Co because P Smith has endorsed it *and* delivered it to the company. If it had been intercepted by another person, that person could in theory obtain payment of the cheque as it is payable to the bearer.

Because of the rights of endorsement in blank, P. Smith would have been better advised to make a **special endorsement** by writing 'Pay ABC & Co' and signing the back of the cheque. This would mean that the cheque would still be an order cheque.

The practice of endorsing cheques is getting rarer now.

7.3 Crossing cheques

Crossings on cheques are used to **restrict the use** that can be made of the cheque.

When a cheque is **uncrossed** (R Jones's cheque to P Smith is uncrossed), then the payee may **cash** the cheque at the bank without having to pay the money into another bank account.

A cheque is **crossed** when two parallel lines are pre-printed on or added to a cheque, as shown below. Banks will issue uncrossed cheques on request; usually they preprint crossings. There are four types of crossing, each of which has a different effect.

- **General** (just two lines). This tells the paying bank to make payment *only* to another bank (on behalf of its customer).

Southern Bank
17 CHISWICK HIGH ROAD, LONDON W4 6EG

_____ 20 ___

20-27-48
SOUTHERN BANK PLC

Pay _____

                                      or order

£ [   ]

R. JONES ESQ

Cheque No.   Branch No.   Account No.

⑈101129⑈ 20⵰2748⵰ 30595713⑈

254

- **Special** (two lines with receiving bank's name). This tells the paying bank to make payment only to the bank shown by the special crossing.

- **Not negotiable**. This means that whoever has the cheque cannot have a better claim to it than the person who gave the cheque to him.

- **A/c (account) payee**. This tells the bank to pay only to another bank for the account of the **original** payee: Cheques Act 1992.

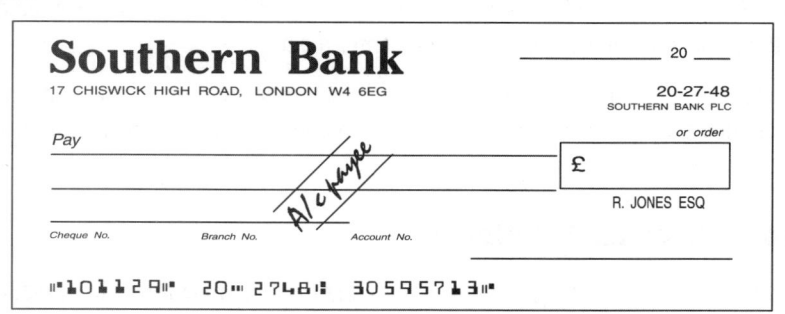

Most banks issue cheques which already have 'only' instead of 'or order' *and/or* an 'account payee' crossing pre-printed on the cheques. **This effectively outlaws the practice of endorsing cheques**.

The old type of cheque is still available, but the banks are keen to do away with endorsing as they suffer a higher incidence of fraud with so-called 'third party' cheques.

7.4 Forgery

If the **drawer's signature is forged** then the cheque is invalid and worthless. If the bank does not realise in time that the signature is a forgery, then it cannot (normally) take the money out of the drawer's account.

PART B   ACCOUNTING FOR RECEIPTS

If an **endorsement is forged**, the previous holder (whose endorsing signature was forged) can recover the cheque, or its value, from the person in possession of it.

7.5 Signatories

A person may sign a cheque under a **business name** which he uses or even under an assumed name. If he does so he is liable as if he had signed in his personal or real name.

An **agent** who signs a cheque should also state 'for' or 'on behalf of' his **principal**, otherwise he might be liable for the cheque.

A cheque may be signed in the name of a **partnership** and it is usual for partnership cheques to be signed this way. It is equivalent to all the signatures of all the individual partners. Hence a firm such as KPMG would have cheques signed 'KPMG'.

A **director** who signs his own name on a cheque for a **company** in accordance with the **mandate** is signing as the **company's representative**, and the company is liable on it.

The company name must appear clearly on the cheque and the name **must** be correct (although 'Co' instead of 'Company' is acceptable). If the company name does not appear, or it appears wrongly, **the director is personally liable if the company does not pay.**

7.6 Incomplete and altered cheques

Cheques may be issued with just the signature of the drawer but they are **incomplete without the name of the payee** or the **amount**. The holder can enter these details as long as it is done as the drawer wished and within a reasonable time. If there is no **date** on the cheque then the holder can enter a date.

Unless all parties to a cheque agree to it, if a cheque has been **altered** then it makes the cheque invalid, except against anyone who sanctioned the alteration and any person who endorses it after the alteration was made.

7.7 Stale and out-of-date cheques

Banks consider that a cheque expires (becomes 'stale'), **six months after the date of issue**. After six months the bank would return the cheque marked 'stale cheque' or 'out of date'.

7.8 Post-dated cheques

Post-dated cheques can be issued, meaning that the date on the cheque is later than the date the cheque was drawn. If the cheque is presented before the date on the cheque then the bank **should** refuse to pay it. Unfortunately banks, usually by oversight, may pay such cheques early.

7.9 Dishonoured cheques

If a cheque is presented for payment at the proper place and is not paid, it is then **dishonoured for payment**. When this happens the holder of the cheque must tell the drawer (and any endorser) within a reasonable time (normally 24 hours). The holder can recover the amount of the cheque plus interest from any liable party. We shall look in more detail at dishonoured cheques in Chapter 11.

7.10 Cheque guarantee cards

When receiving a **personal** cheque, it is usual to accept it only when it is supported by a **personal cheque guarantee card**. This card has on it a specimen of the account holder's signature and it will guarantee that a cheque written by the card holder will be **honoured** (cashed) by the bank **up to the amount** stated on the guarantee card. This is usually £50, although it is possible to obtain £100 and even £250 cheque guarantee cards.

If the cheque is written for an amount **greater** than that on the guarantee card then **the bank is not bound to honour it**. Although the cheque will normally be honoured if there are sufficient funds in the account and if the cheque is otherwise in order.

A typical cheque guarantee card looks like this.

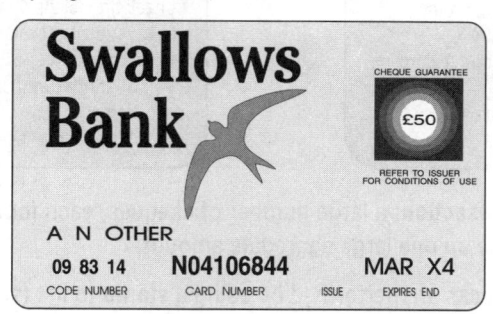

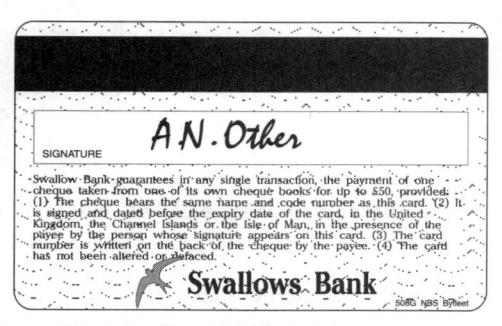

It shows many details that are on a cheque: sort code, account number and name, but it also has a **unique card number**. When the card is used to support a cheque this number will be written on the back of the cheque to prove to the bank that the cheque was guaranteed by a card.

PART B   ACCOUNTING FOR RECEIPTS

8 Receipt of cheque payments

8.1 Cheque payments

It is best practice to follow these procedures when an individual customer pays by cheque supported by a cheque guarantee card.

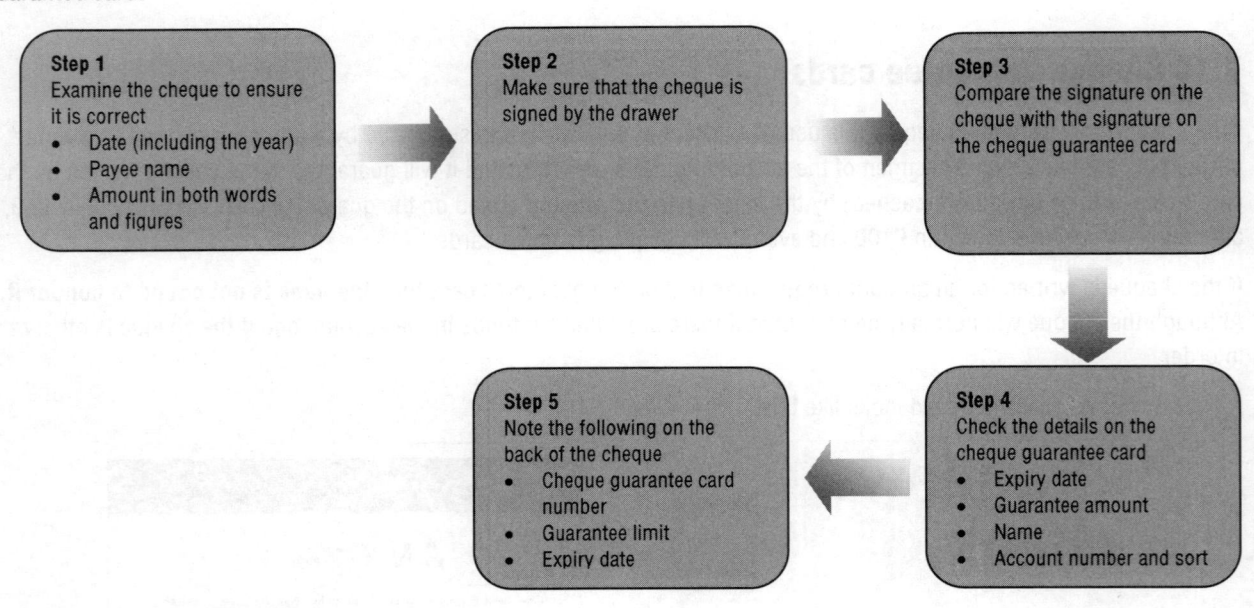

Step 1
Examine the cheque to ensure it is correct
- Date (including the year)
- Payee name
- Amount in both words and figures

Step 2
Make sure that the cheque is signed by the drawer

Step 3
Compare the signature on the cheque with the signature on the cheque guarantee card

Step 4
Check the details on the cheque guarantee card
- Expiry date
- Guarantee amount
- Name
- Account number and sort

Step 5
Note the following on the back of the cheque
- Cheque guarantee card number
- Guarantee limit
- Expiry date

Note that **only one guaranteed cheque can be used in one transaction;** a large number of cheques, each for an amount within the limit on the guarantee card, cannot be issued to make up one large aggregate amount.

Some businesses help their staff to make sure that all these checks are performed by using a **stamp** to list them on the back of the cheque. The cashier has to sign off or tick each check as it is performed.

Cheques received through the **post**, from credit customers or individuals, will not be supported by cheque guarantee cards. Only Steps 1 and 2 above need be performed.

8.2 Cheques: security procedures

Banks recommend and carry out various security precautions with regard to cheques.

(a) Customers are asked to keep **cheque books and cards separate**, although this is not always easy or convenient.

(b) The **number of cheques** in a book is kept to a minimum.

(c) Cheque cards tend to be sent by **registered post** so that customers must sign for their receipt.

(d) The **card remains the property of the bank** and it can be withdrawn if it is being improperly used. New customers may not be issued with a cheque card until they have proved their reliability.

Activity 10.3

Aroma has one shop, and accepts the following methods of payment.

(a) Cash
(b) Cheque, if supported by a cheque guarantee card
(c) Credit cards (Visa and Mastercard). A floor limit of £100 applies, above which an authorisation code must be obtained.

Staff working on the tills sometimes need to ask for guidance on procedures for receiving payments.

A new member of staff, Barry, has started work at the shop. He is required to obtain authorisation for all transactions by cheque and credit card, although it is his responsibility to check that the amount paid agrees with the till roll record.

On 7 August 20X7, Barry presents the documentation as detailed below on three different transactions by cheque (a), (b) and (c) for authorisation.

Task

In each case, consider whether you would authorise the transaction. State clearly the steps, if any, which need to be taken before authorisation can be given. You may assume that the signature has been correctly checked by Barry and that he has entered the number of the cheque card on the back of the cheque. You may also assume that the name on the cheque guarantee card agrees with that printed on the cheque.

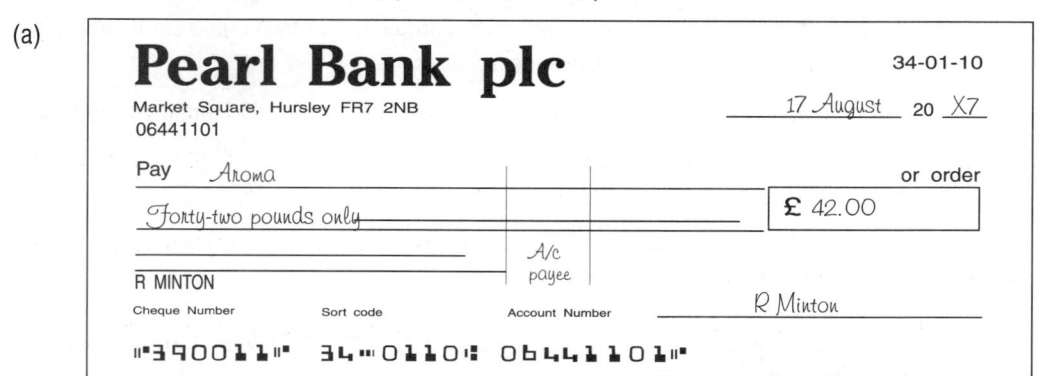

(a)

Pearl Bank plc
Market Square, Hursley FR7 2NB
06441101
34-01-10
17 August 20 X7

Pay Aroma — or order
Forty-two pounds only
£ 42.00
A/c payee
R MINTON
R Minton

Cheque Number: 390011 Sort code: 34-01-10 Account Number: 06441101

Cheque guarantee card (£100 limit): code number 33 04 40; card number E03131042; expires end 03/X9

(b)

Peninsula Building Society
424 Almsgate, Peersley UK4 7PR
00104219
79-21-49
17 August 20 X7

Pay Aroma — or order
Forty-seven pounds only
£ 47.90
S & R MAIDMENT
S P Maidment

Cheque Number: 600057 Sort code: 79-21-49 Account Number: 00104219

Cheque guarantee card (£50 limit): code number 79 21 49; card number 20572358; valid from 08/X6; expires end 07/X7

PART B   ACCOUNTING FOR RECEIPTS

(c)

First Region Bank plc   72-27-27

PO Box 424, Fen Street, Swindon SN99 7PL
70707716

7 August 20___

Pay Aroma   or order

Twenty-four pounds 72   £ 24.72
                          E Co

L WONG   Lee Wong

Cheque Number   Sort code   Account Number

"720718"   72"2727"   70707716"

Cheque guarantee card (£50 limit): code number 72 27 27; card number 1306749265; valid from 09/X7; expires end 08/X9

9 Receipt of card payments

Plastic card payments have become progressively more popular as methods of payment over the last few years. They are used **primarily by individuals**, rather than by companies (although companies do own credit cards which are allocated to members of staff for their use to pay business expenses).

Most retail outlets which accept credit and charge cards now use EFTPOS (Electronic Funds Transfer at Point of Sale). However, some small shops and restaurants still use manual processing which is described in this section. We will examine EFTPOS procedures in Section 10.

9.1 Plastic cards

A typical plastic card will consist of a piece of plastic approximately 8½cm × 5½cm upon which various pieces of information are imprinted, etched or moulded.

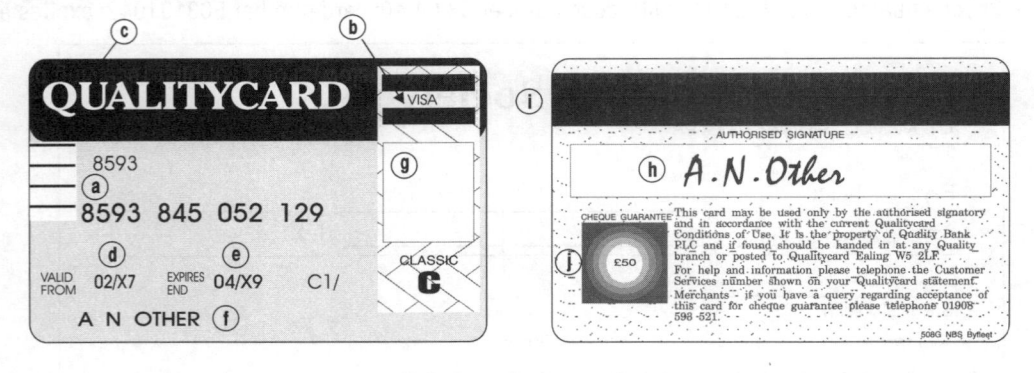

10: RECEIVING AND CHECKING MONEY

Key

(a)	Card number	Each card issued has a unique number allocated to it.
(b)	VISA	This is the type of credit card (which could be VISA or MasterCard).
(c)	Qualitycard	This is the issuing company. There are many different issuing companies (mainly banks and building societies).
(d)	02/X7	This is the date from which the card can be used, in this case 1 February 20X7.
(e)	04/X9	This is the date on which the card expires, so the last date it can be used is 30 April 20X9.
(f)	A N Other	The name of the card holder.
(g)	Hologram	This is a special security device which seeks to prevent forgery of the card. A hologram (a 3-dimensional image) can only be reproduced by sophisticated machinery and its requirement deters casual forgers. Some cards now have photos of their owners.
(h)	Signature strip	This holds the specimen signature of the card holder.
(i)	Magnetic strip	This black strip holds all the information on the card (except the signature) in code enabling a computer to read it.
(j)	£50	This is a cheque guarantee limit. Some cards double up as cheque guarantee cards.

The card number, the 'valid from' and 'expires end' dates, and the card holder name are all **raised lettering** so that when the card is imprinted onto a transaction voucher these details will appear on the voucher (see below).

It is worth splitting the types of card which can be obtained into four categories.

- Credit cards
- Charge cards
- In-house store cards
- Debit cards

We shall look at each of them in turn.

9.2 Credit cards

A **credit card payment** involves three transactions and three parties (see below). For a supplier receiving payment in this way, credit card payments are treated as cash.

Transaction	Comments
Purchase of goods from a supplier by card holder	On producing his card to a **supplier** for goods and/or services, the **card holder** can obtain what he requires without paying for it immediately.
Payment of supplier by card issuer	The **supplier** recovers from the **card issuer** the price of goods or services less a commission which is the card issuer's profit margin.
Payment of card issuer by card holder	At monthly intervals the **card issuer** sends to the **card holder** a statement. The card holder may either settle interest-free within 28 days or he may pay interest on the balance owing after 28 days. He is required to make a minimum payment, which differs between card issuers.

PART B ACCOUNTING FOR RECEIPTS

Card issuers may charge a flat yearly **membership fee** as well as charging **interest.**

The credit cards issued in the UK include **Visa** and **MasterCard.** Most banks, building societies and finance houses issue either Visa or MasterCard credit cards; some issue both. American Express issues its own credit cards.

Suppliers are allowed to charge more for goods purchased by credit card than the same goods purchased by cash or cheque. This reflects the **cost to the supplier** of accepting the credit card as payment.

The card issuers charge the supplier a percentage of the supplier's credit card receipts (perhaps between ½% and 4%, depending on volume) for processing.

Differential pricing of credit card purchases has not so far become widespread as it deters customers who wish to use credit cards.

Many card issuers issue special charity cards called **affinity cards** which are connected to a specific charity or cause. When a customer applies for and receives such a card, the issuer will donate, say £5, to the charity. Each time the card is used a small percentage of the purchase price of the item bought (say 0.25%) is also donated to the charity.

9.2.1 Accepting a credit card receipt

Credit card transactions can be accepted over the telephone or in person over the counter. If goods are ordered by credit card over the **telephone** then either:

(a) The goods must be sent to the address of the cardholder
(b) The goods must be collected in person by the cardholder (eg, theatre tickets)

Example: How to accept a credit card receipt in person

Let us follow the procedure using an example where a hand machine is used.

You are gaining some experience on the retail side of the DIY business you work for as an accounting technician. You are currently working on one of the tills. You have processed the goods a customer wishes to buy and he now gives you the credit card with which he wishes to pay. The total amount payable is £157.85. How do you proceed?

You begin by filling in a **credit card voucher** for the transaction. The voucher is in four parts: the original or top copy and three copies underneath. There is carbon paper between the pages to allow details to be passed to all three copies. The top copy is given to the customer and the bottom three are retained when the transaction has been processed.

Here is an example of all the parts of a blank voucher.

10: RECEIVING AND CHECKING MONEY

PART B   ACCOUNTING FOR RECEIPTS

You should fill in the details of the transaction on the voucher as follows.

Southern FASTPASS

Date: 3/5/X2
Dept.: 3
Sales No.: 1
Initials: KC
Quan./Descrip.: DIY GOODS
Amount: 157 85
Total £: 1 5 7 8 5

The details on the card need to be **imprinted on the voucher**. At the same time as this happens, details about the place of purchase will appear. This is done using a very basic machine.

- A plate is fixed to the machine which holds the information about the place of purchase.
- The credit card is slotted into a place on the machine face up.
- The voucher is placed on top of both and a roller is pushed over the top of the voucher causing the plate and the card to be imprinted onto the voucher.

10: RECEIVING AND CHECKING MONEY

```
 0410 6807 3593 1004              Southern
                                    FASTPASS
 3476   11/X1  02/X3         Date 3/5/X2   Send?   Take?
 A N OTHER                   Dept.       Sales No.  Initials
                                 3           1       KC
 922 8754 93                 Quan./Descrip.
                                    DIY GOODS
 MR HANDYMAN
 SEXTON STREET
 LONDON  NW2 6HH             Amount    157    85

 RETAILER: CHECK THE SIGNATURE!

 Sale confirmed - Cardholder's signature  Authorisation code  Total
       A. N. Other                                            £    1 5 7 8 5
 CARDHOLDER: PLEASE
 RETAIN THIS COPY
```

You now ask the customer to **sign the voucher** where indicated. Hold the card while the customer signs. You should be suspicious of hesitancy and printed signatures.

The transaction is nearly complete, but there are certain **security checks** that you must make before you can accept the credit card as payment.

Security check	Comments
Rub your thumb over the signature panel	It should be flush with the card, not raised (if it is not flush with the card then it may have been tampered with).
Compare the customer signature on the card with that on the voucher	They will not normally match exactly but the likeness should be close enough to leave no doubt.
Check whether the card is stolen against the warning lists regularly issued by the card issuing companies	These lists should be kept up to date and close to all tills where credit cards are accepted. Remember that there is currently a £50 reward for recovering a stolen credit card!
Check that the card is valid by the date	If the current date is past the expiry date, or if it is before the 'valid from' date, then the credit card is not valid. Also, if the 'valid from' date is the current month you should be wary as much fraud occurs on newly issued cards.
Check that the transaction does not exceed the business **floor limit**	When a credit card company allows a business to accept its cards as payment it will set a **floor limit** for the shop or business. Up to this limit the business can process all credit card transactions without any authority. If you want to accept a credit card for a purchase above that amount then you must ring the credit card company up to ask for **authorisation**. If there is no problem then the credit card company will give you an authorisation code which you need to enter in the relevant box.

PART B ACCOUNTING FOR RECEIPTS

Security check	Comments
Final checks	These are all worth checking, even for the second time. • Customer signature • Figures are correct • All details imprinted • Floor limit/authorisation code • Dated correctly

The telephone check system can also be used for other queries. A retailer can ring up if he is suspicious of the validity of the card and use a code to warn the credit card company that he is worried. The credit card company staff can then double check their records and they may also ask questions of the retailer and/or the customer to prove the identity of the customer.

The last procedure in the transaction is to tear off the **top copy of the voucher** and give it to the customer along with the credit card. The carbon paper between the copies should be removed and discarded. The other copies will be put in the till together. They are usually not separated out until they are banked (see Chapter 11).

```
0410 6807 3593 1004                    Southern
                                       FASTPASS
3476   11/X1   02/X3          Date 3/5/X2   Send?  Take?
A N OTHER                     Dept.    Sales No.   Initials
          FASTPASS              3         1          KC
922 8754 93                   Quan./Descrip.
                                       DIY GOODS
MR HANDYMAN
SEXTON STREET
LONDON  NW2 6HH               Amount    157    85

RETAILER: CHECK THE SIGNATURE!
Sale confirmed - Cardholder's signature   Authorisation code  Total
       A.N.Other                               3859          £  1 5 7 8 5
CARDHOLDER: PLEASE
RETAIN THIS COPY
```

Credit card fraud is becoming a major problem. As a result, when a business rings for authorisation, credit card companies will increasingly ask to speak to the customer to carry out security checks. This is nothing to be alarmed about.

New generation credit cards are being developed where the customer's details are kept in an electronic chip. Customers will no longer be asked to sign vouchers, but will have to key their PIN (personal identification number) into a terminal in order to complete a transaction.

9.3 Charge cards

The term **charge card** covers cards such as American Express and Diners Club.

Features	Credit card	Charge card
Cost	Issued free or with an annual 'membership' fee. Interest charged on outstanding balance	Enrolment fee, plus annual 'membership' fee. No interest charged.
Payment	Monthly or by instalments. Credit period may be up to six weeks.	Full balance must be cleared monthly. No credit period allowed after date of account.
Credit limit	Set individually, according to customer's circumstances.	No limit (in theory).

Charge cards are popular for paying **business expenses**. The main advantage is that they overcome the problem of the limit on cheque guarantee cards (usually £50) or spending limits on credit cards (which could come into play for a visit to the USA with air fares, hotel expenses, meals, etc).

The step procedure for accepting payment by charge card is the same as for credit cards, except that the **authorisation process is unnecessary**.

9.4 In-house store cards

In-house store cards are issued and operated by large retail chains such as Marks & Spencer and the John Lewis Partnership. These chains will often, but not always, refuse to accept other credit or charge cards.

The cards operate in the same way as a credit card but they tend to be more expensive for the customer (higher interest rates).

Again, the same procedure for accepting them as payment applies.

9.5 Debit cards

Debit cards are designed for customers who like paying by plastic card but who do not always want credit.

(a) The customer **signs a voucher** at the point of sale.

(b) This is then either **processed** through the credit card system (for example Barclays Connect card is a Visa card) and/or through an EFTPOS system (see below).

(c) The amount of the transaction is **deducted directly from the customer's bank account.**

If the debit card is accepted for a purchase where the transaction has to be processed manually then the voucher used is very similar to the vouchers used for credit card transactions. The same procedure applies as for credit cards.

PART B ACCOUNTING FOR RECEIPTS

10 EFTPOS

10.1 What is EFTPOS?

EFTPOS (Electronic Funds Transfer at Point of Sale) allows the automatic transfer of funds from a customer's bank account to a business, by means of a debit card, at the same time as the customer purchases goods (or services) from it. It is also used simply for automatic processing of credit card, charge card and store card transactions.

EFTPOS is an established system of payment for goods and services, in almost universal use throughout the UK. The effect has been to reduce the number of cheques written, as transactions are settled more and more frequently by plastic.

10.2 The EFTPOS system

Most types of **credit card**, **charge card**, **store card** and **debit card** can be processed through the EFTPOS terminal which sits on or by the retailer's counter. The terminal can read the magnetic strips on the backs of cards automatically.

The terminal allows businesses to deal with card transactions **electronically,** which has many **advantages** over the manual system outlined above.

(a) When a retailer carries out an EFTPOS transaction, it will automatically telephone the appropriate card company and seek **authorisation**, eliminating the need to ring them for approval of transactions above the floor limit.

(b) At the same time the transaction will also be **accepted** by the card company for processing and subsequent payment direct to the retailer's account.

The terminal prints a **two part receipt** for the customer to sign that is used in place of the manual vouchers discussed above. The **details of the card**, the **transaction amount** and the **supplier details** are all printed on the receipt. The customer receives the top copy of this receipt and the retailer keeps the bottom part for his records.

If you need to use an EFTPOS terminal in the workplace, you will receive detailed instructions in its use.

Note that, even though the terminal carries out most checks for you, you should still consider carrying out all the **security checks** as computers have been known to get it wrong!

10.3 Reports

The reports which can be requested will usually include:

(a) Transactions processed through the terminal for **each card issuer** since the last report.
(b) **'End of day' procedures**, which we will discuss in Chapter 11.

11 Other receipts

There are some more **specialised kinds of receipts** which are used by certain businesses. They use these methods because it suits their particular business.

11.1 Banker's draft

```
Quality Bank          Date_____ 20 ____  20-27-48N
                      Branch _____

On demand pay _____ or order
_____ £
_____ on account of this Office

To Quality Bank plc          _____ Manager
Head Office
London W5 2LF                _____ Countersignature
     "101131"  20"2748"  4731822 1"
```

This method of payment is available from banks on request (and on payment of a fee) to customers who need to eliminate the risk of a cheque being 'bounced'.

Paying by **banker's draft** is common when a customer is buying property and needs a guarantee that the payment **cannot be dishonoured** in order to complete the purchase.

The customer must have sufficient cleared funds to cover the debit made by the bank to his account in return for the issue of the draft, which is effectively a cheque drawn on the bank by itself, payable to a person specified by the customer. This is a *fast* way of getting money to someone.

An alternative to a banker's draft is a **building society cheque**.

This is *not* a personal cheque issued by an individual on his building society account. It is where a customer withdraws money from his building society account and asks for the money as a cheque. He may specify to whom the cheque is made payable and **the cheque cannot be stopped.**

11.2 Standing orders and direct debits

These types of payment are **regular payments** (usually monthly). **A standing order** is an instruction for the payer's bank to pay a set amount into the recipient's bank account. In the case of a **direct debit**, the recipient's bank seeks the payment from the payer's bank. The amount of a **standing order** can only be changed by the payer, but the amount of a **direct debit** can be changed by the receiver as well (so is suitable where payments change eg mortgage payments).

- Banks and building societies: mortgage and other loan repayments

PART B ACCOUNTING FOR RECEIPTS

- Insurance companies: insurance and personal pension premiums
- Local authorities: rates and community charge instalments
- Credit card companies: minimum amounts due to credit card issuers
- Large clubs/associations: subscriptions
- Utilities (gas, electricity, telephone): especially when customers are paying a fixed monthly amount reviewed annually
- Hire companies: equipment rental and maintenance

Where there are a large number of relatively small amounts to be collected and processed, it is better to use standing orders or direct debits as the bank will process them automatically.

11.3 CHAPS and BACS

These are methods of transferring funds electronically direct from the payer's account to the recipient's account. They are dealt with in detail in Chapter 13.

BACS is particularly useful for making payments to a number of people (employees, suppliers) on the same day, without having to write a large number of cheques.

Activity 10.4

Imagine that you are employed in various different businesses, as detailed below. In each case, a customer or potential customer telephones you with a query about how a payment or payments may be made.

Task

State what you would say in response to the customer, making any assumptions about the policies of the businesses which you consider appropriate. You should explain your reasons as part of your response.

The customers' queries are as follows.

(a) **Business: electricity company**

'I am a domestic customer, and receive a bill from you each quarter. I want to continue to pay quarterly, but I don't want to go the trouble of writing out a cheque or making a special trip (for example to a bank or your office) to pay the bill. However, I do need to know how much the bill is going to be before I am due to pay it. What method of payment would you suggest?'

(b) **Business: house builder**

'If I buy one of your houses, I'll be getting a mortgage, and so some of the funds will be coming from my building society. However, some will be due from me when the sale is completed. How will that need to be paid?'

(c) **Business: mail order company**

'I want to place an order with you. I don't have a bank account, building society account or a credit card, so I suppose that I'll need to send you the amount due by cash through the post. Is that OK?'

(d) **Business: DIY retailer**

'I want to call in to your store to buy something costing £34 for a friend. I understand that you accept cheques supported by a cheque guarantee card. My friend has made out and signed the cheque and given me her cheque guarantee card. I'd like to bring the cheque and card in when I collect the goods.'

PART B ACCOUNTING FOR RECEIPTS

Key learning points

- Receipts have to be well **controlled** to ensure a good cash flow. There are three key features of control.
  - **Banking** (performed promptly and correctly)
  - **Security** (avoiding loss or theft)
  - **Documentation** (remittance advice)

- Trade customers usually send a *remittance advice* with their payment.

- **Till receipts** or **written receipts** are *prima facie* proof of purchase and they must contain certain information.

- There are various ways a company can **receive money**. The main ones are:
  - Cash
  - Cheque
  - Credit, debit or charge card

- The **timing and types of receipt** a business experiences will depend on:
  - The type of business
  - The type of sale
  - Seasonal and economic trends

- **Holding cash** creates problems and careful security procedures are required.

- A **cheque** is: 'an unconditional order in writing addressed by a person to a bank, signed by the person giving it, requiring the bank to pay on demand a sum certain in money to or to the order of a specified person or to bearer'.

- **Cheque guarantee cards** are issued to guarantee personal cheques up to a certain limit. Strict procedures should be followed when accepting a personal cheque as payment.

- **Strict procedures** should also be followed when accepting credit, debit or charge cards as payment.

- **EFTPOS** is a means of allowing a transaction to be recorded immediately on customer bank accounts or credit card statements, while at the same time authorising the transaction.

- Other means of electronic receipts include direct debit, standing order, BACS and CHAPS

Quick quiz

1. Control over cash receipts will concentrate on which three key areas?
2. A remittance advice shows which .... a payment covers. *Complete the blank.*
3. Why is it important to give the correct change to customers?
4. What is fidelity insurance?
5. Which three parties are always required for a cheque to be valid?
6. What is the effect of an 'endorsement in blank'?
7. What are the four possible types of cheque crossing?
8. When is a cheque 'stale'?

    A   When it is grubby
    B   When it is three months old
    C   When it is six months old
    D   When it is a year old

9. How many guaranteed cheques can be used in one transaction?

    A   1
    B   2
    C   3
    D   4

10. A retailer can use differential pricing for credit card purchases. True or false?
11. What does EFTPOS stand for?
12. A banker's draft cannot be dishonoured. True or false?

Answers to quick quiz

1. Receipts should be banked promptly, correctly recorded and loss or theft should be prevented.
2. A remittance advice shows which **invoices** a payment covers.
3. Giving correct change prevents customer annoyance and loss of money by the business.
4. Fidelity insurance allows businesses to reclaim stolen money from an insurer when a member of the business's staff has been dishonest.
5. A cheque must name: a drawer; a drawee; and a payee.
6. An endorsement in blank converts a cheque from an order cheque to a bearer cheque.
7. The four types of crossing are: general; special; not negotiable; and a/c payee.
8. **C**. A cheque is stale (out of date) six months after the date of issue.

PART B ACCOUNTING FOR RECEIPTS

9   **A**. Only one cheque can be used per transaction.

10 True, although the practice of differential pricing is not widespread.

11 EFTPOS = Electronic Funds Transfer at Point of Sale.

12 True.

Activity checklist

This checklist shows which performance criteria, range statement or knowledge and understanding point is covered by each activity in this chapter. Tick off each activity as you complete it.

Activity

10.1	☐	This activity deals with Range Statement 1.2.1: receipts: cash and Knowledge and Understanding point 20: methods of handling money.
10.2	☐	This activity deals with Performance Criteria 1.2.A and Range Statement 1.2.1 receipts: cash.
10.3	☐	This activity deals with Performance Criteria 1.2.D and Range Statement 1.2.3 unusual features: wrongly completed cheques.
10.4	☐	This activity deals with Range Statement 1.2.1 receipts: cash; cheques; an automated payment.

Note that, although knowledge and understanding point 8 requires knowledge of automated payments (CHAPS; BACS; direct debits and standing orders), the Range Statement 1.2.1 requires **evidence** of only **one automated payment method**. This is an important change under the new standards.

Note also that range statement 1.2.3 on unusual features no longer requires evidence of under payments, over payments or cheques returned to sender.

chapter 11

Banking monies received

Contents

1 The problem
2 The solution
3 The banking system
4 The banker/customer relationship
5 Procedures for banking cash
6 Procedures for banking cheques
7 Procedures for banking plastic card transactions
8 Banking and EFTPOS
9 Banking other receipts

Performance criteria
1.2.C Prepare paying in documents and reconcile to relevant records
1.2.D Identify unusual features and either resolve or refer to the appropriate person

Range statement
1.2.3 Unusual features: wrongly completed cheques; out of date cheques; credit and debit card limits exceeded; disagreement with supporting documentation

Knowledge and understanding
1 Types of business transactions and documents involved
7 The use of banking documentation
8 Automated payments
19 Credit card procedures
20 Methods of handling and storing money, including the security aspects
27 Banking and personal security procedures

PART B   ACCOUNTING FOR RECEIPTS

> **Signpost**
> The topics covered in this chapter are relevant to **Unit 1**.

1 The problem

The main problem with banking monies received is the **security** of the funds.

It is very easy for money to go missing, unless good controls are in place.

2 The solution

Receipts must be banked promptly and the person doing the banking should be different from the person recording the receipts.

Banking procedure and control system

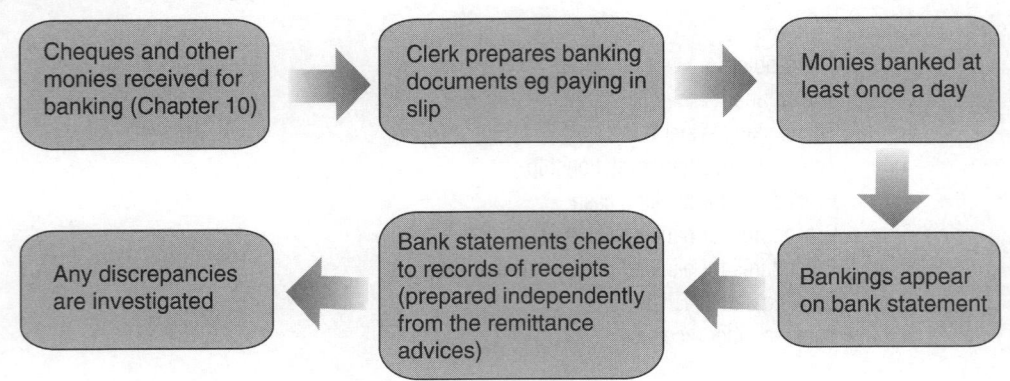

Cheques and other monies received for banking (Chapter 10) → Clerk prepares banking documents eg paying in slip → Monies banked at least once a day → Bankings appear on bank statement → Bank statements checked to records of receipts (prepared independently from the remittance advices) → Any discrepancies are investigated

In this chapter, we are only going to look at the banking procedure.

The control system is not part of the Unit 1 standards and is only shown to make you aware of the complete system. You will study the control system of checking bank statements in Unit 3.

3 The banking system

This chapter covers the **practical aspects of banking** the payments received by a business.

Before dealing with these aspects, however, it would be useful to understand some background details about two areas:

- The **clearing bank system** and how it operates (this section)
- The **legal relationship between the customer and the banker** (Section 4)

3.1 The banking system

The banking system in the UK consists of the following components.

- The **Bank of England** is the British **central bank** which controls or polices the banking industry in this country. Among many other functions, the Bank of England acts as banker to the other banks.

- **Clearing** or **retail banks**. There are four major high street banks.
    - Barclays
    - Lloyds TSB
    - HSBC
    - NatWest

- Smaller retail banks
    - Co-operative Bank
    - Yorkshire Bank
    - Abbey National

    Various former building societies have taken advantage of legislation and have turned themselves into banks (as Abbey National did).

3.2 The clearing system

Clearing is the way of obtaining payment for cheques.

Banks settle cheques and credits through the **clearing system**. The value of the cheques passed between the banks at the end of a particular day is determined and the resulting debts arising between the banks are settled.

Example: Clearing

Lloyds TSB may be asking for settlement of £20m worth of cheques drawn on Barclays bank paid in by its customers at Lloyds TSB branches. In turn, Barclays may have £25m worth of Lloyds cheques paid into branches of Barclays.

	£m
Lloyds TSB owes Barclays	25
Barclays owes Lloyds TSB	20
Net debt: Lloyds TSB owes Barclays	5

In short, at the end of a day, **banks owe money to other banks and are owed money in return**. These debts are settled through accounts which the banks maintain at the Bank of England. The balances on these accounts are termed **operational balances**.

The diagram on page 278 explains how the cheque clearing system operates.

If the paying bank **dishonours a cheque** (refuses to pay it, usually because the paying bank's customer has insufficient funds), it marks on the cheque the **reason for its refusal to pay** and returns it by post **direct** to the receiving bank branch.

PART B ACCOUNTING FOR RECEIPTS

The amount of the cheque will have been included in the total value of cheques passing from the receiving bank to the paying bank at the central clearing. The transaction between the receiving and paying banks is **cancelled** by the receiving bank branch sending in an **unpaid claim** for processing through the clearing system.

The clearing system

Alpha, a customer of Barclays Bank, Penzance, writes a cheque to Beta. Beta is a customer of Lloyds TSB Bank, Stoke and pays the cheque into his branch at Stoke on Monday.

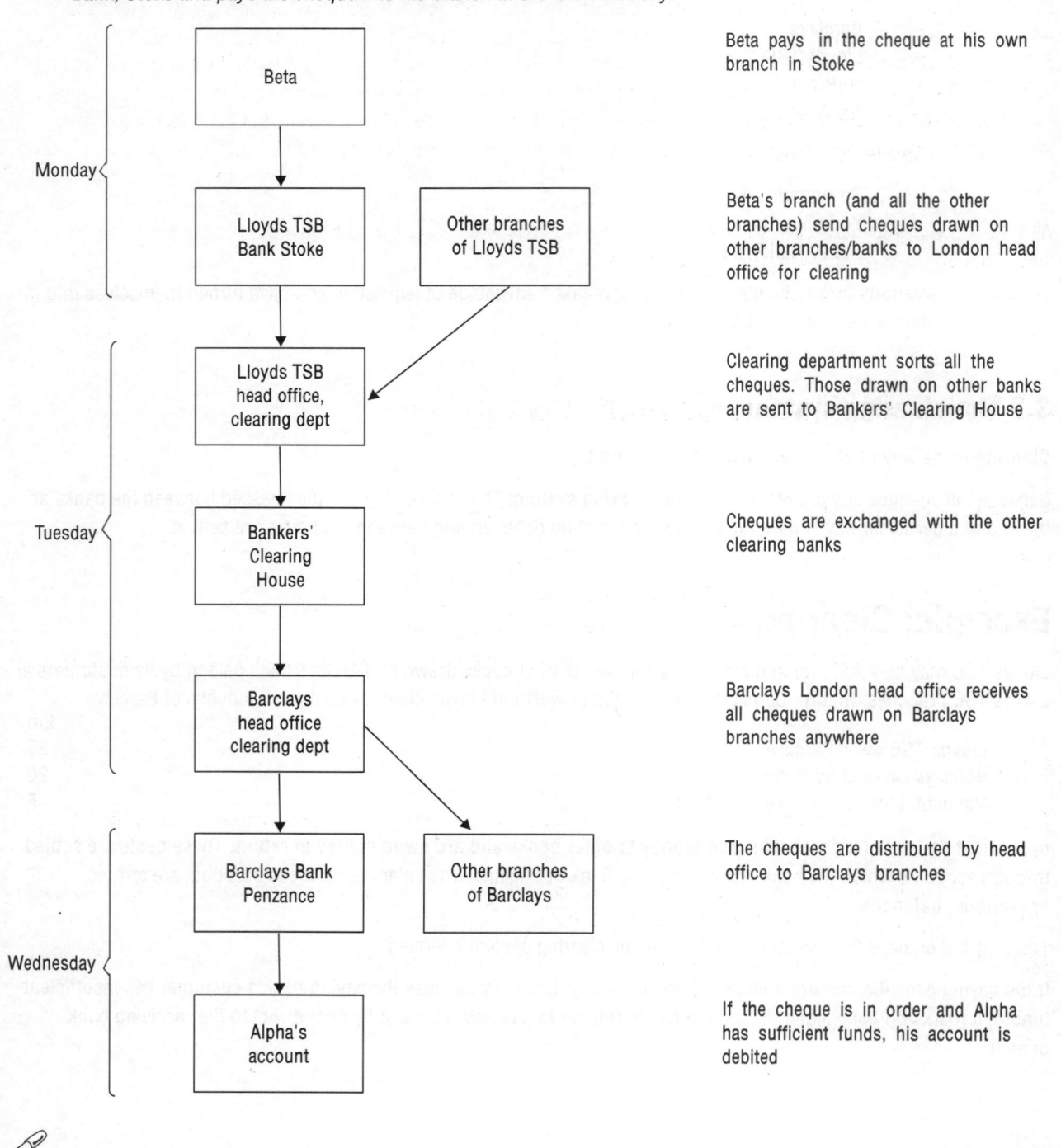

Monday

- Beta → Beta pays in the cheque at his own branch in Stoke
- Lloyds TSB Bank Stoke / Other branches of Lloyds TSB → Beta's branch (and all the other branches) send cheques drawn on other branches/banks to London head office for clearing

- Lloyds TSB head office, clearing dept → Clearing department sorts all the cheques. Those drawn on other banks are sent to Bankers' Clearing House

Tuesday

- Bankers' Clearing House → Cheques are exchanged with the other clearing banks

- Barclays head office clearing dept → Barclays London head office receives all cheques drawn on Barclays branches anywhere

- Barclays Bank Penzance / Other branches of Barclays → The cheques are distributed by head office to Barclays branches

Wednesday

- Alpha's account → If the cheque is in order and Alpha has sufficient funds, his account is debited

278

Activity 11.1

You work in the Yarm branch of Dosh Bank. You receive a telephone call from Mrs Skint, who maintains a current account at your branch. She has the following query.

'I don't usually pay cheques into my current account as normally the only money going in is my pension which is paid by bank transfer. But two days ago I received a cheque for £100 made out to me by my son and I paid it into the bank on that day. Before paying in the cheque, my account balance was £9.62. When I called into the bank yesterday to draw out the £100 from my son, the cashier said I couldn't as I could only draw cleared funds. I asked a friend about this but he couldn't explain, so I'm calling you now to get some explanation. What is this 'clearing' business? My son is a very reputable person so I don't think there should be any reason for you to doubt his creditworthiness. I was wondering if the fact that he had written 'not negotiable' across the cheque had created some problem.'

Task

Write down what you would say in reply to Mrs Skint, including in your answer an explanation of the term 'cleared funds' and of the effect of the words 'not negotiable' on the cheque.

4 The banker/customer relationship

4.1 What is a banker?

A **banker** is someone who will:

- Put money and cheques **received** into a customer's account.
- Take out all cheques and orders **paid** from the customer's account
- **Keep accounts**, such as current accounts, on the customer's behalf which can be used for paying in or taking out.

4.2 What is a customer?

A person becomes a **customer** in respect of cheque transactions as soon as the bank opens an account for him in his name.

In any other situation, for example when investment advice is given, a person becomes a **customer** as soon as the bank accepts his instructions and undertakes to provide a service.

It is important to know if a person is a customer, because banks owe many **legal duties** to customers and can be **sued** if they do not carry out these duties adequately.

PART B   ACCOUNTING FOR RECEIPTS

4.3 The contractual relationships

The relationship between bank and customer arises from legal **contracts** between them which it is necessary to understand.

4.3.1 Creditor/debtor relationship

When a bank lends money to a customer: the **customer is a debtor** who must at some stage repay the **bank, who is the creditor**. Similarly when a customer pays money into a bank, the bank owes that money to the customer, so the **customer is a creditor of the bank** and the **bank is the debtor of the customer.**

Activity 11.2

Obtain a bank statement, one of your own will be sufficient. Check how the bank statement shows the following transactions and work out why.

Transaction	Debit/Credit?	Reason
Money paid into the account		
Cheques paid out of the account		
Interest paid by the bank		
A positive bank balance		
An overdrawn bank balance		

4.3.2 The bailor/bailee relationship

A bank may offer a **safe deposit service** to customers. When it accepts the customer's property, the bank has an obligation:

- To take **'reasonable' care to safeguard** it against damage and loss.
- To **redeliver** it to the customer, or some other person authorised by him and not to any other person.

In law this type of arrangement is known as a **bailment. The customer is the bailor, the bank is the bailee.**

4.3.3 Principal/agent relationship

The bank may act as **agent for its customers**; it may also employ agents (for example stockbrokers) to handle certain business. The bank can act as agent when it arranges insurance for the customer; the bank is acting as an insurance broker and is the agent of its customer.

4.3.4 Mortgagor/mortgagee relationship

A customer may ask a bank to give a loan secured by a charge (or **mortgage**) over the customer's assets eg property. The **customer (mortgagor)** grants the **bank (mortgagee)** a mortgage.

The customer is the debtor, and the bank is the creditor for the amount of the loan. If the customer does not pay back the loan, the bank can sell the asset or assets to recover its money.

4.3.5 Summary of relationships

Contractual relationship	Transaction	Customer	Bank
Creditor/debtor	Customer deposits cash at bank	Creditor	Debtor
Debtor/creditor	Bank gives customer money on overdraft	Debtor	Creditor
Bailor/bailee	Customer stores property in bank's safes deposit facilities	Bailor	Bailee
Principal/agent	Bank arranges insurance for customer	Principal	Agent
Mortgagor/mortgagee	Bank lends money to customer with a mortgage on customer's property as its security	Mortgagor (Debtor)	Mortgagee (Creditor)

There is **no duty for the customer** to ensure that he keeps records of the account and he has **no duty to check the statements he gets from the bank**.

This means that it is the bank's responsibility to ensure transactions are correct. If it gives too much money to the account the customer *may* not have to return it (provided he acted in good faith).

If it takes too much money away from the account, then the customer's reputation may be damaged (by the bank's 'libel') if cheques he has drawn are not honoured by the bank. The bank may then have to compensate him for the damage, particularly if he is a business customer with a valuable credit standing.

5 Procedures for banking cash

5.1 The paying-in slip

When a business or an individual pays money into the bank, then a **paying-in slip** must be used. The bank treats this as a summary document which 'totals up' the cash (and cheques) which are being banked.

A paying-in slip will look similar to the one shown here.

PART B   ACCOUNTING FOR RECEIPTS

[Bank giro credit slip for ABC & Co, Quality Bank, Ealing Broadway Branch, A/C no. 47318221]

This is a preprinted form; the details of the company (ABC & Co) have already been entered. Banks also hold completely **blank forms** for customers to use.

The slip is laid out in such a way that, **for cash**, all you have to do is to **fill in the amounts of each denomination and add them up**.

5.2 Counting the cash

Notes should be paid in with the **Queen's head uppermost and to the right**.

Most banks have special machines which count bundles of notes automatically. For the machine to work properly all the notes have to be of the same denomination (for instance, all £20 notes) and the same way up.

Care should be taken to check that the **totals counted are correct** and notes should be put into **bundles** totalling £100 or £500, where possible. This means that it can take quite a long time for a business to prepare the cash for banking.

Coins should be counted and inserted into the plastic paying-in bags supplied.

You may need to leave a **float** in the till for the next day's trading. If so, not all the cash should be paid into the bank.

5.3 Filling in a paying-in slip

The following procedures are good practice to use when preparing bankings.

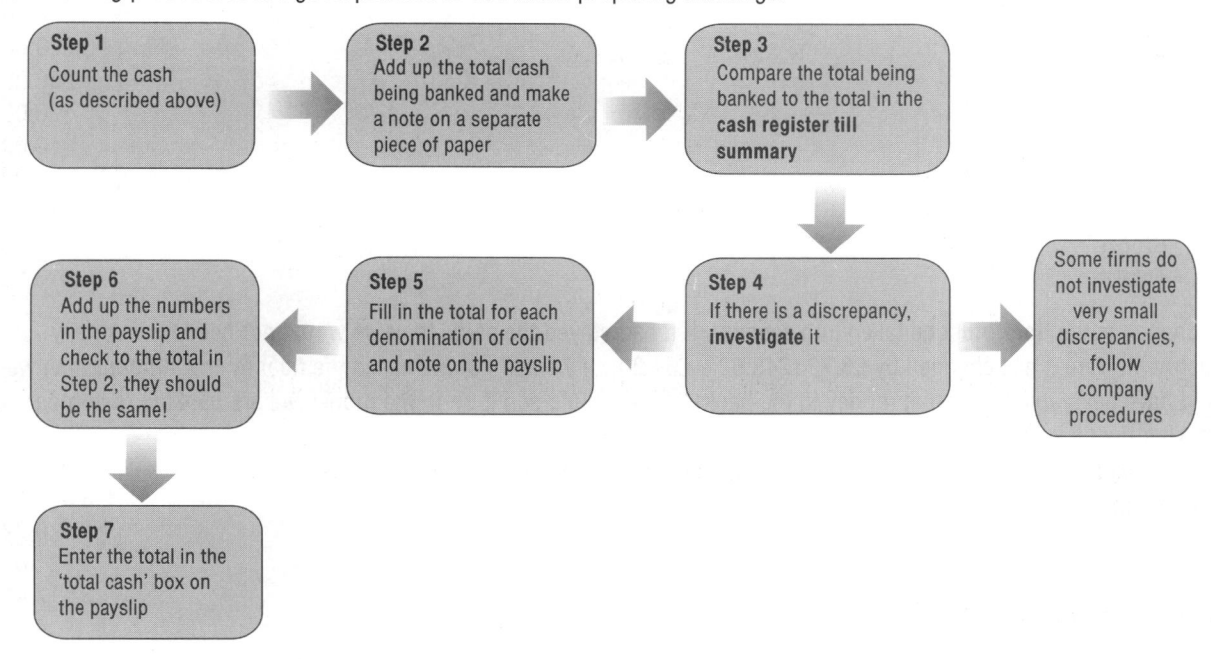

Step 1 Count the cash (as described above) →
Step 2 Add up the total cash being banked and make a note on a separate piece of paper →
Step 3 Compare the total being banked to the total in the **cash register till summary** ↓
Step 4 If there is a discrepancy, **investigate** it →
Some firms do not investigate very small discrepancies, follow company procedures

Step 5 Fill in the total for each denomination of coin and note on the payslip ←
Step 6 Add up the numbers in the payslip and check to the total in Step 2, they should be the same! ↓
Step 7 Enter the total in the 'total cash' box on the payslip

Example: Banking cash

You are preparing the day's takings for banking. When you have sorted and counted the notes you find you have the following.

(a) Five £50 notes
(b) 110 £20 notes
(c) 560 £10 notes
(d) 40 £5 notes
(e) Six bags each containing 20 £1 coins
(f) Two bags each containing 10 50p coins
(g) Ten bags each containing 50 20p coins
(h) Other silver worth £32.20
(i) Bronze worth 93p

The **float** left in the till was £34.90 at the end of yesterday and £43.62 at the end of today. The till summary states that £8,517.41 was received today.

PART B ACCOUNTING FOR RECEIPTS

The amounts of money to be banked are worked out on a separate piece of paper.

	£
5 × £50	250.00
110 × £20	2,200.00
560 × £10	5,600.00
40 × £5	200.00
6 × 20 × £1	120.00
2 × 10 × £0.50	10.00
10 × 50 × £0.20	100.00
Other silver	32.20
Bronze	0.93
Total	8,513.13

The change in the **float** must be taken into account. If it had stayed the same then we would not need to make any adjustment. Here it has changed by £8.72 (£43.62 – £34.90). If we had not increased the float by that amount then we would have been able to put that money in the bank. So we should add it on to the money we are banking to compare it with what the till says we have taken.

	£
Money to be banked	8,513.13
Add increase in the float	8.72
Day's takings	8,521.85
Receipts according to the till	8,517.41
Difference	4.44

This difference is very small and would be ignored (or **written off**). The business should set a limit, for instance £5, over which investigations are made. We will now complete the paying-in slip.

```
Date 23/6/X5        Date 23/6/X5        bank giro credit              Notes  £50    250  00
A/c                 Cashier's stamp                Paid in by/Customer's Reference      £20  2,200  00
                    and initials                                                        £10  5,600  00
Notes £50   250  00                                                                     £5     200  00
      £20 2,200 00                         6   83048231    92057419            Coins    £1     120  00
      £10 5,600 00                                                                      50p     10  00
      £5    200  00                            Quality Bank                             20p    100  00
Coins £1    120  00                                                                  Silver    32  20
      50p    10  00                          EALING BROADWAY BRANCH                  Bronze        93
      20p   100  00
   Silver    32  20   Fee                                                            Cash £ 8,513 13
   Bronze       93                                                                   Cheques
  Cash £  8,513 13   No of Cheques           AB BROWNE & CO                          £       8,513 13
  Cheques
    £    8,513 13                            Please do not write or mark below this line

   101131        ⑈101131⑈  20⑆ 2748⑉ 4731822 1⑈
```

Note that there is space to add in the total of any cheques to be banked (see Section 6)

5.4 Security procedures when banking cash

Generally, the **security procedures** below should be considered and implemented where possible.

(a) **Vary both the time** of the visit to the bank and **the member of staff** taking the money there.

(b) **Send more than one person.** This is particularly important when using the night safe; the banks advise that one person should drive and then watch over the other person, who carries the money and puts it into the night safe.

(c) If very large amounts of cash are banked regularly, then consider employing a **security firm** to collect the money and deliver it to the bank.

(d) It is always wise to fill in the left hand side of the paying-in slip, which is retained by the customer as a **record** of the deposit. You can record the information elsewhere if you wish.

6 Procedures for banking cheques

6.1 Paying-in

The same paying-in slip is used for cheques as for cash, but this time we also need to look at the **back of the paying-in slip**.

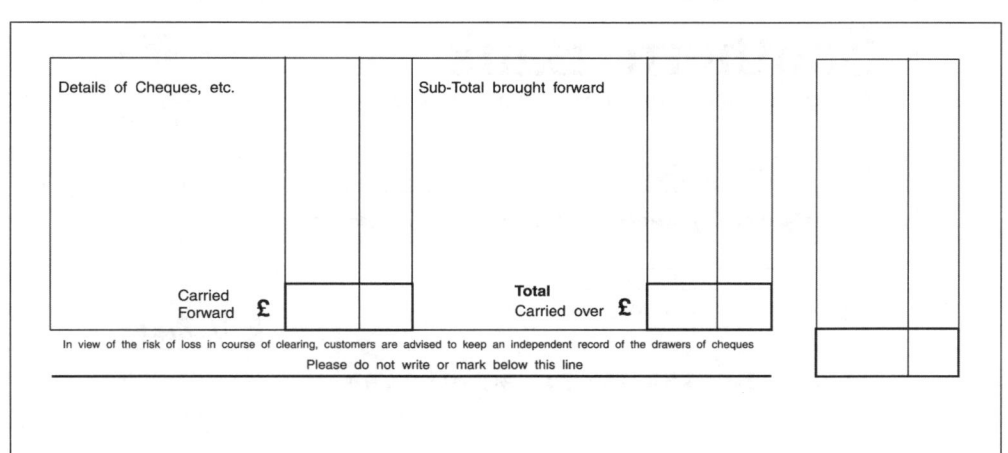

[Paying-in slip form showing: Details of Cheques, etc.; Sub-Total brought forward; Carried Forward £; Total Carried over £. Note: "In view of the risk of loss in course of clearing, customers are advised to keep an independent record of the drawers of cheques. Please do not write or mark below this line"]

The bank has to have a **list of the cheques** being paid in. The details required are usually only:

- The **drawer** (the person who signs the cheque)
- The **amount**.

Many of the procedures for banking cheques are the same as for cash. Let us use an example to work out how to fill in the paying-in slip.

PART B   ACCOUNTING FOR RECEIPTS

Example: Banking cheques

At the end of a business day, you are asked to bank the cheques which have been received that day. Here are just two of the cheques you must bank.

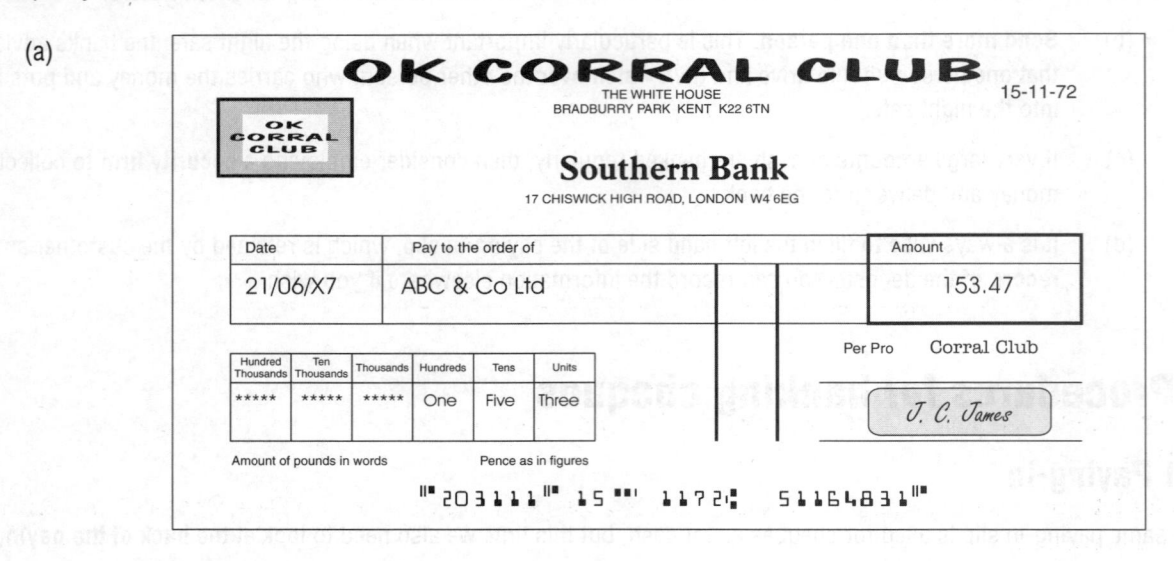

(a)

OK CORRAL CLUB
THE WHITE HOUSE
BRADBURRY PARK KENT K22 6TN
15-11-72

Southern Bank
17 CHISWICK HIGH ROAD, LONDON W4 6EG

Date	Pay to the order of	Amount
21/06/X7	ABC & Co Ltd	153.47

Hundred Thousands	Ten Thousands	Thousands	Hundreds	Tens	Units
*****	*****	*****	One	Five	Three

Amount of pounds in words   Pence as in figures

Per Pro   Corral Club

J. C. James

"203111" 15 "" 1172: 51164831"

(b)

Southern Bank
CHISWICK BRANCH 17 HIGH ROAD, LONDON W4 6RG

22 June 20 X7

15-11-72
SOUTHERN BANK PLC

Pay   M. R. Jones
Forty-eight pounds and seventy-three pence

£ 48-73

or order

MR R. U. BENT

R. U. Bent

Cheque No.   Branch No.   Account No.

"102172" 15" 1172: 30595713"

On the reverse of the cheque made out to M R Jones, it says 'Pay to the order of ABC & Co' and it is signed M R Jones.

11: BANKING MONIES RECEIVED

The back of the slip is filled in as shown below with the **details of the cheques**. Note that a postal order is banked in the same way as a cheque.

Details of Cheques, etc.			Sub-Total brought forward	717	19		153	47
OK Corral Club	153	47					48	73
M. R. Jones	48	73	L. M. Star	11	00		379	20
XYZ & Co	379	20	P. Brook	24	92		22	40
A. Allen	22	40	S. Cope	15	37		13	45
P. Turner	13	45	Postal order	15	00		57	82
A. R. Sears	57	82					42	12
J. J. Rook	42	12					11	00
							24	92
							15	37
Carried Forward £	717	19	Total Carried over £	783	48		15	00
							783	48

In view of the risk of loss in course of clearing, customers are advised to keep an independent record of the drawers of cheques. Please do not write or mark below this line

It is advisable to keep a record of all the drawers of the cheques banked. The easiest way may be to photocopy the rear of the paying-in slip, if no carbon copy is taken.

Now the **total** is transferred to the front of the slip. The number of cheques is entered in the appropriate box on the slip (11 in this example).

[paying-in slip: Date 23/6/X5, Quality Bank, Ealing Broadway Branch, ABC & CO, A/C no 47318221, No of Cheques 11, Cheques £783 48]

The back of the paying-in slip is only capable of holding a certain number of cheques. It is acceptable to list a **larger number of cheques** on a separate piece of paper if necessary.

For customers regularly receiving a large number of cheques, the banks provide larger paying in slips in special paying in books.

PART B ACCOUNTING FOR RECEIPTS

Activity 11.3

Aroma has the following amounts to pay in to the bank.

Cheques	£	Cash
B Wyman	940.00	2 × £50 notes
Pacific Ltd	1,721.50	5 × £20 notes
S McManus	94.26	97 × £10 notes
A Singh	19.29	42 × £5 notes
P L Ferguson	57.37	804 × £1 coins
Dex Ltd	42.91	80 × 50p coins
M Green	12.50	120 × 20p coins; £34.85 silver (10p/5p); £9.28 bronze (2p/1p)
Postal order from		
S R Sykes	15.00	

Task

Complete the paying-in slip and counterfoil below for presentation to the bank on 10 June 20X7.

6.2 Returned/dishonoured cheques

The bank may return a cheque to you and remove its amount from your bank account, because the cheque has been **dishonoured for payment**. You may incur some bank charges when this happens.

Below is a list of reasons the bank may give for dishonouring the payment. We shall look in detail at the two main ones - insufficient funds and stolen cheques.

- Insufficient funds
- Stolen cheque/cheque guarantee card
- Refer to drawer
- Refer to drawer, please represent
- Refer to drawer, trustee in bankruptcy appointed
- Drawer's signature required
- No account
- Out of date
- Signature requires drawer's confirmation
- Signature differs
- Orders not to pay
- Telephone orders not to pay
- Drawer deceased
- Mutilated cheque

6.2.1 Insufficient funds

There may **not be enough money in the customer's account to cover the cheque.** Normally the banks **will** honour a cheque in these circumstances *if*:

> Cheque is for an amount lower than the cheque guarantee card amount

+

> There is evidence that the cheque guarantee card has been inspected eg the card number is written on back of the cheque

When a cheque is dishonoured in this way, your bank will **represent** the cheque twice. If the cheque is still not paid, then it will be returned to you marked 'refer to drawer'. It is up to you to contact your customer (the drawer) and obtain the money from him in some other way.

Banks are very careful about saying whether there are insufficient funds in an account. If sufficient funds were, or should have been, in the account and the bank is at fault, then it may have made a 'libel' against its customer (damaging his reputation). They will probably only say 'refer to drawer'.

PART B   ACCOUNTING FOR RECEIPTS

6.2.2 Stolen cheques and cheque guarantee cards

If a cheque is accepted where the cheque is stolen and the signature of the drawer is **forged**, then **the cheque is invalid and worthless**.

Even if a cheque is accepted with a cheque guarantee card and all details appear to agree, it is still worthless and will be returned with 'cheque book and cheque guarantee card reported stolen, signatures differ', or something of a similar nature, marked on it.

The person who accepted the cheque has no recourse to the bank; he must pursue the person who actually owes him the money (the person who forged the cheque).

6.3 Bulk banking

Consider the large volume of small receipts supermarkets have to **bulk bank**. For the large chains of supermarkets, the problems are multiplied by the number of stores they own across the country. What do they do?

(a) Use a **central bank and cash centre** where all their cash is sorted.

(b) **Bank locally**, using whichever of the major banks is most convenient in each location. Banking is done **daily**.

(c) **Cheques** are not usually presented in a detailed listing by drawer; just an add-list from an adding machine is given. **Notes** are banked by denomination as usual.

(d) Most retailers **do not bank their** coins as this is always needed for the tills.

(e) Money is **removed from the tills** regularly (often through a chute into strong boxes). It is kept segregated on a till-by-till basis. At the end of the day a printout from each till showing all the takings will be matched with the money removed.

(f) **Security carriers** are used to move cash from the premises.

Activity 11.4

(a) Your firm, Steve, Beppe & Co, provides professional services and bills its clients on completion of the work. The bank has returned unpaid three of its customers' cheques. The following had been written on the three cheques respectively.

First cheque: 'Drawer's signature required'
Second cheque: 'Re-present on due date'
Third cheque: 'Refer to drawer'

Your colleague is unclear as to what these various words mean.

Task

Explain to your colleague what is meant by the words on the three cheques and advise her what action should be taken, if any.

(b) The bank has made a charge for dealing with each of the three returned cheques. The General Manager of your firm has noted this charge on the bank statement and has asked you to recommend how, in the light of each of these three items, your firm might reduce the number of returned cheques and therefore reduce the likelihood of future such charges being levied.

Task

Prepare a memorandum to the General Manager on this matter.

7 Procedures for banking plastic card transactions

7.1 Card vouchers

Card vouchers (for credit, debit, charge and store cards) are **processed through the banking system**.

Where the retailer processes transactions manually, he pays the vouchers into his bank account and his bank will present the vouchers to the card issuers for payment.

The **same paying-in slip** is used to bank the card transactions, but other documents must be prepared first.

7.2 Card summaries

The card issuers require a **summary of all transactions on a summary voucher**.

The summary voucher consists of an original or 'top copy' and two copies with carbon paper in between. The bottom copy is the **processing copy**. There is a place to list the vouchers on the back of it.

PART B ACCOUNTING FOR RECEIPTS

Top copy summary voucher

> HAVE YOU IMPRINTED THE SUMMARY WITH YOUR RETAILER'S CARD?
>
> BANK Processing (White) copy of Summary with your Vouchers in correct order:
> 1. SUMMARY
> 2. SALES VOUCHERS
> 3. REFUND VOUCHERS
> KEEP Retailer's copies (Blue & Yellow)
> NO MORE THAN 200 Vouchers to each Summary
> DO NOT USE Staples, Pins, Paper Clips
>
> | | ITEMS | AMOUNT |
> |---|---|---|
> | SALES VOUCHERS (LISTED OVERLEAF) | | |
> | LESS REFUND VOUCHERS | | |
> | DATE | TOTAL £ | |
>
> SUMMARY - RETAILER'S COPY
>
> Southern Bank **BANKING**
> **FASTPASS** **SUMMARY**
>
> RETAILER'S SIGNATURE
>
> COMPLETE THIS SUMMARY FOR EVERY DEPOSIT OF SALES VOUCHERS AND ENTER THE TOTAL ON YOUR NORMAL CURRENT ACCOUNT PAYING-IN SLIP

Bottom (processing copy) summary voucher: front

> **3200**
>
> | | ITEMS | AMOUNT |
> |---|---|---|
> | SALES VOUCHERS (LISTED OVERLEAF) | | |
> | LESS REFUND VOUCHERS | | |
> | DATE | TOTAL £ | |
>
> SOUTHERN BANKING SUMMARY - PROCESSING COPY
>
> RETAILER'S SIGNATURE

Bottom (processing copy) summary voucher: back

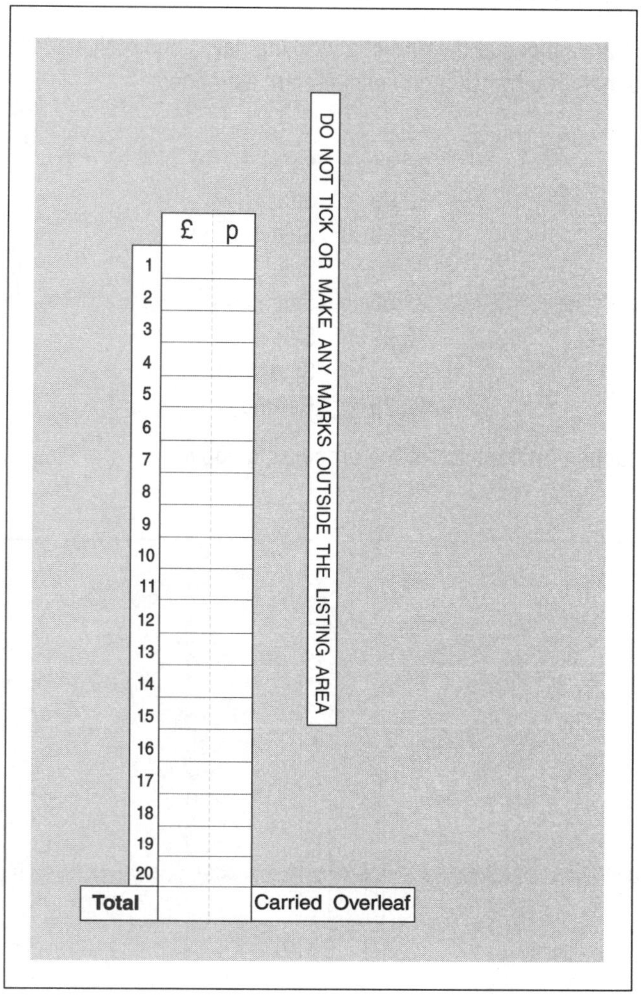

DO NOT TICK OR MAKE ANY MARKS OUTSIDE THE LISTING AREA

	£	p
1		
2		
3		
4		
5		
6		
7		
8		
9		
10		
11		
12		
13		
14		
15		
16		
17		
18		
19		
20		
Total		Carried Overleaf

The **summary voucher** has to be imprinted with the retailer's plastic card using the same machine as for credit card sales. It contains all the relevant information about the business, including an account number.

Unlike cheques, **only the amount of the card transaction** needs to be entered on the back of the processing copy of the summary voucher - names are not needed.

PART B   ACCOUNTING FOR RECEIPTS

Example: Banking card vouchers

You are asked to bank all card transactions at the end of a working day. You receive all the card vouchers for the day and you obtain a summary voucher. The transaction vouchers are as follows.

	£		£
Sale	26.41	Sale	12.95
Sale	32.99	Sale	14.48
Sale	32.99	Sale	136.48
Sale	100.40	Sale	12.95
Sale	22.00	Sale	112.95
Sale	46.99	Sale	11.80
Sale	37.80	Sale	56.71
Sale	12.95	Refund	22.00

Enter the amount of each transaction on the back of the processing copy

Back of processing copy

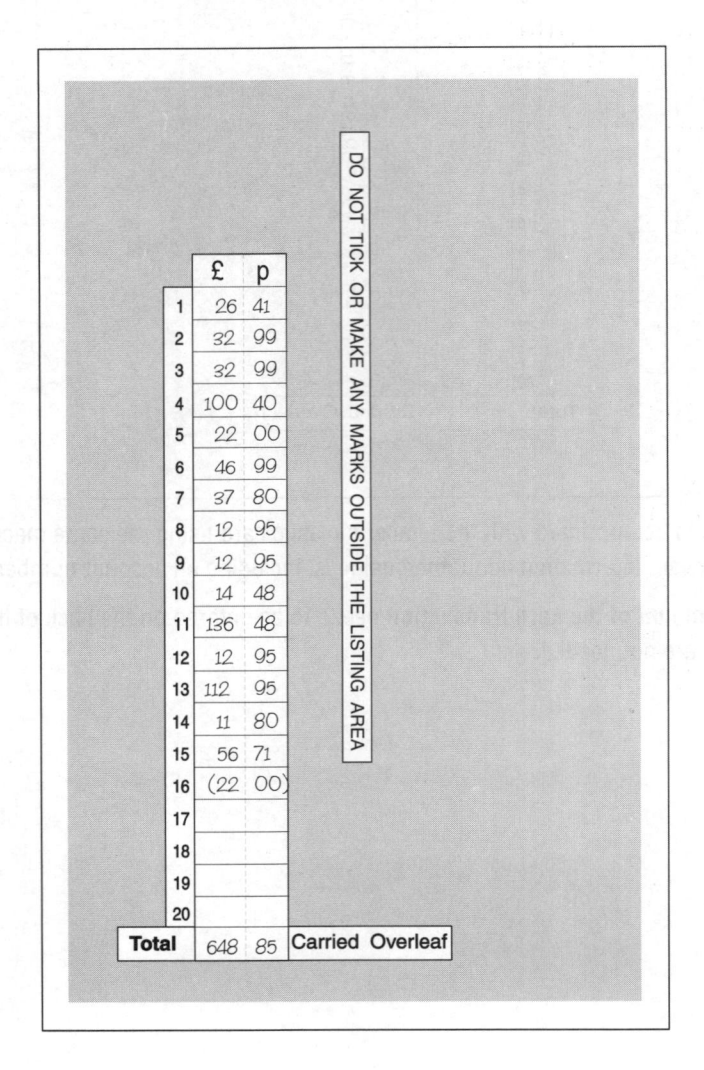

	£	p
1	26	41
2	32	99
3	32	99
4	100	40
5	22	00
6	46	99
7	37	80
8	12	95
9	12	95
10	14	48
11	136	48
12	12	95
13	112	95
14	11	80
15	56	71
16	(22	00)
17		
18		
19		
20		
Total	648	85

Carried Overleaf

DO NOT TICK OR MAKE ANY MARKS OUTSIDE THE LISTING AREA

11: BANKING MONIES RECEIVED

Transfer the total amount and number of transactions to the front of the **top copy** and the carbon will transfer this through to the front of the processing copy. Imprint the retailer card details on the summary voucher.

Top copy

HAVE YOU IMPRINTED THE SUMMARY WITH YOUR RETAILER'S CARD?

7849 950 1725 05

BANK Processing (White) copy of Summary with your Vouchers in correct order.
1. SUMMARY
2. SALES VOUCHERS
3. REFUND VOUCHERS
KEEP Retailer's copies (Blue & Yellow)
NO MORE THAN 200 Vouchers to each Summary
DO NOT USE Staples, Pins, Paper Clips

ABC & CO
LONDON W12

950 1725 05

ABC & CO
LONDON W12

Southern Bank **BANKING**
FASTPASS **SUMMARY**

	ITEMS	AMOUNT	
SALES VOUCHERS (LISTED OVERLEAF)	15	670	85
LESS REFUND VOUCHERS	1	22	00
DATE 26/6/X6	TOTAL £	648	85

A. N. Other
RETAILER'S SIGNATURE

SUMMARY - RETAILER'S COPY

COMPLETE THIS SUMMARY FOR EVERY DEPOSIT OF SALES VOUCHERS AND ENTER THE TOTAL ON YOUR NORMAL CURRENT ACCOUNT PAYING-IN SLIP

Front of processing copy

3200

7849 950 1725 05

ABC & CO
LONDON W12

950 1725 05

ABC & CO
LONDON W12

	ITEMS	AMOUNT	
SALES VOUCHERS (LISTED OVERLEAF)	15	670	85
LESS REFUND VOUCHERS	1	22	00
DATE 26/6/X6	TOTAL £	648	85

A. N. Other
RETAILER'S SIGNATURE

SOUTHERN BANKING SUMMARY - PROCESSING COPY

PART B ACCOUNTING FOR RECEIPTS

Separate the two top copies from the processing copy. Enter the total of the summary voucher onto a normal paying-in slip, as if it were a cheque.

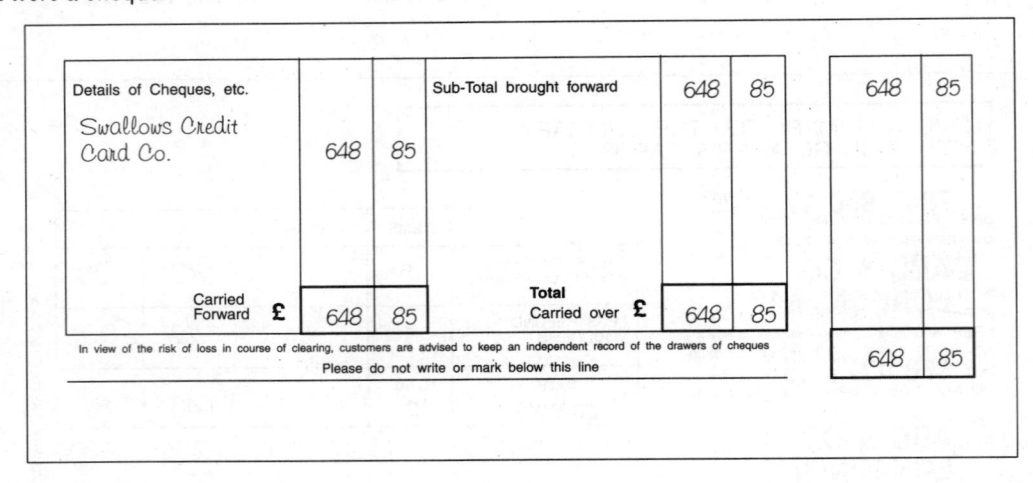

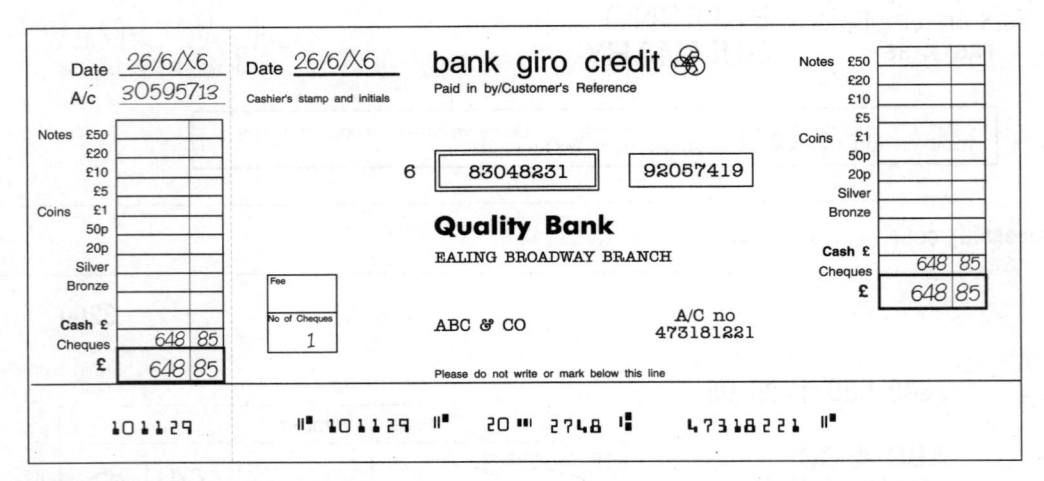

Details of Cheques, etc.			Sub-Total brought forward	648	85	648	85
Swallows Credit Card Co.	648	85					
Carried Forward £	648	85	Total Carried over £	648	85	648	85

In view of the risk of loss in course of clearing, customers are advised to keep an independent record of the drawers of cheques. Please do not write or mark below this line

Bank giro credit slip:
- Date: 26/6/X6
- A/c: 30595713
- bank giro credit — Quality Bank, EALING BROADWAY BRANCH
- ABC & CO, A/C no 473181221
- No of Cheques: 1
- Cheques: 648 85
- £ 648 85
- 83048231 92057419
- 101129 101129 20 2748 473 18221

The documents are then dealt with as follows.

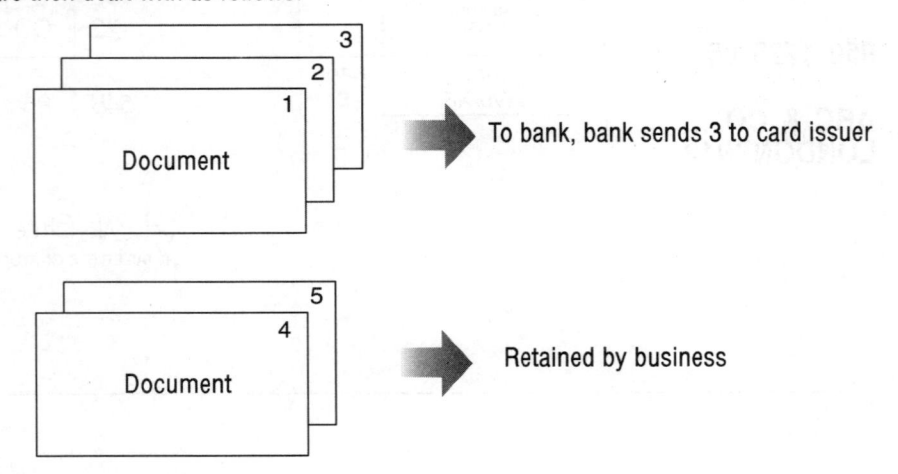

Documents 1, 2, 3 → To bank, bank sends 3 to card issuer

Documents 4, 5 → Retained by business

11: BANKING MONIES RECEIVED

Key

1. Paying-in slip
2. Top copy of the summary voucher
3. Processing copy of summary voucher, plus the processing copies of the card transaction vouchers
4. Middle copy of summary voucher
5. Second copies of card transaction vouchers

7.3 Queries arising from card transactions

Problem with card receipts	Action
Stolen cards	As a general rule where a retailer has followed all proper security procedures (Chapter 10) the card issuer will honour the transaction even if the card is stolen.
Transactions taking place **above the shop's floor limit**	The card issuer may refuse to honour the transaction as the retailer has been negligent in not obtaining authorisation.
Transaction below floor limit but takes customer over their **card limit**	The card issuer may refuse to honour the transaction, even though the business has followed all the security procedures. The business will have to pursue the customer for payment by another means.
Errors in completing the card voucher **Non-processing** in error by the card issuer	Discrepancies which arise as a result of error can usually be dealt with quite quickly and efficiently by correspondence directly between the business and the card issuer.

Activity 11.5

Aroma's retail shop receives payment by cash, cheque and credit card. Each day's takings are stored in a secure safe for banking on the following working day. Credit card vouchers are summarised daily on the bank's credit card summary.

The following summary relates to the week commencing Monday 27 November 20X7.

	Cash float at start of the day £	Cash/cheques for banking £	Cash float at end of day £	Credit card sales vouchers £	Credit card refund £
Monday	24.16	684.08	37.05	104.28	-
Tuesday	37.05	504.27	12.60	202.96	-
Wednesday	12.60	691.41	19.40	124.17	37.26
Thursday	19.40	729.62	32.42	291.41	-
Friday	32.42	840.50	26.91	342.09	41.20

The till summaries show total sales for the week of £4,439.28.

PART B ACCOUNTING FOR RECEIPTS

Tasks

(a) Prepare a schedule of each day's sales, showing cash/cheque sales and credit card sales separately for each day, and showing totals for the week. Compare the total to the total per the till summaries. Use the grid below. (Remember sales are bankings adjusted for the cash float movement!)

Day	Cash and cheque sales	Credit card sales	Total for day	Total for week so far
Monday				
Tuesday				
Wednesday				
Thursday				
Friday				

(b) Three credit card sales vouchers and one credit card refund voucher were issued on Wednesday 29 November. Using the blank form below, complete for signature the retailer's banking summary for that day's credit card transactions.

```
HAVE YOU IMPRINTED THE SUMMARY
WITH YOUR RETAILER'S CARD?

BANK Processing (White) copy of              ITEMS    AMOUNT
Summary with your Vouchers in
correct order:                       SALES VOUCHERS
1. SUMMARY                           (LISTED OVERLEAF)
2. SALES VOUCHERS
3. REFUND VOUCHERS                   LESS REFUND
KEEP Retailer's copies (Blue & Yellow)  VOUCHERS
NO MORE THAN 200 Vouchers to each
Summary                              DATE        TOTAL
DO NOT USE Staples, Pins, Paper Clips             £


First Region Bank    BANKING
FASTPASS             SUMMARY            RETAILER'S SIGNATURE

COMPLETE THIS SUMMARY FOR EVERY DEPOSIT OF SALES VOUCHERS AND ENTER THE
TOTAL ON YOUR NORMAL CURRENT ACCOUNT PAYING-IN SLIP
```

(c) State what should be done with the banking summary you have prepared in (b).

Activity 11.6

The following credit card receipts were processed on 22 May 20X7.

Customer		Amount £
1		28.42
2		69.18
3		99.81
4		57.48
5	Refund	(21.14)
6		93.14
7		31.18
8		72.87
9	Refund	(34.69)
10		17.81

Task

Complete the credit card summary voucher and bank paying-in slip shown below.

11: BANKING MONIES RECEIVED

PART B ACCOUNTING FOR RECEIPTS

	£	p	
1	26	41	
2	32	99	
3	32	99	
4	100	40	
5	22	00	
6	46	99	
7	37	80	
8	12	95	
9	12	95	
10	14	48	
11	136	48	
12	12	95	
13	112	95	
14	11	80	
15	56	71	
16	(22	00)	
17			
18			
19			
20			
Total	648	85	Carried Overleaf

DO NOT TICK OR MAKE ANY MARKS OUTSIDE THE LISTING AREA

bank giro credit
Paid in by/Customer's Reference

8 83048231 92057419

Quality Bank
EALING BROADWAY BRANCH

A. B. BROWNE & CO   A/C no 30494713

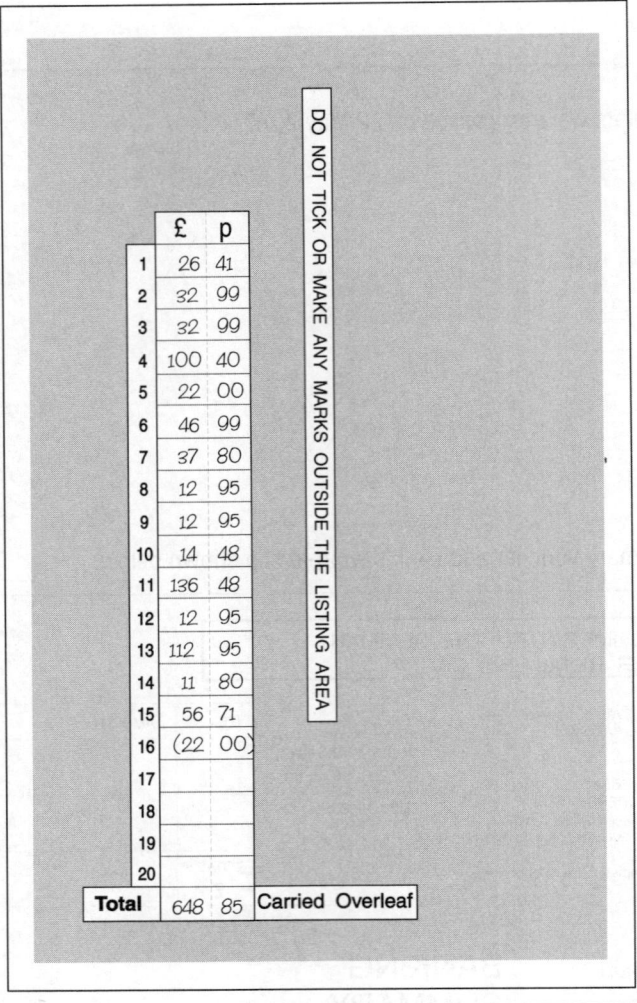

Date ____   Date ____
A/c ____   Cashier's stamp and initials
Cashier's stamp and initials

Cash ____
Cheques etc ____
Fee
No of Cheques
£ ____

Notes £50, £20, £10, £5
Coins £1, 50p, 20p
Silver
Bronze
Cash £
Cheques
£

Please do not write or mark below this line

101129   101129   20 2748 30494713

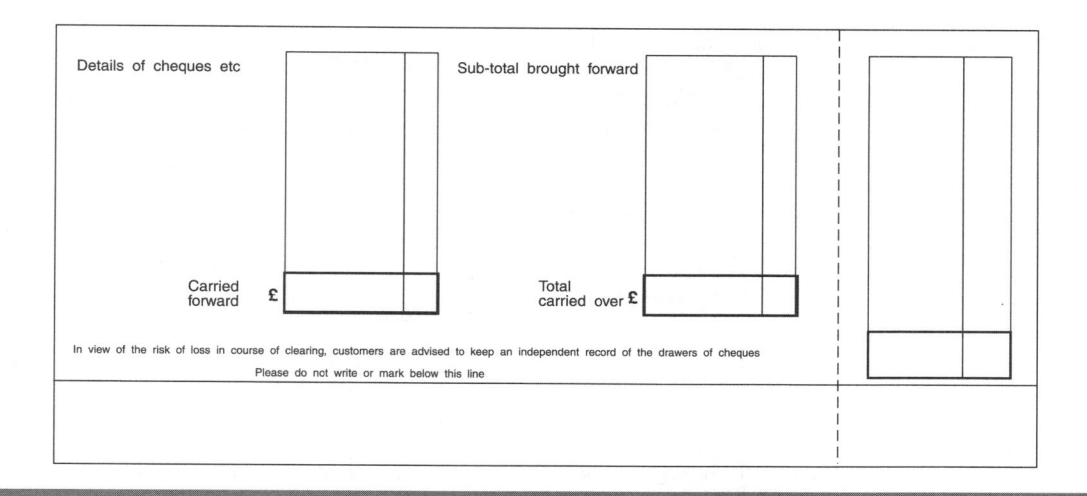

8 Banking and EFTPOS

8.1 Banking EFTPOS transactions

Where businesses use **EFTPOS** to process card receipts, there is no need to deposit the sale slips at the bank.

The sales (and returns) are processed by the card issuers and credited **directly to the business bank account**, usually within two or three days.

The narrative on the bank statement next to the entry indicates the type of service (eg Switch, Visa and MasterCard).

8.2 'End of day' procedure

The retailer only knows what will be paid into his bank account if he has carried out the **'end of day' procedure**. This produces a **summary report of transactions** undertaken during the day. It should be carried out after closing time and can then be matched against amounts appearing on the bank statement.

If you have to use an EFTPOS machine, you will be instructed how to do the 'end of day' procedure.

A summary report of transactions will look something like this.

```
A MERCHANT
HIGH STREET
ANYTOWN

          RECONCILIATION
-------------------------------

VISA
M 1234567
T06500015                    R0023


VISA
PREVIOUS
0005                        £0.89DR
0000                        £0.00CR
TOTAL 0012-0018
                              £0.89

CURRENT
0002                       £50.50DR
0001                       £25.25CR
TOTAL 0019-0023
                             £25.25

COMPLETED

SESSION TOTALS AGREED

DATE 06/07/X4                  19:31
```

8.3 Retention of documents

In the event of queries on individual transactions or bank account credits, the retailer will need to produce relevant copies of the vouchers. Therefore it is essential that all copy vouchers are kept in a safe place, preferably in date order, for a **minimum period of 6 months** and sometimes even longer.

The best way is to attach the day's sales and refund slips to the **end of day reconciliation** and then to keep these in date order.

9 Banking other receipts

Some receipts, by their very nature, require no action on the part of the business. These include **direct debits, standing orders, BACS payments, CHAPS payments** and **telegraphic transfers**, as the amounts are transferred straight into the business's bank account.

9.1 Banker's drafts

Banker's drafts are paid into the bank by the business in the same manner as cheques.

9.2 Bank giro credits

Bank giro credits can be paid into a bank account by the **customer of the business**, in which case the amounts will appear automatically on the business's bank statement.

PART B   ACCOUNTING FOR RECEIPTS

Key learning points

- ☑ You should note the important theoretical and legal aspects of **banks, bankers and their relationship with their customers.**
  - How the clearing system works
  - Relationships between banker and customer
- ☑ **Banking procedures** for various kinds of receipts should be fully understood and you should observe real transactions wherever possible.
- ☑ When **banking cash receipts**:
  - Cash must be properly counted and sorted
  - Notes and coins must be listed by denomination on the paying-in slip
- ☑ The details required on the paying-in slip when **cheques are banked** include:
  - Name of drawer (or endorser)
  - Amount of cheque
  - Total value of cheques banked
  - Number of cheques banked
- ☑ **Plastic card transactions** which are processed manually must be listed on a summary voucher for banking purposes. The processing copies are sent to the bank while the retailer retains a copy of the summary voucher and each transaction voucher.
- ☑ Credit, charge or debit card receipts via **EFTPOS** are credited directly to the retailer's bank account. He can agree the amounts received to the 'End of day' reconciliation produced by the terminal.

Quick quiz

1. What is 'clearing' in banking terms?
2. How long does a cheque take to clear?
3. What are the four types of relationship which may exist between a banker and customer?
4. How should coins be banked?
5. Which details from cheques should be included on the paying-in slip?
6. If you accept a stolen cheque in good faith, it is worth nothing to you. True or false?
7. What happens if you accept a stolen credit card for an amount below your floor limit?

    A   The card issuer will never honour the transaction
    B   The card issuer will always honour the transaction
    C   The card issuer will honour the transaction, provided usual security procedures are followed
    D   The card issuer will only honour the transaction if authorisation was obtained

Answers to quick quiz

1. Clearing is obtaining payment for cheques.
2. Cheques take three working days to clear.
3. The relationships are: debtor/creditor; bailor/bailee; principal/agent; mortgagor/mortgagee.
4. Coins should be banked in the plastic paying-in bags supplied by banks, with the correct number of coins as shown on the bag.
5. The drawer and the amount should be noted on the paying-in slip.
6. True. You must pursue the person who forged the cheque to honour the debt.
7. **C**. If all security procedures have been followed, the issuer will usually honour the transaction.

PART B ACCOUNTING FOR RECEIPTS

Activity checklist

This checklist shows which performance criteria, range statement or knowledge and understanding point is covered by each activity in this chapter. Tick off each activity as you complete it.

Activity		
11.1	☐	This activity deals with Knowledge and Understanding point 1: types of business transactions.
11.2	☐	This activity deals with Knowledge and Understanding point 1: types of business transactions.
11.3	☐	This activity deals with Performance Criteria 1.2.C, concerning preparation of paying-in documents
11.4	☐	This activity deals with Performance Criteria 1.2.D
11.5	☐	This activity deals with Performance Criteria 1.2.C, concerning reconciling to relevant records, and Knowledge and Understanding point 7: the use of banking documentation
11.6	☐	This activity deals with Knowledge and Understanding point 19: credit card procedures

chapter 12

Recording monies received

Contents

1. The problem
2. The solution
3. The cash book
4. Cash registers
5. Cash received sheets (remittance lists)
6. Posting cash receipts to the main ledger

Performance criteria

- 1.2.A Check receipts against relevant supporting information
- 1.2.B Enter receipts in appropriate accounting records
- 1.2.D Identity unusual features and either resolve or refer to the appropriate person

Range statement

- 1.2.1 Receipts: cash; cheques; an automated payment
- 1.2.2 Accounting records: manual cash book; manual main ledger and subsidiary ledger; computerised records
- 1.2.3 Unusual features: wrongly completed cheques; out of date cheque; credit and debit card limits exceeded; disagreement with supporting documentation

PART B   ACCOUNTING FOR RECEIPTS

Knowledge and understanding

1   Types of business transactions and documents involved
12 Accounting for receipts from credit customers and customers without credit accounts
14 Operation of manual accounting systems
15 Operation of computerised accounting systems, including output
16 Use of the cash book as part of the double entry system or as books of prime entry
18 Relationship between accounting system and the ledger
25 Organisational procedures for filing source documents

> **Signpost**
>
> The topics covered in this chapter are relevant to **Unit 1**.

1 The problem

A business needs to know the following.

- All receipts have been correctly banked
- All receipts have been recorded
- All monies received from debtors are correctly recorded in the sales ledger accounts
- All cash sales (that is non-credit sales) are correctly recorded
- All capital receipts are correctly recorded (see Section 6)

The controls over recording receipts must be as good as those for banking the receipts, otherwise the business will not know whether it has received all the money due to it.

2 The solution

As we have seen in the previous two chapters, **security** is vital for receipts.

Whenever possible, duties must be **segregated**, so that the person **banking receipts** is a different person from the one who **records** the receipts.

An ideal system includes the following checks.

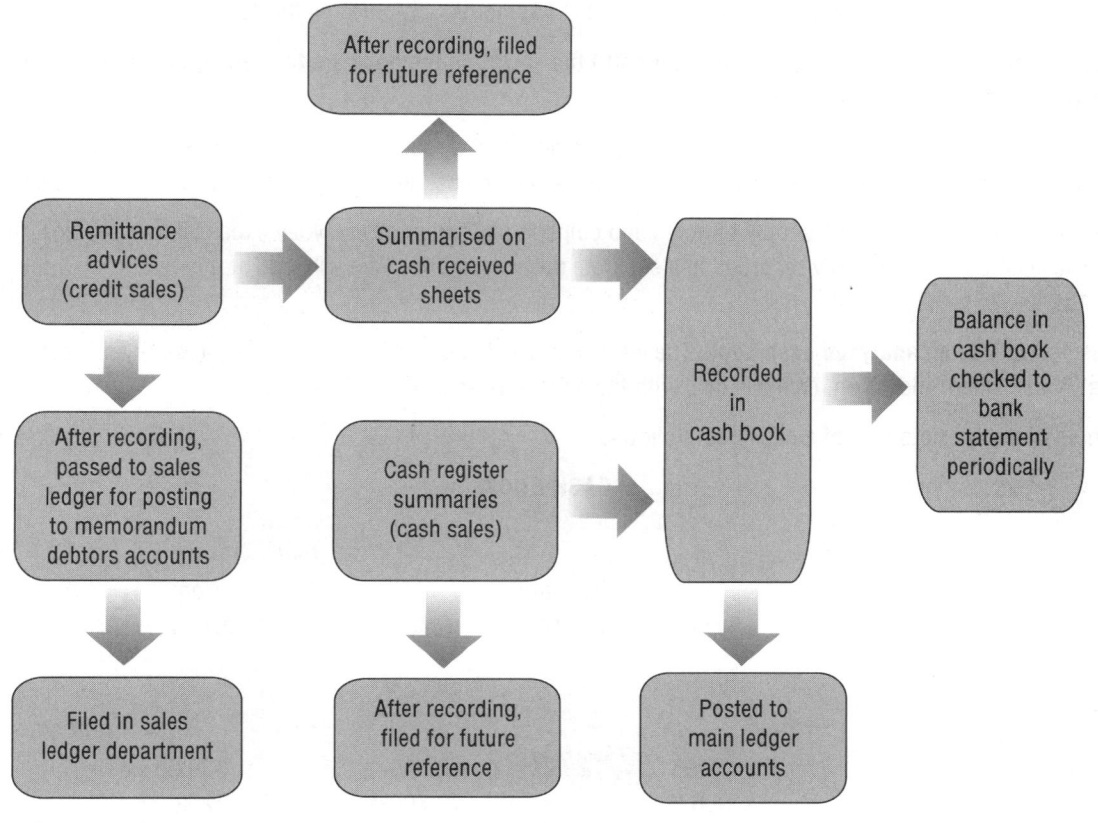

```
Remittance advices (credit sales) 
  → Summarised on cash received sheets 
    → After recording, filed for future reference
    → Recorded in cash book
      → Balance in cash book checked to bank statement periodically
      → Posted to main ledger accounts
  → After recording, passed to sales ledger for posting to memorandum debtors accounts
    → Filed in sales ledger department

Cash register summaries (cash sales)
  → Recorded in cash book
  → After recording, filed for future reference
```

Note the following points.

- The person recording the receipts does not handle the cash or cheques received.
- The balance on the cash book is periodically checked to the balance on the bank statement (see your Unit 3 studies). This ensures that all receipts have been banked.
- The source documents (remittance advices, cash received sheets, cash register summaries) are all filed for future reference.

3 The cash book

3.1 What is the cash book?

Remember the double entry rule for assets.

ASSET ACCOUNT	
DR	CR
INCREASE	DECREASE

The cash book records the **cash balance** of the business and so records an **asset**.

PART B ACCOUNTING FOR RECEIPTS

The left hand side of the cash book (the **debit** side) is used to record amounts of monies **received** by the business, while the right hand side (the **credit** side) is used to record **payments** of monies by the business.

Periodically (often daily but perhaps only once a month) the entries in the book are totalled and the **balance of cash** available to the business is determined.

The main cash book usually records the amounts received and paid through the **business bank account**. The 'cash' referred to may consist mostly of cheques, rather than notes and coins, depending on the nature of the business.

However, most businesses need a supply of notes and coins to pay for small everyday expenses (eg postage, tea and coffee). These amounts are usually recorded in a separate **petty cash book**. We will look at the petty cash book in Chapter 15.

Most businesses use an **analysed cash book**. The left hand page has columns in which receipts are analysed as 'Debtors', 'Cash sales' and so on. (We will deal with the payments analysis in Chapter 14.)

An example of the receipts side of a cash book follows.

CASH BOOK

RECEIPTS

Date 20X7	Narrative	Folio	Discount allowed	Total	Output VAT on cash sales	Receipts from debtors	Cash sales	Other
01-Sep	Balance b/d			900.00				
	Cash sale			80.00	11.91		68.09	
	Debtor pays: Hay	SL96	20.00	380.00		380.00		
	Debtor pays: Been	SL632		720.00		720.00		
	Debtor pays: Seed	SL501	40.00	960.00		960.00		
	Cash sale			150.00	22.34		127.66	
	Fixed asset sale			200.00				200.00
			60.00	2,490.00	34.25	2,060.00	195.75	200.00

The fixed asset sale means the sale of an asset used in the business, for example, a computer. This is not the usual trade of the business and so it needs to be separately recorded. We will return to this in Section 6.

3.2 Discounts allowed

The discount allowed column above shows **how cash discounts are recorded**.

The discount allowed column shows why the **full amount of a debt** has not been received from a customer.

The debts owed by a customer are recorded in the **sales ledger**. The discount allowed will be posted to the individual's account, clearing the **total** debt. So the account of Hay will show cash received of £380 plus discount allowed of £20, to clear a total debt of £400.

A **summary** posting will be required to the sales ledger control account of the total cash received from debtors (£2,060) and the total discounts allowed (£60).

The double entry postings are dealt with in detail in Section 6.

Activity 12.1

Which of the following will *not* be entered in the receipts side of the cash book?

(a) Cheque received
(b) Payment from sales ledger customers
(c) Supplier's invoice
(d) Credit note
(e) Debit note
(f) Bank interest received
(g) Payment for a fixed asset sold
(h) Refund received from a supplier

4 Cash registers

4.1 Cash received

The cash book is not always the first place that receipts are recorded. Sometimes it is more practical to **record receipts elsewhere** and then **summarise them in the cash book**.

- Cash registers (this section)
- Cash received sheets or remittance lists (see Section 5)

Cash registers have been in use for a long time in retail shops. They used to be mechanically operated, but today most are computerised.

The more sophisticated and larger stores have cash registers which are connected to a central computer. The cash registers update the computer automatically as a sale takes place, and each cash register can be updated for price changes.

If you have to use a cash register in practice, you will be instructed in its use.

PART B ACCOUNTING FOR RECEIPTS

4.2 Till receipts

The cash register will print a receipt for the customer (and a record of the transaction on a second till roll which is kept in the printer).

```
        *** ARNIE'S ***
       VAT NO  423 4895 26


              20  01  X3

       Water          .1.00
       Mixers         .2.00
       Sherry         .3.00
       Spirits        .4.00
                     .10.00 ST
                     .20.00 CA TD
                     .10.00 CG


           110000042

        004           15:00
```

The sales comes to a total of £10 and a £20 note has been tendered to pay for the goods. The register calculates that £10 change is due.

Cash registers can also deal with sales where the customer tenders two, or even three, **different forms of payment** (cash and cheque, cash and credit card, etc).

4.3 Recording cash received by the register

At the end of the day, the register will produce a readout of the day's sales. It will then be 'reset' to clear the register ready for the next day's sales.

The readout will look something like the example below.

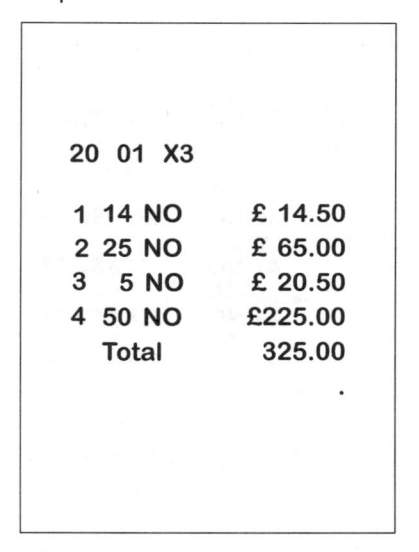

```
20  01  X3

1  14 NO      £ 14.50
2  25 NO      £ 65.00
3   5 NO      £ 20.50
4  50 NO      £225.00
   Total       325.00
```

The first column shows the type of sale, the second column the number of sales and the third column the value of those sales. The total sales for the day are shown at the bottom. This is a simplified example.

Some organisations may take readings more frequently than daily eg hourly in a busy supermarket.

The readout is used as follows.

- A check on the amount of money in the till
- To record the receipts in the cash book

The entry in the cash book will be the total amount of cash received. This will be analysed into sales and VAT, so that it can be **posted to the main ledger** (see Section 6 of this chapter).

PART B   ACCOUNTING FOR RECEIPTS

Activity 12.2

The summary below analyses the number and value of sales made hourly on a particular day. The summary is printed each day at the close of business. The store opens daily at 9.00 am.

```
09:00 → 10:00
          14 NO      £77.41
10:00 → 11:00
          29 NO      £541.25
11:00 → 12:00
          35 NO      £1,096.99
12:00 → 13:00
          41 NO      £857.18
13:00 → 14:00
          24 NO      £1,148.58
14:00 → 15:00
          21 NO      £467.79
15:00 → 16:00
          33 NO      £405.26
16:00 → 17:00
          39 NO      £715.22
```

Tasks

The store manager wants certain information on the day's trading. Use the information from the summary to answer the following questions.

(a) What value of sales was made between 3.00 pm and 5.00 pm?

(b) In which two-hour period ('hour-to-hour') was there:

   (i) The highest number of sales
   (ii) The highest value of sales

(c) All sales were for cash except for £319.25 cheque and credit card sales. The cash float at the start of the day was £25.00. How much cash would you expect to find in the till at 5.00 pm? (*Note:* A cash float is the amount of money in the till before business starts, in order to be able to give change to the first customers.)

Activity 12.3

During the day, different members of staff are on duty at the computerised till in Activity 12.2. When a new member of staff takes over the till, the outgoing and incoming staff members are expected to count the contents of the till and put small change in bags for specified amounts provided by the bank. These bags are left in the till until the end of each day.

At 5.00 pm when Ali Alaqat finished a two hour period on the till, it was found that the money in the till is £17.42 short. The amounts counted in the till at previous changes of duty during the day were as follows.

Time	Outgoing till operator	Amount counted £
11.00 am	John Walton	625.66
3.00 pm	Surinda Patel	4,196.20

Tasks

(a) Use the information given in Activities 12.2 and 12.3 to calculate when the cash shortage arose. Show any workings.

(b) Suggest what procedures could be adopted to make it possible for discrepancies in the amount of cash in the till to be discovered earlier and more easily than the procedure you have used in part (a).

5 Cash received sheets (remittance lists)

Businesses which do not have a cash register still need to record money received from sales they have made.

Very small shops or businesses may write down on a piece of paper the money received as they sell something. This is a basic **cash received sheet.** It will show cash, cheques and credit card receipts.

Larger non-retail companies may have **pre-printed cash received sheets** or **remittance lists** on which they record receipts that arrive through the post.

CASH RECEIVED SHEET 7141 (b)

DATE 10/4/X5   (a)

ARC BUILDING SUPPLIES LTD

NAME		ACCOUNT	AMOUNT
P Jones and Son	1	00437	169.00
S Car & Co	2	01562	62.70
H M Customs & Excise	3	00002	55.00
Moblem Ltd	4	02137	3,233.99
Lobells plc	5	05148	244.91
Cannery Whiff	6	02420	9,553.72
Lymping Ltd	7	09370	62.20
Yorker plc	8	09682	322.41
Mowley Ltd	9	01433	43.30
Regalia plc	10	03997	978.50
Herod & Sons	11	05763	71.40
Forman & Co	12	07211	4,288.52
Thatchers	13	04520	610.00
Eggary & Co	14	08871	4,823.50
Redwood & Sons	15	08759	420.68
TOTAL		10000 (c)	24,939.83 (d)

PART B ACCOUNTING FOR RECEIPTS

Key

(a) **Account number**. This is the ledger account number of the customer in the **sales ledger**. For non-sales ledger receipts, the code of the account in the main ledger is used. In this case 00002 is the code for Customs & Excise refunding VAT.

(b) **Cash received sheet number**. Preprinted cash received sheets should be sequentially numbered. This helps to ensure that all receipts have been recorded, as a check can be made that all cash received sheets are present.

(c) **Cash account number (10000)**. This is the ledger account number of the cash account in the main ledger.

(d) **Total receipts**. The money received is summarised here and only the totals need to be recorded in the cash book.

Activity 12.4

Aroma's business is expanding. All monies received are now entered on cash received sheets which record details in separate columns, headed as follows.

(a) **Date**

(b) **Name**, showing the name of the firm or person from whom the money is received

(c) **Account number**, showing:
- For sales ledger receipts, the account number of the customer in the sales ledger, or
- For other receipts, the code for the ledger account to be credited

(d) **Amount**

In the week commencing 20 April 20X7, the post includes the items listed below. All cheques received were accompanied by a remittance advice.

20.4.X7	A cheque for £492.70 from Jill's Kitchen Co. A cheque for £242.98 from G Edwards & Son. A credit note for £124.40 from a supplier, Extrans Ltd.
21.4.X7	A cheque for £892.76 from Crystal Water Co. A VAT repayment cheque of £487.50 from HM Customs & Excise. A cheque for £500 from Green Gourmet Co, being part payment against invoice No 17201 which was for a total amount of £1,024.20.
22.4.X7	A cheque for £1,700.00 from BRM Motors in payment for a secondhand motor vehicle. A cheque for £1,920.70 from Jennan Tonic Ltd.
23.4.X7	A cheque for £400 from Oliver's Organic Foods. A debit note for £92.00 from Fender Foods plc. A cheque for £3,208.00 from Parkers Preserves Ltd.
24.4.X7	A cheque for £4,920.75 from Pennine Springs Ltd A statement of account from British Telecom plc, showing a balance of £382.44, to be paid by direct debit.

The following is a list of sales ledger account numbers.

	Account number		Account number
Crystal Water Co	C101	Jill's Kitchen Co	J211
Denny's Ltd	D024	Oliver's Organic Foods	O301
G Edwards & Son	E102	Parkers Preserves Ltd	P002
Fender Foods plc	F108	Pennine Springs Ltd	P004
Green Gourmet Co	G105	Spring Bottlers plc	S003
Jennan Tonic Ltd	J110	West, Key & Eiss	W402

The following list shows certain ledger account codes.

Cash	1000
Value added tax	1600
Motor vehicle disposals	1720
Telephones	1924
Sales ledger control account	1200

Tasks

(a) Draw up and total the cash received sheet for the week, using the blank sheet below. The last sheet used was number 1522.

(b) State how you would expect the cash receipts to be recorded in the cash book.

Cash received sheet		Number	
Date	Name	Account No.	Amount
			£
	Total	1,000	

PART B ACCOUNTING FOR RECEIPTS

6 Posting cash receipts to the main ledger

6.1 Sales and debtors

The aim of the accounting system is to document, record, summarise and present the financial transactions of a business. It is only when we **post the receipts side of the cash book to the main ledger that we have accounted for cash receipts.**

Book of prime entry		Ledger accounts
Cash book	P O S T → I N	Cash (or bank) account Sales account(s) VAT account Sales ledger control
Records cash receipts	G	*Accounts for cash receipts*

Provided all the procedures have been followed correctly in preparing the cash book, posting it to the main ledger should be straightforward.

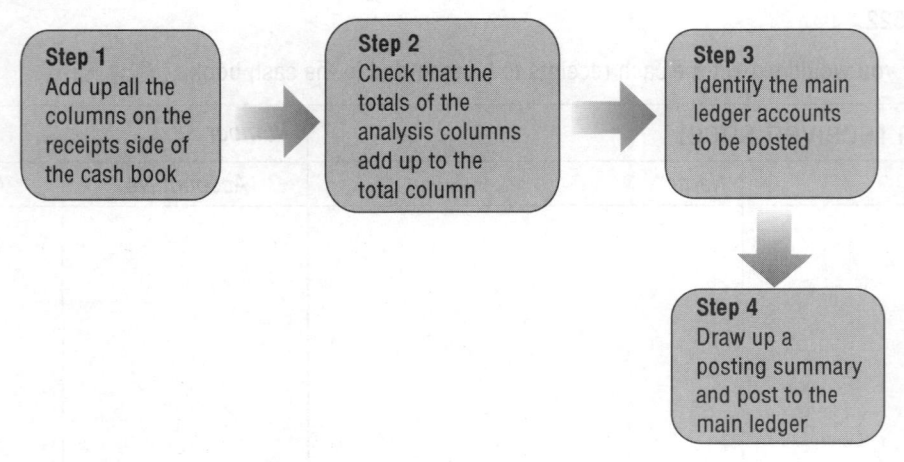

Step 1 Add up all the columns on the receipts side of the cash book → **Step 2** Check that the totals of the analysis columns add up to the total column → **Step 3** Identify the main ledger accounts to be posted → **Step 4** Draw up a posting summary and post to the main ledger

Example: posting the main ledger from the cash book

Robbie Jackson wants to post his cash received for 1 September 20X7 to his main ledger. The relevant main ledger accounts are as follows.

CASH ACCOUNT   CA01

		£		£
1 Sept	Balance b/d	900.00		

12: RECORDING MONIES RECEIVED

SALES LEDGER CONTROL			SLCA01
	£		£
1 Sept Balance b/d	51,795.00		

SALES			SA01
	£		£
1 Sept		Balance b/d	200,403.00

VAT			VAT01
	£		£
1 Sept		Balance b/d	35,070.00

FIXED ASSET DISPOSAL			DIS01
	£		£

DISCOUNT ALLOWED			DA01
	£		£
1 Sept Balance b/d	2,410.00		

Step 1 Add up all the columns. (Note that the 'total' column excludes the balance b/d - we do not want to double count.)

ROBBIE JACKSON: CASH BOOK

RECEIPTS

Date 20X7	Narrative	Folio	Discount allowed	Total	Output VAT on cash sales	Receipts from debtors	Cash sales	Other
01-Sep	Balance b/d			900.00				
	Cash sale			80.00	11.91		68.09	
	Debtor pays: Hay	SL96	20.00	380.00		380.00		
	Debtor pays: Been	SL632		720.00		720.00		
	Debtor pays: Seed	SL501	40.00	960.00		960.00		
	Cash sale			150.00	22.34		127.66	
	Fixed asset sale			200.00				200.00
			60.00	2,490.00	34.25	2,060.00	195.75	200.00
			SLCA01 CR *DA01* DR	*CA01* DR	*VAT01* CR	*SLCA01* CR	*SA01* CR	*DIS01* CR

PART B   ACCOUNTING FOR RECEIPTS

Step 2   **Check the totals**

	£
Output VAT on cash sales	34.25
Receipts from debtors	2,060.00
Cash sales	195.75
Other receipts	200.00
Total cash received	2,490.00

Step 3   **Identify main ledger accounts.** We have marked the folio references for the main ledger accounts on the receipts page above.

- CA01 Cash account
- VAT01 VAT account
- SLCA Sales ledger control account (SLCA)
- SA01 Sales
- DIS01 Disposal of fixed assets
- DA01 Discounts allowed

Step 4   **Draw up the posting summary and post the main ledger.**

			£	£
DEBIT	Cash account	CA01	2,490.00	
	Discounts allowed	DA01	60.00	
CREDIT	SLCA	SLCA01		2,120.00
	VAT	VAT01		34.25
	Sales	SA01		195.75
	Disposal of fixed assets	DIS01		200.00

Being cash book receipts postings summary 1 September 20X7

Note that the credit to SLCA of £2,120 reflects £60 discounts allowed plus £2,060 received from them in cash.

CASH ACCOUNT			CA01
£			£
1 Sept Balance b/d	900.00		
1 Sept Cash book	2,490.00		

SALES LEDGER CONTROL			SLCA01
£			£
1 Sept Balance b/d	51,795.00	1 Sept Cash book	2,120.00

SALES			SA01
£			£
1 Sept		Balance b/d	200,403.00
		1 Sept Cash book	195.75

	VAT		VAT01
	£		£
1 Sept		Balance b/d	35,070.00
		1 Sept Cash book	34.25

	FIXED ASSET DISPOSAL		DIS01
	£		£
		1 Sept Cash book	200.00

	DISCOUNT ALLOWED		DA01
	£		£
1 Sept Balance b/d	2,410.00		
1 Sept Cash book	60.00		

Remember that the main ledger *is* the double entry system and therefore all debits and credits on the posting summary must be equal (check this in the above example).

6.2 Capital and revenue items

Some income will be of a **revenue** nature and some of a **capital** nature. They must be accounted for separately.

In the above example sales are revenue and the sale of fixed assets is capital. They are posted to different accounts.

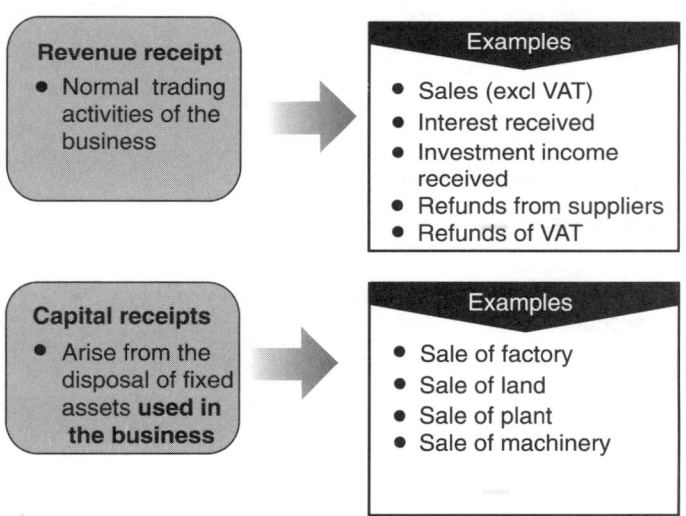

Revenue receipt
- Normal trading activities of the business

→ **Examples**
- Sales (excl VAT)
- Interest received
- Investment income received
- Refunds from suppliers
- Refunds of VAT

Capital receipts
- Arise from the disposal of fixed assets **used in the business**

→ **Examples**
- Sale of factory
- Sale of land
- Sale of plant
- Sale of machinery

Revenue items arise from the day to day trading of the business. They directly affect the **profit** that the business makes (profit = income − expenses).

Capital items arise from the disposal of secondhand assets previously used in the business and no longer needed. As they are not part of the day to day trading and arise irregularly, they are recorded separately in a fixed asset disposal account.

PART B ACCOUNTING FOR RECEIPTS

Capital items are not included in sales, as they would give an inaccurate picture of the profit made by way of trade. For example, a business is doing badly and sells some valuable land. If this were included in sales, it would give a totally inaccurate picture of the business's trade.

6.3 Postings summary

For cash sales:

		£	£
DEBIT:	Cash account (gross)	X	
CREDIT:	Sales account (net)		X
	VAT account		X

For cash sales with a discount allowed:

		£	£
DEBIT:	Cash account	X	
	Discount allowed	X	
CREDIT:	Sales account (net sales **plus** discount allowed)		X
	VAT account		X

For receipts from debtors:

		£	£
DEBIT:	Cash account	X	
CREDIT:	SLCA		X

(Remember that the sale and VAT were recorded when the invoice was sent out and a debtor was set up in the sales ledger control account.)

For receipts from debtors with a discount allowed:

		£	£
DEBIT:	Cash account	X	
	Discount allowed	X	
CREDIT:	SLCA (cash received **plus** discount allowed)		X

For receipts from the sale of fixed assets:

		£	£
DEBIT:	Cash account	X	
CREDIT:	Fixed asset disposal account		X

Activity 12.5

Prepare a posting summary for Aroma for the week commencing 20 April 20X7, using the information given in Activity 12.4.

AROMA POSTING SUMMARY		WEEK COMMENCING	
ACCOUNT	NO	DEBIT	CREDIT
TOTALS			

Activity 12.6

Aria Enterprises is a business selling marketing services to suppliers of opera companies. Most of its sales are to credit customers although there are a small number of cash sales. As at 15 February the receipts side of Aria's cash book was as follows:

ARIA ENTERPRISES

RECEIPTS

Date	Narrative	Folio	Discount allowed	Receipt total	VAT	Debtors	Cash sales	Other
05-Feb	Carmen Carpets	SL0075	112.50	2,137.50		2,137.50		
08-Feb	Placido Players	SL0553		42.00	6.25		35.75	
11-Feb	Mehta Metronomes	SL0712		543.27		543.27		
14-Feb	Luciano Lighting	SL0009	19.00	361.00		361.00		
15-Feb	Tosca Tents	SL0473		4,000.00	595.74		3,404.26	
15-Feb	Magic Flute Instruments	SL0338	475.00	9,025.00		9,025.00		
	Bank interest			42.01				42.01
	Sale of delivery van			2,500.00				2,500.00
	Totals							

The business operates a memorandum sales ledger plus a sales ledger control account in the main ledger. Relevant main ledger codes and balances brought down are as follows:

PART B ACCOUNTING FOR RECEIPTS

Account	Nominal code	Balance at 15/2 £
Cash	CAB 010	76,959 DR
VAT control account	VAT 094	10,500 CR
Sales ledger control account	SLC 040	152,744 DR
Sales discounts allowed	DIS 340	7,050 DR
Sales	SAL 200	372,771 CR
Interest received	INT 270	0
Fixed asset disposal	FAD 028	0

Tasks

(a) Total the receipts side of the cash book and identify the postings to the main ledger.
(b) Prepare a posting summary. Open up the main ledger accounts and post the relevant amounts to them.

6.4 Computerisation of receipts recording

It is quite rare to find a completely **computerised cash book.** Companies with the most sophisticated main ledger computer systems will still often maintain a manual cash book.

What many businesses do have is a **computerised cash book** which *is* the **main ledger cash account**, so the recording of every cash transaction is effectively a posting to the main ledger cash account.

This means that the company does not have to post totals from a book of prime entry, but has the disadvantage of making the main ledger huge in terms of the disk space it takes up.

In a computerised accounting system, it is normal for receipts from trade debtors (who have balances owing on the sales ledger) to be **posted directly from the cash received sheets to the individual account on the computerised sales ledger**. At the end of a period (day or week, or even a month), the computer will produce a **posting summary**. An example is shown below.

SALES LEDGER POSTING SUMMARY 31 MARCH 20X4

	DR	£	CR	£
Sales	SLCA	117.50	Sales	100.00
Output VAT			VAT	17.50
Cash received	Cash	90.00	SLCA	90.00
		207.50		207.50

If sales ledger and main ledger are **integrated,** they are connected and can update each other. So posting the sales ledger and the summary accounts can take place automatically.

If the two systems are **not integrated** then the posting will be input by the computer operator to the accounts in the main ledger.

Miscellaneous receipts will include sales of fixed assets, refunds from suppliers and perhaps VAT refunds from HM Customs & Excise. Such receipts do not normally appear in the sales ledger, as it is unlikely that an invoice has been issued to tell the payer he owes money to the business.

In this case the receipt can be recorded directly in a manual cash book and the cash book will be used to post such transactions to the accounts in the computer main ledger.

Key learning points

- ☑ ***Controls* over the recording of cash receipts** include:
  - Segregation of duties
  - Bank reconciliations
- ☑ **Analysed cash books** show how much money has been received and paid, and what each amount was for, by placing it in the correct column. A cash book is a daybook or book of prime entry.
- ☑ **Cash registers** can be very useful in the control of cash receipts. They are accurate and they can be used to collect different kinds of sales information.
- ☑ **Cash received sheets**, or remittance lists are used to collect receipts ready for recording.
- ☑ **Computerised accounting systems** will often still have a manual cash book. The sales ledger will be used to update the cash book to reflect cash received.
- ☑ The **sales ledger control account** can also be called the **total debtors account** or the **debtors control account.**
- ☑ The **sales ledger** may also be called a **subsidiary ledger.**
- ☑ The **main ledger** is also known as the **general ledger** or the **nominal ledger**.
- ☑ Be prepared for alternative names to be used in the workplace, as well as in assessments.

PART B   ACCOUNTING FOR RECEIPTS

Quick quiz

1. What is 'segregation of duties' when dealing with cash receipts?
2. The cash book reflects the movement of notes and coins through the business. True or false?
3. Why is a discount allowed column required in the cash book?
4. Is it easier for the operator if the computerised sales ledger and main ledger are integrated?

Answers to quick quiz

1. The receiving and recording functions are kept separate to avoid theft.
2. False. The cash book records movements through the business bank account. Notes and coins are recorded in the petty cash book.
3. The discount allowed column shows why the full amount of a debt has not been received, for clearing the total amount in the sales ledger.
4. Yes, because both ledgers can be updated simultaneously for cash receipts from debtors.

Activity checklist

This checklist shows which performance criteria, range statement or knowledge and understanding point is covered by each activity in this chapter. Tick off each activity as you complete it.

Activity		
12.1	☐	This activity deals with Range Statement 1.2.1: receipts.
12.2	☐	This activity deals with Knowledge and Understanding point 1: types of business transaction and the documents involved.
12.3	☐	This activity deals with Performance Criteria 1.2.A and 1.2.D.
12.4	☐	This activity deals with Performance Criteria 1.2.B.
12.5	☐	This activity deals with Performance Criteria 1.2.B.
12.6	☐	This activity deals with Performance Criteria 1.2.B.

PART C

Accounting for payments

chapter 13

Authorising and making payments

Contents

1. The problem
2. The solution
3. Controls over payments
4. Cheque requisition forms
5. Expenses claim forms
6. The timing and methods of payments
7. Payments by cash
8. Payments by cheque
9. BACS
10. Payments by banker's draft
11. Payments by standing order and direct debit
12. Payments by other methods
13. Documentation to go out with payments

Performance criteria

- 2.2.A Calculate payments from relevant documentation
- 2.2.B Schedule payments and obtain authorisation
- 2.2.C Use the appropriate payment method and timescale, in accordance with organisational procedures
- 2.2.E Identify queries and resolve or refer to the appropriate person
- 2.2.F Ensure security and confidentiality is maintained according to organisational requirements

Range statement

- 2.2.1 Payments: creditors
- 2.2.2 Documentation: suppliers' statements; cheque requisitions
- 2.2.3 Payment method: cash; cheques; an automated payment
- 2.2.5 Queries relating to: unauthorised claims for payment; insufficient supporting evidence; claims exceeding authorised limit.

PART C ACCOUNTING FOR PAYMENTS

Knowledge and understanding

- 6 Cheques, including crossing and endorsements
- 7 Automated payments
- 9 Documentation for payments
- 20 Credit card procedures
- 25 The nature of the organisation's business transactions
- 26 Organisational procedures for authorisation and coding of purchase invoices and payments

Signpost

The topics covered in this chapter are relevant to **Unit 2**.

1 The problem

A business needs strict controls over payments. It does not matter how small or how large the payment.

If a business allows any employees to pay out its money without permission, the scope for dishonesty increases alarmingly.

2 The solution

The usual way of controlling payments is to apply three controls.

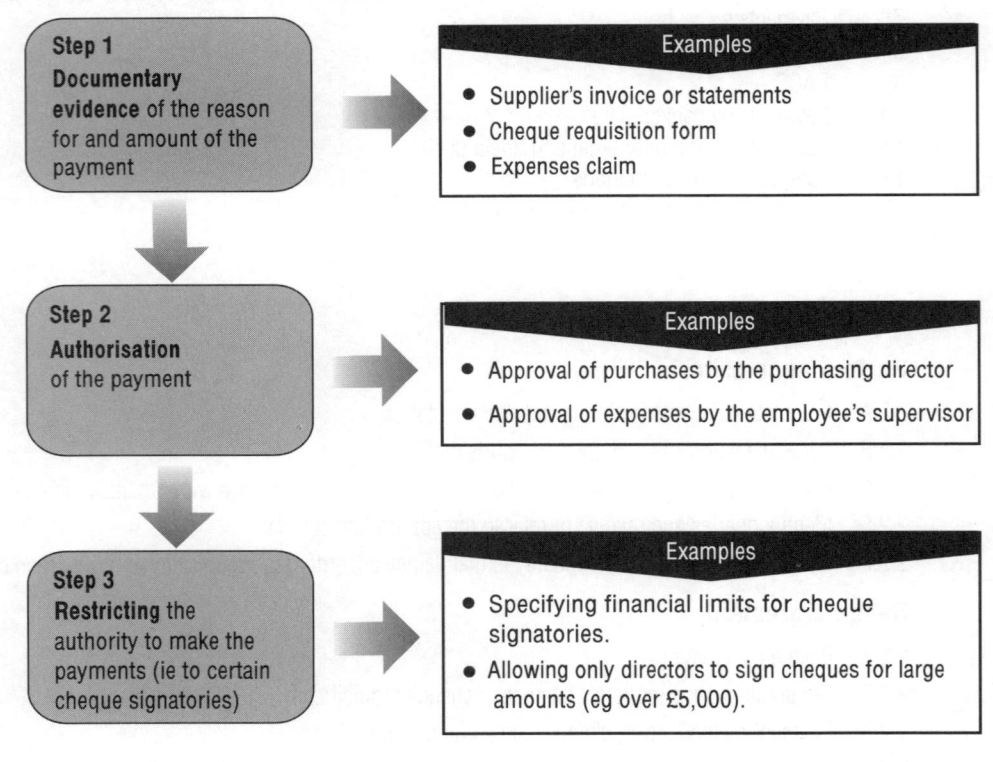

Step 1 Documentary **evidence** of the reason for and amount of the payment

Examples
- Supplier's invoice or statements
- Cheque requisition form
- Expenses claim

Step 2 Authorisation of the payment

Examples
- Approval of purchases by the purchasing director
- Approval of expenses by the employee's supervisor

Step 3 Restricting the authority to make the payments (ie to certain cheque signatories)

Examples
- Specifying financial limits for cheque signatories.
- Allowing only directors to sign cheques for large amounts (eg over £5,000).

Cheque signatories are the people authorised to sign cheques on behalf of the business. Specimen signatures are given to the bank, together with details of the financial limits applying.

Financial limits mean that certain people can only sign cheques up to a certain amount. For example, the chief accountant may be able to sign cheques up to £500. For cheques between £500 and £5,000, the cheque may need a second signature (say the finance director). For cheques over £5,000 only the finance director and managing director can sign.

Usually only the **accounts department** can make payments.

3 Controls over payments

The difference between the three steps in Section 2 can best be illustrated by an example.

Example: Controlling a payment

A company buys goods costing £5,000.

Step 1   Obtaining **documentary evidence**.

The supplier sends an invoice. This is the documentary evidence of the reason for and amount of the payment.

Step 2   **Authorisation** of the payment.

The invoice will be approved by the purchasing director. This approval is the authorisation of the payment.

Step 3   **Restricting the authority to actually make the payment.**

Payment will be made to the supplier by cheque. For a payment of £5,000, perhaps only the finance director and managing director can sign the cheque. Therefore the authority to make the payment is limited to these two people.

3.1 Authorisation

Every payment must be approved by an **authorised person**. This person will often be a manager or supervisor in the department concerned.

Every organisation has its own system to determine the following.

- **Which individuals** can authorise particular expenses
- The **maximum amount** of expenditure that an individual can authorise

As an illustration, the authorisation limits on spending in a company with three departments and a head office might be as follows.

PART C ACCOUNTING FOR PAYMENTS

	Departments			
Limit on expenditure	**Purchasing**	**Production**	**Sales**	**Head Office**
No limit	Chairman or Managing Director	Chairman or Managing Director	Chairman or Managing Director	Chairman or Managing Director
£25,000	Purchasing director Chief accountant	Production director Chief accountant	Sales director Chief accountant	Chief accountant
£5,000	Grade 1 manager	Grade 1 manager	Grade 1 manager	Grade 1 manager
£1,000	Grade 2 manager	Grade 2 manager	Grade 2 manager	Grade 2 manager
£100	Supervisor	Supervisor	Supervisor	Supervisor

A person authorises a payment by putting a **signature** or **recognisable initials** on the supporting document and the date. Supporting documents include the following.

- Supplier's invoice or statement (see Part A)
- Cheque requisition form (see Section 4 below)
- Expenses claim form (see Section 5 below)

Some companies use a **sticker** or **stamp** which they put on invoices received.

```
             INVOICE PAYMENT
              APPROVED BY

    Name ------------------------------------------------

    Dept ------------------------------------------------

    Date ------------------------------------------------
                                  Initials -----------------
```

When the invoice is passed to the accounts department for payment this makes it easier for the accounts department to check that the invoice has been properly authorised for payment.

Without authorisation, the accounts department should **refuse to make the payment**. The document should be returned to the appropriate department for proper approval to be given.

4 Cheque requisition forms

A **supplier's invoice** usually provides the documentary evidence of the reason for a payment, and the amount of that payment.

However, a payment may be required in the following circumstances.

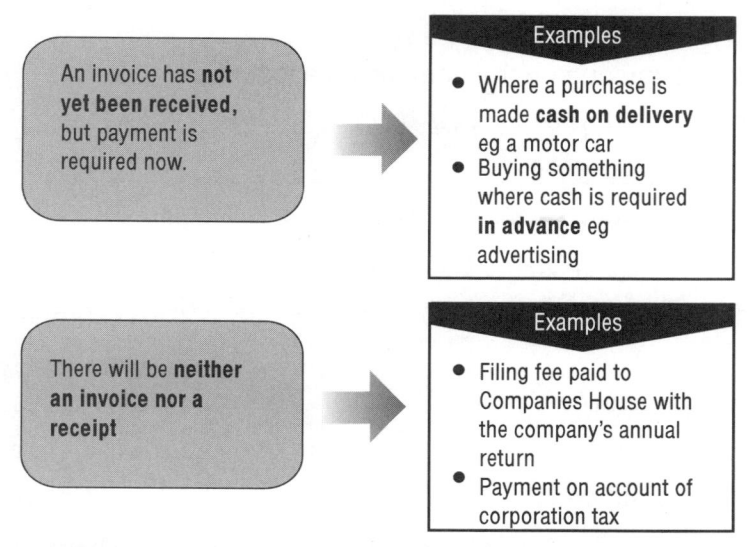

- An invoice has **not yet been received**, but payment is required now. → **Examples**
  - Where a purchase is made **cash on delivery** eg a motor car
  - Buying something where cash is required **in advance** eg advertising

- There will be **neither an invoice nor a receipt** → **Examples**
  - Filing fee paid to Companies House with the company's annual return
  - Payment on account of corporation tax

The circumstances where there is neither an invoice nor a receipt are very rare. They usually concern payments to the Government that are required by law.

Documentary evidence of the reason for, and the amount of, the payment is obtained by completing a **cheque requisition form**.

A cheque requisition form is an **internal document** for use within the business and so there is no standard design. The following example shows a typical layout.

Example: Cheque requisition form

The advertising manager of ABC Ltd wants to put an advertisement into the local weekly newspaper. The newspaper requests payment of £470 (£400 + VAT at 17½%) in advance, by a fax letter. A receipt will be sent later with confirmation that the advertisement has been inserted. The advertising manager needs to complete a **cheque requisition form**.

PART C ACCOUNTING FOR PAYMENTS

ABC LIMITED
CHEQUE REQUISITION FORM

DATE _17 JUNE 20X1_

Please draw a cheque on the company's account

PAYABLE TO _Popular Newspapers Plc_

AMOUNT _£470_

REASON _2 column 5 inch ad in 20 June edition_
of Morning Herald newspaper

Main ledger code (if known) _201/A01101_

Please tick as appropriate

Invoice/receipt to follow	✓
No invoice or receipt	
Other evidence attached	✓ _Fax letter_

Send cheque to _A Davies, Ad Manager, for sending on to Popular Newspapers ASAP_

Signature _A Davies_

Department _15_

Telephone extension _x326_

Note that no mention is made of the VAT. Input VAT can not be claimed until there is a valid VAT receipt.

This is the routine for preparing a cheque requisition form.

Action	Comment
The form must be **signed** by a person who can **authorise** the payment.	This might be the advertising manager personally or his/her superior.
The **main ledger code** is needed to record the payment in the accounts.	The code will be entered by the advertising manager or the accounts department.
Supporting documentation should be attached.	Here fax requesting payment.
The completed and signed **cheque**, will be sent to the person authorising payment.	This is the advertising manger. In some organisations, the accounts department will only send the cheque to the payee direct.
An **invoice/receipt** may follow.	Some organisations may insist on this.

Activity 13.1

Aroma is purchasing a second-hand van for making deliveries. Kris Anthemum needs a cheque made payable to Arthur Daley for £500. Arthur will give him a receipt for the payment, but there is no invoice. Today is 20 June 20X7, complete the following cheque requisition form. Assume that Arthur is not registered for VAT, and that Kris will hand the cheque to him on delivery of the van.

AROMA

CHEQUE REQUISITION FORM

DATE --

Please draw a cheque on the business's bank account:

PAYABLE TO: --
AMOUNT --
REASON: ---

Please tick as appropriate

Invoice/receipt to follow	....
No invoice or receipt	....
Other evidence attached	....

Send cheque to: --
Signature: ---
Position: --

Note that the format is slightly different to that used in the example.

5 Expenses claim forms

In many organisations, employees make **payments out of their own pocket for items of business expense** and then claim reimbursement.

- Money spent on **business travel**
- Cost of **newspapers or magazines** that the employee buys for business use
- Part or all of the employee's **domestic telephone bill**
- **Petrol** (for company cars)
- **Car service and repair bills** (for company cars)

PART C ACCOUNTING FOR PAYMENTS

The claim for reimbursement is made by completing an **expenses claim form.**

Proof is needed of the existence and the amount of the expense, and this is done by attaching **receipts**.

The completed form (together with attached receipts) is given to the employee's supervisor to sign as **approved and authorised.**

The form is then passed to the accounts department for payment.

An **example of an expenses claim form** follows.

ABC LIMITED
Expenses claim form

Name: C. PURVIS   Month: OCTOBER X7

Department: MARKETING

	Nominal ledger code	NET £	VAT £	TOTAL £
MOTOR CAR EXPENSES				
Petrol		49-20	-	49-20
Repairs and service		100-00	17-50	117-50
Parking		5-00	-	5-00
Car tax				
		154-20	17-50	171-70
OTHER TRAVEL COSTS				
(Specify) Taxi		12.00	-	12.00
TELEPHONE EXPENSES				
(Attach telephone bill)		24-00	4-20	28-20
NEWSPAPERS AND JOURNALS				
		12-50	-	12-50
OTHER (Specify)				
Stationery		5-80	-	5-80
TOTAL CLAIMED		208-50	21-70	230-20

Signature of claimant: Claire Purvis   Date: 3 Nov X7

Authorised by: ....   Date: ....

Notes

1. The form still needs to be **authorised** before it can be paid.

2. The nominal ledger (main ledger) codes will be entered by the accounts department. Sometimes codes will be pre-printed.

3. Receipts should be attached to the claim form.

6 The timing and methods of payments

6.1 When should payments be made and to whom?

Suppliers submitting invoices will usually grant a **period of credit** to a customer.

- 'Net 30 days' means payment is due 30 days from the date of the invoice
- Similarly 'net 60 days'/'net 90 days' allow 60/ 90 days from the invoice date
- Some periods of credit may run from the **statement date**
- Some specify the latest date for payment eg 'Payment due by 30 November'

If the invoice is not paid by the due date, it becomes **overdue.** The supplier will send reminders or make telephone calls to chase payment.

6.1.1 Who decides?

Decisions about who should be paid and when are made by a **senior person,** perhaps the chief accountant.

To help in this, an accounts clerk may be asked to draw up an aged creditors list (see Chapter 9).

Example: Who should be paid and when?

At the end of May 20X1, the accounts clerk of ABC Ltd is asked to prepare a list of unpaid invoices. She is asked to indicate which are overdue and which unpaid for over two months.

ABC Ltd's chief accountant will probably pay all the amounts listed in the final column.

Unpaid invoices as at 31 May 20X1

Supplier name	Credit terms	Invoice date	Invoice number	Amount £	Overdue or unpaid for over 2 months £
Archway Ltd	60 days	8.3.X1	32743	535.50	535.50
		15.4.X1	33816	421.80	
B A D Ltd	30 days	11.4.X1	9291	1,100.00	1,100.00
Bray Bros Ltd	60 days	8.4.X1	12534	125.55	
Chalk Ltd	30 days	21.3.X1	0135	245.75	245.75
		31.3.X1	0160	306.35	306.35
		2.5.X1	0297	281.00	
Finsbury Ltd	30 days	16.5.X1	546327	2,427.00	
Jupiter Telephones	-	18.4.X1	83461150	814.39	
Western Water	-	20.3.X1	2778045	650.72	650.72
Willow Ltd	30 days	16.4.X1	W248	173.20	173.20
				7,081.26	3,011.52

Miscellaneous (non-purchase ledger) payments will be made at various dates during the month as they fall due. However **purchase ledger bills tend to be paid at the end of the month.**

PART C   ACCOUNTING FOR PAYMENTS

6.2 Methods of payment

The following are the most common methods of **making payments** for goods and services, wages and salaries, rent and rates etc.

- Cheques
- BACS (especially for salaries and wages)

Other payment methods

- Cash
- Banker's draft
- Standing order
- Direct debit
- Company credit card or charge card
- Mail transfer and telegraphic transfer
- CHAPS

This chapter looks at the procedures for making payments by each of these methods. Small payments by cash are dealt with separately in Chapter 15 on **petty cash**.

Payments of **wages and salaries** are dealt with in Part D on payroll and are not described here.

7 Payments by cash

Cash payments are used quite often by a business.

- For **small payments** out of petty cash (see Chapter 15)
- For **wages** (see Part D)

However, a business should never use cash to pay **large amounts to suppliers**.

- Cash needs to be kept **secure** as it is easily stolen
- Cash can get **lost in the post**
- Difficulty of keeping **control over cash**
- No evidence of a cash payment, unless given a **receipt** (bad for record keeping)

Not surprisingly, the use of cash to make large payments to suppliers is often associated with dishonest dealers.

8 Payments by cheque

The most common method of paying suppliers is by **cheque**.

Cheques are for payments out of a bank **current account**. The accounts department will be provided with cheque books by its bank.

8.1 Security

The accounts department is responsible for the **safekeeping** of the cheque book(s). They should be kept under lock and key, perhaps in a **safe** and at the very least in a **locked drawer**.

Cheque books, or individual cheques from a book, can be stolen by someone to use fraudulently. To prevent fraud, only an **authorised person** should be able to order new cheque books.

8.2 Signatures on business cheques

A bank will not accept a payment by cheque unless it has been **properly signed**.

(a) Only certain **cheque signatories** can sign a cheque. Their names and specimen signatures must be given to the bank on a **bank form or letter**.

(b) Cheques above a certain value must usually have **two authorised signatures**.

(c) The authorised signatories are selected by the business itself, but can include the chairman, all directors and the chief accountant or financial controller.

Revise the legal aspects of cheques, including crossing and endorsements, in Chapter 10.

8.3 Procedures for preparing cheques

The starting point for preparing payments to suppliers, or other creditors, is deciding when to write cheques and **which payments to make**. See the next page for a step by step guide.

PART C   ACCOUNTING FOR PAYMENTS

Example: Cheque payment

Here is an example of a cheque for £1,520.75 made payable to H V Stern Ltd and crossed 'A/c payee'. It has been prepared on 6 January 20X9 and is a payment of invoice 12345. Cheques over £1,000 need two authorised signatures.

```
                    6 Jan  20X9      Southern Bank              6 Jan      20X9
                 To                   CHISWICK BRANCH                   20-27-48
                    H V Stern Ltd  17 HIGH ROAD, LONDON W4 6RG      SOUTHERN BANK PLC
                    Invoice 12345                                          or order
                                    Pay    H. V. Stern Ltd
                                    One thousand five hundred and twenty pounds 75p    £  1,520-75
                                                              A/c                       FOR ABC LTD
                                                             Payee
                    This   £ 1,520.75  Cheque No.   Branch No.   Account No.     J. B. Turner
                    Cheque                                                       W J Eccles
                    ⑈101129⑈      ⑈101129⑈   20⑆2748⑈   30595713⑈
```

> The **accounting procedures** for recording the payment in the ledgers will be described in the next chapter.

8.4 Discounts for early settlement

If a cash discount is taken, it must be deducted from the payment to be made.

Example: Cash discount

The supplier will indicate the availability of a **cash discount** on each invoice, but the method of showing the discount will vary. Here is just one example.

13: AUTHORISING AND MAKING PAYMENTS

Step 1 Prepare a list of payments due — For example, by a list of aged creditors. Discounts receivable may influence decisions (See Chapter 2).

Step 2
- Payments authorised
- Sufficient funds available

The authorised payments must not take the business over its authorised overdraft limit

Step 3 Check invoices to be paid

The accounts clerk finds the relevant invoices in the unpaid invoices file and carries out the following cheques
- Invoice is **properly authorised** for payment
- Main ledger **codes** are entered (if not, it should be done now)
- There is a **remittance advice** (either the supplier's own or prepare one now)

Step 4 Prepare the cheques
- From the information on the invoice
- Keep a record by completing the counterfoil (name, date, amount, etc)
- Follow any supplier specification eg cross cheque 'A/c Payee'

Step 5
- Attach invoice and remittance advice to cheque
- Pass to **signatories** for signature

- Attaching the invoice to the cheque provides documentary evidence of the **reason, amount and authorisation** of the payment
- Signatories carry out an **independent check** of the validity of the payment before signing the cheque
- Signatories also can check the remittance advice to ensure the payment is being sent to the correct person

Step 6 Mark invoice 'PAID'
- Detach invoice from cheque and stamp it PAID
- Record details of date of payment and cheque number on the invoice
- File for reference if queries arise

Step 7 Send off cheque with remittance advice
- Send cheque to payee with **remittance advice**
- Remittance advice gives details of what the payment covers
- Keep a copy of the remittance advice in case of queries

PART C ACCOUNTING FOR PAYMENTS

BANGLES LTD
Jewel House
Richmans Road
LONDON SE1N 5AB

INVOICE

Invoice Number: 123456
Tax Point: 01/08/X7
Account Number: 3365

CUSTOMER
ABC Ltd
112 Peters Square
Weyford
Kent CR2 2TA

Telephone Number 01427 123 4567
VAT Registration Number 457 4635 19
Northern Bank plc Code 20-25-43
Account Number 957023

Item Code	Description	Quantity	Unit Price	Net Amount
13579A	Deeks	30	250.00	7,500.00
	Delivery	1	100.00	100.00

Terms of payment are 30 days net. A cash discount of 2.5% is available for payment within 7 days.

SALES VALUE: 7,600.00
VAT AT 17.5%: 1,296.75
AMOUNT PAYABLE: 8,896.75

Settlement discount of £190.00 for payments by 8th August 20X7

Amount payable 8,896.75
Less discount 190.00
Amount payable if payment made by the month of August 20X7 8,706.75

Remember that VAT is calculated on the **sales value net of discount**, regardless of whether the discount is taken.

	£
Sales value	7,600
Less 2.5% discount	(190)
Net sales value	7,410

VAT at 17.5% of £7,410   £1,296.75

ABC Ltd's chief accountant decides to take the cash discount. A cheque is written and despatched not later than 8 August. The amount of the cheque will be £8,706.75, as shown at the bottom of the invoice.

The counterfoil of the cheque should include a note to indicate that a 2.5% settlement discount has been taken. The invoice will be stamped PAID with the date and cheque number. An extra note on the invoice that the 2.5% discount has been taken would be useful.

If payment is delayed beyond 8 August, the **full amount** (£8,896.75) is due.

If a **credit note** is due against the invoice, or has already been received, it should be deducted **before** the cash discount is calculated.

Activity 13.2

One of the major suppliers of Aroma is Avocado Co. Avocado Co offers the following terms.

30 days net
1% discount for payment within 14 days of invoice date
2% discount for payment within 7 days of invoice date

Aroma makes payments to suppliers on Thursday of each week. Although payment of invoices will sometimes be delayed (for example, if a credit note is awaited), it is the general policy of Aroma to pay within suppliers' terms. At each payment date, all invoices which will become overdue during the period up to and including the next payment date (the next Thursday) are paid. Payment is made by hand delivery of a cheque on Thursdays to Avocado's premises nearby.

Avocado has sent a statement of account to Aroma (with which Aroma agrees) showing the following details (amounts are shown before discount).

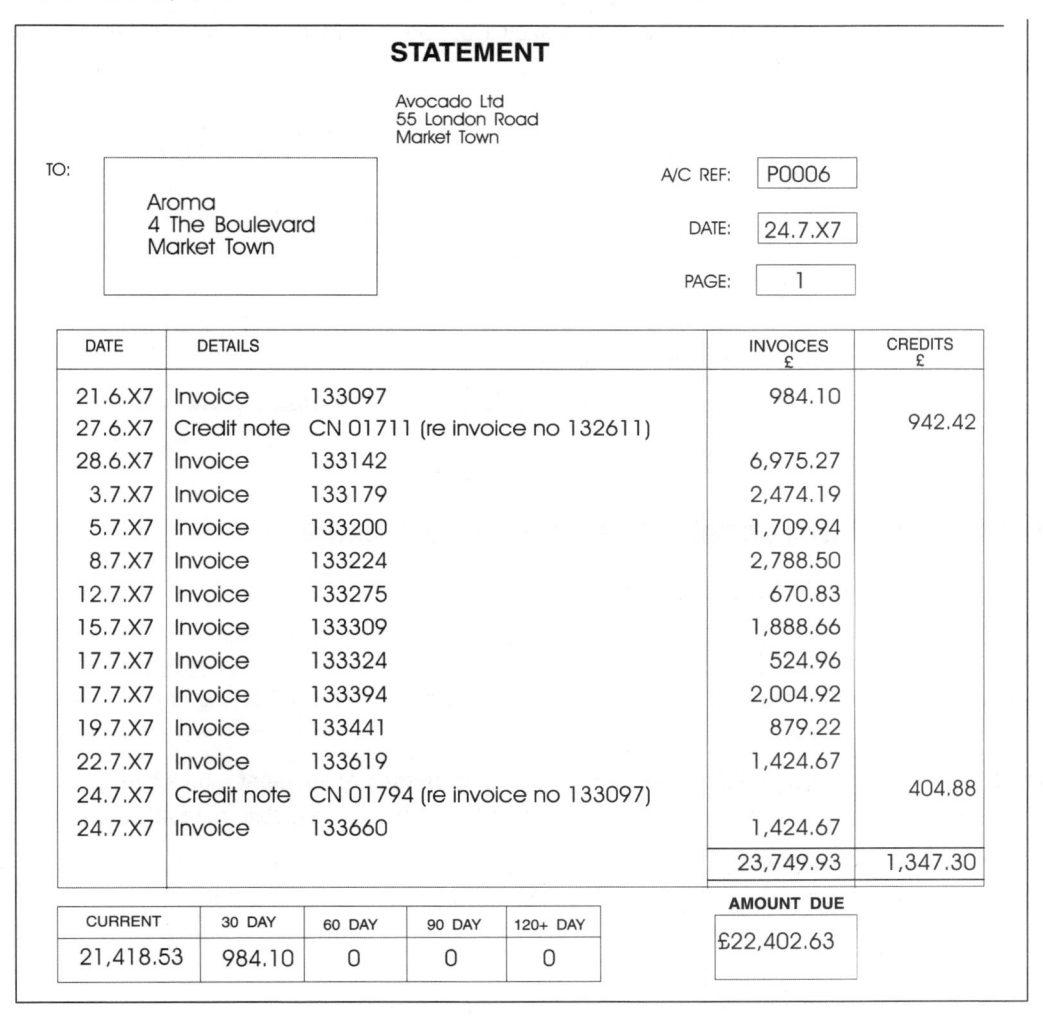

STATEMENT

Avocado Ltd
55 London Road
Market Town

TO: Aroma
4 The Boulevard
Market Town

A/C REF: P0006
DATE: 24.7.X7
PAGE: 1

DATE	DETAILS		INVOICES £	CREDITS £
21.6.X7	Invoice	133097	984.10	
27.6.X7	Credit note	CN 01711 (re invoice no 132611)		942.42
28.6.X7	Invoice	133142	6,975.27	
3.7.X7	Invoice	133179	2,474.19	
5.7.X7	Invoice	133200	1,709.94	
8.7.X7	Invoice	133224	2,788.50	
12.7.X7	Invoice	133275	670.83	
15.7.X7	Invoice	133309	1,888.66	
17.7.X7	Invoice	133324	524.96	
17.7.X7	Invoice	133394	2,004.92	
19.7.X7	Invoice	133441	879.22	
22.7.X7	Invoice	133619	1,424.67	
24.7.X7	Credit note	CN 01794 (re invoice no 133097)		404.88
24.7.X7	Invoice	133660	1,424.67	
			23,749.93	1,347.30

CURRENT	30 DAY	60 DAY	90 DAY	120+ DAY
21,418.53	984.10	0	0	0

AMOUNT DUE
£22,402.63

PART C ACCOUNTING FOR PAYMENTS

Task

Prepare two schedules, following the layouts indicated below, showing the payments to be made to Avocado on 25 July, 1 August, 8 August and 15 August in respect of the items included in the statement of account dated 24 July 20X7, conforming to the following alternative requirements. Ignore VAT.

(a) Payment is to be made as late as possible within suppliers' payment terms, irrespective of whether or not discounts are given.

Ref	Amount £	Due date (invoice date add 30 days)	25.7 Payment date £	1.8 £	8.8 £	15.8 £

(b) Payment is to be made as late as possible such that all available settlement discounts are taken up at the highest possible rate of discount.

Ref	Amount £	Best discount available %	£	25.7 £	Payment date 1.8 £	8.8 £	Ref

Any items which are already overdue should be paid on 25 July.

8.5 Advantages and disadvantages of paying by cheque

Cheques are widely used to pay for supplies and other expenses.

Advantages of cheque payments	Disadvantages of cheque payments
Convenient to use for payments of any amount.	**Security problems** in keeping cheques safe from theft and misuse (forged signatures), but more secure than cash.
Cheque number used to **trace payments**, in case of queries.	**Slow method of payment,** and a supplier might insist on a more prompt and reliable method, eg standing order.
Commonly used and **widely accepted**.	Can get **lost in the post**.

8.6 Lost cheques

The loss of the cheque will not become apparent until the supplier demands payment.

- **Check on the supplier's account** in the purchase ledger, to see if a cheque payment has been made
- If a payment was made, and the date is not recent (recent cheques might be in the post), the cheque is probably **lost or misdirected**

The following actions should be taken, when it appears a cheque has been lost.

Step 1 Confirm the cheque has **not gone through the bank account**, by checking the most recent bank statements or by telephoning the bank.

Step 2 Check the **name and address** to which the cheque was sent, and the name of any particular person to whom the letter was addressed.

One of three things will probably have happened.

Circumstances	Action to take
The cheque **has gone through your bank account** and the supplier has been paid.	The error is in the supplier's records. Give the supplier the details of the payment.
The cheque has been sent to the supplier, but to the **wrong person** in the supplier's organisation.	Inform the supplier so that he can retrieve the cheque.
The cheque has either been sent to the **wrong address** or has been **lost in the post**.	You should *stop* the cheque and prepare a new one.

8.7 Stopping cheques

Businesses need to stop payments of cheques quite often. Some even have a special form for sending stop instructions to the bank.

Sometimes the recipient of the cheque has forgotten to bank it until it is out of date. In this case, the bank should not pay the cheque anyway. However the cheque should be returned to you before a new cheque is issued, as a precaution against the bank paying it in error.

To **stop a cheque from being paid**, you should carry out the following.

Step 1 Telephone your bank with details of the cheque to be stopped.

Step 2 Confirm this instruction in writing.

An example of a 'stop' form is shown below. The accounts clerk will fill in the form, which will then be signed by an authorised signatory for cheques.

If the cheque has been stopped because it was **lost**, the supplier still has the right to be paid. A new cheque should be prepared and signed. Bear in mind the following points.

(a) The 'PAID' supplier's invoice should be **altered** to show the old cheque has been stopped, and the date and number of the **replacement cheque** added.

PART C ACCOUNTING FOR PAYMENTS

(b) Write 'STOPPED' on the **counterfoil of the old cheque** and the date on which this occurred.

(c) The **counterfoil of the new cheque** should refer to the supplier's invoice and indicate that it is a replacement cheque.

(d) The replacement cheque should be **sent to the supplier**, with a covering letter.

ABC LIMITED

3, The Mews
Barking

The Manager
Bank plc
6 Hill Road
Barking

DATE: 23 July 20X9

Dear Sir

ABC LIMITED ACCOUNT NO 2467890

We wish to confirm our request by telephone that the payment of the cheque detailed below is stopped.

Cheque No   009372

Dated   3 July 20X9

Amount £   4,276.83

Payee   A & P Plumb Ltd

We have inspected our statements up to number *493* inclusive and the cheque is not listed on them.

We have drawn a replacement cheque no: 00 9406

Your faithfully

M. P. Jones

FOR ABC LIMITED

Activity 13.3

At 7 October 20X7, the unpaid invoices/credit notes file of Keynes & Milton Builders includes the following items in respect of their supplier, Morton Bricks plc, supplier account number C1109.

Date	Details	Amount £
3.8.X7	Invoice 49492	142.91
24.8.X7	Invoice 50140	2,941.17
2.9.X7	Invoice 50311	642.54
4.9.X7	Invoice 50379	1,421.70
7.9.X7	Invoice 50411	6,997.21
9.9.X7	Invoice 50449	354.72
11.9.X7	Invoice 50457	3,428.88
13.9.X7	Credit note 7211 (re invoice 50114)	(864.75)
18.9.X7	Invoice 50601	824.79
25.9.X7	Credit note 7218 (re invoice 50379)	(842.05)
2.10.X7	Invoice 50888	1,752.94

All the above invoices have been correctly authorised by the purchasing manager.

The records of Keynes & Milton show that as at 15 October 20X7, the only payment made to Morton Bricks since 7 October was on 8 October. This payment was for £4,306.27.

The copy remittance advice shows the following details.

REMITTANCE ADVICE

TO: Morton Bricks plc
London Common
Wallsend
N24 4QP

KEYNES & MILTON BUILDERS
24 HURLE ROAD
HODLEY
NOTTINGHAM NG4 7SA

Account Ref: C1109   Date: 0810X7   Page: 1

DATE	DETAILS		INVOICES	CREDIT NOTES	PAYMENT AMOUNT
3.8.97	Invoice	49492	142.91		142.91
24.8.97	Invoice	50140	2,941.17		2,941.17
2.9.97	Invoice	50311	642.54		642.54
4.9.97	Invoice	50379	1,421.70		1,421.70
25.9.97	Credit note	7218		842.05	(842.05)
	Total		5,148.32	842.05	4,306.27

PART C ACCOUNTING FOR PAYMENTS

Between 7 October and 15 October, the following invoices were received from Morton Bricks. They have been authorised for payment.

Date	Details	Amount £
8.10.X7	Invoice 50991	408.00
	Invoice 51042	189.10

Keynes & Milton has received the following statement of account from Morton Bricks.

MORTON BRICKS PLC
London Common
Wallsend
N24 4QP

Telephone: 01794 424710
Fax: 01794 474770

Account number: 0995
Date of statement: 9 October 20X7

Keynes & Milton Builders
24 Hurle Road
Hodley
Nottingham
NG4 75A

STATEMENT OF ACCOUNT

Details		Amount £
3.8.X7	Invoice 49492	-142.91
24.8.X7	Invoice 50140	-2,941.17
2.9.X7	Invoice 50311	-662.54
4.9.X7	Invoice 50379	-1,421.70
7.9.X7	Invoice 50411	-6,997.21
9.9.X7	Invoice 50449	-357.42
11.9.X7	Invoice 50457	-3,428.88
18.9.X7	Invoice 50601	-824.79
25.9.X7	Credit note 7218	+842.05
2.10.X7	Invoice 50888	-1,752.94
8.10.X7	Invoice 50991	-408.00
Total amount due(-)		-18,095.51

Terms: 30 days net
E & OE

You work as an Accounts Assistant with Keynes & Milton Builders. You are asked whether there are any errors or discrepancies on Morton Bricks plc's statement.

Tasks

(a) List the apparent errors and discrepancies which you find in the statement of account.

(b) (i) Calculate the payment which should be made on 15 October 20X7 to clear all unpaid items shown in your firm's records as being over thirty days old.

(ii) Using the blank form provided below, prepare a cheque for signature to make the payment, crossing the cheque 'Not negotiable'. Assume that the payment calculated in (b)(i) has been authorised by the Chief Accountant and there are sufficient funds in the bank to cover it.

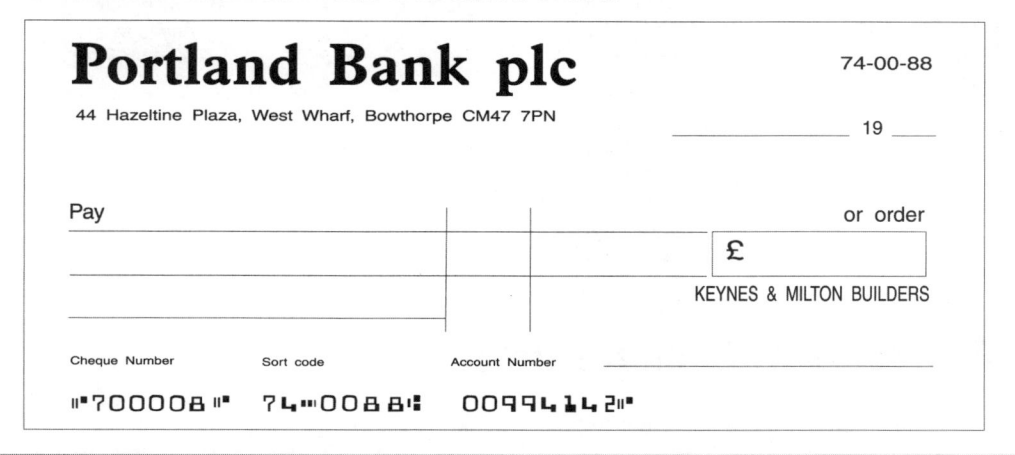

Portland Bank plc 74-00-88
44 Hazeltine Plaza, West Wharf, Bowthorpe CM47 7PN
_____ 19 ____

Pay _____ or order

_____ £ _____

_____ KEYNES & MILTON BUILDERS

Cheque Number   Sort code   Account Number
⑈700008⑈   74⑈0088⑉   0099414 2⑈

9 BACS

9.1 What is BACS?

BACS stands for **Bankers Automated Clearing Services**. It is a company owned by the high street banks which operates the electronic transfer of funds between bank accounts.

When a business uses BACS, it sends information to BACS for processing.

BACS is used for processing of the following.

- Standing orders
- Direct debits
- Salaries (monthly)
- Wages (weekly)
- Some one-off payments

Many businesses use BACS. Even small businesses can do so because their bank helps to organise the information needed.

The most important advantage of the BACS system is that it operates with **very reduced amounts of paperwork**. Large amounts of paperwork cause expense, delay and can lack a great deal in the way of security.

9.2 Procedures for using BACS

A company wishes to pay its salaries using BACS. The procedure is as follows.

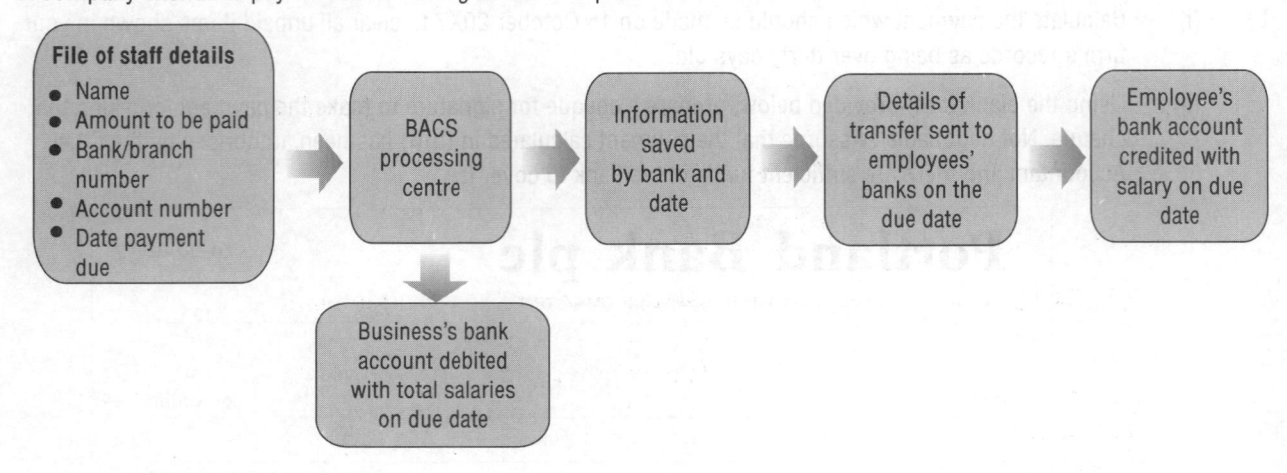

```
File of staff details          BACS            Information         Details of           Employee's
• Name                      processing    →    saved         →    transfer sent to →   bank account
• Amount to be paid    →    centre             by bank and        employees'           credited with
• Bank/branch                                  date               banks on the         salary on due
  number                                                          due date             date
• Account number                 ↓
• Date payment
  due                       Business's bank
                            account debited
                            with total salaries
                            on due date
```

10 Payments by banker's draft

A supplier can sometimes ask a customer to pay by **banker's draft**.

Unlike normal cheques, a banker's draft **cannot be stopped or cancelled after it has been issued** and so payment is guaranteed. Banker's drafts are only used when a large payment is involved, such as for the purchase of a car.

Example: Payment by banker's draft

One of your managers wants to buy a car from Fittipaldi Motors, for £33,334.45.

Step 1 Prepare an **application for a banker's draft** to be provided by your bank to pay the car supplier. Although applications for a banker's draft can be made by letter, banks also provide standard forms that can be used instead. A standard form is shown below, filled in by the accounts clerk of the business.

Step 2 **Signatures of (probably two) authorised officials** are required.

Step 3 The signed form is **sent to the bank**.

Step 4 The bank **returns the form to the business with the draft** (see below).

Step 5 The form is signed to **acknowledge receipt of the draft** and returned to the bank.

Step 6 The draft is then sent or taken to the **car supplier**, who will release the car to the business.

13: AUTHORISING AND MAKING PAYMENTS

Application for Inland Draft

To Swallows Bank plc

EDGWARE   Date _3.6.X8_

Kindly supply a crossed Draft. *~~Marked 'account payee'~~

Payable to _FITTIPALDI MOTORS_

£ _33,334.45_   amount in words _Thirty three thousand, three hundred and thirty four pounds - 45p_

*Please debit my/our account no

| 8 | 2 | 3 | 7 | 4 | 1 | 1 | 6 |

*~~Herewith cash to cover~~
*~~Herewith cheque to cover~~

Charges (if any) to be   *~~deducted~~/charged to me/us   Delete as necessary

Signature(s) _JP MACHUGH_   _B CLIVE_

Names(s) _JP MACHUGH_   _B CLIVE_

Address (if not a customer) _____

I/We acknowledge receipt of the above mentioned Draft number _123455_
Signature _____

(Tot be signed by an authorised person in the business and returned to the bank)

Swallows Bank
Swallows Bank Plc
Head Office
London EC3V 1AB

15-14-12T

Date _4th June 20X8_

Fittipaldi Motors Limited

the sum of _Thirty Three Thousand Three Hundred and Thirty Four Pounds and Forty Five Pence only_

£ _33,334 - 45_

NOT NEGOTIABLE

For Swallows Bank Plc
EDGWARE BRANCH
BR Dowding
SV Pritchard

⑈123455⑈ 15⑆ 1412⑆ 000345 6⑈

PART C   ACCOUNTING FOR PAYMENTS

11 Payments by standing order and direct debit

11.1 Standing orders

Standing order payments are used by a business to make **regular** payments of a **fixed** amount. Examples include the following.

- **Hire purchase** (eg an asset bought under an HP agreement)
- **Rental payments** to the landlord of a building occupied by the business
- **Insurance premiums**

Although the supplier (the HP company, landlord, or insurance company) may request payment by standing order, **it is up to the paying business to set up a standing order arrangement.**

The business must specify the following to its bank.

- It wants a standing order arrangement for **regular payments** from its account
- The **fixed amount** of each payment
- The **frequency** of each payment (eg monthly) and the due date
- **Banking details of the supplier** to which the payments should be made

If the business subsequently needs to alter the amount of each payment, or to stop future payments, it must send the relevant instructions to the bank **in writing**.

A standing order request can be sent in a letter, but banks also supply standard forms called **Standing Order Mandates**. An authorised cheque signatory will need to sign the request form.

It is likely that an accounts clerk will be asked to prepare the mandate form ready for signature.

Example: Standing order mandate

ABC Ltd buys some office furniture on hire purchase, arranging to make monthly payments of £240.25 to the HP company, whose banking details are as follows.

HP company	Smooth Finance Ltd
Bank of HP company	Barminster Bank plc
	Richmond-upon-Thames branch
	Sort code 22-33-44
Bank account number	11742538

ABC Ltd banks at the Weyford branch of Lowlands Bank plc, 5 High Street, Weyford, Kent CR1 1GG, account number 36274859.

The first payment is due on 15 June 20X4 and the final payment on 15 May 20X6.

A Standing Order Mandate would be prepared for signature as follows.

Standing Order Mandate

TO _LOWLANDS_ BANK

Address _5 HIGH STREET, WEYFORD, KENT_

Please pay

Bank	Branch Title (not address)	Sorting Code Number
BARMINSTER	RICHMOND-UPON-THAMES	22-33-44

for the credit of

Beneficiary's Name	Account Number
SMOOTH FINANCE LIMITED	11742538

the sum of

Regular amount in figures	Regular amount in words
£ 240-25	TWO HUNDRED AND FORTY POUNDS & 25 PENCE

commencing

Date and Amount of First Payment	and thereafter every	Due Date and Frequency
15 JUNE 20X7 £ 240-25		15TH OF EACH MONTH

*until

Date and Amount of Last Payment	*until you receive further notice from me/us in writing and debit my/our account accordingly.
15 MAY 20X9 £ 240-25	

quoting the reference _OFFICE FURNITURE_

This instruction cancels any previous order in favour of the beneficiary named above, under this reference.

Special instructions:

Account to be debited	Account Number
ABC LIMITED	3 6 2 7 4 8 5 9

Signature(s) _____   Date _____

*Delete if not applicable

The **reference** (ABC office furniture) will appear on Smooth Finance's bank statements. It will not appear on ABC Ltd's bank statement. A reference for Smooth Finance is not essential and is only supplied at ABC Ltd's choice. An alternative would be a reference **number,** such as the agreement number.

11.2 Direct debits

Direct debits, like standing orders, are used for **regular payments**. They differ from standing orders in the following ways.

- The **person who *receives* the payments initiates each payment**, informing the paying bank of the *amount* of each payment
- Payments can be for a **variable amount** each time and at irregular intervals

An example of a completed direct debit instruction follows. This is returned to the **supplier** not the bank. The supplier then makes arrangements with its own bank to collect the payments.

PART C ACCOUNTING FOR PAYMENTS

British Gas
South Midlands

British Gas plc (South Midlands)
Gas Payment Plan
Freepost
Coringham CV6 3TT

Gas Payment Plan Direct Debit Instruction

Instructions to your Bank/Building Society to pay direct debits

Please complete parts 1 to 5 to instruct your Bank/Building Society to make payments directly from your account.

When completed please return the form direct to us.

1. The Manager

| WESTLAKE | Bank/~~Building Society~~ |

(Full Address of your Bank/Building Society)

| 3 Great Way, Dudentry |
| South Midlands |
| DD1 1BC |

2. Name of account holder(s)

| LARKSPUR LIMITED |

3. Bank/Building Society Account Number

| 3 | 5 | 1 | 4 | 9 | 7 | 5 | 5 |

4. Sort-Code

| 6 | 2 | - | 3 | 1 | - | 9 | 5 |

Originator's Identification Number
916258

Instruction Number
Branch use only

Account Reference Number

| 00137200123468 |

Revenue Officer
British Gas plc South Midlands
PO Box 78
Coringham CV6 3TT

After completion the Bank/Building Society branch should detach this part of the form and return it to the address above.

I/We would like to start a Gas Payment Plan and have completed a Direct Debit Mandate

Please send the whole form to the reply address overleaf

5. Your instructions to the Bank/Building Society and signature

- I/We instruct you to pay direct debits from my/our account at the request of British Gas South Midlands.
- The amounts are variable and may be debited on various dates.
- I/We understand that British Gas South Midlands may change the amounts and dates only after giving prior notice.

British Gas South Midlands
Account Reference Number

| 00137200123468 |

- I/We will inform the Bank/Building Society in writing if I/We wish to cancel this instruction.
- I/We understand that if a debit is paid which breaks the terms of the instruction, the Bank/Building Society will make a refund.

Signature(s)	Date
R. C. Watson	8/9/X3
J. Keats	8/9/X3

- Banks/Building Societies may decline to accept Direct Debits from some types of account.

FOR BANK/BUILDING SOCIETY USE ONLY

Branch Title _____

Sort Code

A/c no.

A/c name

(maximum 18 characters)

Direct debits in respect of our customer's instruction under the reference number quoted should be made out as above.

Standing Order mandate cancelled. _____
Last payment made on _____
Standing Order mandate not traced _____

For _____ Bank/Building Society
Manager _____ Date _____

03/09/X3 DIST. 24

LARKSPUR LTD
12 BONNY STREET
DUDENTRY
SOUTH MIDLANDS DD1 2ER

00137200123468

Payments by direct debit include regular bills, such as telephone, gas, electricity and water. The company being paid by direct debit will inform the payer of the amount and date of each payment in a printed statement.

12 Payments by other methods

Other methods of payment will be comparatively rare and depend on the type of business involved.

12.1 Business credit, debit or charge cards

Some businesses have credit, debit or charge card schemes (with MasterCard or Visa, Delta and American Express or Diners Club respectively).

Under such a scheme, selected individuals within the business are given a card which they use to pay for their business expenses.

- **Limits** can be placed on the amount of spending on an individual card
- Cardholders will normally be **directors**, senior managers and **sales representatives**

Individuals using a business card to pay for goods and services, should obtain both **a card sales voucher** and **a receipt** from the supplier. These should be given to the accounts department regularly.

- **Receipts** are evidence of payment for Value Added Tax purposes
- **Card sales vouchers** are used to check the card company's statements

Every month, the card company will send a **statement of account** to the business. It will ask for payment **in full** and the payment will usually be made by **cheque**.

The statement will cover the period since the previous monthly statement.

- A summary of the **total amount payable** for all the business cards issued
- A statement of all the **individual items** of spending on each individual card

An extract from a **monthly statement** for a business card scheme is illustrated below.

(a) **The total amount payable**

```
DINERS EXPRESS Cards        SUMMARY OF ACCOUNT          Payment  Diners Express Europe Limited
                                                         Address  PO Box 22
                                                                  Bournton
                                                                  England BO3 1YR

        PLEASE CHECK THAT THE CARD IS IN YOUR POSSESSION.
        REPORT LOST AND STOLEN CARDS IMMEDIATELY
                ON BOURNTON 01234 456789

                                        PLEASE PAY THIS AMOUNT IN STERLING
    J J JAGGER                           £    1,427.58
    XYZ LIMITED
    13 BANBURY ROAD                     INCLUDES PAYMENTS AND CHARGES
    OXFORD OX2 8PB                      RECEIVED BY          03/10/X7
                                        MEMBERSHIP NUMBER
                                          3463-517420-64215
```

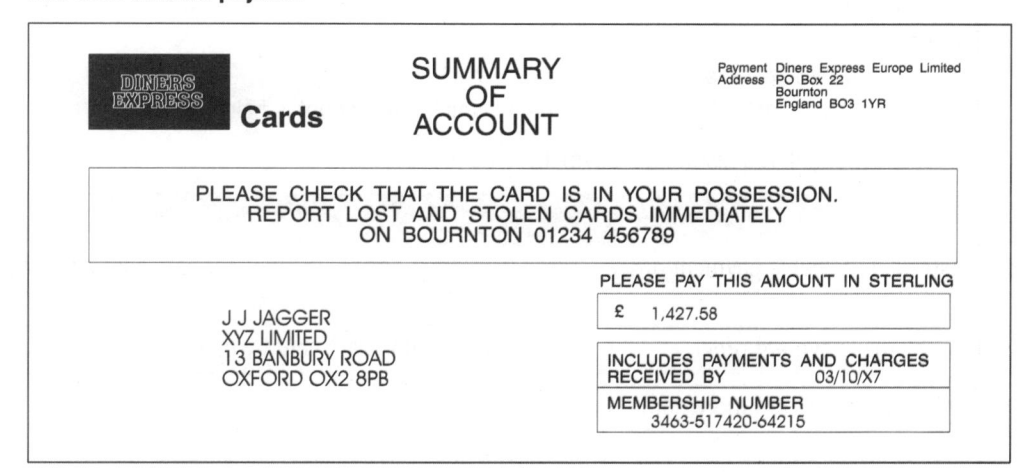

PART C   ACCOUNTING FOR PAYMENTS

(b) **Extract from listing of charges for each card**

```
                    STATEMENT OF ACCOUNT        Page  1
  DINERS
  EXPRESS    Cards                         PREVIOUS BALANCE
 REFERENCE                                      2,244.88
  NUMBER
 1354222   PAYMENT RECEIVED ON 15/09/X2 - THANK YOU    2,244.88CR
                   TOTAL FOR CARD 00
 1230652   MOLIVIANO UK LTD, HEATHROW, MIDDX            41.90
 1240672   BETTAPETROL UK LTD, OXFORD                   24.50
 1250672   SWIFT GARAGE, HEADINGTON                    325.15
 1420672   BISTRO SARTRE, OXFORD                        82.00

 PREVIOUS              NEW              NEW            NEW
 BALANCE  2,244.88  CHARGES  473.55  CREDITS 2,244.88 BALANCE 473.55

 Please quote your Membership Number 3463-517420-64215  with any query.
 You are welcome to telephone us directly on   PLEASE SEE OVERLEAF

 Cheque No _____ Date Paid _____          PLEASE SEE OVER
```

The **itemised listing** for each card should be checked against the vouchers sent to the accounts department by the cardholder. Any discrepancies or missing vouchers should be queried.

- With the **cardholder** to check whether he still has the voucher or he did incur the expenditure
- With the **card company** for any discrepancies

12.2 Payments by Telegraphic Transfer (TT) or Mail Transfer (MT)

Occasionally, payments can be arranged by means of an **electronic funds transfer** between the payer's and the payee's bank accounts.

Electronic funds transfers are made quickly and so are suitable in cases where a supplier wants **immediate payment**. They will only be used for **large** payments and usually at the insistence of the person being paid.

Electronic funds transfers can be to a payee in a foreign country, as well as within the UK.

When a business agrees to make a payment by a funds transfer, it should obtain the following details from the person to be paid (the payee).

- Bank name and branch
- Sort code
- Payee's name and address
- Payee's bank account number and the name in which the account is held

It must then write to its own bank requesting the payment to be made.

Type of payment	Details
Telegraphic Transfer (TT) or cable payment order	Instructions for the payment are sent from the payer's bank to the payee's bank by cable.
Mail Transfer (MT) or mail payment order	Instructions are sent by mail.

For payments within the UK, TTs are more common.

13: AUTHORISING AND MAKING PAYMENTS

The request for a TT payment can be prepared by an accounts clerk, but it must be signed by (usually two) **authorised persons**. Here is an example of a request letter.

ABC Ltd

112 Peters Square
Weyford
Kent CR2 2TA

Lowlands Bank plc
Weyford Branch
5 High Street
Weyford
Kent CR1 1GG

16 July 20X5

Dear Sir

Request for a payment by telegraphic transfer

We are writing to ask you to arrange a payment from this company's current account by means of telegraphic transfer. Details are as follows.

This company's account number	36274859
Amount of payment	£11,400.00 (Eleven thousand four hundred pounds only)
Beneficiary	T M Peters Limited 25 Crescent Road Canterbury CR3 1XX
Beneficiary's bank	Barminster Bank plc Broad Street Canterbury branch Sort code 45-67-89
Beneficiary's bank account no	38252849

in the name T M Peters Limited.

Signed on behalf of ABC Ltd

.... (R Griffiths)

.... (P W Border)

The bank will subsequently **confirm in writing** that the payment has been made.

12.3 CHAPS

CHAPS (Clearing House Automated Payment System) is used to transmit high value, guaranteed sterling payments for same day settlement. The transfer can only be done by computer and the security procedures are rigorous.

PART C   ACCOUNTING FOR PAYMENTS

Activity 13.4

Aroma has to make the following payments.

(a) £6.29 for office cleaning materials bought from a nearby supermarket.

(b) £231.40 monthly, which represents hire purchase instalments on a new van. The payments are due to Marsh Finance Ltd over a period of 36 months.

(c) £534.21 to Southern Electric plc for the most recent quarter's electricity and standing charge. A bank giro credit form/payment counterfoil is attached to the bill. There is no direct debiting mandate currently in force.

(d) £161.50 monthly for ten months, representing the business rates payable to Clapperton District Council, which operates a direct debiting system.

(e) £186.60 to Renton Hire Ltd for a week's hire of a car on company business by Kris from Edinburgh Airport. Kris must pay on the spot, and does not wish to use a personal cheque or cash.

(f) £23,425.00 to Selham Motors Ltd for a new car. Selham Motors will not accept one of the company's cheques in payment, since Aroma wishes to collect the vehicle immediately upon delivering the payment in person and Selham Motors is concerned that such a cheque might be dishonoured.

Task

Recommend the method of payment which you think would be most appropriate in each case, stating your reasons.

13 Documentation to go out with payments

When a payment is made, it is usual to send a document with the payment to show what the payment is for and who it is from. This document might be any of the following.

- A **remittance advice** either created by the payer or issued by the supplier
- An **order form**, when payments are sent with the order itself
- A **pro-forma invoice**, provided by the supplier for payments with order
- A **bank giro credit form** for telephone, electricity and other similar bills
- A **covering letter** when other forms of documentation do not exist

13.1 Remittance advices

The **remittance advice** should include the following information.

- The name and address of the customer
- The name and address of the supplier
- The customer's account number or code (as specified by the supplier) and/or the supplier code (as specified by the customer)

- The invoice number(s)
- The invoice amount(s)
- The invoice date(s)
- The date of payment
- The total amount of the payment

Remember that there are **two** types of remittance advices.

- Sent with the **supplier's statement** (eg a separate form, or a tear-off slip)
- Prepared by the **customer's accounts department** and sent to the supplier with the payment (with a copy kept for reference)

The example below is of a remittance advice **prepared** by ABC Ltd's accounts clerk for the payment of three invoices less a credit note. The total payment is £1,185.50.

ABC Ltd
112 Peters Square
Weyford
Kent CR2 2TA
Telephone: 01329 456272

REMITTANCE ADVICE

Rapid Supplies Ltd
63 Canterbury Road
Weyford
Kent CR3 6UX

Supplier code
603

Date of payment
8/9/X0

Invoice/ credit note date	Details	Invoices £	Credit notes £	Payment amount £
3/8/X7	Invoice 062074	375.80		375.80
10/8/X7	Invoice 063015	405.20	120.00	405.20
15/8/X7	Credit note CR2752			(120.00)
24/8/X7	Invoice 063240	524.50		524.50
	Total payment			1,185.50

Note. The supplier code is the code used by ABC Ltd to identify Rapid Supplies Ltd in its own accounting system.

The remittance advice is sent to the supplier with a cheque for £1,185.50. A copy of the advice is kept in the accounts department of ABC Ltd.

If the supplier sent remittance advices with each invoice and credit note, these should also be sent back with the payment. In this example, the letter posted to the supplier would contain the following.

- A cheque
- ABC Ltd's own remittance advice
- The remittance advice(s) from Rapid Supplies Ltd

PART C   ACCOUNTING FOR PAYMENTS

Activity 13.5

Aroma is due to pay (or claim credit in the case of credit notes) the following items in respect of two creditors. The date shown is the date of the invoice or credit note.

		Goods £	VAT £	Total £
Feathers Ltd (Ref F011)				
30.3.X7	Invoice 07114	74.40	13.02	87.42
6.4.X7	Credit note CR084 (re invoice 07101)	142.25	24.89	167.14
7.4.X7	Invoice 07241	248.71	43.52	292.23
9.4.X7	Invoice 07249	724.94	126.86	851.80
14.4.X7	Invoice 07302	141.17	24.70	165.87
22.4.X7	Credit note CR087 (re invoice 07241)	101.24	17.72	118.96
22.4.X7	Invoice 07487	421.00	73.68	494.68
28.4.X7	Credit note CR099 (re invoice 07114)	74.40	13.02	87.42
7.5.X7	Invoice 07714	98.94	17.31	116.25
The Furniture People (Ref F017)				
2.4.X7	Invoice 734282	3,742.28	654.90	4,397.18
23.4.X7	Invoice 735110	6,141.04	1,074.68	7,215.72
27.4.X7	Invoice 735192	842.92	147.51	990.43
27.4.X7	Invoice 735204	1,241.70	217.30	1,459.00
4.5.X7	Credit note 274221 (re invoice 732118)	942.41	164.92	1,107.33

The creditors' addresses are as follows.

Feathers Ltd, 247 Marconi Road, Chelmsford, Essex CM1 4PQ

The Furniture People, 4 Kane Street, Northampton NN3 4SR

The procedures manual of Aroma specifies the following cheque signatories.

Cheque signatories

C Taylor	Financial Controller
R Hare	Financial Accountant
J Mackie	Finance Director
B Mitchell	General Manager
J Knight	Managing Director
K Anthemum	Chairman

Two signatures are required on all cheques.

Cheques up to £1,000	Any two signatories
Cheques up to £10,000	Any two directors
Cheques over £10,000	Chairman or managing director, plus one other director

Tasks

(a) Prepare remittance advices for the payments to be made on 2 June 20X7 to each of the two creditors. You should use the blank forms provided below.

(b) Show the total of the payments to be made.

Aroma

**4 The Boulevard
Market Town
MT2 3AB**
Telephone: 01279 33942
Fax: 01279 33920

REMITTANCE ADVICE

Supplier account number

Date of payment:

Invoice/ credit note date	Details	Invoices £	Credit notes £	Payment amount £
....	....	....	....	....
....	....	....	....	....
....	....	....	....	....
....	....	....	....	....
....	....	....	....	....
....	....	....	....	....
....	....	....	....	....
....	....	....	....	....

Aroma

**4 The Boulevard
Market Town
MT2 3AB**
Telephone: 01279 33942
Fax: 01279 33920

REMITTANCE ADVICE

Supplier account number

Date of payment:

Invoice/ credit note date	Details	Invoices £	Credit notes £	Payment amount £
....	....	....	....	....
....	....	....	....	....
....	....	....	....	....
....	....	....	....	....
....	....	....	....	....
....	....	....	....	....
....	....	....	....	....
....	....	....	....	....

PART C ACCOUNTING FOR PAYMENTS

Activity 13.6

Carrying on from Activity 13.5, you establish that the following cheque signatories are available in the office today and tomorrow: R Hare, B Mitchell, K Anthemum and C Taylor. J Knight is expected back in the office tomorrow.

Tasks

(a) Complete cheques for the payments to be made, using the crossing 'A/c payee'.

(b) State what action you will take to get each of the cheques signed.

(c) State what you would do to the invoices and credit notes now that they have been paid, giving reasons.

Portland Bank plc 74-98-76
7 The Square, Bishop's Stortford, Hertfordshire CM23 1NP   20

Pay   or order

£

FOR AND ON BEHALF OF AROMA

Cheque Number   Sort code   Account Number

720088   74-9876   64196419

Portland Bank plc 74-98-76
7 The Square, Bishop's Stortford, Hertfordshire CM23 1NP   20

Pay   or order

£

FOR AND ON BEHALF OF AROMA

Cheque Number   Sort code   Account Number

720089   74-9876   64196419

Key learning points

- It is very important to apply **controls over payments**. Three key features of controls are as follows.
    - Documentation (invoice, statement, cheque request form, expenses claim form)
    - Authorisation of the expenditure item (passing it for payment)
    - Authorised signatures for cheques and payment instructions to banks

- A **cheque requisition form** is a request for a cheque to be drawn to make a payment.

- **Cheque requisition forms** are used when primary documentation such as an invoice has not been received. Cheque requisition forms help to ensure authorisation and recording of payments.

- **Expenses claim forms** contain an itemised list of expenses to be reimbursed to an employee.

- It is important to establish **proper authorisation procedures**, with each person in authority having written limits.

- A business will use a variety of **methods to make payments**. Ignoring payroll (wages and salaries) and petty cash, the most common and convenient methods of payment are by **cheque** and by **BACS**.

- Regarding **cheques**, you should know how to do the following.
    - Prepare a cheque for payment
    - Deal with lost cheques
    - Stop cheques

- **BACS** is a useful method of making and recording payments. It can save a business a lot of time.

- **Other payment methods** are often arranged at the insistence of the supplier.
    - Banker's drafts
    - Standing orders
    - Telegraphic transfers (TT payments)

- **Direct debits** are not often used for payments by businesses, but might occasionally be used for convenience.

- The **timing of payments** may depend on credit terms offered by suppliers, including **discounts** for prompt payment.

- A business should send proper **explanatory documentation** with all payments to avoid confusion. Copies of the relevant documents should be filed in such a way that the documents are easy to retrieve.

- The **accounts department** must carry out the following duties.

    - Make all payments and send these to suppliers with remittance advices.

    - Have a system for being able to trace each payment in the case of queries. (By writing the invoice number on the cheque counterfoil and the cheque number on the invoice. Stamping invoices PAID with the date of payment).

    - Keep a filing system for paid and unpaid invoices, standing orders, credit card company statements and any other documentation.

    - Record payments in the accounts (see the next chapter).

PART C ACCOUNTING FOR PAYMENTS

Quick quiz

1. What are the three main steps in applying controls over payments?
2. When might documentary evidence not be available for a payment?
3. A cheque requisition form is an internal document requesting that a _____ be drawn for payment. *Complete the blank.*
4. What is an expenses claim form used for and by whom?
5. Which methods of payment are most commonly used by businesses?
6. Cash can be sent by post. True/false?
7. What should you do to stop a cheque?
8. Which of the following statements about a standing order and a direct debit are true?

    A   Standing orders are for a set amount, direct debits can vary
    B   Standing orders are for a variable amount, direct debits are for a set amount
    C   Both standing orders and direct debits are for set amounts
    D   Both standing orders and direct debits are for variable amounts

9. When might payment be made by Telegraphic Transfer?
10. What is the document most usually sent with a payment by a business?
11. What does BACS stand for?

Answers to quick quiz

1. The three steps are: obtaining documentary evidence; authorisation of payments; restricting authority to make payments.
2. When an invoice has not yet been received or there will be no invoice or receipt.
3. A cheque requisition form is an internal document requesting that a cheque be drawn for payment.
4. Employees use an expenses claim form to obtain reimbursement for expenses.
5. Cheques and BACS are the most common.
6. False. It might get lost, and there would be no proof of the amount sent and no means of retrieving it.
7. Telephone the bank saying you want the cheque stopped and then confirm the instruction in writing.
8. **A**. Standing orders are always for the same amount, whereas direct debits can be for a different amount each time.
9. A TT is most suitable when payment of a large amount is required immediately.
10. A remittance advice is usually sent with a payment.
11. Bankers Automated Clearing Services.

Activity checklist

This checklist shows which performance criteria, range statement or knowledge and understanding point is covered by each activity in this chapter. Tick off each activity as you complete it.

Activity

13.1	☐	This activity deals with Range Statement 2.2.2 documents: cheque requisitions.
13.2	☐	This activity deals with Performance Criteria 2.2.A and 2.2.B.
13.3	☐	This activity deals with Performance Criteria 2.2.A, 2.2.B, 2.2.C and 2.2.E, together with Range Statement 2.2.3 payment method: cheques.
13.4	☐	This activity deals with Range Statement 2.2.3 payment method: cash; cheques; and automated payment.
13.5	☐	This activity deals with Performance Criteria 2.2.A and 2.2.B, and Knowledge and Understanding point 9: documentation for payments.
13.6	☐	This activity deals with Performance Criteria 2.2.C and 2.2.F.

PART C ACCOUNTING FOR PAYMENTS

chapter 14

Recording payments

Contents

1. The problem
2. The solution
3. Controls over recording payments
4. The cash book: recording payments
5. Posting cash payments to the main ledger
6. Returned cheques

Performance criteria

2.2.D   Enter payments into accounting records
2.2.E   Identify queries and resolve or refer to the appropriate person

Range statement

2.2.4   Accounting records: manual cash book; manual main ledger; manual subsidiary ledger; computerised ledger

Knowledge and understanding

11. Double-entry bookkeeping, including balancing accounts
12. Accounting for payments to credit suppliers, and to suppliers where a credit account is not available
13. Capital and revenue expenditure
15. Operation of manual accounting systems
16. Operation of computerised accounting systems, including output
17. The use of the cash book as part of the double entry system or as books of prime entry
19. Relationship between accounting system and ledger
24. Relevant understanding of the organisation's accounting systems and administrative systems and procedures

PART C   ACCOUNTING FOR PAYMENTS

> **Signpost**
> The topics covered in this chapter are relevant to **Unit 2.**

1 The problem

When recording payments, a business needs to know that:

- All payments made have been recorded
- No unauthorised payments have been made

If an unauthorised payment has been made (eg someone has stolen a cheque), then they will try to cover it up. The easier way to do this is by ensuring that the payment is not recorded.

Controls are needed to ensure that this cannot happen.

2 The solution

The main way of making sure that all payments are recorded is to carry out a **bank reconciliation**, at regular intervals.

A bank reconciliation compares the entries in the cash book with the bank statement. You will deal with this in Unit 3.

Other ways of preventing misuse of payments include the following controls.

14: RECORDING PAYMENTS

Fraud
- An unauthorised payment
- The nature of the payment to be hidden

→ **Controls**
- All payments are properly **authorised**
- **C**hecks are made to **supporting documents**
- **Segregation of duties** so that whoever writes the cheques does not record them
- Senior staff check the day's payments for **unusual items**
- A **minimum number** of cheque books used at the same time (preferably one)

Completeness
- All payments are recorded

→ **Controls**
- Only **one cheque book** used at a time
- Cheques are issued **in sequence**
- A **sequence check** is made on the cash book by a senior staff member (to ensure no cheques are missing)
- All **direct debit** and **standing order** payments are recorded in the cash book

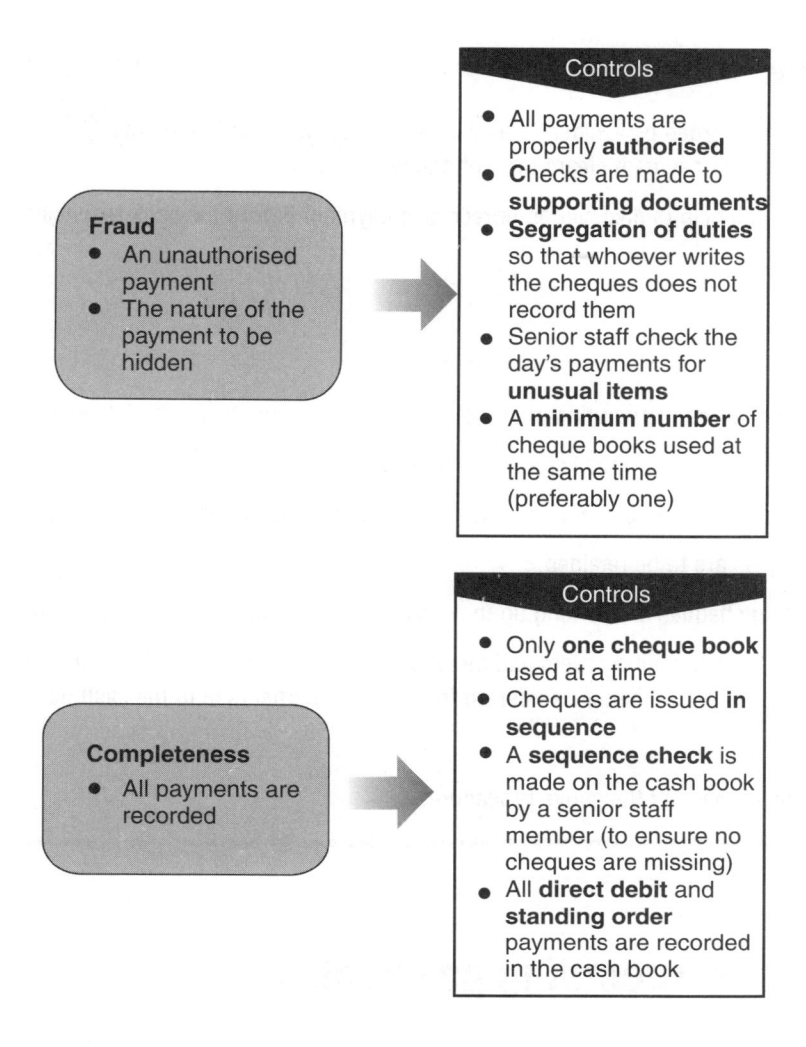

3 Controls over recording payments

3.1 Fraud

Someone who makes an **unauthorised payment** (to himself or a third party) will want the payment to be recorded, because of the bank reconciliation, but the **nature of the payment to be hidden**.

The controls in Section 2 will help to prevent this.

It is always possible that someone might organise an unauthorised payment and disappear before the inevitable discovery.

However most frauds are carried out over a period of time and involve relatively small individual amounts. Most people could not carry out a one-off fraud large enough to keep them for the rest of their life.

PART C ACCOUNTING FOR PAYMENTS

3.2 Completeness

If a payment has not been recorded by accident, this will become apparent during the bank reconciliation. It will only be discovered, however, when the payment clears through the bank account.

The controls in Section 2 will help to discover an unrecorded payment **before** the bank reconciliation takes place.

Activity 14.1

At Aroma, among the procedures in operation over the recording of payments are the following.

(a) Only one cheque book is to be in use at any one time.

(b) Numbers of all cheques are to be entered in the cash book even where the cheque is cancelled.

(c) All cancelled cheques are to be retained.

(d) The tasks of writing cheques and writing up the cash book are to be carried out by different people.

(e) Authorised details of all standing orders and direct debits are to be filed and the details of any such payments are to be agreed to the file before being transferred from bank statements in to the cash book.

Task

Comment on the reasons for each of the above procedures.

4 The cash book: recording payments

4.1 Analysing payments

The cash book is usually analysed into different types of payment. Different businesses will do this in different ways depending on several factors.

- **How many categories** of purchases they have
- **How often** they purchase goods in each category
- The way the business is **split up** into separate segments
- How **complicated** the cash book may become

In the example shown on Pages 372 and 373, there are columns for three different types of purchases, as well as sundry expense and capital payments.

Payments are divided between **capital** and **revenue** items.

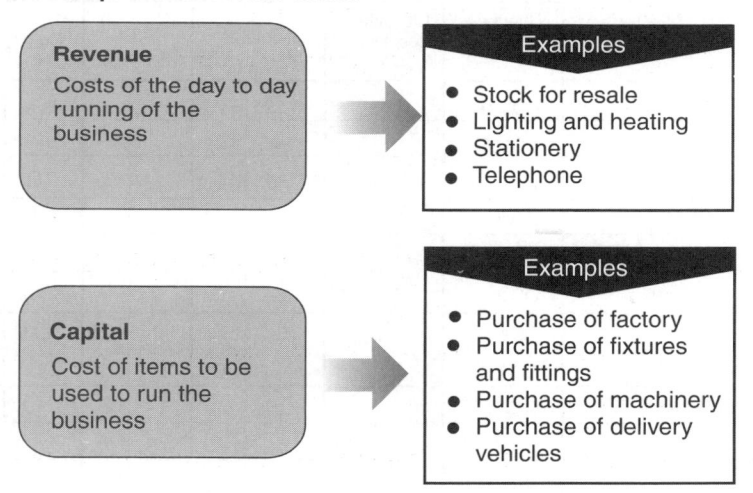

Revenue
Costs of the day to day running of the business

Examples
- Stock for resale
- Lighting and heating
- Stationery
- Telephone

Capital
Cost of items to be used to run the business

Examples
- Purchase of factory
- Purchase of fixtures and fittings
- Purchase of machinery
- Purchase of delivery vehicles

Discounts received are recorded in a separate column, a memorandum column which is not part of the cash book balance.

In a computerised system, the payments will be automatically analysed by means of the main ledger coding entered on the invoice (see Chapter 13).

Type of payment	Treatment in the cash book
Cash purchases	The columns for cash purchases are **analysed** by type, as this is the first record of the purchases.
Payments to creditors	These are not analysed as the analysis has already been made in the purchase day book. (See Chapter 4).
VAT	Input VAT on credit purchases is already recorded in the purchase day book. **VAT on cash purchases** and sundry expenses must be recorded in the cash book as it is **not** recorded elsewhere.
Cancelled cheques	These are entered in the cash book to allow a complete sequence check, and to make sure the cheque does not pass through the bank account. **Spoiled cheques** should be retained.
Extent of analysis	This cash book is analysed in detail. This is not always necessary, but it makes it easier to post to the ledger accounts.
Non-cheque payments	The **standing orders, direct debits**, etc are entered at the end of the page, even though some transactions are dated earlier in the month. This is acceptable and shows that this information is extracted from the bank statements monthly. The validity of all standing orders and direct debit payments must be checked against a **control list** (a complete record of all current standing orders and direct debits, maintained by a responsible person).

PART C ACCOUNTING FOR PAYMENTS

FEBRUARY - PAYMENTS

	Date	Details	Cheque number	Discounts received		Total		VAT		Creditors		Cash purchases - paper etc	
1	1/2/X7	Sharp & Co (creditor)	00349	222	96	4,236	27			4,236	27		
2	1/2/X7	Petty cash	00350			827	35						
3	4/2/X7	H E Co Garage - MD's car	Bnks Dft			22,460	00						
4	4/2/X7	Dye Light (creditor)	00351			327	20			327	20		
5	6/2/X7	Paper Press (trade journal)	00352			550	00						
6	7/2/X7	Sharp & Co (creditor)	00353	277	37	5,270	05			5,270	05		
7	11/2/X7	MRC & Co (creditor)	00354	111	58	4,351	44			4,351	44		
8	12/2/X7	Couinces (cash purchase)	00355			244	00	36	34			207	66
9	12/2/X7	Xerxes Ltd (creditor)	00356			2,372	49			2,372	49		
10	12/2/X7	Telecom	00357			327	40	48	76				
11	14/2/X7	Factory insurance y/e 15/2/95	00358			15,349	50						
12	14/2/X7	Ensa & Co (creditor)	00359			3,297	28			3,297	28		
13	18/2/X7	Oak & Elm Ltd (creditor)	00360			1,005	00			1,005	00		
14	19/2/X7	Post office (franking)	00361			220	00						
15	19/2/X7	Cheque cancelled	00362			-							
16													
17	19/2/X7	HCB's Ltd (cash purchase)	00363			347	20	51	71				
18	19/2/X7	Olivia & Co (cash purchase)	00364			199	90	29	77			170	13
19	21/2/X7	Viola Ltd (creditor)	00365			6,340	00			6,340	00		
20	22/2/X7	London Water plc	00366			4,729	80						
21	26/2/X7	Sharp & Co (creditor)	00367	245	78	4,669	80			4,669	80		
22	26/2/X7	Janus Ltd (creditor)	00368			379	46			379	46		
23	26/2/X7	Ermine & Trude (cash purchase)	00369			127	98	19	06				
24	28/2/X7	February salaries and wages	BACS			33,497	28						
25	4/2/X7	London Electricity plc	S/O			250	00	37	23				
26	7/2/X7	London Gas plc	S/O			300	00	44	68				
27	19/2/X7	Borough of Hackbern	D/D			125	00						
28	27/2/X7	Bank interest	-			273	94						
	27/2/X7	Bank charges	-			192	76						
		TOTAL		857	69	112,271	10	267	55	32,248	99	377	79

14: RECORDING PAYMENTS

Cash purchases - dye		Cash purchases - sundry		Bank charges interest		Light, heat and phone		Rent, rates and insurance		Motor expenses		Print, post and stationery		Wages and salaries		Fixed assets		Petty cash	
																		827	35
										120	00					22,340	00		
												550	00						
						278	64												
								15,349	50										
												220	00						
295	49																		
								4,729	80										
		108	92																
														33,497	28				
						212	77												
						255	32												
								125	00										
				273	94														
				192	76														
295	49	108	92	466	70	746	73	20,204	30	120	00	770	00	33,497	28	22,340	00	827	35

PART C   ACCOUNTING FOR PAYMENTS

Activity 14.2

State whether each of the two statements below is TRUE or FALSE.

(a) Cheque payments are recorded in the cash book only when they have been presented at the bank because it is only then that payment is made from the bank account.

(b) Standing order payments made by the bank should normally be entered in the cash book, but not where they represent payments in advance for goods or services not yet received.

Activity 14.3

You are involved in training some new members of staff at your firm on the recording of payments.

Task

Explain briefly each of the following terms.

(a) Cancelled cheque
(b) Stopped cheque
(c) Paid cheque

4.2 Three-column cash book

An alternative format for a cash book is the **three-column cash book**, which is found in businesses which do not bank all their cash receipts each day. They keep the cash in the till and occasionally bank some of it, the remainder being used to pay expenses.

The three columns are for cash payments, bank payments and discounts received. There are analysis columns, which together equal the total of the cash payments and bank payments columns.

Activity 14.4

On 4 May 20X7 Aroma's cash book showed a cash balance of £224 and an overdraft of £336. During the week ended 9 May the following transactions took place.

May 4   Withdrew £50 of cash from the bank for business use

May 5   Repaid a debt of £120 owing to R Hill, taking advantage of a 10% cash discount. The payment was by cheque

May 6	Sold £45 of goods for cash
May 7	Paid a telephone bill of £210 by cheque
May 8	Received a cheque from H Larkin for £180. Larkin has taken advantage of a £20 cash discount offered to him
May 8	Purchased £135 of goods from Honour Ltd by cheque
May 9	Received a cheque from D Randle for £482

Ignore VAT.

Tasks

Enter the above transactions into the cash book shown below.

The records should be totalled off at the end of the week and balances c/f. Folio numbers are not required.

Receipts   *Payments*

Date	Details	Discount	Cash	Bank	Date	Details	Discount	Cash	Bank

5 Posting cash payments to the main ledger

5.1 Manual postings

It is only when we **post the payments side of the cash book to the main (general or nominal) ledger that we can be said to have accounted for cash payments.** This is because the posting completes the double entry.

Remember that the cash account is an asset account. Payments out of the account will reduce the asset and so are **credits**.

The following steps apply to posting payments.

PART C   ACCOUNTING FOR PAYMENTS

Step 1	Add up all the columns.
Step 2	Check that the analysis columns (excluding the discount received memorandum column) add up to the total cash paid column.
Step 3	Identify the main ledger accounts by marking against the cash book account.
Step 4	Draw up the posting summary and post the main ledger.

Example: Posting the main ledger

We wish to post Robin Plenty's cash payments for 1 September 20X7.

ROBIN PLENTY CASH BOOK

Date	PAYMENTS Narrative	Folio	Total	Input VAT on cash purchases	Payments to creditors	Expenses	Fixed assets
20X7							
01-Sep	Creditor paid: Kew	PL543	120.00		120.00		
	Creditor paid: Hare	PL76	310.00		310.00		
	Telephone expense		400.00			400.00	
	Gas expense		280.00			280.00	
	Plant & machinery purchase		1,500.00				1,500.00
	Cash purchase: stationery		97.00	14.44		82.56	
			2,707.00	14.44	430.00	762.56	1,500.00

The entry for Hare should reflect a discount taken of £10, as only £300 of the debt of £310 was actually paid out. The relevant main ledger accounts are set out below.

```
                       CASH ACCOUNT                              CA01
                            £    |                                £
  1 Sept   Balance b/d  2,900.00 |

                 PURCHASE LEDGER CONTROL                        PLC01
                            £    |                                £
                                 | 1 Sept   Balance b/d     42,972.00

                         EXPENSES                                XP01
                            £    |                                £
  1 Sept   Balance b/d 170,249.00|

                           VAT                                  VAT01
                            £    |                                £
                                 |          Balance b/d     35,070.00

                       FIXED ASSETS                              FA01
                            £    |                                £
```

376

14: RECORDING PAYMENTS

DISCOUNT RECEIVED		DR01
£		£

Robin Plenty's amended payments side looks like this.

ROBIN PLENTY CASH BOOK

PAYMENTS

Date	Narrative	Folio	Discount received	Total	Input VAT on cash purchases	Payments to creditors	Expenses	Fixed assets
20X7								
01-Sep	Creditor paid: Kew	PL543		120.00		120.00		
	Creditor paid: Hare	PL76	10.00	300.00		300.00		
	Telephone expense			400.00			400.00	
	Gas expense			280.00			280.00	
	Plant & machinery purchase			1,500.00				1,500.00
	Cash purchase: stationery			97.00	14.44		82.56	
			10.00	2,697.00	14.44	420.00	762.56	1,500.00
			DR01 CR PLC01 DR	CA01 CR	VAT01 DR	PLC01 DR	XP01 DR	FA01 DR

Step 1   **Add up the columns** (see above)

Step 2   **Check the totals**

	£
Input VAT on cash purchases	14.44
Payments to creditors	420.00
Expenses	762.56
Fixed asset purchases	1,500.00
	2,697.00

Step 3   **Identify the main ledger accounts**. The folio references for the main ledger accounts are marked on the payment page above.

Step 4   Draw up the **posting summary** and post the main ledger.

PART C ACCOUNTING FOR PAYMENTS

			£	£
DEBIT	Purchase ledger control (420 + 10)	PLC01	430.00	
	VAT	VAT01	14.44	
	Expenses	XP01	762.56	
	Fixed assets	FA01	1,500.00	
CREDIT	Cash	CA01		2,697.00
	Discounts received	DR01		10.00

Cash book payments posting summary on 1 September 20X7

CASH ACCOUNT — CA01

		£			£
1 Sept	Balance b/d	2,900.00	1 Sept	Cash book	2,697.00

PURCHASE LEDGER CONTROL — PLC01

		£			£
1 Sept	Cash book	430.00	1 Sept	Balance b/d	42,972.00

EXPENSES — XP01

		£		£
1 Sept	Balance b/d	170,249.00		
1 Sept	Cash book	762.56		

VAT — VAT01

		£			£
1 Sept	Cash book	14.44		Balance b/d	35,070.00

FIXED ASSETS — FA01

		£		£
1 Sept	Cash book	1,500.00		

DISCOUNTS RECEIVED — DR01

	£			£
		1 Sept	Cash book	10.00

Activity 14.5

The payments side of the cash book for Aria Enterprises is shown on the following page as at 15 February.

The business has a memorandum purchase ledger for suppliers plus a purchase ledger control account in the main ledger. Relevant main ledger codes and balances are as follows.

14: RECORDING PAYMENTS

ARIA ENTERPRISES

PAYMENTS

Date	Narrative	Folio	Discount received	Payment total	VAT	Creditors	Salaries	O'heads	Fixed assets	Sundry expenses
01-Feb	Smallsoft Software	PL0054	110.00	2,090.00		2,090.00				
02-Feb	Mailhouse Ltd	PL0467		569.02		569.02				
02-Feb	Champagne (cash)			65.00	9.68					55.32
04-Feb	Stationery Box	PL0503	250.00	4,750.00		4,750.00				
05-Feb	Pacific Computers Ltd			32,894.00					32,894.00	
08-Feb	PR Reps Ltd	PL0004		5,501.40		5,501.40				
09-Feb	Champagne (cash)			19.95	2.97					16.98
09-Feb	Flowers R Us Ltd	PL0962	1.75	33.25		33.25				
10-Feb	BG (for 3 Spring Street)			178.99				178.99		
13-Feb	Window cleaner			25.00	3.72					21.28
14-Feb	Jan/Feb salaries			46,987.65			46,987.65			
14-Feb	CopyRight Ltd	PL0775		36.48		36.48				
15-Feb	Data Warehouse Ltd	PL0087		10,237.95		10,237.95				
	London Electricity (HO)			1,016.00				1,016.00		

PART C   ACCOUNTING FOR PAYMENTS

		Balance at 15.2
Cash	CAB 010	95,609.78 DR
VAT control	VAT 094	11,102.00 CR
Sundry expenses	SUN 490	567.92 DR
Fixed asset cost	FAC 020	272,972.00 DR
Utility costs	UTI 470	1,509.72 DR
Salaries	WAG 510	45,207.69 DR
Purchase discounts received	DIS 350	279.48 CR
Purchase ledger control	PLC 110	112,221.80 CR

Tasks

(a) Total the payments side of the cash book and identify the postings to the main ledger.

(b) Prepare a posting summary. Open up the main ledger accounts and post the relevant amounts to them.

5.2 Computerisation of payments recording

Cheques will usually be printed in batches or runs for convenience, on a periodic basis, perhaps weekly.

It is usual to obtain a printed list of the cheques issued as a record. The total amount paid will be shown on the printout.

- If a manual cash book is kept, then this total is entered in the cash book.

Date	Details	Cheque Nos	Total	Purchases
12.7.X2	Purchase ledger cheques	000375-87	£4,276.14	£4,276.14

- A computerised cash book will be updated automatically.

The print outs of the cheque runs should be filed in case any query arises, as they are probably the only detailed list of the contents of all the cheques.

The computerised cash book will be part of the double entry system, whereas the manual cash book is a book of prime entry.

Activity 14.6

Sisyphus Ltd is in the quarrying business. The company uses a computerised accounting system, in which the Bank Account (code 10000) acts as a control account. A manual cash book is operated in parallel. Receipts and payments are not analysed in the cash book.

On Monday 1 May 20X7, there are four creditor balances on the purchase ledger. All creditors are paid on the Wednesday preceding the week in which the invoice becomes 45 days old.

A schedule has been prepared at 1 May 20X7 of the invoices of each supplier due for payment at different dates in May 20X7. This schedule is set out below.

Creditor	Invoice ref	Invoice amount £	Payment date
ACM Crushers Ltd (A001)	20127	2,012.42	3.05.X7
	20134	7,018.00	10.05.X7
	20182	1,721.29	10.05.X7
	20242	982.00	31.05.X7
Benzade Ltd (B008)	B4241	101.24	3.05.X7
	B4921	94.27	10.05.X7
	B5288	172.19	24.05.X7
	B5298	242.17	24.05.X7
Gadd Ltd (G004)	722421	621.00	17.05.X7
	723724	92.50	17.05.X7
	723890	1,927.91	31.05.X7
Quaygate Ltd (Q001)	31427	205.00	3.05.X7
	31572	700.50	3.05.X7
	31591	401.15	31.05.X7

For payments to creditors, a single entry is made in the cash book for each weekly payment run.

Other payments to be made in the month May 20X7 are as follows.

(a) On the first of the month, the petty cash imprest is to be made up by drawing a cheque of £127.00 for cash.

(b) Payments are to be made where applicable under the following standing order instructions.

　(i) £192.00 on 15 February 20X6 and quarterly thereafter (six payments in total), in favour of Turnmead Ltd.
　(ii) £342.00 on 30 April 20X7 and monthly thereafter until further notice, in favour of Icarus Ltd.

(c) The month's salaries, amounting to £5,842.45, are to be paid by BACS transfer on the last Monday of the month.

Cheques are always drawn in numerical sequence. As at Monday 1 May 20X7, the last cheque which had been used was numbered 400601.

Tasks

(a) Show the payments to be made *by cheque* during the month of May 20X7, indicating for each payment the cheque number, date, payee and amount. (Deal with each creditor's payment in alphabetical order by creditor name as shown above.)

(b) List *all* of the payments to be made by Sisyphus Ltd in May 20X7 as you might expect to see them in the manual cash book, and calculate a total for the month's payments.

6 Returned cheques

Returned cheques are cheques which have been drawn by the business, paid, processed by the bank and then returned to the business.

Banks will return cheques on request, although they charge for the service. The cheque will have been processed and this means that the cheque will have the following additions.

- A 'crossing stamp' on the front identifying which bank and branch it was paid in at
- Encoded along the bottom with the amount of the cheque for bank processing

Advantages of receiving returned cheques

- Extra guard against fraud by checking the signature, the amounts and the payee on the cheque (someone might have altered the cheque after signature)
- Extra guard against bank error
- Proof of payment, if the supplier later queries this

Disadvantages of receiving returned cheques

- Bank charges for this service may become very high and so the cost will outweigh the benefit
- Large numbers of cheques are difficult and costly to file and store
- Queries where holding the returned cheque would be useful are very low; as long as the other controls are in place, then keeping returned cheques should not be necessary

Key learning points

- **Controls** over recording payments are important to avoid fraud and to ensure completeness.
- The **bank reconciliation** is the most important control.
- Analysis of payments in the cash book will help to control the expenditure of the business.
- **Posting** the payments side of the cash book to the **main ledger**.
    - Add up the cash book columns
    - Check that the analysis columns add up to the total
    - Identify relevant main ledger accounts
    - Draw up the posting summary and post to the main ledger
- Receiving **returned cheques** is not necessarily of great value for control purposes, although some businesses may find it useful.
- In a **computer system**, updating the purchase ledger for payments will usually cause the cash book to be automatically updated.
- Remember **BACS** is a useful method of making and **recording** payments; it can save a business quite a lot of time.

PART C   ACCOUNTING FOR PAYMENTS

Quick quiz

1 What is the best control over cash payments?

2 What other controls will help to prevent fraud involving payments?

3 Discounts received are shown in a memorandum column in the cash book. True or false?

4 Returned cheques are both a check against _____ and a check against _____ by the bank. *Complete the blanks*.

Answers to quick quiz

1 The bank reconciliation is the best control over payments.

2 Other controls include: authorisation of payments; supporting documentation; segregation of duties; checks for unusual payments; one cheque book in use.

3 True. The column is there so that the total amount owed to creditors can be posted to the purchase ledger, not just the amount paid.

4 Returned cheques are both a check against **fraud** and a check against **mistakes** by the bank.

Activity checklist

This checklist shows which performance criteria, range statement or knowledge and understanding point is covered by each activity in this chapter. Tick off each activity as you complete it.

Activity		
14.1		This activity deals with Knowledge and Understanding point 24: relevant understanding of the organisation's accounts systems and administrative systems and procedures.
14.2		This activity deals with Performance Criteria 2.2.D.
14.3		This activity deals with Performance Criteria 2.2.E.
14.4		This activity deals with Performance Criteria 2.2.D and Knowledge and Understanding point 11 concerning balancing accounts.
14.5		This activity deals with Performance Criteria 2.2.D, and Range Statement 2.2.4 accounting records: manual cash book; manual main ledger.
14.6		This activity deals with Performance Criteria 2.2.D and Range Statement 2.2.4 accounting records: computerised records; manual cash book.

chapter 15

Maintaining petty cash records

Contents

1 The problem
2 The solution
3 The purpose of petty cash
4 Security and control of petty cash
5 The imprest system
6 Petty cash vouchers
7 The petty cash book
8 Recording and analysing petty cash transactions
9 Recording petty cash transactions: VAT
10 Topping up the float, balancing off and posting petty cash

Performance criteria

2.2.A Calculate payments from relevant documentation
2.2.B Schedule payments and obtain authorisation
2.2.C Use the appropriate payment method and timescales in accordance with organisation procedures
2.2.D Enter payments into accounting records
2.2.E Identify queries and resolve or refer to the appropriate person
2.2.F Ensure security and confidentiality is maintained according to organisational requirements

Range statement

2.2.1 Payments: petty cash
2.2.2 Documentation: petty cash claims
2.2.3 Payment methods: cash
2.2.4 Accounting records: manual petty cash book
2.2.5 Queries relating to: unauthorised claims for payment; insufficient supporting evidence; claims exceeding prescribed limit

PART C   ACCOUNTING FOR PAYMENTS

Knowledge and understanding

11   Double entry bookkeeping, including balancing accounts

1.16 & 2.17
    The use of the petty cash book as part of the double entry system or as books of prime entry

1.21 & 2.21
    Petty cash procedures: imprest and non imprest methods; analysis

23   Methods of handling and storing money from a security aspect

> **Signpost**
>
> The topics covered in this chapter are relevant to **Unit 2.** However they also cover knowledge and understanding for Unit 1, as noted above.

Chapter 15 scenario – Aroma. This scenario applies to all the activities in this chapter.

You are the petty cashier at Aroma. An imprest of £150 is operated for petty cash, with a limit of £25 applying to individual petty cash payments. The imprest float is made up at the end of each week.

The office procedures manual states that you may authorise payments of up to £10, provided they are supported by receipts. Requests for larger sums and for payments which are not supported by receipts must be referred to the Administration Manager.

1 The problem

Petty cash means the notes and coins kept on the business premises to pay small expenses eg tea and coffee, stamps.

Although petty cash payments are small, they still need to be controlled.

2 The solution

Like all payments, the petty cash system needs controls.

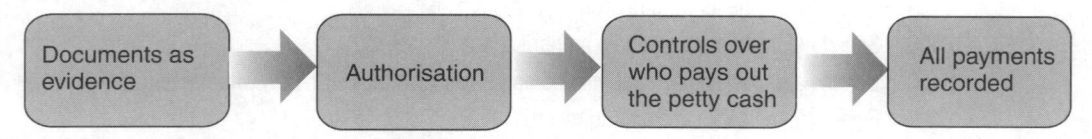

Documents as evidence → Authorisation → Controls over who pays out the petty cash → All payments recorded

As the amounts involved are small, the petty cashier may well be able to authorise small amounts supported by receipts.

For larger amounts and expenses with no receipts, authorisation will usually be needed by a third party, such as the Administration Manager or Chief Accountant.

3 The purpose of petty cash

3.1 What items are paid for out of petty cash?

- **Small** items of expense for which payment in notes and coin is required
- Many businesses **specify what** can be paid for out of petty cash
- **Informal system of judgement** by the petty cash officer or his supervisor

Here are some typical expenses, limits and recipients for payments out of petty cash.

Typical expense to be paid for	Typical maximum amount	Who directly receives the cash?	Who ultimately receives the cash?
Travel expenses of employee on official business	5.00	Employee	Travel company
Weekly milk bill	10.00	Milkman	Milkman
Items from local shop,			
eg tea, coffee	5.00	Employee	Shop
emergency stationery	5.00	Employee	Shop
stamps	5.00	Employee	Shop
Monthly office window cleaner	20.00	Window cleaner	Window cleaner

3.2 Who gets paid out of petty cash?

From the table in Section 3.1, payments out of petty cash for expenses go:

- To **employees** (to reimburse them for out of pocket expenses)
- To small **suppliers**, such as the milkman or window cleaner

Sometimes employees will ask for petty cash **in advance**. This may occur because they do not have enough cash themselves to pay for the item.

3.2.1 Watch out for casual labour

If **casual labour** is paid from petty cash (eg the office cleaner), the Inland Revenue will want to know. Your organisation could be liable to pay **National Insurance Contributions** (NICs) and **income tax** for this person, on top of their cash 'wages'.

Payments out of **petty cash for casual labour** should therefore be **sanctioned by an office manager**. The manager will need to record the name and address of the person receiving the cash wage, to satisfy Inland Revenue requirements.

It is best if all employees (even casual labour) are paid through the payroll system **not** petty cash.

PART C ACCOUNTING FOR PAYMENTS

Activity 15.1

Would you say that the items, amount and recipient below are acceptable for petty cash payments at Aroma?

Expense item	Amount	Direct recipient	Acceptable?
Portable air conditioning unit	£75.99	Sam Gardner, office manager	
Coffee filters for office coffee machine	£2.99	Raj Devi, PA	
Bunch of flowers for Valentine's day	£18.00	Orlando Orseo, Sales	
Metro ticket to Plastics Today conference	£2.60	Orlando Orseo, Sales	

4 Security and control of petty cash

4.1 The petty cashier

Looking after petty cash should be the responsibility of one individual called the **petty cash officer** or **petty cashier**. However a 'deputy' or 'stand-in' is needed when the petty cashier is absent on holiday, through illness etc.

The petty cashier has the following responsibilities.

- Ensure the cash is **held in a safe place**
- **Make the actual payments of cash**
- Ensure that all **payments are properly authorised** and are for **valid reasons**
- Ensure that all payments are **recorded**

4.2 The petty cash box

Petty cash must be kept **secure**. It is usual to keep it in a lockable box or tin.

The box or tin is then kept in a locked drawer or the office safe. The key to the petty cash box (and the key to the desk drawer) will be held by the petty cashier.

No one should be allowed access to the petty cash box except the petty cashier, the 'deputy' and the office supervisor.

In some offices, you will find that more individuals have access to petty cash. This is poor office practice because it encourages a lack of proper control and security for cash.

4.3 Why are only small items paid for out of petty cash?

Petty cash should not be used for large expenses, such as office furniture, large restaurant bills or aeroplane tickets because of **security**.

- A large amount of cash is an obvious target for theft
- Payments of large items from petty cash could be abused

4.4 Limiting the size of petty cash payments

There should be a **maximum limit** to the amount of any individual payment. For example, an organisation might have a £40.00 limit. Requests for larger payments should be refused by the petty cashier.

Larger payments can be obtained by another method.

- An employee should submit an **expenses claim** or **cheque request form**
- An external supplier (eg the milkman or window cleaner) should submit **invoices** for payment by cheque

4.5 Authorisation and authorisation limits

Payments out of petty cash should be **properly authorised by the appropriate person.**

- The petty cashier can authorise individual payments up to a certain limit, say £20.00, but only if a receipt is provided
- For larger amounts up to the petty cash limit, the authorisation should be by the petty cashier's supervisor
- Exceptionally, a petty cash payment in excess of the maximum limit might be permitted, subject to authorisation by a nominated senior person

4.6 Receipts

A request for payment out of petty cash should be supported by a **receipt**, as proof of purchase.

The receipt might simply be a till roll, showing the name of the shop or supplier and the amount of the payment. It is good practice to write down the nature of the item purchased on the receipt, if it does not show this already.

4.6.1 VAT receipts

If VAT has been paid, which can be reclaimed from Customs & Excise, a **VAT receipt** is needed showing these details.

- The total payment
- The VAT paid (not essential, the petty cashier can calculate the VAT)
- The supplier's name, address and VAT registration number
- The date of the transaction

Customs & Excise do allow VAT to be reclaimed in cases where the total amount (including VAT) is **£25 or less, without a VAT invoice.**

- Telephone calls from public or private telephones
- Purchases through coin-operated machines

PART C   ACCOUNTING FOR PAYMENTS

- Car park charges
- Single or return toll charges

4.6.2 No available receipts

Sometimes petty cash claims will be submitted without a receipt, eg travelling expenses. Employees are not always required to provide proof of a taxi, bus or train fare.

However, the payment should be sanctioned by an authorised person, eg by the supervisor or manager of the individual concerned.

Activity 15.2

Orlando Orseo suggests that it would be much more convenient if you could leave an amount, say £30, in a 'kitty box' by Reception. Then employees who are short of cash for parking meters, phones or Metro fares could 'dip in' without all 'that receipt fuss'. Outline for him why this is not such a good idea.

Activity 15.3

Raj Devi brings you the following petty cash claims. Which can you pay immediately and which need further action?

(a) £22.00 train travel to a conference, which has not been authorised by the Administration Manager.
(b) £5.20 spent on tea bags, supported by a valid receipt.
(c) £30.00 taxi fare, authorised by the Administration Manager.
(d) £6.25 biscuits for the office, supported by a valid receipt.
(e) £20.00 stationery, with no receipt but authorised by the Administration Manager.
(f) £11.99 spent on office milk, with a valid receipt.
(g) £2.20 spent on postage stamps, with no receipt.

5 The imprest system

5.1 What is an imprest system

The **imprest system** has a maximum amount of money in petty cash, the imprest amount. The imprest amount varies from one organisation to another, and might be enough to make petty cash payments for about one month.

Example: Imprest system

The maximum amount for petty cash in company A is £500.00. At the start of the month, the petty cash box contains this amount. As payments are made out of petty cash, the amount of cash left will diminish. Eventually the petty cashier will decide that petty cash needs to be 'topped up' again to the imprest amount of £500.00.

5.2 Topping up

Topping up petty cash can occur whenever the need arises. However, it is usually done regularly, once each week or once each month.

In order to top up petty cash to the imprest amount, cash is drawn from the bank equal to the amount of petty cash payments.

We will cover the procedure for topping up in Section 10 of this chapter. However an example follows to illustrate the method.

Example: Topping up the imprest

		£
1 May	Imprest amount	1,000.00
1-31 May	Petty cash payments (total of 57 receipts)	(826.40)
31 May	Petty cash in tin at month end	173.60
31 May	Top up drawn from bank (equal to receipts)	826.40
31 May	Restored imprest amount	1,000.00

In a non-imprest system the petty cash is topped up to any amount without reference to the petty cash vouchers. The maximum amount of petty cash can vary from month to month depending on likely expenditure; for example £300 January, £150 February, £250 March.

Activity 15.4

You have the following vouchers in the petty cash box at 30 November. By how much should the balance in the box be topped up?

Date	Expense	Amount £
3 November	Tea bags	1.99
6 November	Light bulbs	5.99
11 November	Train fare	10.50
17 November	Teapot and cups	24.99
22 November	Desk lamp	19.99
25 November	Stamps book	10.00

PART C ACCOUNTING FOR PAYMENTS

6 Petty cash vouchers

6.1 Vouchers

The initial record of payment is the **petty cash voucher**.

A voucher must be prepared whenever a payment is requested. The receipt(s) should be firmly attached to the voucher.

When completed, a voucher should contain the following details.

- (a) **Details** of the purpose for which the money was spent
- (b) The **amount(s)** paid
- (c) The **name of the person receiving the cash** (who should acknowledge receipt by signing the voucher)
- (d) The **signature** of the person authorising the payment
- (e) The **date** of payment
- (f) The **number** of the voucher (see Paragraph 6.8 below)
- (g) The relevant **receipt(s)** stapled to it

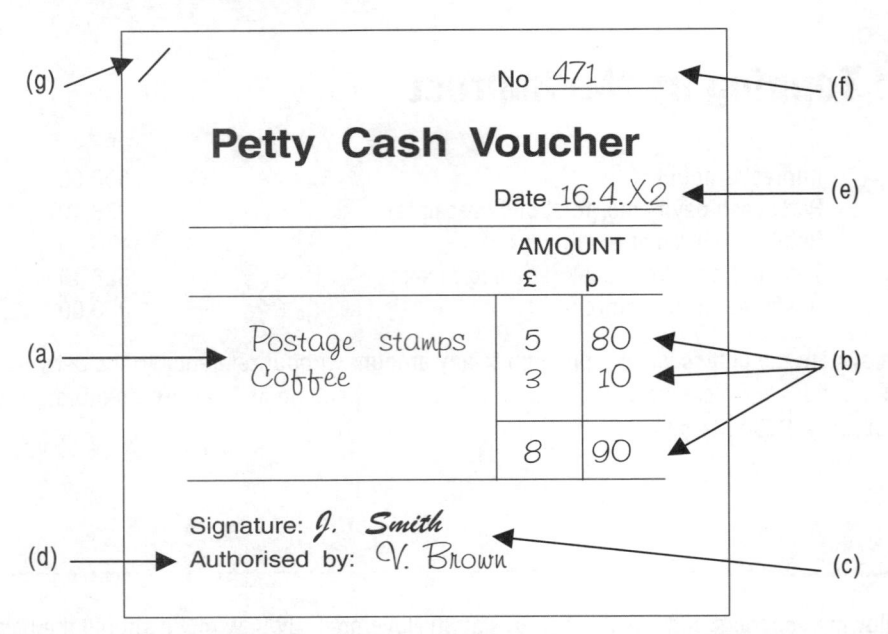

Petty Cash Voucher

No 471 (f)
Date 16.4.X2 (e)

	AMOUNT £	p
Postage stamps	5	80
Coffee	3	10
	8	90

Signature: J. Smith
Authorised by: V. Brown

(g) (a) (b) (d) (c)

J Smith should give the petty cashier a receipt for the coffee. There should also be some evidence of purchase of the stamps (a receipt from the shop or Post Office).

Otherwise she will need a note from her manager confirming that the stamps have been obtained for office, not personal, use.

Example: Petty cash vouchers

The petty cash system in company B provides for a maximum individual payment of £100.00. The petty cashier can authorise individual payments up to £25.00. Payments between £25.00 and £100.00 must be authorised by the accounts supervisor, R Greene. On 18 December 20X2 a petty cash claim is made for expenses for an office Christmas party. Receipts from a supermarket for food and drink total £82.56. Payment is to be made to the office manager, D Porter.

The petty cashier writes out the voucher. However the supervisor R Greene must sign the voucher to authorise payment.

The petty cash voucher (not yet given its voucher number) would be as follows.

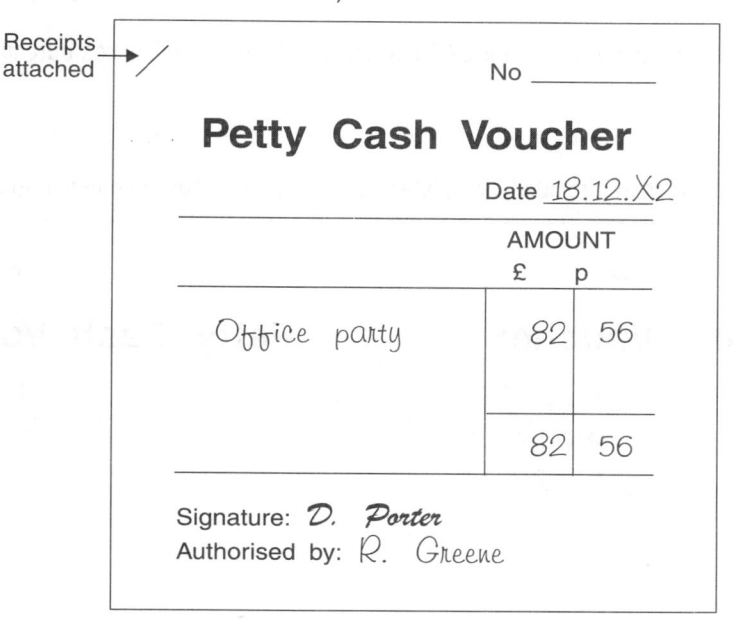

```
Receipts attached ──►  ✓                          No _____

                    Petty Cash Voucher
                                        Date  18.12.X2
                                        ─────────────────
                                             AMOUNT
                                           £        p

                    Office party         82     56

                                         82     56

                    Signature:  D. Porter
                    Authorised by:  R. Greene
```

6.2 Voucher numbers

Every petty cash voucher is given a **unique voucher number**. They are numbered in sequence, starting at 1. Usually the number sequence restarts from 1 with the first voucher **each year**.

Numbering the vouchers allows the following checks.

- Vouchers traced from the petty cash book to where they are **filed**
- **Completeness check** to ensure no vouchers are missing or not recorded

The voucher's number is inserted at either of the following stages.

- When the payment is made
- When the vouchers are used to write up the petty cash book (Section 7)

After payment has been made, the completed voucher is attached securely to the relevant receipt(s) and put in the petty cash box. It is kept in the petty cash box until the next 'top up' to the imprest amount.

After the 'top up', the vouchers should be filed for future reference.

PART C ACCOUNTING FOR PAYMENTS

Activity 15.5

On Monday 14 December 20X7 you receive the following requests for reimbursement. The last voucher used the previous week was numbered 100.

(a) The receptionist, Mrs A Clarke, produces a receipt for postage stamps purchased for office use to the value of £6.25.

(b) The sales manager produces a receipt for £7.50 in respect of a return rail ticket, purchased in order to visit a customer.

Task

Using the blank petty cash vouchers provided, complete vouchers for the above two items. Ignore VAT.

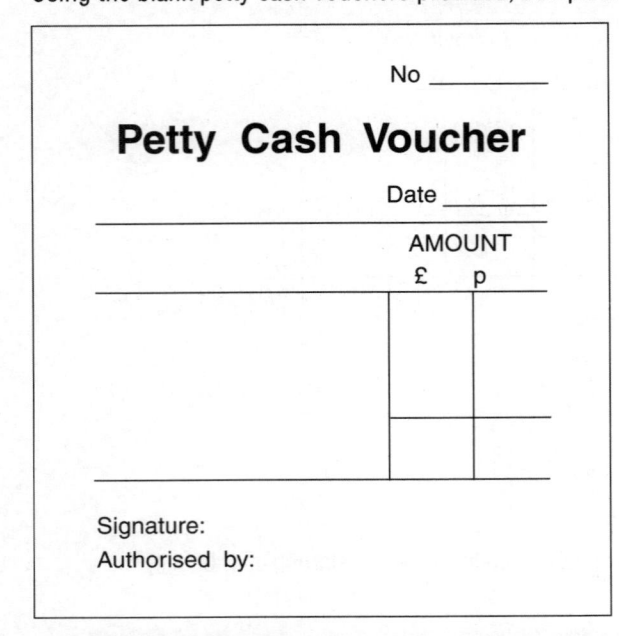

	No _____
Petty Cash Voucher	
Date _____	
	AMOUNT
	£ p
Signature:	
Authorised by:	

	No _____
Petty Cash Voucher	
Date _____	
	AMOUNT
	£ p
Signature:	
Authorised by:	

6.3 Petty cash payments for expenses not yet incurred

There will be occasions when someone needs a petty cash advance.

(a) **Payments in advance** must be authorised by a supervisor or office manager.

(b) The petty cashier writes out a petty cash voucher marked 'cash advance' and gets the recipient's signature.

(c) When the receipt and the change are eventually received, the petty cashier should **alter the voucher** to show the exact amount of the payment.

Example: Petty cash advances

A director of company C needs money to pay for a taxi and asks for £20.00 from petty cash on 5 July 20X0. The payment is sanctioned by the accounts supervisor, T Roberts. The next day, the director returns with a taxi cab receipt for £15.50 and gives back change of £4.50.

The petty cash voucher should be prepared initially as follows.

```
                                        No _____
            Petty Cash Voucher
                                  Date  5.7.X0
                                    AMOUNT
                                    £      p
     Taxi fare                     20    00
     (CASH ADVANCE)

                                   20    00

     Signature: P. Perkins (Director)
     Authorised by: T. Roberts
```

On 6 July the original voucher is altered by the petty cashier.

```
                                        No _____
            Petty Cash Voucher
                                  Date  5.7.X0
                                    AMOUNT
                                    £      p
     Taxi fare                     2̶0̶   0̶0̶
     (C̶A̶S̶H̶ A̶D̶V̶A̶N̶C̶E̶)             15    50

                                   2̶0̶   0̶0̶
                                   15    50

     Signature: P. Perkins (Director)
     Authorised by: T. Roberts
```

PART C ACCOUNTING FOR PAYMENTS

The change is put into the petty cash box, together with the amended voucher and (attached to the voucher) the receipt. However, if a further amount is required, then either a new voucher is prepared or the old voucher amended to show that the **adjusted figure is authorised**.

6.4 Checks on petty cash and vouchers

Each week, the petty cashier may make a large number of payments. For security and control reasons, there ought to be **regular checks** on the following.

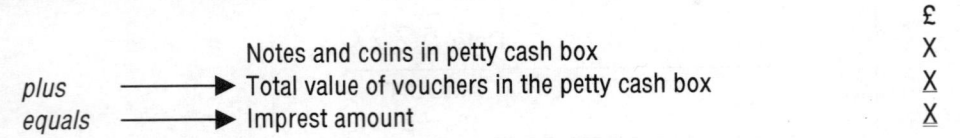

		£
	Notes and coins in petty cash box	X
plus →	Total value of vouchers in the petty cash box	X
equals →	Imprest amount	X

If the amount of cash plus the value of the vouchers does **not** equal the imprest amount, something has gone wrong. The petty cashier should inform his or her supervisor immediately.

Possible reasons for the discrepancy

- **Mistake** in the cash paid out (eg paid out £10.00 for a voucher of only £9.80)
- **Theft** from the petty cash box

6.5 IOUs and petty cash

In some organisations, individuals may be permitted to borrow money from petty cash. They must, of course, pay it back.

When someone borrows cash, they must put an **IOU** into the petty cash box.

> I owe petty cash £10.00
>
> J. Smith
> 15/10/X5

When checking the petty cash, **IOUs are equivalent to cash**.

		£
	Notes and coins in petty cash box	X
plus →	Total value of IOUs	X
plus →	Total value of vouchers in the petty cash box	X
equals →	Imprest amount	X

When the borrowed amount is returned to petty cash, the IOU is given to the borrower marked 'paid'. It is not good practice to allow borrowing from petty cash. However, it does happen and therefore must be properly controlled.

6.6 Receiving money into petty cash

Occasionally, **money is put into petty cash** apart from top ups.

- An employee paying for office stamps used for personal letters
- Employees paying for private calls made from an office phone
- Money from a cash sale may be used to boost petty cash

When money is paid into petty cash in this way, the petty cashier inserts a **voucher for the money received**. For example, C Trickey pays £1.10 for stamps used for his private mail.

Petty Cash Voucher

No _____
Date 17.9.X8

	AMOUNT £	p
Cash received for sale of postage stamps to C Trickey	1	10
	1	10

Signature: *V. Brown (Petty cashier)*
Authorised by:

Practice varies, but usually vouchers for cash received are **not** sequentially numbered.

If a check is made after money has been paid into petty cash in this way, then the following should apply.

			£
	Notes and coins in petty cash box		X
plus	→	Total value of IOUs	X
plus	→	Total value of vouchers for payments out of petty cash	X
less	→	Total value of vouchers for receipts of cash into petty cash	(X)
equals	→	Imprest amount	X

PART C ACCOUNTING FOR PAYMENTS

Activity 15.6

On Tuesday 15 December 20X7, you receive the following requests for reimbursement.

(a) The new office clerk presents bus tickets for amounts totalling £3.60 to support a request for payment for his first week's travel to work.

(b) Ten new typewriter ribbons have been received costing £5.50 each. An invoice has been sent with the goods and a receipt will be issued on payment.

(c) The office caretaker asks for £5 to pay as a gratuity to the refuse collectors, as has been customary in previous years.

(d) A clerk says that the administration manager asked him to purchase coffee, tea and sugar for the office kitchen. The receipt shows a total cost of £15.40.

Task

Using the blank petty cash vouchers provided, complete vouchers for any of the above items which you are able to authorise. Indicate what action you would take in respect of any requests for which you have not completed vouchers.

No _____	No _____
Petty Cash Voucher	**Petty Cash Voucher**
Date _____	Date _____
AMOUNT £ p	AMOUNT £ p
Signature:	Signature:
Authorised by:	Authorised by:

```
            No _____                              No _____
   Petty Cash Voucher                      Petty Cash Voucher
                    Date _____                          Date _____
   _____                      _____
                  AMOUNT                                  AMOUNT
                   £    p                                  £    p
   _____|___|___|            _____|___|___|
                      |   |   |                               |   |   |
                      |___|___|                               |___|___|
                      |   |   |                               |   |   |
   _____|___|___|            _____|___|___|

   Signature:                                Signature:
   Authorised by:                            Authorised by:
```

7 The petty cash book

The next step is to record cash put into the petty cash box and payments out of the petty cash box. This record is the **petty cash book,** which is a book of prime entry.

The purposes of the petty cash book

- To **provide an accounting record** of every petty cash transaction
- To allow for **posting petty cash expenses to the main ledger**

The petty cash book is a bound book with a large number of columns on each double page.

Left hand side: debit side	Right hand side: credit side
Used to record **cash receipts** into the petty cash box. It consists of about two to four columns.	Used to record and analyse **cash payments**. The number of analysis columns can be quite large.

There is a column in the **middle** for showing the **date of each transaction**.

Each petty cash transaction is recorded on a **separate line** in the petty cash book. An example of a petty cash book is illustrated on the next page.

PART C   ACCOUNTING FOR PAYMENTS

8 Recording and analysing petty cash transactions

Writing up the petty cash book should be done fairly regularly, depending on how often petty cash is used in the organisation.

- Typically, every two to four weeks
- **Must** be written up before the float is topped up

8.1 Recording petty cash payments

The petty cashier transfers details of **payments** from the vouchers into the book, on the right side of the double page. Entries in the petty cash book are listed in voucher number order *and* date order.

There may be several vouchers and, usually, it is at this stage that the vouchers are given their **sequential number**. If there are 20 vouchers and the number of the last voucher written up is 963, the 20 vouchers should be numbered 964-983.

Remember that the vouchers must first be sorted into date order **before** they are given their sequential number.

8.1.1 Columns on the payment side

The payments side (the **credit** side) will have the following columns.

(a) One column showing the **voucher number**.

(b) One column showing the **total payment** on a voucher.

(c) Several columns **analysing** each payment. Typical column headings are shown on the example.

(d) One column will be for **sundry items**.

(e) One column will be for **value added tax** (VAT).

(f) There should be a **'Details'** column. This is used to explain the reason for the payment. **All sundry items** should be explained.

Receipts							Payments						
(j) Details	(i) Net receipt £	(h) VAT £	(g) Total £	Date	(f) Details	(a) Voucher No	(b) Total £	(c) Analysis of payments				(d) Sundry £	(e) VAT £
								Travel £	Postage £	Enter-tainment £	Office supplies £		

PART C ACCOUNTING FOR PAYMENTS

8.2 Writing up the payments side

Entering the details of petty cash expenses in the book should normally be a fairly simple process.

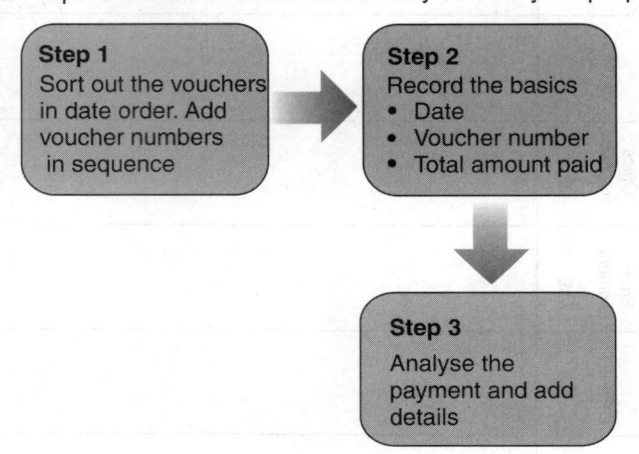

Step 1
Sort out the vouchers in date order. Add voucher numbers in sequence

→

Step 2
Record the basics
- Date
- Voucher number
- Total amount paid

↓

Step 3
Analyse the payment and add details

Example: Writing up petty cash book payments

The following four vouchers were taken from the petty cash box, sorted into date order and numbered in sequence 1461 to 1464.

	No 1461
Petty Cash Voucher	
Date 22.2.X3	

	AMOUNT £	p
Postage	15	20
	15	20

Signature: *B Travis*
Authorised by: *Admin Manager*

	No 1462
Petty Cash Voucher	
Date 24.2.X3	

	AMOUNT £	p
Coffee	5	50
Biscuits	3	50
	9	00

Signature: *P Sayles*
Authorised by: *Office Manager*

```
                                  No  1463                                          No  1464

        Petty Cash Voucher                          Petty Cash Voucher
                             Date  1.3.X3                                     Date  5.3.X3

                             AMOUNT                                           AMOUNT
                            £       p                                        £       p

  Taxi fare                  6      40         Bus fares                      1      35
                                               Payment to charity            10      00
                                               collectors
                             6      40
                                                                             11      35

  Signature: R Olney                           Signature: P Sayles
  Authorised by: Petty Cashier                 Authorised by: Office Manager
```

The petty cash book should be written up as follows. (You would normally see a VAT column here, but we deal with this in Section 9.)

Date	Details	Voucher no	Total £	Travel £	Postage £	Stationery £	Sundry £
20X3							
22.2	Stamps	1461	15.20		15.20		
24.2	Coffee, biscuits	1462	9.00				9.00
1.3	Taxi	1463	6.40	6.40			
5.3	Bus fares, payment to charity	1464	11.35	1.35			10.00

Activity 15.7

Assume that items (c) and (d) in Activity 15.6 above have now been duly authorised on vouchers 103 and 104 respectively.

PART C ACCOUNTING FOR PAYMENTS

Task

Write up the payments side of the petty cash book below to reflect the authorised petty cash expenditure on 15 December 20X7.

Date	Details	Voucher No	Total £	Analysis of payments		
				Travel £	Postage £	Sundry £
20X7						

8.3 Recording receipts of money into petty cash

If there have been some receipts of money into petty cash, these should be recorded on the left-hand side (**debit** side) of the petty cash book.

8.3.1 Columns on the receipts side

The receipts side will have the following columns.

- (g) A column for the **total receipt** on a voucher
- (h) A column for **VAT**
- (i) A column for the **net receipt**
- (j) A **details** column

There is a receipt voucher for £4.70 from an employee for a personal telephone call. The £4.70 is a net payment of £4.00 plus 70p for VAT at 17½%.

The receipt would be recorded in the petty cash book as follows (and the opening balance is also shown).

Details	Net receipt £	VAT £	Total £	Date
Balance b/d Telephone	4.00	0.70	400.00 4.70	20X9 1.8 12.8

9 Recording petty cash transactions: VAT

In some petty cash systems, the VAT on payments or receipts is ignored completely. This is on the grounds that the VAT is immaterial and accounting for it is more trouble than it is worth.

The VAT element in petty cash transactions should be accounted for separately. However, **the transaction must be accompanied by a VAT receipt** (unless the total amount including VAT is less than £25 (4.6.1)).

Accounting for VAT payments

- The total payment column shows the payment **inclusive** of VAT
- The amount of VAT paid is entered in the VAT column
- The net amount is entered in the analysis column(s)

Example: Petty cash payments including VAT

Here are two receipts for payments that include a VAT element. A claim from petty cash is made separately for each. How would these be recorded as petty cash vouchers and in the petty cash book?

```
           XYZ Ltd
    3 High Street, Kingston

    VAT Reg No. 228 4135 62
    Date 20/4/X4
                               £
    Electric plugs and fuses   22.00
    VAT @ 17.5%                 3.85
    Total                      25.85
```

```
           ABC Ltd
    14 Low Street, Richmond

    VAT Reg No. 221 4685 27
    Date 22/4/X4


    Paid £42.30 for stationery,
    inclusive of VAT @ 17.5%
```

In the case of receipt from ABC Ltd, the actual amount of VAT is not shown and needs to be worked it out.

PART C ACCOUNTING FOR PAYMENTS

$$\text{VAT} = \frac{17.5\%}{117.5\%} \times \text{total payment}$$

$$\text{Payment exclusive of VAT} = \frac{100\%}{117.5\%} \times \text{total payment}$$

(a) $\text{VAT payment} = \frac{17.5}{117.5} \times £42.30$

$\qquad\qquad\quad = £6.30$

(b) The payment exclusive of VAT is (£42.30 − £6.30) = £36.00, or

$$\frac{100}{117.5} \times £42.30 = £36.00$$

Note. For ease of calculations in future you should note that 17½/117½ is equivalent to the fraction 7/47.

No 371		
Petty Cash Voucher		
Date 20.4.X4		
	AMOUNT	
	£	p
Plugs and fuses	22	00
VAT	3	85
	25	85
Signature: *J. Smith*		
Authorised by: *V. Brown (Petty cashier)*		

No 372		
Petty Cash Voucher		
Date 22.4.X4		
	AMOUNT	
	£	p
Stationery	36	00
VAT	6	30
	42	30
Signature: *R. Greene*		
Authorised by: *D. Nuttall (Supervisor)*		

Here our petty cash book only shows analysis columns for stationery, sundry items, and VAT, in order to keep the illustration as simple as possible.

Date	Details	Voucher no	Total £	Analysis of payments		
				Stationery £	Sundry £	VAT £
20X4						
20.4	Plugs and fuses	371	25.85		22.00	3.85
22.4	Stationery	372	42.30	36.00		6.30

Activity 15.8

The following petty cash vouchers were processed during the remainder of the week ending 18 December 20X7.

Petty Cash Voucher — No 105
Date 16.12.X7

	AMOUNT £	p
Stationery	10	81
	10	81

Signature: SM BODY
Authorised by: Admin Manager

Petty Cash Voucher — No 106
Date 17.12.X7

	AMOUNT £	p
Sundry expenses	5	17
	5	17

Signature: A Clarke
Authorised by: Petty Cashier

PART C ACCOUNTING FOR PAYMENTS

No 107		
Petty Cash Voucher		
Date 17.12.X7		
	AMOUNT £	p
Repairs	22	09
	22	09
Signature: *A Person*		
Authorised by: Administration Manager		

No 108		
Petty Cash Voucher		
Date 17.12.X7		
	AMOUNT £	p
Stationery	4	23
	4	23
Signature: *NE Body*		
Authorised by: Petty Cashier		

No 109		
Petty Cash Voucher		
Date 17.12.X7		
	AMOUNT £	p
Sundry expenses	2	82
	2	82
Signature: *Anne Onymus*		
Authorised by: Petty Cashier		

No 110		
Petty Cash Voucher		
Date 18.12.X7		
	AMOUNT £	p
Sundry expenses	6	58
Stationery	1	41
	7	99
Signature: *C Happe*		
Authorised by: Petty Cashier		

15: MAINTAINING PETTY CASH RECORDS

PETTY CASH BOOK

Receipts

Details	Net receipt £	VAT £	Total £
Balance b/d			150.00

Payments

Date	Details	Voucher No	Total £	Analysis of payments					
				Travel £	Postage £	Stationery £	Repairs £	Sundry £	VAT £
20X7									
14.12	Postage	101	6.25		6.25				
14.12	Travel	102	7.50	7.50					
15.12	Sundry	103	5.00					5.00	
15.12	Sundry	104	15.40					15.40	

PART C   ACCOUNTING FOR PAYMENTS

All of the expenses listed on vouchers 105 to 110 included VAT at 17.5%, and VAT receipts were presented in each case.

Task

Make appropriate entries in the petty cash book (payments side) on page 409, to record petty cash vouchers 105 to 110.

Activity 15.9

During the week beginning 14 December 20X7 the following cash sums were received into the petty cash.

- 15.12.X7   Cash sale: £29.14 (including VAT at 17½%)
- 16.12.X7   £1.88 received from a member of staff to pay for personal telephone calls
- 18.12.X7   Cash sale: £13.16 (including VAT at 17½%)

Task

Write up the petty cash book (receipts side) on the previous page for the week beginning 14 December 20X7.

10 Topping up the float, balancing off and posting petty cash

Whenever the imprest float is **topped up** by drawing more cash from the bank, the petty cash book must be **balanced off**.

10.1 Procedure

These steps should be followed.

Step 1	**Add up** the payments in all columns. The analysis columns should **cross-cast** to the total column.
Step 2	Check **amount left** in petty cash box.

		£
	Notes and coins in petty cash box	X
plus	IOUs	X
plus	payment vouchers	X
less	receipt vouchers	(X)
equals	imprest amount	X

All discrepancies, however small, should be investigated and discussed with the petty cashier's supervisor.

Step 3 Prepare cheque requisition for the difference between the imprest amount and the amount of cash left.

		£
	Imprest amount	X
less	Cash in petty cash box	(X)
	Cheque requisition	X

Step 4 Draw cash from bank, specifying the notes and coins required, and place in box. Enter amount on left-hand (debit) side of petty cash book.

Step 5 Balance off PCB. This completes the double page in the book and starts the next one.

Step 6 Ensure that the balancing off is checked by the accounts supervisor, who should sign and date the balanced off pages. This shows that the correct amount of cash has been drawn.

Step 7 Post the totals to the main ledger.

PART C ACCOUNTING FOR PAYMENTS

PETTY CASH BOOK

Receipts

Details	Net receipt £	VAT £	Total £
Balance b/d			250.00
Sale of postage stamps	1.10	—	1.10

Payments

Date	Details	Voucher No	Total £	Travel £	Postage £	Enter-tainment £	Office supplies £	Sundry £	VAT £
19X0									
5.3	Light bulbs	635	19.27				16.40		2.87
8.3	Taxi fares	636	49.50	25.00		24.50			
12.3	Entertainment	637	56.80			56.80			
14.3	Window cleaner	638	47.00				40.00		7.00
20.3									
21.3									
22.3	Stamps	639	6.60		6.60				
24.3	Magazines	640	12.30					12.30	
29.3	Bus fares	641	3.65	3.65					

Example: Topping up, balancing off and posting

The imprest amount is £250, and at the end of March the petty cashier decides to top up the float in the petty cash box. Using the example on page 412.

Step 1 Add up the payments in all columns. The analysis columns should cross-cast to the total columns.

Cross-cast check

	£
Travel	28.65
Postage	6.60
Entertainment	81.30
Office supplies	56.40
Sundry	12.30
VAT	9.87
Total payments	195.12

Step 2 Check amount left in petty cash box.

If there are no discrepancies, the cash in the box should amount to £55.98. This is because:

		£
	Imprest amount	250.00
plus	receipts	1.10
		251.10
less	total payments	195.12
equals	cash in box	55.98

Step 3 Prepare a cheque requisition for the difference between the imprest amount and the amount of cash left.

The amount of cash needed to top up the petty cash to the imprest amount can be calculated in either of two ways.

Method 1		Method 2	
	£		£
Imprest amount	250.00	Total payments	195.12
Cash in the box	(55.98)	Less receipts	(1.10)
Cash needed	194.02	Cash needed	194.02

A cheque requisition form should be prepared by the petty cashier. In this example, the cheque requisition should be for £194.02.

An example of a completed form is given below.

PART C   ACCOUNTING FOR PAYMENTS

Cheque requisition

DATE: 31/X/X0
PAYABLE TO: Cash
AMOUNT: £194.02
DETAILS: Petty cash imprest float
SIGNED: Petty cashier
AUTHORISED BY: Accounts supervisor

The cheque should then be prepared, taken to the bank and cashed.

NEWROSE INTERNATIONAL
1 Bower street, The Garden, W4 9EG   22 29 48

NEWROSE INTERNATIONAL

STAG BANK
Forest Lane, The Dell

Date	Pay to the order of			Amount
31/03/X0	Cash			**** 194.02

Hundred Thousands	Ten Thousands	Thousands	Hundreds	Tens	Units
******************			One	Nine	Four

Amount of pounds in words   Pence as in figures

Per Pro NEWROSE INTERNATIONAL

A Rose

⑈101127⑈ 22⑈2948⑈ 50195733⑈

15: MAINTAINING PETTY CASH RECORDS

Step 4 — Draw cash from bank, specifying the notes and coins required, and place in box.

When the cheque is cashed, the petty cashier should decide the denomination of notes and coins. Since petty cash is for small payments, the petty cashier might decide to ask for the £194.02 to be made up as follows

	Number	£	
£20 notes	3	60.00	
£10 notes	7	70.00	
£5 notes	10	50.00	
£1 coins	9	9.00	
50p coins	6		3.00
20p coins	5		1.00
10p coins	4		0.40
5p coins	7		0.35
2p coins	10		0.20
1p coins	7		0.07
			194.02

The receipt of the money into petty cash must be recorded as follows.

- The cash book (as a cheque payment)
- The petty cash book (as a receipt)

In the petty cash book, the entry should include a reference to the corresponding folio number or entry number in the cash book. CB 324 in this example.

Step 5 — Balance off PCB.

The left-hand (debit) side of the petty cash book is completed as follows.

- Enter the details of the cash receipt (Step 4)
- Total the columns for receipts
- On the payments side, insert an entry in the total column for the amount of cash in petty cash. This balance carried down is the imprest amount. Then total the payments
- The total for receipts, including the balance brought forward, must be equal to the total for payments plus the balance carried down.
- Show the balance brought down, which should be the imprest amount, on the next page of the petty cash book.

These entries are shown on Page 418.

PART C   ACCOUNTING FOR PAYMENTS

Step 6 Ensure that the balancing off is checked by the accounts supervisor, who should sign and date the balanced off pages.

The supervisor will probably already have checked the amount of cash in the petty cash box when the cheque requisition form was authorised. The check that is carried out now should be to ensure the following.

- The columns have been properly totalled and cross-cast
- The analysis of payments seems correct
- There are vouchers and receipts for all the payments. The amount on each voucher corresponds with the amount shown in the petty cash book

If the supervisor is satisfied, he or she should sign and date the page.

Step 7 Post the totals to the main ledger.

This can be done by drawing up a posting summary of the totals from the petty cash book. The ledger codes show where in the general ledger the amounts have been posted. In this example, A041 is the petty cash account, the 'E' accounts are expenses and the 'R' account is revenue or income.

```
POSTING SUMMARY
Day book: Petty cash
Date: 31.3.X0
                          General ledger
                          Account          Dr          Cr
                                           £           £
Petty cash                A041             1.10        195.12
Travel                    E151             28.65
Postage                   E153             6.60
Entertainment             E155             81.30
Office supplies           E164             56.40
Sundry expenses           E180             12.30
VAT                       E247             9.87
Sundry income             R302                         1.10
                                           196.22      196.22
```

Every item of petty cash expense (or income) should be allocated to an account in the general ledger. There should be a separate account for each of the expenditure items for which there is an analysis column in the petty cash book.

Study the completed petty cash book on the following page and make sure that you can follow through each and every entry. The circled numbers refer to the steps outlined above.

10.2 Drawing cash against a crossed cheque

Did you spot that the cheque in Step 4 above is made out to cash and yet is also a crossed cheque? Crossed cheques should normally only be paid into another bank account. The bank may ignore the instruction of the crossing, however, under certain circumstances.

The drawer or some representative well known to the bank (eg the petty cashier) may present a crossed cheque for payment in cash. The banks can ignore the crossing on the grounds that there is no risk of the money passing to a person not entitled to it.

This is an example of practical business and banking needs overriding the rules relating to cheques and banking.

10.3 Archive records

When the recording is complete, all the completed vouchers and receipts in the petty cash box must be removed.

The vouchers must not be thrown away, but kept for at least seven years. It must be possible for an auditor to find any voucher for which an entry has been made in the petty cash book. The petty cashier needs a system of archiving used vouchers.

PART C ACCOUNTING FOR PAYMENTS

PETTY CASH BOOK

Receipts

Details	Net receipt £	VAT £	Total £
Balance b/d			250.00
Sale of postage stamps	1.10	—	1.10
Ledger code A041 ⑦	⑤ 1.10		④ 194.02
Cash book folio CB32 ④		⑤	⑤ 445.12
Ledger code	⑦ P303		

Payments

Date	Details	Voucher No	Total £	Travel £	Postage £	Enter-tainment £	Office supplies £	Sundry £	VAT £
20X0									
5.3	Light bulbs	635	19.27				16.40		2.87
8.3	Taxi fares	636	49.50	25.00		24.50			
12.3	Entertainment	637	56.80			56.80			
14.3	Window cleaner	638	47.00				40.00		7.00
20.3	Stamps	639	6.60		6.60				
21.3	Magazines	640	12.30					12.30	
22.3	Bus fares	641	3.65	3.65					
	⑦		① 195.12	① 28.65	① 6.60	① 81.30	① 56.40	① 12.30	① 9.87
31.3	Balance c/d	Ledger code A041	250.00	⑤	⑤	⑦	⑦	⑦	⑦
			445.12	£151	£153	£155	£163	£183	£247

Practice will vary but the normal system for **holding archive records** follows.

(a) The vouchers (with attached receipts) should be filed together in number order.

(b) Until the accounts for that year have been audited, the voucher files are kept available, clearly labelled to show the numbers and dates covered.

(c) After the annual audit, the vouchers can be archived.

Activity 15.10

(a) Total the petty cash book on Page 40 for the week ended 18 December 20X7.

(b) Complete the cheque requisition form below to top up the imprest float.

(c) Balance off the petty cash book and bring down the balance at the start of the week beginning 21 December 20X7.

Cheque requisition

Date ....

Payable to ....

Amount ....

Details ....

....

....

Signed ....

PART C ACCOUNTING FOR PAYMENTS

Key learning points

- ☑ Petty cash is used to make **small payments** with notes and coins. The cash must be kept **safe**, in a **locked box or tin**, and its **security is the responsibility of a petty cashier**. Payments must be properly **authorised**, and all transactions should be supported by **receipts** and **vouchers**.

- ☑ There is usually an **imprest system** for petty cash, whereby a certain amount of cash is held in the box, say £200. At regular intervals or when cash runs low, vouchers are added up and recorded, and the total of the vouchers is used as the amount by which to top up the imprest to £200 again.

	£
Cash in box	X
Total of vouchers = top-up	X
Imprest amount	X

- ☑ All **payments** out of petty cash must be **properly authorised**. This is evidenced by a **voucher**, signed by both the person receiving the payment and the person authorising it. Claims for payment must be supported by a **receipt** whenever possible.

- ☑ If there is **no receipt** to support a claim for payment, the petty cashier should refer the claim to his or her supervisor.

- ☑ At regular intervals, details of payments out of petty cash are recorded from the vouchers into the **petty cash book**. Vouchers should be in date order and **numbered sequentially** and they should be entered into the petty cash book in this order.

- ☑ When the **VAT element in petty cash expenditure** is recorded, there must be a VAT receipt.

- ☑ A **new page** in the petty cash book is started whenever the imprest float is topped up.

- ☑ When the **imprest float** is topped up, a sequence of procedures must be followed.

    - The total **expenses and analysis columns** in the book should be added up, and these totals checked to ensure that they cross-cast.

    - The amount of cash in the petty cash tin must be **counted**, and a check made to ensure that the amount needed to top up petty cash to the imprest amount equals the total of voucher payments (minus any receipts).

    - A **cheque requisition form** must be prepared and authorised.

    - The cash withdrawal is entered in the **cash book** (payment) and the **petty cash book** (receipts side).

    - The page of the petty cash book should be **checked** by the accounts supervisor.

    - Prepare a **posting summary**.

    - The petty cashier must remove the reimbursed vouchers from the petty cash box and transfer them to an **'archive'** file.

Quick quiz

1. Why do organisations need petty cash?
2. Who is responsible for the safety and security of the petty cash box?
3. What is the nature and purpose of the imprest system?
4. (a) What details are shown on petty cash vouchers?
   (b) What information is usually only added to petty cash vouchers when the petty cash book is about to be written up?
   (c) What should be attached to a petty cash voucher?
5. What items are recorded on the left-hand side of the petty cash book? And what on the right?
6. Why might money be received into petty cash?
7. The VAT element of petty cash vouchers must always be analysed. True or false?
8. State the 7 steps for topping up, balancing off and posting petty cash.

Answers to quick quiz

1. Small items of expense need to be paid for out of notes and coins.
2. The petty cashier; a 'deputy' in his or her absence.
3. The imprest system is designed to keep control of petty cash. The imprest amount is the maximum amount in the petty cash box; payments are made out of this and vouchers created for the payments. The difference between the amount of cash in the petty cash box and the imprest amount is the amount that needs to be paid in to 'top up'. It should also be the sum total of the vouchers.
4. (a) Purpose of payment; amount paid; name and signature of recipient; name and signature of person authorising payment; date of payment.
   (b) Voucher number
   (c) Receipt
5. Receipts of money into petty cash (debit side). Payments of money from petty cash (credit side).
6. Payments from employees for personal use of company property; cash sales (rarely)
7. False. It may be company policy to ignore VAT on petty cash items.
8. (i) Cast and cross-cast columns in petty cash book
   (ii) Count cash and vouchers in petty cash box
   (iii) Calculate amount of, and prepare, cheque requisition and cheque
   (iv) Specifying notes and coins required, cash cheque at bank and put cash in box, enter in petty cash book
   (v) Balance off petty cash book
   (vi) Supervisor checks balancing off
   (vii) Post totals to main ledger

PART C　ACCOUNTING FOR PAYMENTS

Activity checklist

This checklist shows which performance criteria, range statement or knowledge and understanding point is covered by each activity in this chapter. Tick off each activity as you complete it.

Activity

15.1	☐	This activity deals with Performance Criteria 2.2.C
15.2	☐	This activity deals with Performance Criteria 2.2.F and Knowledge and Understanding point 23: methods of handling and storing money from a security aspect.
15.3	☐	This activity deals with Performance Criteria 2.2.A and 2.2.E, also Range Statement 2.2.5 on queries.
15.4	☐	This activity deals with Knowledge and Understanding point 21: imprest methods.
15.5	☐	This activity deals with Performance Criteria 2.2.A, and Range Statement 2.2.2: documentation: petty cash claim.
15.6	☐	This activity deals with Performance Criteria 2.2.A, 2.2.B, and 2.2.E.
15.7	☐	This activity deals with Performance Criteria 2.2.D.
15.8	☐	This activity deals with Performance Criteria 2.2.D.
15.9	☐	This activity deals with Performance Criteria 2.2.D.
15.10	☐	This activity deals with Performance Criteria 2.2.A, 2.2.D. and Knowledge and Understanding point 21 on the imprest system.

PART D

Payroll

chapter 16

Paying wages and salaries and updating records

Contents

1. The problem
2. The solution
3. The payslip
4. Payment in cash
5. Cheque payments
6. Direct credit
7. Bank giro credit
8. Updating the records
9. Payments to the Inland Revenue

Performance criteria

- 2.2.A Calculate payments from relevant documentation
- 2.2.B Schedule payments and obtain authorisation
- 2.2.C Use the appropriate payment method and timescales in accordance with organisational procedure
- 2.2.D Enter payments into accounting records
- 2.2.F Ensure security and confidentiality is maintained according to organisational requirements

Range statement

- 2.2.1 Payments: payroll
- 2.2.2 Documentation: payslips
- 2.2.3 Payment methods: cash, cheques, an automated payment

Knowledge and understanding

22 Payroll accounting procedures: accounting for gross pay and statutory and non-statutory deductions through the wages and salaries control account and payments to external agencies; security and control; simple gross pay to net pay calculations but excluding the use of tax and NI tables

23 Methods of handling and storing money from a security aspect

PART D   PAYROLL

> **Signpost**
> The topics covered in this chapter are relevant to **Unit 2**.

1 The problem

Paying wages and salaries in cash creates **extra security** problems.

Also there are time limits for paying statutory deductions (tax and national insurance) to the Inland Revenue.

Therefore **extra vigilance** is needed in paying wages and salaries.

2 The solution

You do not need to know in detail how to calculate tax and national insurance deductions from pay. For the purposes of Unit 2, you just need to know how to pay the net amount to employees.

You will also need to know about the processes of paying **statutory deductions** (ie deductions required by law) to the Inland Revenue.

The controls needed in the paying of wages and salaries include the following.

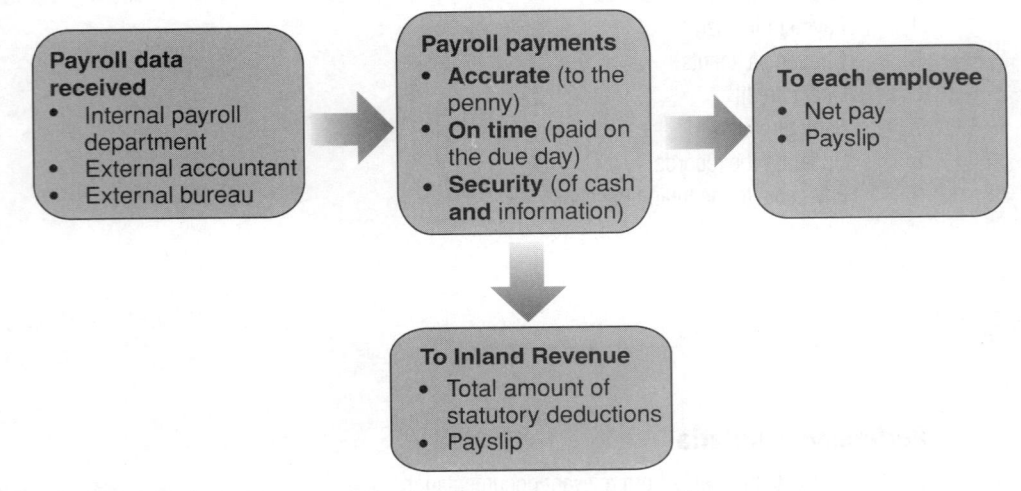

Payroll data received
- Internal payroll department
- External accountant
- External bureau

→

Payroll payments
- **Accurate** (to the penny)
- **On time** (paid on the due day)
- **Security** (of cash **and** information)

→

To each employee
- Net pay
- Payslip

↓

To Inland Revenue
- Total amount of statutory deductions
- Payslip

For the purposes of payroll payments, it is the **net pay** that goes to the employee.

| Gross pay | − | Deductions | = | Net pay |

Deductions can be statutory (tax, national insurance) or voluntary (pension contributions, company savings scheme).

3 The payslip

An employee has a **legal right** to receive a payslip. By law, the payslip must show the employee's gross pay, all deductions and the net pay due to the employee.

It is not always necessary to **itemise** deductions. **Fixed deductions** (ie those which do not change from month to month) can be shown as one deduction provided an employee has been informed of them beforehand. Such a statement must be reissued every 12 months.

Broadly speaking, however, a payslip should state the following.

Compulsory disclosures (unless aggregated fixed deductions)	Not compulsory but usually disclosed
The employer's name	The employee's tax code
The employee's name	NICs to date (ie in the current tax year)
Gross pay, showing how made up	The employee's payroll number
Additions to and deductions from pay	The employee's National Insurance number
Employee's pension contributions, if any	The method of payment
Statutory Sick Pay, if any	
Statutory Maternity Pay, if any	
Tax paid to date (ie in the current tax year)	
Tax in the period	
NICs for the period	
Date	
Net pay	
The method of payment for each segment of net pay, if they are paid in different ways	

There is **no standard format for a payslip**, but you might find that yours looks something like the example below.

PART D   PAYROLL

120 MR A.N. OTHER			EXAMPLE LTD		
NI No: WE123456C Tax Code: 433L Pay By: EFT			Date: 21/02/X0	Tax Period:	Mt 11
DESCRIPTION			AMOUNT	THIS YEAR	
01 BASIC SALARY			1,350.00		
02 OVERTIME			10.00		
TOTAL PAY >>>			1,360.00	14,960.00	
INCOME TAX - PAYE			213.29	2,347.11	
EMPLOYEE'S NI (EMPLOYER 121.88) TABLE A			107.40	1,181.40	
SEASON TICKET LOAN			40.00		
(HOL PAY ACCRUED 0.00) TOTAL NET PAY >>>			999.31		

The payslip can be produced

- **Manually**
- By **computer**

Example: Calculating net pay

> **Tutorial note.** The AAT have stated that candidates need to be able to calculate net pay from gross figures, using information given on tax codes, tax rates and NIC rates. There will be **no** tax tables involved. Therefore, it is unlikely that questions will be any harder than this example.

Joe Bloggs has an annual gross salary of £25,000 pa. His tax code for the year 2003/04 is 465L. Calculate his net annual salary given the following information.

(a)   The tax-free pay for code 465L is £4,659 for the year.

(b)   Any taxable amount over the tax-free pay is taxed at the following rates.

   (i)   First £5,000 at 10%
   (ii) Balance at 22%

(c)   The NIC rate is 11% for employees.

	£
Annual salary	25,000
Tax-free pay for year	(4,659)
Taxable pay	20,341

Tax due:

First	£5,000	@ 10%	500.00
Next	£15,341	@ 22%	3,375.02
	£20,341		3,875.02

NIC due:

£25,000 @ 11%   £2,750.00

Therefore net pay for the year is as follows:

	£
Gross pay	25,000.00
Tax	(3,875.02)
NIC	(2,750.00)
Net pay	18,374.98

4 Payment in cash

4.1 Wages in cash

Employees taken on **since 1 January 1987** do not have the right to demand payment in cash. Employees engaged before that date may insist on payment in cash if this is stipulated in the contract of employment.

Cash payment is still quite common in the cases of **part-time employees, temporary staff and casual labour**. Employers are slowly abandoning cash payment for the following reasons.

- **Counting notes and coins is time consuming** and requires more payroll staff
- **Employees have to count their pay** on receipt and **sign for the amount**, causing long queues on pay day
- Cash required for an employee's pay has to be **worked out in detail** and ordered from the bank
- The handling and transport of large amounts of cash pose **security problems**.

Activity 16.1

Although employers prefer not to pay wages in cash, can you think of any reason why employees might prefer it? List as many as you can.

However, you might be involved in paying cash wages, so this is described below.

4.2 Ordering money

As stated above, the cash required to pay an employee has to be **worked out in detail** before the bank can be told what to send. To do so, a **coinage analysis** might be prepared for each employee. An example is given below.

PART D   PAYROLL

MONARCH BUILDERS LTD

NAME	NET WAGE £	p	£50	£20	£10	£5	£2	£1	50p	20p	10p	5p	2p	1p
L Bourbon	178	41	3	1		1	1	1		2				1
C Windsor	99	63	1	2		1	2		1		1		1	1
N Romanov	121	15	2	1				1			1	1		
F Habsberg	156	21	3			1		1	1					1
A Osman	174	51	3	1			2		1					1
R Rajah	180	62	3	1	1				1		1		1	
M Incah	79	90	1	1		1	2		1	2				
VALUE	990	43	£800	£140	£10	£20	£14	£3	£2	£1	30p	5p	4p	4p
NUMBER			16	7	1	4	7	3	4	5	3	1	2	4

Remember that some employees may not want a note larger than £20.

Where employees are paid in cash, it is quite common for a breakdown of the notes and coin with which the employee is paid to be added to the documentation. Sometimes it will be **printed on the payslip** next to, or after, the figure for net pay.

A very simple example, for an employee who received £156.88 net pay for a week, would be.

Notes/Coins		£
£50	× 2	100.00
£20	× 2	40.00
£10	× 1	10.00
£5	× 1	5.00
£1	× 1	1.00
50p	× 1	0.50
20p	× 1	0.20
10p	× 1	0.10
5p	× 1	0.05
2p	× 1	0.02
1p	× 1	0.01
Net pay		156.88

Activity 16.2

Prepare a note and coin analysis for the following employees.

Name	Net wage due £
Bigg	120.12
Little	36.05
Large	129.71
Small	87.04
Stout	276.94
Thynne	110.25
Fatt	89.71
Skinnie	122.43
	972.25

The employees do not want to receive £50 notes, preferring lower denominations.

Once the analysis is completed, a cheque requisition form for the total amount will need to be prepared, the payment **authorised** and the cheque prepared and signed.

4.3 Handing cash over

Each employee should **count** the money and then **sign** for it. There are pay packets available which allow this to be done without opening the packet.

(a) If an employee is **unable to collect** their wage packet (eg because of illness), the **unclaimed wages packet** is held in a **safe** until it is collected.

(b) If the employee sends someone else to collect the wages, the employee should send **written authority** naming the person collecting the wages, and that person should provide **proof of identity**.

4.4 Payment out of petty cash

Part-time or **casual** workers are sometimes paid out of **petty cash.** This is not good practice because it can lead to problems with the **Inland Revenue**.

If a person works regularly, then maybe he or she falls into one of the following categories.

- **Self-employed,** in which case no deductions are made
- An **employee**, in this case PAYE, NICs and so on are payable

It is the duty of the employer to ensure that PAYE and NICs are paid in such a case. Failure to record all payments to employees can result in **penalties** for the employer, and can mean that the employer is liable to pay the PAYE and NICs which should have been deducted.

PART D PAYROLL

4.5 Allowances

Petty cash is sometimes used to make **informal advances** to employees. If this is the case, the borrower should sign an IOU.

Money cannot be deducted from pay unless there is a **specific agreement** to do so. So, if an IOU is to be repaid in this way, the employee should also sign a form expressly authorising payroll to reclaim the loan from pay.

Otherwise, the amount of the IOU should be repaid directly by the employee.

Activity 16.3

You made the following payments out of petty cash this month. What should you, as Petty Cashier, do about each one?

(a) Gina Chatterjee received £50 for looking after the plants in the reception area and meetings room. She receives this sum every month. She works for several other local businesses providing the same service. She does not provide an invoice.

(b) Jo Kent received £100 as an advance of salary. She signed a petty cash voucher. A copy of this has been passed to you.

	No. 291 Petty Cash Voucher	
		Date: 10.3.X7
	AMOUNT	
	£	p
Advance of salary for March	100	00
Signature: *Jo Kent*		
Authorised by: *Alison Brown*		

(c) Lewis Taylor received £30 for helping out in the post room on several occasions recently, when a member of staff was off sick. Lewis is a full-time student with various part-time jobs. He signed no receipt.

5 Cheque payments

A **cheque** is the simplest form of **cashless pay**. The cheque shows the **name** of the employee, and the **amount** to be paid which agrees exactly to the payslip.

The payroll must be **authorised** by the payroll manager before it is passed for payment. Therefore, a copy of the authorised payroll and the payslips, should be passed to the **cheque signatories** so that they can check payment is to genuine employees.

It is likely that directors' pay cheques will be **highly confidential** and so will only be signed by senior personnel. Remember that pay is a highly sensitive issue and details of an individual's pay **must not be given to anyone without authority.**

The problem with cheque payments is that so much **time** is spent preparing them. Also, while the **security problems** with cheques are less than with cash, there is still the possibility of **theft** or **fraud** (see Chapter 13).

Sometimes paycheques are **printed**, so that only the signature is necessary. Printing the cheque can be the final run of the normal payroll processing.

Some organisations have a system where the **cheque** is the second half of a perforated sheet of paper which has the **pay slip** on top. The employee receives both, tears off the cheque and takes it to the bank. An example is given below.

PART D PAYROLL

EMPLOYEE	NAME	CODE	MONTH	BLOGGS AND CO	
0152	A. WORKER	404L	11		21/2/X0

Narrative	Amount		Year To Date	
	£	p	£	p
BASIC PAY	1,000	00	11,000	00
GROSS PAY	1,000	00	11,000	00
INCOME TAX	142.24		1,563.49	
NICs	78.38		862.18	
NET PAY	779.38			

Any Bank
449 SOMEWHERE ROAD, LONDON W5 2LF

21 2 20 X0

20-27-48
SOUTHERN BANK PLC

Pay A. WORKER   or order

SEVEN HUNDRED AND SEVENTY-NINE POUNDS AND THIRTY-EIGHT PENCE

£ 779-38

ACCOUNT PAYEE

Authorised signature *Any Body*
Authorised signature *Some Body*

Bloggs and Co

Cheque No.   Branch No.   Account No.
⑈101129⑈ 20⑈2748⑈ 3059571 3⑈

The cheques must be **numbered in sequence**, and must be kept under **strict control**.

Even though cheques are used less as **automated payment systems** take over, they will still be used for **exceptional circumstances**.

- An **employee leaving** part way through the month
- A **new employee** joining during the month
- **Advances of salary**

6 Direct credit

Most companies now use some form of **automated payment system**. So instead of filling up pay packets with cash, or preparing large numbers of cheques, the whole operation is done speedily and automatically through the banking system.

Direct Credit is a system which enables you to make payments by electronic transfer directly into bank or building society accounts.

An organisation can use Direct Credit in one of two ways.

(a) **Indirect access:** the organisation uses a **bureau service** provided by its bank or by a computer bureau. You provide the payroll information by fax, telephone, post or PC input and, in return for a fee, the bureau transmits the data to BACS. The bureau may also provide payslips or a full payroll service.

(b) **Direct access:** the organisation has a direct telecommunications link to BACS, called **BACSTEL**. You need a PC, appropriate modem and the required software. Your transmission is secured using **passwords** and a confirmation receipt comes back from BACS so that you know your transmission was successful. This may be faster and cheaper than indirect access but you incur the initial costs of the software, etc.

Whichever method you adopt, use the following procedure.

Day 1 Send off a list of employees with the amount of net pay, sort code of their bank or building society and their account numbers.

Day 2 Your payment instructions are processed overnight for distribution by the banks and building societies on Day 3.

Day 3 Payment day. Your bank account is debited with a **single entry** covering the value of all the payments made, and simultaneously the accounts of all individual employees are credited.

Benefits to employers	Benefits to employees
Greater security	Their pay is in their accounts on pay day as **cleared funds** (guaranteed to be available for withdrawal straight away, unlike cheques)
Reduced costs of cheque stationery or cash handling	Increased security
Less administration	**No time wasted** checking pay packet or paying a cheque in
Increased control of cash flows, as the date of the debit is known exactly (pay day), not before (as with cash payments)	**No difficulty in collecting pay** whilst on holiday or off sick

PART D PAYROLL

The **disadvantage to employees** could be that they have to open a bank or building society account to get paid. However, 80% of the UK population now have a current account at a bank or building society, and over 70% of all salary and wage payments are now made by direct credit.

Some **smaller employers** may not consider it worthwhile to use Direct Credit if they only have a small workforce. Others, especially if they have computerised all other aspects of their accounting systems, may see this as a logical next step.

Suppliers can also be paid by Direct Credit (see Chapter 13), so the initial expense of establishing a BACSTEL link can be spread between Purchase Ledger and Payroll administration.

The monthly payment of **PAYE** and **NICs** (see Section 9) can be made by Direct Credit as well.

Activity 16.4

You have just started work with a brand new software company which has taken on 20 staff in all. They are all going to be paid monthly. The company's accounting systems will all be computerised (including payroll). What method of payment would you recommend the company adopts for payroll? List the advantages and disadvantages of:

(a) Cash
(b) Cheque
(c) Direct Credit

Example: Direct credit

Arnold Bax is an employee. His net pay was £1,380 in June. Arnold Bax banks at Natlays Bank. The sort code of his branch is 17-31-98, and his bank account number is 12345678.

Of the information above, what would you transmit to BACS?

Arnold Bax. £1,380. 17 – 31 – 98. 12345678

7 Bank giro credit

Bank giro credit (BGC) is being replaced as a form of payment by **BACS**, as BGC has none of BACS' advantages.

Summary of procedure

- **One cheque is signed** for the total value of the payments to be made.
- A **credit slip** is prepared for **each** employee, with the employee's name, bank sort code, account number and net pay.
- This paperwork is then processed by the bank.

In this system the amount of **paperwork** is the same as for writing cheques. The only difference is that none of the credit transfer slips has to be signed by the authorised signatories (although they should still see them as evidence to support the cheque).

8 Updating the records

Keeping the payroll records is outside the scope of your studies. However you do need to know how to post the payroll payments into the main ledger.

8.1 Payroll ledger accounts

Entering payroll data into the correct **ledger account** is normally quite straightforward.

- Payroll is normally only done **weekly** or **monthly**.
- **Same types of entry** take place every period.
- The **wages control account** helps to ensure that the entries are being made correctly.

After all the wages items have been posted, the balance on the wages control account should be NIL.

Example: Payroll ledger accounts

Comecon Ltd pays its workers every month. In Month 1, the payroll details are as follows.

	£
Gross wages	31,200
Employer's NICs	2,000
Net wages paid to workers via Direct Credit (BACS)	25,000
Deductions for PAYE made from workers' wages	4,000
Deductions for employees' National Insurance	1,000
Employees' contributions to the pension fund	1,200
Employer's contributions to the pension fund	1,500

Assume there was £50,000 in the bank at the beginning of Month 1 (an asset of £50,000). Details of these items are beyond the scope of your studies, but you need to know how to post the payments to the main ledger.

Let's post the entries to the accounts below, doing one entry at a time. The T accounts are shown later. For convenience here we shall show the entries in **journal** form.

Step 1   Entry for **gross pay**.

	Debit £	Credit £
Staff costs (gross wages)	31,200	
Wages control		31,200

PART D PAYROLL

Step 2 — Wages costs do not only include gross wages, so some more entries are necessary, an entry for other **employer's costs**.

	Debit £	Credit £
Staff costs (employer's NICs)	2,000	
Staff costs (employer's pension contributions)	1,500	
Wages control		3,500

Step 3 — **Net wages** paid to employees out of cash must be entered.

	Debit £	Credit £
Wages control	25,000	
Cash (net paid)		25,000

Step 4 — The **Inland Revenue** must be paid soon after the month end. However, they do not have to be paid at the same time as the workers, so let us enter that into a liability account. This is because we will pay the Inland Revenue at a future date.

	Debit £	Credit £
Wages control	4,000	
PAYE account: Inland Revenue for PAYE		4,000

Step 5 — We also have to set up a creditor for NICs, as we have collected money as **employees' NICs** which must be paid to the Inland Revenue.

	Debit £	Credit £
Wages control	1,000	
PAYE account: Inland Revenue for NICs		1,000

Step 6 — Do the same again for **employer's NIC**

	Debit £	Credit £
Wages control	2,000	
PAYE account: Inland Revenue for NICs		2,000

Step 7 — Then there are **deductions from employees' wages for pension fund contributions**. The amount owed to the pension fund is a liability, as it is owed money. Pension funds are separate legal entities.

	Debit £	Credit £
Wages control	1,200	
Pension fund		1,200

16: PAYING WAGES AND SALARIES AND UPDATING RECORDS

Step 8   Finally there are the **employer's contributions to the pension fund**.

	Debit £	Credit £
Wages control	1,500	
Pension fund		1,500

By making these entries:

(a) All the amounts owing to **external agencies** have been collected in their own **liability accounts** for them to be dealt with later.

(b) The employees' **gross pay**, together with the other payroll related costs of **employer's NICs and pension contributions**, have been collected in a **staff costs expense account**.

We had better look at the T accounts now to see which accounts have a balance. Don't forget that we had £50,000 cash to start with.

STAFF COSTS ACCOUNT

	£		£
Gross wages	31,200		
Employer's NICs	2,000		
Employer's pension contributions	1,500	Balance c/d	34,700
	34,700		34,700
Balance b/d	34,700		

WAGES CONTROL ACCOUNT

	£		£
Cash – net pay	25,000	Gross wages	31,200
PAYE liability	4,000	Employer's NICs and pension	
NICs liability – employees'	1,000	contributions (2,000 + 1,500)	3,500
NICs liability – employer's	2,000		
Pension fund liability – employees'	1,200		
Pension fund liability – employer's	1,500		
	34,700		34,700

(Note that both sides have the same total, and so there is no balance to carry forward.)

CASH ACCOUNT

	£		£
Balance b/d	50,000	Wages control – net pay	25,000
		Balance c/d	25,000
	50,000		50,000
Balance b/d	25,000		

PART D PAYROLL

PAYE LIABILITY

	£		£
Balance c/d	4,000	Wages control – PAYE	4,000
		Balance b/d	4,000

NICs LIABILITY

	£		£
		Wages control – employees' NICs	1,000
Balance c/d	3,000	Wages control – employer's NICs	2,000
	3,000		3,000
		Balance b/d	3,000

PENSION FUND LIABILITY

	£		£
		Wages control – employees' contributions	1,200
Balance c/d	2,700	Wages control – employer's contributions	1,500
	2,700		2,700
		Balance b/d	2,700

Study the T accounts carefully and make sure that you can find both entries for each transaction: number them according to the steps shown.

The end result is that we have balances of £34,700 on the staff costs account (representing the total staff costs for the month), £25,000 less in cash, liabilities of £4,000 and £3,000 to the Inland Revenue for PAYE and NIC respectively, and another liability of £2,700 to the pension fund.

The liabilities will be settled by payment over the next week or two, clearing the various accounts as with any other creditors.

	Debit	Credit
	£	£
PAYE liability	4,000	
NICs liability	3,000	
Pension fund liability	2,700	
Cash account		9,700

The balance on the **staff costs account** stays there – this is the record in the ledger accounts of the payroll expenses for the month. Next month, Month 2's staff costs will be added to it.

8.2 Proforma wages control account

The wages control account contains entries as in the proforma shown below.

16: PAYING WAGES AND SALARIES AND UPDATING RECORDS

WAGES CONTROL ACCOUNT

	£		£
Cash – net wages	X	Staff costs	
PAYE liability	X	– gross wages	X
NIC liability – employees'	X	– employer's NICs	X
NIC liability – employer's	X	– employer's pension contributions	X
Pension fund liability – employees'	X	– other staff costs	X
Pension fund liability – employer's	X		
Other deductions liability accounts	X		
	X		X

Terminology

Strictly wages are weekly paid and salaries are monthly paid, so the wages control account is also known as the **wages and salaries control account**.

Activity 16.5

Aroma has the following payroll details in Month 1. Write out the double entry for these transactions and show the wages control account at the end of all the transactions.

		£
Gross wages and salaries:	Administrative staff	102,531
	Sales and marketing staff	226,704
	Production staff	1,067,895
Employer's NICs		104,782
Employees' NICs		83,829
PAYE deductions		351,826
Pension deductions:	Employer's	41,728
	Employees'	37,860
Net wages and salaries		903,893
GAYE donations		10,180
Season ticket loan repayments		9,542

9 Payments to the inland revenue

9.1 Paying the Collector

Most employers must pay to the Collector **within 14 days of the end of the tax month** the amounts collected as PAYE and NICs for that month.

Tax Month 2, for example, ends on **5 June**. Payment must be made by **19 June**.

PART D PAYROLL

The only exception is for **small employers**, who are allowed to pay **every quarter**.

Quarter ending	Payment due by
July 5	July 19
October 5	October 19
January 5	January 19
April 5	April 19

A **small employer** is one whose **average** monthly payment for the year is likely to be **under £1,500**.

Activity 16.6

Aroma employs a small staff of full and part-time assistants and therefore has to deduct PAYE and NICs from their wages. Kris estimates that the total of these deductions each month will be as follows:

	£		£
January	1,500	July	750
February	900	August	700
March	900	September	900
April	900	October	1,200
May	900	November	1,500
June	900	December	2,000

Can Kris pay his PAYE and NICs every quarter instead of every month?

9.2 Form P30B

A **P30B payslip** is a sort of bank giro credit which details how much is paid to the Collector of Taxes at the Accounts Office split between:

- Income tax
- National Insurance

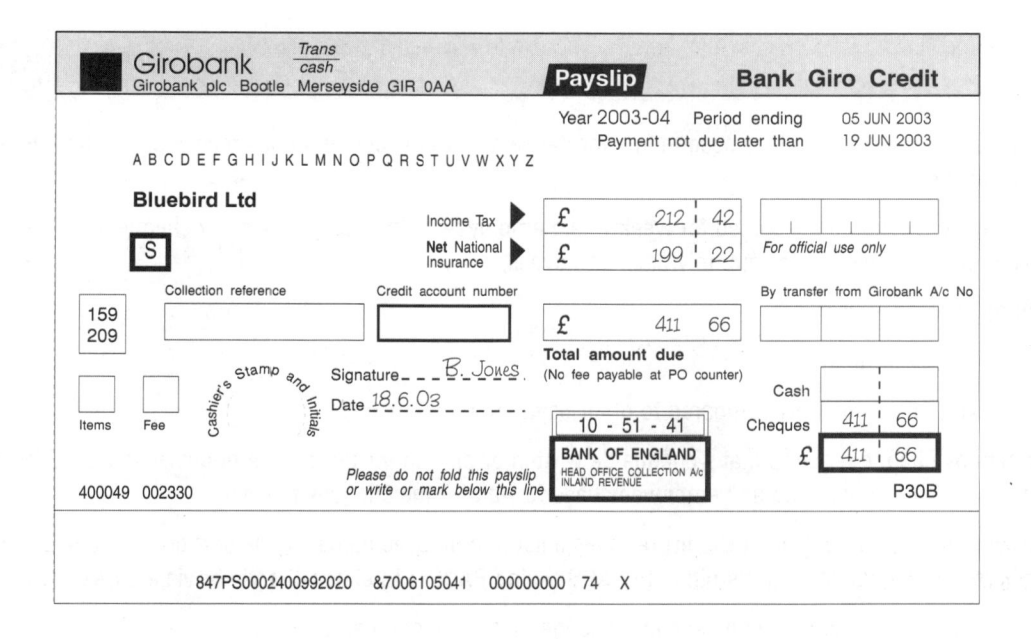

16: PAYING WAGES AND SALARIES AND UPDATING RECORDS

Step 1 Enter in the **Income Tax box** what is due from employees as PAYE, net of any refunds in the month.

Step 2 To find net **National Insurance** first add together the total:

- Employees' NICs
- Employer's NICs

Then subtract the total of any **SSP** or **SMP** that you are entitled to recover. **You do not need to know the details of this for the purposes of Unit 2.**

There may be occasions where the total due is a negative figure.

Step 1 Write NIL on the P30B and send it in as normal.

Step 2 Deduct the amount from next month's payment.

Activity 16.7

The following has been extracted from the Month 1 payroll of Aroma.

	£
Income tax deducted (gross)	40,000
Income tax refunded	500
Employees' NICs	7,000
Employer's NICs	14,000

What should be paid to the Inland Revenue Accounts Office?

Key learning points

- For the employee the payslip is second in importance only to the actual money received. Certain things must be shown on a payslip.
- Cash payment is sometimes used for weekly paid employees, although payment by cheque and Direct Credit are most common especially for monthly paid employees.
- Cash payment involves:
  - security problems
  - extra time and effort compared to other payment methods
- Payment by cheque requires that a cheque be written or printed for the exact amount of an employee's net pay. This can be time consuming and employees have to wait for the cheques to clear.
- Payment through BACS (Direct Credit) requires a list of employee names, bank sort codes, bank account numbers and net pay to be transmitted to BACS (using BACSTEL) either directly or via a bureau or bank.
- Payroll costs must also be recognised in the ledger accounts of an enterprise.
  - Total wages cost is an expense of the business.
  - A business deducts tax and NICs from employees' wages on behalf of the government. Until it pays, these amounts are liabilities as they are owed by the business.
  - The business must also make NI contributions on its own behalf, which also must be paid to the government. This gives rise to an expense and a liability.
- One way of ensuring that every payroll expense is properly analysed is to use a wages control account, in which every payroll transaction is collected in total.

Quick quiz

1. An employer is legally obliged to provide payslips to all employees. True or false?
2. All deductions from pay must be itemised on the payslip. True or false?
3. List as many disadvantages as you can of paying employees in cash.
4. Prepare a note and coin analysis for an employee who will receive net pay of £187.46 this week and who does not want to receive large denomination notes (over £20).
5. Your office cleaner has been paid £50 per week out of petty cash every week for over a year now. These payments are never put on the payroll. What enquiries should you make about this?
6. List three types of cashless pay.
7. What is the double entry to account for the employer's pension contributions in April, due to be paid into the pension scheme account in May? (Ignore the wages control account here.)
8. When all the entries relating to the payroll have been made, what should be the balance on the wages control account?

Answers to quick quiz

1. True
2. False. If deductions are the same every month (such as Trade Union subscriptions, GAYE donations or SAYE payments) then the employee can be given an annual statement itemising all such fixed deductions and they need not also be itemised on the payslip.
3. Security risks for employer and employees; time consuming to prepare wage packets; expensive in staff time, bank charges and security measures; time consuming distributing them and ensuring employees check them; employees off sick, on holiday or away from site face delays in receiving wages.
4.

Denomination	£20	£10	£5	£2	£1	50p	20p	10p	5p	2p	1p
Quantity	9	–	1	1	–	–	2	–	1	–	1
Total value	£180	–	£5	£2	–	–	40p	–	5p	–	1p

5. You or your supervisor should find out from whoever authorises these payments whether the cleaner is self-employed or operating/employed by a limited company. In either case, the cleaner should be submitting invoices showing the full business name. If the cleaner is, in the Inland Revenue's eyes, an employee of your company then he/she should be on the payroll and should have the appropriate deductions made from his/her wages. If the Inland Revenue find out about the cleaner and consider that he/she is an employee, then all the PAYE and NIC that should have been deducted since employment began can be reclaimed. This might also spur the Inland Revenue on to investigate whether there are any other payments missing from the payroll.

PART D   PAYROLL

6 Payment by cheque; direct credit; bank giro credit.

7 Debit   Staff costs (or pension costs, or any other suitably named expense account).
  Credit   Pension scheme account (a creditor – the money is due to the administrator).

8 NIL. The account should balance exactly. If it doesn't, a mistake has been made somewhere.

Activity checklist

This checklist shows which performance criteria, range statement or knowledge and understanding point is covered by each activity in this chapter. Tick off each activity as you complete it.

Activity		
16.1	☐	This activity deals with Range Statement 2.2.3 payment methods: cash
16.2	☐	This activity deals with Performance Criteria 2.2.A and Range Statement 2.2.3 payment methods: cash
16.3	☐	This activity deals with Performance Criteria 2.2.C
16.4	☐	This activity deals with Performance Criteria 2.2.C and Range Statement 2.2.3 payment methods: cash; cheque; an automated payment
16.5	☐	This activity deals with Performance Criteria 2.2.D and Knowledge and Understanding point 22 regarding the wages and salaries control account
16.6	☐	This activity deals with Knowledge and Understanding point 22 concerning payments to external agencies
16.7	☐	This activity deals with Knowledge and Understanding point 22 concerning payments to external agencies

PART E

Basic law

chapter 17

Business law

Contents

1 Introduction: contract law
2 Formation of a contract
3 Contracts for the sale of goods

Knowledge and understanding

1.2 & 2.2   Basic law relating to contract law, and UK Sale of Goods Act

Signpost
The topics covered in this chapter are relevant to **Units 1 and 2**.

PART E BASIC LAW

1 Introduction: contract law

All organisations do business by entering into **transactions** with individuals and with other organisations.

- For the buying and selling of materials and goods
- For the provision of services
- For securing labour
- For receiving and offering payment for any or all of the above

1.1 Contract law

These transactions are conducted by **agreement** between the parties involved.

A standard framework controls the terms and fulfilment of business agreements, so that people do not:

- Promise one thing and deliver another
- 'Take the money and run'
- Take the goods and run *without* paying!

This is where the **law of contract** comes in.

Contract law is the main area of the law relevant to these Units. You need to have some grasp of:

- What particular laws are trying to achieve
- Broadly how the laws work

1.2 Criminal and civil law

The English legal system distinguishes between two branches of the law.

- **Criminal law** deals with conduct which is **prohibited by law**.
- **Civil law** exists to **regulate disputes over the rights and obligations of persons dealing with each other**.

	Criminal law	Civil law
Parties to a case	State - prosecution Individual - accused	Individual - plaintiff Individual - defendant
Burden of proof	With prosecution, beyond reasonable doubt	With plaintiff, on the balance of probability
Objective	Punishment	Settlement
Examples	Murder, fraud, drink-driving	Contract, divorce

Example: Civil and criminal wrongs

A business person is on his way to visit a client after spending an afternoon in the pub. He crashes his car and injures a pedestrian. What type of legal proceedings might ensue?

(a) The police will initiate a **prosecution** for the offence of drunken driving. This would be a **criminal action**.

(b) The pedestrian might wish to sue for compensation for pain and suffering resulting from the wrong. This is a **civil action**.

Contract law is civil law.

There are special provisions for the **sale of goods (see Section 3)**. There are also important general principles defining **what makes a valid contract** (see Section 2).

2 Formation of a contract

A **contract** is an agreement which **legally binds** the parties involved.

You may have a signed **contract of employment**, setting out your hours of work, your holiday entitlement and the required period of notice.

Example: A simple contract

What happens if you buy some paperclips for your employer? You and the retailer do not draw up and sign a written contract. However, if you have paid money, you have a reasonable expectation that you will get your paperclips. If you have the paperclips, the retailer has a reasonable expectation that you will pay for them. There is a mutual agreement here: one party 'agrees' to sell, and the other to buy. **This is a contract**.

A contract does **not** have to be in **writing**, and may not be clear-cut, explicit or specific. So **what makes a contract?**

- Intention to create legal relations
- Offer and acceptance
- Consideration

We will look at each of these elements in turn.

2.1 Intention to create legal relations

Both parties must intend and understand the agreement between them to be **legally binding**. In the majority of contracts this is not explicitly stated, so the courts apply two presumptions.

- **Social, domestic and family arrangements** are *not* usually binding.
- **Commercial agreements** are usually intended to be legally binding.

Sometimes, a commercial agreement may be worded to show that legal relations are *not* intended. In such cases, the burden of proof is on the party seeking to escape liability to show that there was no intention to enter into legal relations.

Example: Legal relations

A company, negotiating over the terms for making an employee redundant, gave him the choice either of withdrawing his total contributions from their contributory pension fund or of receiving a paid-up pension. It was agreed that if he chose the first option, the company would make an *ex gratia* payment to him. He chose the first option; his contributions were refunded but the *ex gratia* payment was not made. He sued for **breach of contract**. The defendant (the company) argued that the use of the phrase *ex gratia* showed no intention to create legal relations. The court decided that this was a commercial arrangement, and the company was not able to rebut the presumption of legal relations: it had to make the payment.

Activity 17.1

Commercial agreements are usually intended by the parties to be legally binding. True or false?

2.2 Offer and acceptance

A binding contract is formed by an offer and acceptance of terms. This means that new terms cannot be introduced afterwards unless both parties agree.

2.2.1 The offer

Case law shows that an offer must be distinguished from:

- An invitation to make an offer (an invitation to 'treat' or negotiate)
- The mere supply of information
- An advertisement

Here are some illustrations of **what does *not* constitute an offer.**

(a) **Invitation to make an offer.** A supermarket selling food is not legally making an 'offer' to you. Instead it is inviting **you** to make an 'offer' to buy the goods. (In the old days, you would bargain, so putting goods on sale is an invitation to negotiate – rather like buying a house.)

(b) **Supply of information.** For example you may receive details of goods through the post. The seller may decide not to sell you the goods: the supply of information in a catalogue, say, is not an 'offer' strictly speaking.

(c) **Advertisement.** An advertisement of goods for sale is an attempt to induce people to offer to buy the goods and is therefore classified as an invitation to make an offer.

Example: Offer and acceptance

Can you identify the offer and the acceptance in the following typical business transaction?

(a) Grant publishes an advertisement showing a range of goods and the prices of each item.
(b) Hurley telephones Grant in response to the advertisement.
(c) Grant sends a complete price list or quotation to Hurley.
(d) Hurley sends a completed purchase order to Grant.
(e) Grant supplies the goods to Hurley.
(f) Grant invoices Hurley.
(g) Hurley pays for the goods.

Grant's initial **advertisement** is not an offer. Neither is his sending of a price list, since this can be described as a **supply of information**. Hurley's **purchase order** constitutes an offer. Grant's **supply of the goods** constitutes **acceptance**.

Consider what would happen if either the advertisement or the supply of information *did* constitute an offer: by sending a purchase order, Hurley would have accepted the offer and created a binding contract. However, a supplier of goods usually obtains credit references in respect of new customers. It will also wish to check the status of the account of an existing customer before despatching goods, as the customer may have exceeded its credit limit or may have failed to pay off the due balance on its account. The supplier would be unfairly penalised if it had to satisfy every purchase order it received at risk of breach of contract! This is not the commercial position which the law seeks to achieve.

2.2.2 The acceptance

Acceptance of an offer forms a contract, provided:

- It is in response to an offer
- There is some act on the part of an offeree to signal acceptance
- It is unqualified (not a counter-offer)
- It is communicated to the offeror
- It is not subject to contract

Acceptance of an offer may be by express words. It may also be **implied** from the conduct or actions of the accepting party. There must be **some act on the part of the offeree** to indicate his acceptance, passive inaction is not acceptance.

Acceptance must be **unqualified agreement** to the terms of the offer. Acceptance which introduces any new terms is defined at law as a **counter-offer**. This is treated as a rejection of the original offer.

There are laws about the sending of **unsolicited** (un-asked-for) goods; the recipient is not bound to accept such goods.

Acceptance must be **communicated to the offeror**.

- Acceptance by a letter is effective as soon as the letter is posted - even if it is then delayed or lost in the post. This is called the **postal rule**.
- If an offer is made over the telephone, the offeree must ensure that his acceptance is understood. If interference on the line prevents the offeror from hearing the reply, no contract is formed.
- The offeror may **call for acceptance by specified means**, but he must state very precisely that this is the only means that will suffice.

Acceptance **subject to contract** is neither acceptance, rejection nor a request for information. It means that the offeree is agreeable to the terms of the offer but that the parties should negotiate a formal (usually written) contract. Neither party is bound until the formal contract is signed.

2.2.3 Termination of offer

An offer might be terminated by:

- **Rejection**, either outright or by the making of a counter-offer
- **Expiring after a specified time** set in the offer
- **Expiring after a reasonable time** if there is no express time limit set
- The offeror **revoking (withdrawing) the offer at any time before acceptance and actually communicating revocation to the offeree**

The offer may be revoked by an **express statement**, or by some **action** by the offeror indicating that he no longer regards the offer as in force. The **communication of the revocation takes effect only when it is received** (ie the postal rule does not apply here).

Activity 17.2

As an accounts assistant, it is your responsibility to dispose of any motor vehicles which are surplus to the company's requirements. You place an advertisement in the local paper asking a price of £4,000 for a car. Jenson telephones you saying he will buy the car for £3,000. You say that you would accept £3,500 and he tells you he will need to think about it but would like to have a test drive at the weekend. Then you receive a call from Eddie and agree to sell him the car for £3,300. When Jenson rings back to arrange the test drive he is furious to hear that the car has been sold and threatens you with an action for breach of contract.

(a) Was there at any point a valid contract between Jenson and you? Yes/No

(b) Explain briefly the reason for your answer

Activity 17.3

You advertise a consignment of goods for sale at the standard price of £600 per batch. Ajax telephones you and you offer to sell him the goods at £550 per batch. He says he will pay £480 but you refuse to reduce your price. The following day you receive an order by post from Ajax for five batches at £550 each.

(a) Has a valid contract been formed? Yes/No

(b) Explain briefly the reason for your answer.

Activity 17.4

You are assistant to the chief accountant at Bold & Co. Vim, the site administration manager, rings you to say that he has received a telex directory with a note which says that unless it is returned within fourteen days it will be assumed that the recipient has bought it for £49.95.

(a) Does a valid contract exist? Yes/No

(b) Explain briefly the reason for your answer.

2.3 Consideration

The third essential element for a binding contract is **consideration**. To be binding, a promise cannot be 'free': something must be given in exchange.

Someone telephones you and tells you that, as a special promotion, he will clean your car free of charge on the following day. If he then fails to turn up, you cannot sue him for breach of contract. There is **no contract**. You have not provided any consideration.

There is one exception to this rule. A promise for free is binding if it is made by **deed**. An example is an annual payment to a charity, made by **deed of covenant**.

PART E BASIC LAW

Activity 17.5

Harry of Super Sounds Ltd has recently sent out a quotation to Sally at The Music Store offering to sell her 20 CD players for £85 each plus VAT. In reply she sends him a fax saying that The Music Store would like to accept the offer provided that the units can be delivered by Saturday.

(a) At this stage, does a valid contract exist between the two companies? Yes/No

(b) Briefly explain the reason for your answer.

Activity 17.6

Super Sounds Ltd has placed a display advertisement in a hi-fi magazine for a new line of car CD players. The price stated in the magazine is £29.99 for each CD player, but an error has been made by the printer and the price should have been £129.99. Harry of Super Sounds Ltd receives a phone call from Billy who wants to place an order for 30 CD players. Chris tells him of the mistake but Billy insists that the company must honour its offer and supply them at £29.99 each.

(a) Does Super Sounds Ltd have to supply the CD players at £29.99 each? Yes/No

(b) Explain briefly the reason for your answer.

Activity 17.7

Suzy of Security Ltd telephones Jeanne of Home Designs Ltd on 12 August, offering to sell her 30 burglar alarm systems which are being disposed of as a special offer because they are surplus stock. Jeanne, on being told that the offer is open for ten days, expresses interest and so Suzy faxes full details, including price and contract terms, on 13 August. On 14 August Jeanne faxes back saying she is 'definitely interested' and will reply by post within a week. She posts an acceptance of the offer on 16 August and Suzy receives this on 19 August. The alarm systems are despatched on 21 August, invoiced on 23 August and delivered on 24 August. Home Designs Ltd pays by credit transfer on 2 September.

(a) On what date was a contract for the sale of the burglar alarm systems formed between Security Ltd and Home Designs Ltd?

(b) Briefly explain the reason for your answer.

Activity 17.8

Security Ltd receives an enquiry from Great Fires Ltd to purchase 230 smoke alarms. A quotation is sent out offering to supply these for £2.20 each. Two days later, Suzy of Security Ltd realises that a mistake has been made and that the quoted price should have been £3.20 each. She writes to Great Fires Ltd telling them of the mistake and saying that the smoke alarms cannot be supplied as per the quotation. The following day, Julius telephones from Great Fires Ltd, thanks her for her letter and tells her that he wants to accept the offer contained in the original quotation. He insists that Security Ltd must honour the contractual price of £2.20.

(a) Does a valid contract exist between Security Ltd and Great Fires Ltd? Yes/No

(b) Explain briefly the reason for your answer.

Activity 17.9

Wang sees an advertisement placed by his local electrical retailer in his local paper for a multimedia PC for £1,025 including VAT. He immediately rushes along to the shop to buy one. One of the store assistants tells him that they are out of stock but that they can supply one at the advertised price on the next day: Henry agrees and signs an order form.

(a) Does a valid contract exist between Henry and the retailer? Yes/No

(b) Explain briefly the reason for your answer.

3 Contracts for the sale of goods

3.1 Sale of Goods Act

An important area of contract law is the law concerning the **sale of goods**.

The Sale of Goods Act 1979 also covers contracts where the **supply of services** is the major part of the contract. For example, contracts of repair, where the supply of goods may be incidental to the provision of a service.

There must be a **money consideration**, or **price**.

A situation in which goods are exchanged for other goods does not give rise to a 'sale of goods'. However, if **some money** changes hands - as with a trade-in arrangement for a car - there is a contract for the sale of goods.

Imagine that you are about to enter into a contract for the purchase of some goods. What might you be concerned about?

- You may want the goods delivered for a particular occasion or **date**.
- Are the goods stolen, ie does the seller have a **right to sell the goods**?

- You would expect the goods to be the same type and quality as the description or any sample.
- The goods should be of **reasonable quality** and **suitable for their purpose**.

The Sale of Goods Act covers these matters and a number of other important issues. Its provisions are regarded as **implied terms** of most contracts for the sale of goods.

3.2 Implied terms

A sale of goods is subject to the following provisions of the Sale of Goods Act.

- The effect of delay in performance (s 10)
- Title, or the seller's right to sell the goods (s 12)
- Description of the goods (s 13)
- Quality of the goods (s 14(2))
- Fitness of the goods for the purpose for which they are supplied (s 14(3))
- Sale by sample (s 15)

3.2.1 Time of performance

If goods arrive too late, they may be useless.

The terms of the contract will determine whether a particular timescale is a condition of performance. If it is, a breach of such terms entitles the injured party to treat the contract as discharged.

In commercial contracts for the supply of goods for business or industrial use, it will be assumed that **time is of the essence**, even where there is no express term to that effect.

3.2.2 Seller's title

You cannot sell something that is not yours to sell. It is an implied condition that the seller has a **right to sell the goods**, or will have, at the time of sale.

If the seller delivers goods without having the right to sell, the buyer does not get to own the goods, which is the essential basis of the contract. If the buyer subsequently has to return the goods to the real owner, he may recover the entire price from the seller.

Example: Seller's title

R bought a car from D, which D had unknowingly bought from a thief. When this was discovered, the car was returned to the true owner. R sued D for the return of the full purchase price (as damages). The court decided that, although R had used the car for several months, he had not had ownership of it, which is what he had paid for. D therefore had to repay the full amount.

3.2.3 Goods to correspond with contract description

If you have agreed to buy certain goods on the basis of the description (whether the buyer's or the seller's), you expect the goods to correspond to the description.

This is implied, under the Act, in any contract for sale of goods 'by description'. The description may be of ingredients, components, age, date of shipment, packing, quantity etc.

Example: Sale by description

A seller advertised a second-hand reaping machine, describing it as new the previous year. The buyer bought it without seeing it. When it arrived he found that it was much more than a year old and rejected it. The seller sued for the price. It was held that this was a sale by description, the goods had not corresponded to the description, and the buyer was therefore entitled to reject the goods.

The provisions of the Trade Descriptions Act 1968 may also be relevant if the seller uses a **false description**: this is a *criminal* offence.

3.2.4 Satisfactory quality

All goods supplied under a contract for the sale of goods **in the course of a business** must be of **'satisfactory quality'**. They should meet the standard that a reasonable person would regard as satisfactory, taking account of any description of the goods, the price and other relevant circumstances (the Sale and Supply of Goods Act 1994).

In deciding whether goods are of satisfactory quality, the following should be taken into account.

(a) **Fitness for all the purposes for which goods of the kind in question are commonly supplied.** A hot water bottle that deteriorated when filled with hot water, for example, would not be of satisfactory quality. A bucket needs to hold a variety of substances, and be handled in a variety of ways, without leakage, damage, immediate deterioration and so on.

(b) **Appearance and finish**. Previous to 1994 goods with superficial damage, but which operated properly in the main, could be of merchantable quality. Satisfactory quality includes freedom from dents, marks, scratches and so on - unless they have clearly been allowed for in the description and price.

(c) **Freedom from minor defects**.

(d) **Safety**.

(e) **Durability**. They have to remain of satisfactory quality for a period which could be expected by a reasonable person.

Activity 17.10

Peter buys an electronic keyboard from his local catalogue store. He pays £199 for it. He returns to the store the next day complaining that, although the main keys work, none of the pre-set rhythm buttons seem to function. He demands an immediate refund. The sales assistant refuses to given him a refund or take back the goods, and instead gives him a card with the name and address of the manufacturer, suggesting that Peter contacts them to obtain a refund or a replacement.

(a) Was the sales assistant legally justified in refusing to give a refund? Yes/No

(b) Give briefly a reason for your answer.

3.2.5 Fitness of goods for a disclosed purpose

If you tell a seller (explicitly or by implication) that you intend to use goods for a particular purpose, you expect the goods supplied to be reasonably fit for that purpose.

This is an implied term, under the Act, unless it can be shown that the seller may not have known whether the goods were suitable for a purpose which was not familiar to him and the buyer may have been in a better position to tell.

Like 'satisfactory quality', this condition only applies to goods sold **in the course of a business**.

3.2.6 Sale by sample

If you have agreed to buy goods after inspecting a sample, you have the implied right to expect that:

(a) The bulk of the delivery will be of the **same quality** as the sample.

(b) You will have a reasonable opportunity to **compare** the bulk of the delivery with the sample.

(c) The bulk of the goods contain no defects (rendering their quality unsatisfactory) which would not be noticeable from reasonable **inspection** of the sample.

Example: Sale by sample

A child buys a catapult. Because of its faulty construction, it breaks, causing him to lose an eye. He successfully sues the shopkeeper, under the Act, for failure to supply goods which are of satisfactory quality and fit for the purpose for which they were supplied. The shopkeeper had bought the catapults by relying on a sample, which he had tested by pulling on the elastic. He sues the wholesaler for breach of the implied terms related to sale by sample under the Act. The court would find that the shopkeeper made a reasonable examination, which did not reveal the defect: the wholesaler would be liable to the shopkeeper.

3.2.7 Complaints

The law has recently been amended if a customer has a complaint.

- Goods must be faulty at **time of purchase**
- If complaint is within 6 months, the retailer has to prove that goods were not faulty
- If complaint is after 6 months, the customer has to prove that the goods were faulty

3.3 Passing of property and risk

Another important issue in any transaction for the sale of goods is determining **the point at which property (ownership) passes** from one person to another.

This is important because the **risk (and cost) of accidental damage or loss is, usually, borne by the owner of goods.**

The key rules are as follows.

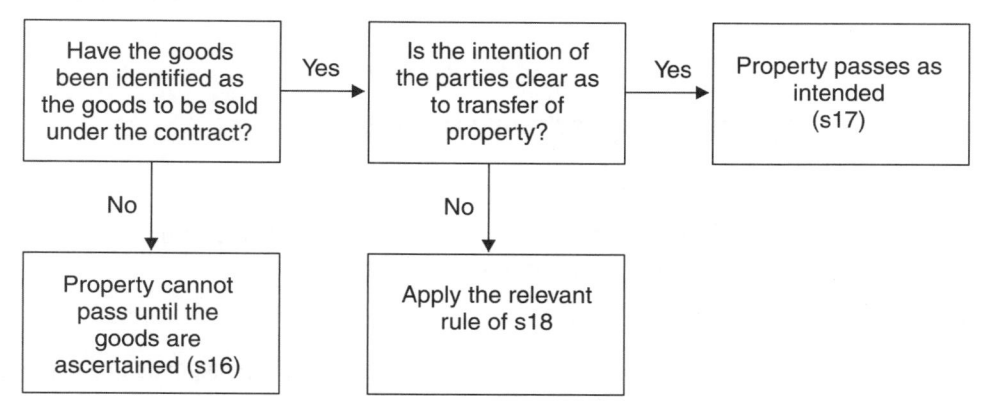

```
┌─────────────────────┐      ┌─────────────────────┐      ┌─────────────────────┐
│ Have the goods      │      │ Is the intention of │      │ Property passes as  │
│ been identified as  │ Yes  │ the parties clear as│ Yes  │ intended            │
│ the goods to be sold├─────▶│ to transfer of      ├─────▶│ (s17)               │
│ under the contract? │      │ property?           │      │                     │
└──────────┬──────────┘      └──────────┬──────────┘      └─────────────────────┘
           │ No                         │ No
           ▼                            ▼
┌─────────────────────┐      ┌─────────────────────┐
│ Property cannot     │      │ Apply the relevant  │
│ pass until the      │      │ rule of s18         │
│ goods are           │      │                     │
│ ascertained (s16)   │      │                     │
└─────────────────────┘      └─────────────────────┘
```

Note that **property** is not the same as **possession**. Despite the old adage 'possession is nine-tenths of the law', property (ownership) passes when the parties *intend* it to pass - not necessarily when possession of the goods change hands.

(a) A buyer may gain ownership of goods (property), while the seller retains possession of them: prior to delivery, for example.

(b) A buyer may gain possession of goods (by delivery), while the seller retains property in them: for example, under a contract stating that the seller retains title/ownership until the buyer has settled all debts due to him.

Such clauses are known as **retention of title** or **Romalpa** clauses (after an important 1976 case in this area). You may well find similar terms printed on the back of invoices which you process in your everyday work.

If the intention of the parties is not clear as to the transfer of property, **the rules of section 18 are applied to ascertain the point of transfer**. As brief examples of the detailed provisions:

(a) **Rule 2** states that where there is a contract for the sale of specific goods, and the seller has to do something to the goods in order to get them into a **deliverable state**, the property does not pass until that thing is done *and* the buyer has notice that it has been done. (Your company has entered into a contract for the purchase of a new machine, to which certain safety hoods are to be fitted prior to delivery. Before the suppliers can do this work, the machine is destroyed by a fire at their warehouse. They still demand payment from you, since you had effectively purchased the machine. Relying on rule 2, you could claim that the goods had not reached a deliverable state, and that property had therefore not yet passed.)

(b) **Rule 3** states that where there is a contract for the sale of specific goods in a deliverable state *and* the **seller** is bound to **weigh, measure or test them to fix the price**, property passes when he has done so and the buyer has notice of it.

PART E   BASIC LAW

Activity 17.11

Your company has entered into a contract for the purchase of some envelopes. Under the contract the envelopes are to be stamped with the company logo by the supplier. Before the supplier can do this work, the envelopes are damaged in a flood at the supplier's warehouse; he brings an action for the price against you. What is your legal position?

3.4 Acceptance and rejection of goods or services

The third important area in sale of goods contracts is **acceptance and rejection**.

Once you have 'accepted' goods, it is (in general) too late to claim a breach of contract for breach of an implied condition (such as satisfactory quality). A buyer is deemed to have accepted goods if :

- He informs the seller that he accepts them
- He acts in a way that implies he owns them, for example by re-selling the goods to a third party
- After the lapse of a reasonable time, the buyer retains the goods without informing the seller that he has rejected them

Obviously, you want to discover any defects or breaches of conditions **before** you do or say anything that implies acceptance (like signing for a delivery)! Under the Act, the **buyer must be given a reasonable opportunity to examine the goods on delivery**, before accepting them.

Example: Acceptance of goods

A company buys goods from a manufacturer and resells them to a customer, with delivery direct from manufacturer to customer. The customer complains that the goods are defective. In these circumstances, the company would be permitted to reject the goods - despite the resale - because it had not been given the opportunity, as buyer, to inspect them.

3.5 Remedies for non-payment

If a buyer wrongfully neglects, or refuses, to pay for goods, the seller may pursue one of a number of remedies.

(a) **Remedies against the buyer**. The seller has a right to sue the buyer for the **price** of the goods. This can be pursued if property in the goods has passed to the buyer

(b) **Remedies 'against the goods'**, or 'real remedies'.

 (i) **Lien** is the right to retain physical possession of the goods. The seller may refuse to hand the goods over until the buyer pays for them.

 (ii) **Stoppage in transit** is the right to recover the goods from an independent carrier to whom they have been entrusted, and to hold them until the buyer pays for them.

(iii) **Right of resale** is the right, under certain circumstances (for example, where the goods are perishable), to sell the goods to a third party.

Activity 17.12

A customer fails to pay for goods which he ordered from you and which you have supplied. What remedy for breach of contract are you most likely to pursue?

3.6 The Sale and Supply of Goods to Customers Regulations 2002

A customer has the legal right to choose one of the following if a fault appears within 6 years of purchase (5 years in Scotland) and it is reasonable for goods to last that long.

- Repair
- Replacement
- Partial or full refund
- Compensation

PART E   BASIC LAW

Key learning points

- ☑ The English legal system recognises a distinction between **criminal law** and **civil law**, each of which has different objectives.

- ☑ You are unlikely to be assessed on contract law. It is more likely that you will need to show an understanding of business law within your portfolio.

- ☑ A **contract** is an agreement which legally binds the parties to it. The essential elements of a contract are that there is an **intention to create legal relations** and that it is an agreement made by **offer and acceptance** in which the obligations assumed by each party are supported by **consideration**.

- ☑ The most important single topic in the law of **contracts for the sale of goods** is the protection given to a buyer of goods by the conditions implied by ss 12-15 of the Sale of Goods Act 1979.

- ☑ These are designed to ensure that a buyer can obtain goods which are of **satisfactory quality** and **in accordance with his requirements**. The second key area is the question of **when property passes** and so of who bears the loss if goods are damaged or destroyed while the transaction is in progress.

- ☑ There is in practice an overlap between the basic law of contract and the law relating to sale of goods. This is to be expected, as the sale of goods is really a particular, and common, kind of contract.

- ☑ **Basic contract law** is therefore of as much importance as statutory rules in any sale of goods.

Quick quiz

1. What are the three essential elements which make a contract?
2. When is an offer taken to have been accepted in such a way as to create a binding contract?
3. List the aspects of goods subject to implied conditions, under sections 10-15 of the Sale of Goods Act.
4. What are the criteria for defining goods as being of 'satisfactory quality' under the Sale and Supply of Goods Act 1994?
5. Under section 17 of the Sale of Goods Act, when is property in ascertained goods transferred to the buyer?
6. What remedies (a) against the buyer and (b) against the goods does a seller have when the buyer refuses to pay for the goods?

Answers to quick quiz

1. In order to create a contract:
   (a) There must be an intention to create legal relations
   (b) There must be offer and acceptance
   (c) The obligations assumed by one party must be supported by consideration given in exchange by the other.

2. An offer is taken to have been accepted when there is some expression or act on the part of the offeree, indicating unqualified agreement to the terms of the offer, which is communicated to the offeror by any suitable means. (Under the postal rule, acceptance dates from the time of posting of an acceptance by means of a correctly stamped and addressed letter, where this is recognised by both parties as a reasonable means of reply.)

3. A sale of goods may be subject to conditions with regard to:
   (a) The time of (or effect of delay in) performance
   (b) Title, or the seller's right to sell the goods
   (c) Description of the goods
   (d) Satisfactory quality of the goods
   (e) Fitness of the goods for a particular (disclosed) purpose
   (f) Sale by sample

4. Goods of 'satisfactory quality' must be:
   (a) Fit for all purposes for which they are commonly supplied
   (b) Adequate in appearance and finish
   (c) Free of minor defects
   (d) Safe
   (e) Durable

   With reasonable regard to description, price and other relevant circumstances.

PART E   BASIC LAW

5   Property in ascertained (identified) goods is transferred at the time when the parties intend (as deduced from the terms of the contract) that it be transferred.

6   Remedies against the buyer: action for the price, action in damages. Remedies against the goods: lien, stoppage in transit, right of resale.

Activity checklist

This checklist shows which performance criteria, range statement or knowledge and understanding point is covered by each activity in this chapter. Tick off each activity as you complete it.

Activity

17.1	☐	This activity deals with Knowledge and Understanding point 2: basic law relating to contract law and Sale of Goods Act
17.2	☐	This activity deals with Knowledge and Understanding point 2: basic law relating to contract law and Sale of Goods Act
17.3	☐	This activity deals with Knowledge and Understanding point 2: basic law relating to contract law and Sale of Goods Act
17.4	☐	This activity deals with Knowledge and Understanding point 2: basic law relating to contract law and Sale of Goods Act
17.5	☐	This activity deals with Knowledge and Understanding point 2: basic law relating to contract law and Sale of Goods Act
17.6	☐	This activity deals with Knowledge and Understanding point 2: basic law relating to contract law and Sale of Goods Act
17.7	☐	This activity deals with Knowledge and Understanding point 2: basic law relating to contract law and Sale of Goods Act
17.8	☐	This activity deals with Knowledge and Understanding point 2: basic law relating to contract law and Sale of Goods Act
17.9	☐	This activity deals with Knowledge and Understanding point 2: basic law relating to contract law and Sale of Goods Act
17.10	☐	This activity deals with Knowledge and Understanding point 2: basic law relating to contract law and Sale of Goods Act
17.11	☐	This activity deals with Knowledge and Understanding point 2: basic law relating to contract law and Sale of Goods Act
17.12	☐	This activity deals with Knowledge and Understanding point 2: basic law relating to contract law and Sale of Goods Act

PART F

Computerised accounting systems

chapter 18

Computerised accounting systems

Contents

1 Introduction
2 Computerised accounting systems
3 Data protection legislation
4 Assessment of computerised accounting systems

Knowledge and understanding

1.10 & 2.10   Basic law relating to data protection
1.15 & 2.16   Operation of computerised accounting systems, including output

PART F COMPUTERISED ACCOUNTING SYSTEMS

1 Introduction

Most accounting systems are run by computer. Even the corner shop owner is likely to produce his accounts using a computer package.

The important point to remember is that the rules of double entry are the same whether the system is manual or computerised.

2 Computerised accounting systems

Throughout this text, we have concentrated on manual accounting systems. However we have also looked at computerised systems in order to highlight the similarities as well as the differences.

3 Data protection legislation

3.1 Why is privacy an important issue?

In recent years, there has been a growing popular fear that **information** about individuals which was stored on computer files and processed by computer could be **misused**.

In particular, it was felt that an individual could easily be harmed by the existence of computerised data about him or her which was inaccurate or misleading and which could be **transferred to unauthorised third parties** at high speed and little cost.

In the UK the current legislation is the **Data Protection Act 1998**. This Act replaced the earlier Data Protection Act 1984.

3.2 The Data Protection Act 1998

The Data Protection Act 1998 is an attempt to protect the **individual**.

3.2.1 Definitions of terms used in the Act

In order to understand the Act it is necessary to know some of the technical terms used in it.

(a) **Personal data** is information about a living individual, including expressions of opinion about him or her. Data about other organisations (eg supplier or customer companies) is not personal data, unless it contains data about individuals who belong to those other organisations.

(b) **Data users** are organisations or individuals who control the contents of files of personal data and the use of personal data which is processed (or intended to be processed) automatically – ie who use personal data which is covered by the terms of the Act.

(c) A **data subject** is an individual who is the subject of personal data.

3.2.2 The data protection principles

Data users must comply with the Data Protection Principles contained in the Act. These are shown in the following table.

	DATA PROTECTION PRINCIPLES
1	Personal data shall be processed fairly and lawfully and, in particular, shall not be processed unless:
	(a) At least one of the conditions in Schedule 2 is met. (See Section 3.3(c) of this Chapter.)
	(b) In the case of sensitive personal data, at least one of the conditions in Schedule 3 is also met. (See Section 3.3(d) of this Chapter.)
2	Personal data shall be obtained only for one or more specified and lawful purposes, and shall not be further processed in any manner incompatible with that purpose or those purposes.
3	Personal data shall be adequate, relevant and not excessive in relation to the purpose or purposes for which they are processed.
4	Personal data shall be accurate and, where necessary, kept up to date.
5	Personal data processed for any purpose or purposes shall not be kept for longer than is necessary for that purpose or those purposes.
6	Personal data shall be processed in accordance with the rights of data subjects under this Act.
7	Appropriate technical and organisational measures shall be taken against unauthorised or unlawful processing of personal data and against accidental loss or destruction of, or damage to, personal data.
8	Personal data shall not be transferred to a country or territory outside the European Economic Area unless that country or territory ensures an adequate level of protection for the rights and freedoms of data subjects in relation to the processing of personal data.

3.2.3 The coverage of the Act

Key points of the Act can be summarised as follows.

(a) With certain exceptions, all **data users** and all computer bureaux have had to **register** under the Act with the **Data Protection Registrar**.

(b) **Individuals** (data subjects) are awarded certain **legal rights**.

(c) **Data holders** must adhere to the **data protection principles**.

3.2.4 Registration under the Act

The Data Protection Registrar keeps a Register of all data users. Each entry in the Register relates to a data user or computer bureau. Unless a data user has an entry in the Register he may not hold personal data. Even if the data user is registered, he must only hold data and use data for the **purposes** which are registered. A data user must apply to be registered.

3.3 Features of the 1998 legislation

(a) Everyone now has the right to go to court to seek redress for **any breach** of data protection law, rather than just for certain aspects of it.

(b) Filing systems that are structured so as to facilitate access to information about a particular person now fall within the legislation. This includes systems that are **paper-based** or on **microfilm** or **microfiche**. Personnel records meet this classification.

(c) Processing of personal data is **forbidden** except in the following circumstances.

  (i) With the **consent** of the subject (person).
  (ii) As a result of a **contractual arrangement.**
  (iii) Because of a **legal obligation.**
  (iv) To **protect the vital interests** of the subject.
  (v) Where processing is in the **public interest.**
  (vi) Where processing is required to exercise **official authority.**

(d) The processing of **'sensitive data'** is forbidden, unless express consent has been obtained or there are conflicting obligations under employment law. Sensitive data includes data relating to **racial origin**, **political opinions**, **religious beliefs**, physical or mental **health, sexual proclivities** and **trade union** membership.

(e) Data subjects have the right to a **copy of data** held about them and also the right to know **why** the data are being processed.

4 Assessment of computerised accounting systems

The new standards include a greater emphasis on computerised accounting systems in Units 1 and 2.

However the AAT do not have any plans to introduce computer based testing for the simulations. Therefore the skills based tests will continue to concentrate on manual systems. It is likely that students will be expected to know how computerised systems differ and the types of report that can be produced This is dealt with throughout this Text.

Knowledge of computerised systems will be evidenced in the Portfolio, either by work based evidence or work produced at college during IT sessions.

BPP have produced a CD-ROM and workbook called *Foundation Bookkeeping with Sage and Spreadsheets with Excel.*

You may also find the BPP book *Building your portfolio* helpful.

Both items can be ordered using the order forms at the back of this Text or online at www.bpp.com/aat.

Answers to Activities

Chapter 1

Answer 1.1

Aroma

4 The Boulevard
Market Town
MT2 3AB

Quotation No 762

To: Dax Office Supplies Ltd

Address: 6 High Street
Market Town
MT5 2LH

Date: 15 March 20X7

DETAILS	PRICE EXCL VAT
Provision and care of 4 large evergreen shrubs in separate containers (4 × £40 per month)	160.00
Provision and care of 6 small flowering plants in one container (£75 per month)	75.00
Sales	235.00
VAT @ 17.5%	
Total	

Answer 1.2

Aroma

4 The Boulevard
Market Town
MT2 3AB

ORDER ACKNOWLEDGEMENT 1724

To: Dax Office Supplies Ltd

Address: 6 High Street
Market Town
MT5 2LH

Date: 20 March 20X7

Sales order no: 543

DETAILS	PRICE EXCL VAT
Provision and care of 4 large evergreen shrubs in separate containers (4 × £40 per month)	160.00
Provision and care of 6 small flowering plants in one container (£75 per month)	75.00

Provision of plants to commence on 1 April 20X7

Sales 235.00
VAT @ 17.5% _____
Total _____

Answer 1.3

Aroma

4 The Boulevard
Market Town
MT2 3AB

SALES INVOICE NO 1762

To: Dax Office Supplies Ltd

Address: 6 High Street
Market Town
MT5 2LH

Date: 1 May 20X7   FOR THE MONTH OF: APRIL 20X7

DETAILS	PRICE
Provision and care of 4 large evergreen shrubs in separate containers (4 × £40 per month)	160.00
Provision and care of 6 small flowering plants in one container (£75 per month)	75.00

Payment terms: 30 days

Sales 235.00
VAT @ 17.5% _____
Total _____

E & OE

Answer 1.4

This is an example of a block code. Although there is an element of order in that the 500,000 series are used for expenses and the 100,000 codes for fixed assets, it is not a significant digit code. (**Note**. The term fixed assets will be explained in Chapter 5, but refers to assets used to run the business.)

ANSWERS TO ACTIVITIES

Answer 1.5

	£
March sales	2,000
Trade discount (5% × £2,000)	(100)
Net sales	1,900

Settlement discounts

	£
£500 paid on 7 April (5% × £500)	25
£1,000 paid on 14 April (2½ % × £1,000)	25
£500 paid on 30 April	-
	50

(**Tutorial note.** It may seem that Country Marquees have overpaid their bill by £150. However VAT needs to be added, as you will see in Section 7.)

Answer 1.6

(a) If Country Marquees delays more than 20 days, there will be no cash discount.

	£
Sales	22,000
Trade discount (10% × £22,000)	2,200
To pay before VAT is added	19,800

(b) If Country Marquees pays within 20 days, then the cash (settlement) discount applies.

	£
Sales	22,000
Trade discount (as in part (a))	2,200
	19,800
Settlement discount (2½% × £19,800)	495

(c) Description

	Price £
Flowers - list price	22,000
- less trade discount (10%)	2,200
Sales	19,800

Terms:

Net 30 days
Discount 2½% if paid within 20 days

478

ANSWERS TO ACTIVITIES

Answer 1.7

Product A

Gross price £705.60 **includes** VAT. Therefore VAT is $\frac{17.5}{117.5} \times £705.60 = £105.08$.

Product B

Net price £480.95 **excludes** VAT. Therefore VAT is $17.5\% \times £480.95 = £84.16$.

Answer 1.8

The point to remember is that VAT is calculated after allowing for the maximum discount **even if it is not taken**. Therefore the answers to (a) and (b) are the same

	£
Sales	22,000
Trade discount	2,200
	19,800
Cash discount	495
Amount on which VAT is charged	19,305
VAT (17.5% × £19,305)	3,378.37

Answer 1.9

Did you remember to calculate the VAT assuming a settlement discount of 5% on the whole amount?

	£
Sales	2,000
Trade discount (as in 1.5)	100
	1,900
Settlement discount (5% × £1,900)	95
Amount on which VAT is charged	1,805
VAT (17.5% × £1,805)	315.87

ANSWERS TO ACTIVITIES

Aroma 🌸

4 The Boulevard
Market Town
MT2 3AB

SALES INVOICE NO: 1763

To: Country Marquees

Address: Crown Estate
                The Links
                Market Town
                MT5 6QQ

Date/Tax point: 31 March 20X7

DETAILS	PRICE
March Sales	2,000.00
Trade discount (5%)	(100.00)

Terms and conditions:		
5% discount within 7 days	Sales	1,900.00
2½% discount within 14 days	VAT @ 17.5%	315.87
Net 30 days	Total	2,215.87

E & OE

VAT Registration No: 987 6543 21

Answer 1.10

VAT is calculated as follows.

	£
Sales after trade discount	25,200.00
Cash discount (2½% × £25,200)	(630.00)
Amount on which VAT is charged	24,570.00
VAT (17.5% × £24,570)	4,299.75

Aroma

4 The Boulevard
Market Town
MT2 3AB

SALES INVOICE NO: 1775

To: Country Marquees

Address: Crown Estate
The Links
Market Town
MT5 6QQ

Date/Tax point: 30 April 20X7

DETAILS		PRICE
5,000 Mixed carnations		2,500.00
10,000 Red roses		15,000.00
3,000 Yellow roses		3,000.00
4,000 Mixed fern		7,500.00
		28,000.00
Trade discount (10%)		(2,800.00)
Terms and conditions:		
	Sales	25,200.00
2 1/2% discount within 20 days	VAT @ 17.5%	4,299.75
30 days net	Total	29,499.75
E & OE		
VAT Registration No: 987 6543 21		

ANSWERS TO ACTIVITIES

Answer 1.11

Did you remember that the VAT is calculated on the **discounted price**, as in the original invoice.

	£
Sales returned	1,500.00
Trade discount (10% × £1,500)	(150.00)
	1,350.00
Cash discount (2½ % × £1,350)	(33.75)
Amount on which VAT is charged	1,316.25
VAT (17.5% × £1,316.25)	230.34

Aroma

4 The Boulevard
Market Town
MT2 3AB

CREDIT NOTE NO: C442

To: Country Marquees

Address: Crown Estate
The Links
Market Town
MT5 6 QQ

Date/Tax point: 5 May 20X7

DETAILS	PRICE
1,000 Red roses on Invoice 1775 returned infested with greenfly	1,500.00
Trade discount (10% × £1,500)	(150.00)

Terms and conditions:

2½% discount within 20 days
30 days net

Sales	1,350.00
VAT @ 17.5%	230.34
Total	1,580.34

E & OE

VAT Registration No: 987 6543 21

Answer 1.12

Country Marquees are a good customer with lots of sales. Their credit limit is £40,000 and, after the recently issued invoice of £28,000, this leaves £12,000. The new order for £35,000 exceeds this limit by £23,000. Kris needs to review their account to see if he should raise their credit limit. This will depend on their payment record and, possibly, an external credit agency's rating. If Kris decides to raise their credit limit, then the order can be accepted. However, if Kris has any doubts, he should contact Country Marquees to discuss the situation. It may well be that Country Marquees are willing to pay £23,000 immediately, which will enable Kris to fulfil their order and stay within the credit limit (Invoice £28,000 − Payment £23,000 + New Order £35,000 = £40,000).

ANSWERS TO ACTIVITIES

Chapter 2

Answer 2.1

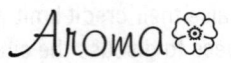

Aroma

4 The Boulevard
Market Town
MT2 3AB

Purchase Order No: 1233

To: Lampley Nurseries

Address: 47 Gorse Road
Lampley
LM2 9PR

Date: 6 April 20X7

VAT reg no: 987 6543 21

DESCRIPTION	CODE	NO OF UNITS	£
Freesias, mixed, small blooms	7050	180	936.00
Roses, white	9248	350	1,820.00
Roses, yellow	9252	200	1,140.00
Carnations, pink	0048	300	855.00
			4,751.00
Trade discount (10%)			(475.10)

DELIVERY INSTRUCTIONS

TO BE DELIVERED BY 13 APRIL 20X7 AT THE LATEST

Sub total	4,275.90
VAT @ 17.5%	748.28
Total	5,024.18

484

Answer 2.2

(a) If there is no purchase order, then Chan will not be able to match the invoice to an order. Therefore she will query the invoice and this could cause delays in paying it.

(b) If Ahmed receives a delivery but has no purchase order to cover it, he should reject the delivery on the grounds that it has not been ordered.

Answer 2.3

PURCHASE	CLASSIFICATION
Electricity for the shop	Business expense
Delivery van	Capital
Red roses	Stock
Gas supply for the shop	Business expense
Stamps	Business expense
Computer for processing purchase orders	Capital
White carnations	Stock
Shelving for displays in the shop	Capital
Repairs to the shop windows	Business expense

Answer 2.4

Blank GRNs could be used to support a bogus invoice. However Chan's request seems reasonable. Ahmed should take a blank GRN and write across it 'Sample for auditors' in ink. This will stop it being misused and fulfil Chan's requirements. Ahmed should remember to keep the warehouse copy, so that a number sequence check can still be made. Only the accounts copy should be given to Chan.

ANSWERS TO ACTIVITIES

Answer 2.5

```
                                                    ACCOUNTS COPY
          GOODS RECEIVED NOTE          WAREHOUSE COPY

       DATE: 10 April 20X7      TIME: 10.00            NO  5565
       ORDER NO: 1233
       SUPPLIER'S ADVICE NOTE NO:  1746           WAREHOUSE A
```

QUANTITY	CAT NO	DESCRIPTION
180 UNITS	7050	Freesias, mixed, small blooms
350 UNITS	9248	Roses, white
200 UNITS	9252	Roses, yellow
200 UNITS	0048	Carnations, pink

Note: A further 100 UNITS of 0048 to COMPLETE PURCHASE ORDER 1233 will be delivered 11 April 20X7

RECEIVED IN GOOD CONDITION: A P   (INITIALS)

Answer 2.6

- Check hours charged to hours on premises as shown in service book
- Check to order that repairs were authorised
- Check calculations on the invoice, including VAT

Tutorial note. These are the minimum checks, if you have thought of others well done!

Answer 2.7

		Trade discount £	*Cash discount* £
Alfred			
	Trade discount (20% × £2,000)	400	-
Bertie			
	Trade discount (10% × £6,000)	600	-
	Cash discount (5% × £3,000)	-	150
Charlie			
	Cash discount (5% of £2,000)	-	100
	(2½ % × £5,000)	-	125
		1,000	375

486

Answer 2.8

(a)
		£
List price		30,000
Trade discount (7½% × £30,000)		(2,250)
To pay		27,750

(b)
		£
Price after trade discount (as in part (a))		27,750.00
Cash discount (2½% × £27,750)		693.75
To pay		27,056.25

Answer 2.9

	£
List price	7,000.00
Trade discount (10% × £7,000)	(700.00)
	6,300.00
Cash discount (5% × £6,300)	(315.00)
Amount on which VAT is charged	5,985.00
VAT (17.5% × £5,985)	1,047.37

Note that the VAT is charged on the amount after **full** cash discount, even though Aroma will not be entitled to that discount (the discount is available only for immediate cash payment and the invoice will not be paid until 10 days after receipt).

Answer 2.10

(a)
- Goods received total £15,500, not £16,000
- Trade discount has been calculated at 0.5% instead of 10%
- VAT has been calculated on £15,920 instead of the price after trade and cash discounts
- VAT has been **deducted** from the total instead of being added
- The cash discount quoted is 5% of the net total, when it should be 5% of the goods ordered less trade discount before VAT

(b)
	£
Goods received (£15,500 + £600)	16,100.00
Trade discount (10%)	(1,610.00)
	14,490.00
VAT @ 17.5%	2,408.96
Net amount due:	16,898.96

Cash discount available if paid immediately upon receipt: £724.50 (5% × £14,490).

VAT is calculated on the discounted price of £13,765.50 (£14,490 - £724.50).

ANSWERS TO ACTIVITIES

Answer 2.11

Re: Invoice 7221

RECEIVED

Checked to Purchase Order No:	1 2 3 3 4 1	
Prices		X
Quantities		X
Checked to GRN No:	G 9 2 4	
Quantities		X
In good condition		X
Supplier terms/discount agreed		X
VAT rate agreed		✓
Calculations: Price extensions		
Additions		
Discount		
VAT		

Exceptions: _Prices incorrect, do not agree to deliveries_

Initials __JR__   Date __30.4.X7__

Payment authorised _____ Date _____

Note. It is not worth completing the rest of the stamp as the invoice does not agree to the order or GRNs.

Re: Invoice 7264

RECEIVED

Checked to Purchase Order No:	1 2 3 3 7 4	
Prices		X
Quantities		X
Checked to GRN No:	G 9 7 7	
Quantities		X
In good condition		✓
Supplier terms/discount agreed		X
VAT rate agreed		✓
Calculations: Price extensions		
Additions		
Discount		
VAT		

Exceptions: _Prices incorrect, do not agree to deliveries_

Initials __JR__   Date __30.4.X7__

Payment authorised _____ Date _____

DISCREPANCY	SUGGESTED ACTION
(1) Goods ordered but not yet delivered P. Order 1241: 1,000 large ferns P. Order 1274: 2,500 white roses 1,500 small ferns	(1) Chase up delivery with Lampley Nurseries
(2) GRN H010: has the wrong code for large ferns (code quoted is for small ferns)	(2) Clarify with warehouse whether the delivery was of small or large ferns
(3) GRN G977: Under-delivery of 1,000 white roses and over-delivery of 1,000 yellow roses re: order 1233	(3) Speak to warehouse about accepting deliveries without a purchase order. Speak to Lampley Nurseries about under/over deliveries
(4) Invoice 7221: Item 0048 – 2,000 delivered but 1,000 returned. Item 9248 price should be £5.20. Only 1% trade discount given – should be 10%.	(4) Contact Lampley Nurseries for credit note to cover these items.
(5) Invoice 7264: Item 1041 not received. Item 9248 not received. Only 1% trade discount given instead of 10%.	(5) Contact Lampley Nurseries for credit note.

Corrections needed

Invoice 7221

	£
Total per invoice	4,051.00
Adjustment for returned pink carnations (100 units × £2.85)	(285.00)
Adjustment for incorrect price for white roses (250 units × £0.50)	(125.00)
Adjusted total	3,641.00
Trade discount (10%)	(364.10)
	3,276.90
VAT @ 17.5%	573.45
Amount due	3,850.35

Invoice 7264

	£
Total per invoice	4,980.00
Adjustment for small ferns not received	(600.00)
Adjustment for white roses not received	(1,425.00)
Adjusted total	2,955.00
Trade discount (10%)	(295.50)
	2,659.50
VAT @ 17.5%	465.41
Amount due	3,124.91

Note. On invoice 7264 the white roses are at the incorrect price but this is ignored, as they have not been received and so the whole amount has to be deducted.

ANSWERS TO ACTIVITIES

Answer 2.12

To: A colleague
From: A Technician
SUBJECT: PURCHASE ORDER FORMS

Date: 7 April 20X7

You have suggested dispensing with Copies 3 and 4 of the purchase order form. This may reduce the burden of administration for purchase order/invoice processing, but it would be at the expense of a potentially serious deterioration in internal control.

Copy 3 of the purchase order, which is sent to the goods inwards department, allows goods inwards staff to check that goods received have been ordered on an authorised purchase order. (They may also help goods inwards staff to identify the internal destination of goods if this is not clear from suppliers' delivery notes.)

The purchase ledger section uses Copy 4 in the accounts department to compare and match goods shown on suppliers' invoices with approved order details. This helps to ensure that only goods which were ordered by someone with the correct authority are paid for. Without this check, goods which have never been ordered at all might be invoiced, or goods might be ordered fraudulently by someone for their own personal use.

Due to these considerations, I feel strongly that the use of four-part purchase order forms should continue.

(You could make an alternative suggestion. A 3-part purchase order could be used with copies being sent to the supplier, the purchasing department and the warehouse. Then on receipt of the goods, the warehouse copy, together with a GRN, could be forwarded to the accounts department to be matched against the invoice.)

Answer 2.13

(a) The supplier is reducing the liability due to him. If there are unpaid invoices outstanding, the account balance will be reduced by the total of the credit note. If Chan has already settled the account by making full payment, the credit will be 'cleared' when Aroma purchases further goods or receives a refund from the supplier.

(b) Any three of the following:

  (i) Wrong goods delivered and rejected.
  (ii) Goods of lower than expected quality, so returned.
  (iii) Wrong price charged when goods invoiced.
  (iv) Invoice does not tie in with GRNs.
  (v) Failure by supplier to give an agreed discount.
  (vi) Goods damaged in transit and so rejected.

(c) (i) The credit note may be cancelling or reducing the amount of the original invoice - so she will need to check that the credit note refers to the right purchase.

  (ii) If the credit note is received for incorrect goods delivered, the GRN will show that the wrong goods were delivered. Checking the GRN lets Chan know that Aroma are getting the full reimbursement.

  (iii) Chan won't need this, as it has nothing to do with a purchase.

  (iv) Aroma are receiving a credit note for goods returned - this is evidence of the quantities sent back.

(v) Chan is informing the supplier that she expects a credit note and for how much. Therefore this is a very useful check.

(vi) This might be useful to trace the transaction back to its origins.

(vii) Again this might be used to check the value of the credit note.

(viii) No marks for guessing why. There is never any harm in checking the arithmetic.

Chapter 3

Answer 3.1

Date	Invoice no	Customer	Net sales	VAT	Gross
16.3.X7	12058	Country Marquees	15,000.00	2,625.00	17,265.00
16.3.X7	12059	ABC Catering	2,500.00	437.50	2,937.50
16.3.X7	12060	Country Marquees	10,250.00	1,793.75	12,043.75

Answer 3.2

AROMA - SALES DAY BOOK

Date	Invoice No.	Customer No.	Total	A	B	C	D	VAT
17/3/X7	I2060	K02	141-00	58-00	62-00			21-00
17/3/X7	I2061	B09	151-62		55-32	62-09	11-63	22-58
17/3/X7	I2062	Cancelled						
17/3/X7	I2063	P11	104-11		34-47	26-31	27-82	15-51
18/3/X7	I2064	A01	141-00		120-00			21-00
18/3/X7	I2065	N04	59-07	50-27				8-80
18/3/X7	I2066	D06	45-98			31-57	7-56	6-85
18/3/X7	I2067	M09	90-60	38-55	38-55			13-50
	TOTAL		733-38	146-82	310-34	119-97	47-01	109-24

Chapter 4

Answer 4.1

Answer: (b). The purchase day book records purchases made on credit.

Answer 4.2

Date	Reference	Supplier	Supplier a/c no	Net	VAT	Gross
16.3.X7	1764	Lampley	L01	2,000.00	350.00	2,350.00
16.3.X7	1765	Alfred	A07	500.00	87.50	587.50
16.3.X7	1766	Bertie	B02	1,000.00	175.00	1,175.00
16.3.X7	1767	Charlie	C05	200.00	35.00	235.00

Answer 4.3

Situations (c) and (h) would be reflected in a purchase returns day book. These are situations in which you have returned goods to the supplier. Items (a) and (d) refer to sales you have made, not your purchases. Item (b) is a different sort of dispute. You have received no goods, and you have not entered the invoice in your accounts. Item (g) is similar to item (b), reflecting over-zealous invoicing by a supplier. Item (e) is an error, but refers to a delivery you have made. Item (f) is just bad luck! The goods were in perfectly good condition when you received them, and you are ordering more.

Answer 4.4

Code	Type of code
Invoice reference numbers	Sequence code
Supplier code numbers	Could be sequence code, but more likely to be a block code

ANSWERS TO ACTIVITIES

Answer 4.5

Date	Reference	Supplier Ref no	Net	VAT	Gross	Roses	Carnations	Potted plants	Sundry
16.3.X7	1764	L01	2,000.00	350.00	2,350.00	1,000.00	300.00	500.00	200.00
16.3.X7	1765	A07	500.00	87.50	587.50		500.00		
16.3.X7	1766	B02	1,000.00	175.00	1,175.00			500.00	500.00
16.3.X7	1767	C05	200.00	35.00	235.00				200.00

Answer 4.6

The main advantage of computerised accounting systems is that a large amount of data can be processed very quickly. A further advantage is that computerised systems are more accurate than manual systems.

Ivan's comment that 'you never know what is going on in that funny box' might be better expressed as 'lack of audit trail'. If a mistake occurs somewhere in the system it is not always possible to identify where and how it happened.

Chapter 5

Answer 5.1

	Asset	Liability	Capital
Bank overdraft		✓	
Factory	✓		
Money paid into a business by the owner			✓
Bank account	✓		
Plant and machinery	✓		
Amounts due from customers	✓		
Amounts due to suppliers		✓	
Stock of goods for sale	✓		

Answer 5.2

```
        Assets              =      Liabilities      +      Capital
Goods           25,000             Creditor  15,000        Capital  20,000
Cash            10,000
(20,000 – 10,000)
                _____                        _____                 _____
                35,000                        15,000                 20,000
```

ANSWERS TO ACTIVITIES

Answer 5.3

Assets		=	Liabilities		+	Capital	
Goods	0		Creditor	15,000		Capital	20,000
Cash	55,000					Profit	25,000
(10,000 + 50,000–						(50,000 –25,000)	
5,000)							
						Drawings	(5,000)
	55,000			15,000			40,000

Answer 5.4

Profit earned in the year	=	Increase in net assets	+	Drawings in current period	–	Capital introduced in the current period
35,000	=	50,000	+	5,000	–	20,000

Answer 5.5

(a) £60,000 (Purchases £75,000 – cash paid £15,000).

(b) £100,000 (Sales £150,000 – cash sales £50,000).

Answer 5.6

		Debit	Credit
(a)	Loan of £5,000 received from the bank	Cash £5,000	Bank loan £5,000
(b)	A payment of £800 cash for purchases	Purchases £800	Cash £800
(c)	The owner takes £50 cash to buy a birthday present for her husband	Drawings £50	Cash £50
(d)	The business sells goods costing £300 for £450 cash	Cash £450	Sales £450
(e)	The business sells goods costing £300 for £450 on credit	Debtors £450	Sales £450

Answer 5.7

CASH						BANK LOAN			
		£			£			£	£
(a) Bank loan		5,000	(b) Purchases		800			(a) Cash	5,000
(d) Sales		450	(c) Drawings		50				

ANSWERS TO ACTIVITIES

PURCHASES				DRAWINGS			
	£		£		£		£
(b) Cash	800			(c) Cash	50		

SALES				DEBTORS			
	£		£		£		£
		(d) Cash	450	(e) Sales	450		
		(e) Debtors	450				

Tutorial note. For items (d) and (e) the relevant amount is the selling price, not the original cost.

Notice that each entry has a narrative that shows where the other half of the double entry has been posted. This makes it easier to trace the other half of transactions and to spot errors.

Answer 5.8

AROMA			No: 121
Posting summary			
Date: 18 March 20X7			
Prepared by: *A Technician*			
Authorised by:			
Account	Code	DR £ p	CR £ p
Sales ledger control account	0210	733-38	
Sales A	2010		146-82
Sales B	2020		310-34
Sales C	2030		119-97
Sales D	2040		47-01
VAT control account	4000		109-24
Totals		733-38	733-38

Answer 5.9

	AROMA			No: 132
Posting summary				
Date: 24 March 20X7				
Prepared by: A Technician				
Authorised by:				
Account	Code		DR £ p	CR £ p
Sales ledger control account	0210			231-60
Sales returns A	2310		38-55	
Sales returns B	2320		158-55	
VAT control account	4000		34-50	
Totals			231-60	231-60

Answer 5.10

(a) (i) £12,572.50 is owed by Aroma to HM Customs & Excise.

(ii) The credit balance on the VAT control account represents a *liability*.

(b)

Account	Credit or debit balance?	Answer
Sales	CREDIT	Revenue
Sales returns	DEBIT	Expense
Sales ledger control account	DEBIT	Asset
Discounts allowed	DEBIT	Expense
Cash	CREDIT	Liability

Note that cash is usually an asset and so would be a debit. A credit balance means that the cash account is overdrawn and so the answer is a liability.

Answer 5.11

(a)

	A	B	C	D	E	F	G	H	I	J
1	Bodgett Purchase day book analysis								Page 41	
2	Date	Ref	Supplier	Supplier account	Total	VAT	Purchase cost	Tools	Painting & decorating	Bathroom items
3										
4	23/11/X7	712	Pitiso Tools	1550	1,858.02	276.72	1,581.30	1,581.30		
5		713	Macin	1310	13,336.25	1,986.25	11,350.00		11,350.00	
6		714	Throne Bathware	2010	2,542.46	378.66	2,163.80			2,163.80
7		715	Payper, Overr, Crackes	1510	1,134.63	168.98	965.65		948.75	16.90
8										
9										
10	Total for 23/11/X7				18,871.36	2,810.61	16,060.75	1,581.30	12,298.75	2,180.70
11										
12										
13										
14										

(b)

ACCOUNT POSTINGS			DR	CR
Account code	Ref		£ p	£ p
4000	PDB41	Tools purchases	1,581.30	
5000	PDB41	Painting & decorating purchases	12,298.75	
6000	PDB41	Bathroom purchases	2,180.70	
0694	PDB41	VAT	2,810.61	
0730	PDB41	Purchase ledger control account		18,871.36
		TOTAL	18,871.36	18,871.36

DATE 23/11/X7

Posted by ....

Helping hand. If you decided that the curtain rails purchased from Paper, Overr, Crackes were for shower curtains and therefore came under the Bathroom category, the relevant totals would be:

| Painting and decorating | £11,678.75 |
| Bathroom | £2,800.70 |

Answers to Activities

Answer 5.12

(a)

Bodgett Purchase returns day book — Page 5

	A	B	C	D	E	F	G	H	I	J	K
1											
2	Date	Debit note ref	Supplier	Supplier account	Total	VAT	Purchase return total	Tools	Painting & decorating	Bathroom items	Purchase ref
3											
4											
5	23/11/97	64	DoItheLot	8523	176.25	26.25	150.00			150.00	613
6		65	C and R	7211	259.67	38.67	221.00		221.00		612
7		66	House Foundation	6644	1,127.51	167.92	959.59			959.59	627
8											
9											
10	Total for 23/11/97				1,563.43	232.84	1,330.59		221.00	1,109.59	
11											
12											
13											
14											

(b)

ACCOUNT POSTINGS

Account code	Ref		DR £ p	CR £ p
0730	PRDB5	Purchase ledger control account	1,563.43	
6050	PRDB5	Purchase returns (bathware)		1,109.59
5050	PRDB5	Purchase returns (painting and decorating)		221.00
0694	PRDB5	VAT		232.84
		TOTAL	1,563.43	1,563.43

DATE   23/11/X7

Posted by ....

Chapter 6

Answer 6.1

Customer	Credit limit			No credit
	High	Medium	Low	
Swansong	✓			
Helping Hands Agency			✓	
Bear and Stag Investments		✓		

These answers may surprise you! However other answers are possible.

Swansong is long established and has a good credit record, therefore it is deserving of a high credit limit. However if Aroma is cautious, it may start with a medium credit limit, to be reviewed after six months, say.

Helping Hands Agency is newly established and the owner has a poor payment record, therefore a low credit limit is appropriate. If Aroma feels that it is unlikely to be paid, it may decide to give no credit limit ie deal on a cash only basis.

Bear and Stag Investments is newly established. The chief adviser may be a City Analyst but has he the experience to run his own business? The credit rating is excellent, but the business has no past payment record and so Aroma should be cautious and start with a medium credit limit. This can be reviewed and increased later if needed.

Answer 6.2

Customer	Delete (Y/N)	Reason
Cash in advance	Y	These are not credit sales but cash sales.
Clears at end of month	N	A record is needed of the invoices issued during the month.

ANSWERS TO ACTIVITIES

Answer 6.3

(a)

CUSTOMER NAME: Arturo Aski

ACCOUNT 001

ADDRESS: 94 Old Comedy Street, Vaudeville, 1BR, W. Meds

CREDIT LIMIT: £2,200

Date	Description	Transaction Ref	DR £	DR p	CR £	CR p	Balance £	Balance p
Brought forward 1/1/X7							2,050	37
1/1/X7	Inv	100	85	00			2,135	37
1/1/X7	Inv	102	16	99			2,152	36
1/1/X7	Inv	106	76	34			2,228	70

CUSTOMER NAME: Maye West

ACCOUNT 030

ADDRESS: 1 Vamping Parade, Holywood, Beds, HW1

CREDIT LIMIT: £1,000

Date	Description	Transaction Ref	DR £	DR p	CR £	CR p	Balance £	Balance p
Brought forward 1/1/X7							69	33
1/1/X7	Inv	101	98	15			167	48

ANSWERS TO ACTIVITIES

CUSTOMER NAME: Naguib Mahfouz

ADDRESS: 10 Palace Walk, London NE9

CREDIT LIMIT: £1,500

ACCOUNT 075

Date	Description	Transaction Ref	DR £	DR p	CR £	CR p	Balance £	Balance p
Brought forward 1/1/X7								
1/1/X7	Inv	104	123	10			123	10

CUSTOMER NAME: Josef Sveik

ADDRESS: 99 Balkan Row, Aldershot

CREDIT LIMIT: £700

ACCOUNT 099

Date	Description	Transaction Ref	DR £	DR p	CR £	CR p	Balance £	Balance p
Brought forward 1/1/X7							353	71
1/1/X7	Inv	105	35	72			389	43
1/1/X7	Cred	C44			353	71	35	72

ANSWERS TO ACTIVITIES

CUSTOMER NAME: *Grace Chang*							ACCOUNT	132

ADDRESS: *Red Dragon Street, Cardiff, Ca4*

CREDIT LIMIT: £1,200

Date	Description	Transaction Ref	DR		CR		Balance	
			£	p	£	p	£	p
	Brought forward 1/1/X7						1,175	80
1/1/X7	Inv	103	20	21			1,196	01

(b) **Double entry**

The sales ledger (ie the list of credit-related transactions analysed by customer) is a memorandum account.

So, the *double entry* from the sales day book and sales returns day book is as follows.

				£	£
(i)	DEBIT		Sales ledger control account	455.51	
	CREDIT		Sales		387.67
			VAT control account		67.84
				455.51	455.51
(ii)	DEBIT		Sales returns	301.03	
			VAT control account	52.68	
	CREDIT		Sales ledger control account		353.71
				353.71	353.71

(c) *Additional items*

(i) Did you check the sales return to the original invoice?

(ii) More importantly, did you notice that Arturo Aski (customer 001) has now exceeded his credit limit? How can this have slipped through the net?

(1) The customer may have told the person who took the order that a cheque was 'in the post'.
(2) The invoice might have been given the incorrect account code.
(3) The person receiving the order might not have checked the customer's credit status.
(4) The credit limit may have been raised, but you have not yet been told about it.

In any case, the matter should be referred to your boss for checking.

(iii) Grace Chang has an outstanding balance of £1,196.01. When she next makes an order, the account must be checked to see that she has reduced the balance outstanding, as it is near her credit limit. In any case, you may wish to monitor the account to ensure that she is not having cashflow problems (and therefore represents a risk to you). If her business is expanding and she is settling debts promptly (which you will be able to ascertain by looking at the ledger history), it may be appropriate to review her credit limit.

Answer 6.4

(a)

CUSTOMER: RANJIT SINGH ACCOUNT 1124
ADDRESS: 19 AMBER ROAD, ST MARY CRAY

Date	Transaction reference	Debit £ p	Credit £ p	Balance £ p
Brought forward				NIL
1/1/X7	236	405.33		405.33
2/2/X7	315	660.72		1,066.05
3/2/X7	317	13.90		1,079.95
5/2/X7	320	17.15		1,097.10
15/2/X7	Cash 004		1,066.05	31.05
21/2/X7	379	872.93		903.98
25/3/X7	Cash 006		500.00	403.98
31/3/X7	443	213.50		617.48
15/4/X7	Cash 007		500.00	117.48
1/5/X7	502	624.30		741.78
15/5/X7	Cash 031		500.00	241.78
	514	494.65		736.43
19/5/X7	521	923.91		1,660.34
20/5/X7	Cash 038		500.00	1,160.34
22/5/X7	538	110.00		1,270.34
20/6/X7	Cash 039		500.00	770.34
22/6/X7	Cash 042		923.91	(153.57)
1/7/X7	618	312.17		158.60
2/7/X7	619	560.73		719.33
8/7/X7	CRN 32		110.00	609.33
		5,209.29	4,599.96	609.33

(b) From the sales ledger which you have reconstructed, it seems that Ranjit Singh owes you £609.33. How is this made up?

	£
Invoices raised	5,209.29
Specific payments	(1,989.96)
Payments on account	(2,500.00)
Credit note	(110.00)
Balance	609.33

ANSWERS TO ACTIVITIES

Working back from the most recent items on the account:

(i)   Credit note number 32 for £110.00 can be matched against an invoice
(ii) Cash receipt ref 042 for £923.91 can be matched against an invoice
(iii) Invoice 619 for £560.73 is not settled
(iv) Invoice 618 for £312.17 is only part settled.

This may look odd - invoice 618 being part settled when the only subsequent credit on the account (the credit note) relates to a different item - but it arises because the cash receipts on 20 June and 22 June led to the account being overpaid, ie it was in credit. This means that the excess credit was allocated against the next available debit, invoice 618.

You might have reached the same position by tracking forward through the account, eliminating 'matched' items and working through the payments on account, as follows.

Payments on account amounted to £2,500. This is deemed to cover the invoices as follows.

		£
Invoice	317	13.90
	320	17.15
	379	872.93
	443	213.50
	502	624.30
	514	494.65
	618 - part (ie balance)	263.57
		2,500.00

The balance remaining is:

618 - unpaid part	48.60
619	560.73
	609.33

(**Note**. Invoice 618 is for £312.17, £263.57 paid and £48.60 unpaid.)

Chapter 7

Answer 7.1

(a) A creditor is owed money by a business, so it is a **liability**.

(b)

Accounts		Purchase ledger (Y/N)
(i)	Personal accounts for suppliers of subcomponents	Y
(ii)	Inland Revenue	N
(iii)	Customs & Excise for VAT	N
(iv)	Suppliers of raw materials stocks	Y
(v)	Bank overdraft	N
(vi)	Long-term bank loan	N
(vii)	Telephone expenses	Y
(viii)	Drawings	N
(ix)	Proprietor's capital	N

Answer 7.2

(a) The *Account name and address update* is used to set up some of the basic details of a supplier account on the computer system.

Updating can include both adding and deleting accounts. To tidy up the ledger, you can rid yourself of old 'dead' accounts.

(b) Many transactions are posted to the purchase ledger accounts, for example:

   (i)   invoices received from suppliers

   (ii) credit notes from suppliers

   (iii) payments to suppliers

   (iv) refunds of cash from suppliers (ie *Debit* Cash, *Credit* Creditors)

   (v)   discounts received

   (vi) correction of mispostings

   (vii) allocation (in open item systems where monies paid are set against individual invoices, rather than simply used to reduce the balance)

ANSWERS TO ACTIVITIES

Answer 7.3

(a) By the open item method, cash paid is matched exactly to invoices.

So, the invoices for which no cash has been paid are:

		£
2/9/X7	P901	453.10
7/9/X7	P904	25.50
30/9/X7	P909	92.70
		571.30

(b) By the balance forward method, cash paid is matched to the oldest invoices, so the outstanding balance is made up as follows.

		£
25/9/X7	P908	478.60
30/9/X7	P909	92.70
		571.30

Answer 7.4

ALFRED

	£		£
Returns	293.75	Invoice	1,175.00

BERTIE

	£		£
		Invoice	587.50

N GAS CO

	£		£
		Invoice	822.50

STANNER SUPPLIES

	£		£
		Invoice	705.00

PURCHASE LEDGER CONTROL A/C

	£		£
Returns DB	293.75	Purchase DB	3,290.00

VAT ACCOUNT

	£		£
Purchase DB	490.00	Returns DB	43.75

PURCHASES ACCOUNT

	£		£
Purchase DB	1,500.00	Returns DB	250.00

GAS ACCOUNT

	£		£
Purchase DB	700.00		

STATIONERY ACCOUNT

	£		£
Purchase DB	600.00		

Answer 7.5

A creditors' age analysis shows how long balances have been outstanding on the purchase ledger accounts. It may indicate that a business is delaying payment longer than is necessary or that it can not pay its liabilities.

Answer 7.6

Postings 28 August 20X7

		Debit £	Credit £
(a)	*Memorandum account adjustment*		
	Purchase ledger - MPV Ltd	97.40	
	Purchase ledger - Kernels Ltd		97.40
	Being correction of misposting of invoice (Kernels' ref 21201)		
(b)	*Memorandum account adjustment*		
	Purchase ledger - ASR Ltd	400.00	
	Purchase ledger - Kernels Ltd		400.00
	Being correction of misposting of 21/8 cash payment to ASR Ltd		
(c)	*Main ledger posting*		
	Purchase ledger control account (£42.84 × 2)	85.68	
	Purchases		85.68
	Being correction of misposting of Kernels Ltd credit note C91004		
	Memorandum account adjustment		
	Purchase ledger - Kernels Ltd	85.68	
(d)	*Main ledger posting*		
	Purchase ledger control account	64.17	
	Purchases		64.17
	Being correction of double posting of invoice 20642		
	Memorandum account adjustment		
	Purchase ledger – Kernels Ltd	64.17	
(e)	*Main ledger posting*		
	Purchase ledger control account	37.50	
	Sales ledger control account		37.50
	Being double entry to reflect contra between Kernels Ltd's sales ledger and purchase ledger accounts.		
	Memorandum account adjustment		
	Purchase ledger – Kernels Ltd	37.50	
	Sales ledger – Kernels Ltd		37.50

ANSWERS TO ACTIVITIES

KERNELS LIMITED

20X7		£	20X7		£
28/08	Misposted credit note (c)	85.68	27/08	Balance b/d	644.26
28/08	Misposted invoice (d)	64.17	28/08	Misposted invoice (a)	97.40
28/08	Contra (e)	37.50	28/08	Misposted cash (b)	400.00
28/08	Balance c/d	954.31			
		1,141.66			1,141.66
			28/08	Balance b/d	954.31

Chapter 8

Answer 8.1

The answer is not £492.22 because a payment was received on 5 May 20X2 which will almost certainly relate to the April balance. The invoices despatched on 3 and 4 May 20X2 are unlikely to have reached Finstar Ltd in time to be included in a payment received by Pickett on 5 May 20X2.

Therefore the outstanding balance b/f from 30.4.X2 and remaining unpaid is £80.05 (492.22 – 412.17).

Answer 8.2

> Finance Director
> ① *Baudrilard*
> Charles House
> Postmodern Industrial Estate
> Frontage, Wilts
>
> ① ②
> Dear Mr *Baudrilard*
> 14/9/X7
> ④ ⑤
> ③ *We've* got problems with your *account* which you will see from the *statement* I sent you *two* weeks ago. *Your* always going *overdrawn* and this month you don't *seem to* have paid us.
> ⑨ ⑥ ⑦ ⑧
>
> Please do *something about* it, or I might have to call in a *soliciter* or debt collector.
> ⑩ ⑪ ⑫ ⑬
>
> ⑭
> I remain, sir, your obedient servant,
>
> ⑮
> Boris Thug, Assistant

(a) 1   (i)   Wrong spelling; should be Baudrillard.
       (ii)   Boris should have used the proper name of the company, J L Baudrillard plc.

   2   The Finance Director, to whom Boris is writing, is called Martin Jacques. (Should the letter go to the Finance Director?)

   3   Who? Boris hasn't used headed notepaper, nor given any address, so the relevant personnel at J L Baudrillard plc are likely to be mystified.

   4   Which account? Both of them? One of them? Boris has not clearly explained what he is referring to.

   5   Again, there are two accounts and so two statements would have been sent.

   6   Better: (i)   To give the precise date you sent them
                     (ii)   To give the statement date, ie 31 August 20X7

   7   You are.

   8   You are not J L Baudrillard plc's banker. Baudrillard has exceeded his credit limit, but an overdraft is when you owe a bank money on your current account.

ANSWERS TO ACTIVITIES

9 Statement is dated 31 August. The letter is dated 14 September. Boris's last enquiry was 7 September. The statement reveals that Baudrillard usually pays on the 10th or 11th of each month. Boris should have waited and checked to see if there were any receipts.

10 Like what? Why not just say 'clear the outstanding debt'?

11 Boris would not be doing that sort of thing, as he is far too junior.

12 Threatening solicitors or debt collectors is completely inappropriate at this stage. This is a first reminder.

13 Solicit*or*.

14 'I remain ... servant' is absurdly pompous in this context. (Boris has obviously been reading the letters page of one of the newspapers.)

15 The letter is unsigned. This is extremely discourteous.

In short, the letter cannot be sent in its current form.

- It fails to identify the sender.
- It does not precisely describe the problem.
- It is not properly addressed.
- It is far too aggressive.
- There are basic errors in spelling and grammar.

(b) While Boris Thug's approach to debtor relations is brutal and potentially disastrous, there are a number of valid questions raised by the situation, and the following actions are appropriate.

(i) Check to see if Baudrillard and/or Baudrillard Robotics have paid in the time which has elapsed since September 7.

(ii) Check that the invoices sent since the last statement and the invoices on the statement have been posted to the correct account (ie Baudrillard plc Head Office or Baudrillard plc Robotics).

(iii) Examine the credit limits offered to Baudrillard, on both accounts.

(1) The 'A' account has never breached the credit limit. The credit limit was reviewed last year.
(2) The Robotics Division's credit limit has not been reviewed for over five years.

(iv) If Baudrillard Robotics is continually breaching its credit limits, the issue is important enough to bring up with Martin Jacques.

(1) It may be that a new arrangement with the company should be negotiated, covering both Head Office and Robotics division.

(2) Alternatively, perhaps a simple solution is that the Robotics Division's credit limit should be raised to reflect the increase.

The matter certainly merits discussion.

(v) If it is simply the case that Baudrillard Robotics holds on to its money for as long as possible, then offering a settlement discount or charging interest on overdue balances might encourage more prompt payment.

Answer 8.3

Account number	Customer name	Balance	Up to 30 days	Up to 60 days	Up to 90 days	Over 90 days
T004	Tricorn Ltd	94.80	0.00	0.00	0.00	94.80
V010	Volux Ltd	997.06	413.66	342.15	241.25	0.00
Y020	Yardsley Smith Ltd	341.77	321.17	20.60	0.00	0.00

Answer 8.4

(a) The goods were mispacked. Beethoven plc has been billed for two Callas Divas when only one was received.

  (i) Check the sales order, and confirmation to see that two Callas Divas were in fact ordered, rather than one Sutherland and one Callas.

  (ii) Check the sales returns day book to see that one Sutherland Diva was returned.

  (iii) Check that you do in fact offer a 10% trade discount to Beethoven plc.

(b) There are a number of ways you could deal with it. The simplest is probably to do the following.

  (i) Issue a credit note for £1,327.44 to cancel, in its entirety, invoice 4321.

  (ii) Issue a new invoice for the Superconductor and the one Callas Diva already received by Beethoven plc, taking the discount into account. This amounts to (£705.99 + £211.88) – 10% = £826.08, + VAT = £970.64.

  (iii) Issue an invoice for the other Callas Diva when it is delivered.

ANSWERS TO ACTIVITIES

&TUNE LTD
Discord Street, Crochety, Sussex

Beethovern plc
Symphony Promenade
Quavertree, Essex

Date   ....
Our Ref   ....
Your Ref ....

Attn: H V Karajan

Dear Mr Karajan,

Re: Invoice 4321

Further to our conversation today, I write to inform you that:

(a) you will be issued a credit note for the entire amount of Invoice 4321 (£1,327.44);

(b) you will also be sent an invoice for the superconductor and the Callas Diva you have already received;

(c) the second Callas Diva is in the course of construction, and will be sent to you when it is completed. You will be billed separately.

As you are entitled to the 10% trade discount, the invoiced amounts will reflect this fact.

Please accept my apologies for any inconvenience caused.

Yours sincerely

A Clerk

A Clerk

Answer 8.5

(a) Basic information needed is as follows.
- Customer name, in full
- Business address and telephone number
- Delivery address, if different from the business address
- Address of registered office
- VAT registration number, for checking purposes
- The name of a person you can deal with
- A reference number

In order to offer credit, you would need to know whether the company is able to use it responsibly. If a substantial amount of credit is requested you might need to know more about the customer's business, such as its profitability and trading history, as these will affect the assessment of how risky it is to give substantial credit. You can also make an assessment of what proportion of their purchases will come from you. If the planned percentage is high, you should consider the company as high risk.

You might insist that Stravinsky trades on a 'cash only' basis for a short period. You can also ask for references, either through the company, who should be asked to nominate other suppliers who you can contact, or from the company's bank or through the trade generally. (Care should be exercised: it has been known for habitual late-payers who withhold payment of bills as long as possible to select two suppliers for regular prompt payment and then to quote these two whenever they are asked for references!)

(b) Setting up an account involves:

   (i) Assigning a code number to the account
   (ii) Writing to the customer detailing the terms on which you operate
   (iii) Setting up the requisite ledger accounts in the accounting system
   (iv) Notifying subordinates of the new account
   (v) Assigning credit limits and payment terms
   (vi) Obtaining all the information in (a) above

Finally, make sure that you have followed your own organisation's procedure for obtaining authorisation to open the account.

The account should be monitored closely for the first, say, six months, to ensure that credit terms are adhered to and Stravinsky pays regularly.

Chapter 9

Answer 9.1

(a) There are a number of reasons why suppliers' statements are useful.

A supplier's statement can be used to check the following.

   (i) That you have *received* everything the supplier says you have
   (ii) That you have *recorded* everything the supplier says you have received
   (iii) That the supplier has *received* payments you have sent
   (iv) That the supplier has *recorded* payments that you have sent
   (v) That both you and the supplier agree on the amount that you owe

In summary, obtaining and checking a supplier statement is a way of checking that both your records are correct. This is why both internal and external auditors, when checking creditor balances, use supplier statements to verify the liability.

(b) Checking a *sample* of 10% might indicate that the system for processing transactions is working and, by implication, that the balances on the other accounts are correct.

Answer 9.2

There are three issues to be considered here.

(a) You are new to the company and, although your boss likes to delegate, you have no prior information about your employer's relationship with Jack Use Ltd.

(b) Being threatened with legal action is quite serious. Your boss should be told about it, even if he does not take the threat seriously.

(c) Jack Use Ltd may themselves be making a terrible mistake - this claim may not be valid.

So, Option 6 is your best choice. It would not hurt to look up the file first to see if there is any relevant information. However it is unlikely that you could tackle this query on your own, which is why option 7 is not the best choice.

Answer 9.3

PAYWELL SERVICES LIMITED
24 Maidstone Road, Taunton TA4 4RP

Ms D Waite
Accounts Department
Recycle Limited
Jarvis Lane
Maidenhead
SL6 4RS

Your ref: DW/SB 42

24 February 20X7

Dear Ms Waite,

Account number - P942

I am concerned at having received your letter of 20 February 20X7 stating that £2,642.50 remains outstanding on the above account for December 20X6.

Our records show that payment of this amount was made by BACS under the usual reference on 31 January. We have not received any acknowledgement of the payment from you.

It would seem that some error has been made, and I would be grateful if you would check whether you have a record of the payment. I note that on previous occasions there have been some problems in matching BACS payments to our account.

I am also concerned that we may not have been credited with the usual 2½% discount for prompt payment. Can you reassure me on this point?

Yours faithfully

A Technician
Senior Accounts Assistant

Answer 9.4

A good deal of thought needs to go into the opening of new files.

(a) Is there already a file for this purpose?

(b) What other files are related to this purpose? In other words, what cross-referencing needs to be done?

(c) Are the documents to be filed of an unusual size or material, requiring special storage facilities?

(d) Are the documents confidential?

(e) Will the documents be needed by you frequently, so that a personal or departmental file would be more appropriate than a central one?

(f) What title should be given to the file to make it clear to all potential users what it contains?

(g) How should documents be arranged within the file?

You may have thought of other points in addition to the above. Point (a) is the most important.

Answer 9.5

The updated file should show the following information.

Company:	Folworth (Business Services) Ltd
Address:	Crichton Buildings
	97 Lower Larkin Street
	London EC4A 8QT
Directors:	Robin Folworth BA ACA
	J..................... Crichton
	Margaret Foster
	Laurence Oldfield MA
	T....................... Scott
	John Thornhill BSc
Purchasing manager:	D Simmonds

Note that space has been left to fill in the new directors' first names.

ANSWERS TO ACTIVITIES

Answer 9.6

Business customers' files	Domestic customers' file	Auditors' file	Miscellaneous file
13, 1	5, 18	3	2, 9
7	11, 12		14
10			
15, 17			

(a) Given its date, document 3 is likely to be relevant to the current year, 2006.

(b) Document 4 may as well be thrown away.

(c) Document 6 should be placed on the auditors' file for 2002.

(d) Documents 8 and 20 can be thrown away, or kept with personnel records, perhaps in a file for 'staff entertainment'.

(e) Document 16 could most appropriately be given to whoever is responsible for cleaning or pinned up on a noticeboard.

(f) Document 19 could be thrown away, or else put in the auditors' file for 1999.

It would be sensible to close the old 'miscellaneous' file and either start a new one or else have a file for 'unusual orders'.

Maintaining a single file for domestic orders seems sensible as these are likely to be 'one-off' purchases. However, it would be helpful if this were arranged alphabetically so that related documents (for example 5 and 18) could be quickly matched.

Chapter 10

Answer 10.1

Customer	Amount of sale £	Amount tendered £	Change due (a) £	Notes/coin in change (b)
1	7.42	10.00	2.58	£2 coin, 50p coin, 5p coin, 2p coin and 1p coin
2	29.21	30.00	0.79	50p piece, 20p piece, 5p piece and two 2p pieces
3	7.98	10.00	2.02	£2 coin and 2p coin
4	44.44	45.00	0.56	50p coin, 5p coin and 1p coin
5	39.25	40.00	0.75	50p coin, 20p coin and 5p coin
6	57.20	57.20	-	-
7	9.46	10.46	1.00	£1 coin
8	10.17	10.50	0.33	20p coin, 10p coin, 2p coin and 1p coin
9	59.62	60.12	0.50	50p coin
10	12.93	20.00	7.07	£5 note, £2 coin, 5p coin and 2p coin
Totals	277.68	293.28	15.60	

The calculations may be checked as follows: £293.28 – £277.68 = £15.60.

Answer 10.2

	£
Cash float at start of the day	36.40
Sales in the day	277.68
Cash held at the end of the day	314.08

Answer 10.3

(a) The date on the cheque is incorrect. However, the cheque cannot be accepted even if the date is corrected because the sort code on the cheque does not agree with the sort code on the cheque card. Barry should ask whether the customer presented a card relating to another account in error.

(b) The date on the cheque is again incorrect. Perhaps Barry has been telling customers the incorrect date! It will be necessary for the customer to sign or initial a change in the date.

The amount in words and the amount in figures do not agree. Again, the customer must initial or sign any change.

The cheque guarantee card expired at the end of July 20X7. The customer needs to use his new replacement card, or some other method of payment entirely.

(c) The year has been omitted from the date. Barry should ask the customer to complete this. The cheque guarantee card details show that the card is not yet valid. This is probably because the customer has only recently been sent the card. Barry should ask the customer whether he has a card covering the period up to August 20X7.

Answer 10.4

(a) 'You can pay by quarterly **direct debit**. You need to complete a direct debit mandate form which authorises us to debit amounts from your bank account. We will send you a bill in the usual way each quarter, and the amount due will be debited from your account 14 days after the date of the bill, so you'll know how much is to be debited well in advance. If an error is made, either the bank or ourselves must put it right.'

(b) 'Normally, any balance due to us when the sale is completed will be paid by **banker's draft** or by **BACS**. A banker's draft or BACS is considered to be as good as cash, and of course cash would be acceptable but it is unusual and not so convenient to pay such a large amount in cash.'

Tutorial note. A builder may accept a cheque for a *deposit* put down on a house, but is very unlikely to accept a cheque when the sale is 'completed', as that is when he must hand over the keys and there is a risk that the cheque could be dishonoured.

(c) 'We do not advise you to send cash through the post, as we cannot accept responsibility if it is lost. We suggest that you pay by **postal order**, obtained from your post office. The post office will charge a fee for this service.'

(d) 'In order to pay by a cheque supported by a **banker's card**, it is necessary for the person whose signature appears on the card to sign and date the cheque in the presence of the payee - in other words, in our store. This rule is a standard rule of all of the banks. Please therefore ask your friend to call in to make the payment herself, unless you wish to pay by some other means, such as cash.'

Chapter 11

Answer 11.1

The cheque from your son is an instruction from your son to his bank to pay to you the sum stated on the cheque. When you pay it in at the branch here, we as the 'collecting' bank need to claim payment of the amount from your son's bank (the 'paying' bank). To deal with the large number of cheques going through the banking system each day, this is done by means of a centralised 'clearing' process. All of the cheques must be sorted, and when your son's bank receives and 'honours' the cheque they will debit the amount to his account and credit us. Only then will we know that the money represents 'cleared funds', and the clearing process usually takes about three working days. This is no reflection on your son's creditworthiness, it is simply a process which all cheques must go through.

Writing 'not negotiable' across the cheque is a way of 'crossing' the cheque. The words mean that if the cheque is stolen, the thief (or anybody he passes the cheque to) cannot become the true owner. Since your son's cheque is made out to you, this presents no problem. If someone had tried to pay the cheque into an account in another person's name, the cashier would need to make some enquiries before accepting it.

Answer 11.2

Transaction	Debit/Credit?	Reason
Money paid into the account	Credit	Increases amount owed by bank
Cheques paid out of the account	Debit	Decreases amount owed by bank
Interest paid by the bank	Credit	Increases amount owed by bank
A positive bank balance	Credit	Amount owed by bank to customer
An overdrawn bank balance	Debit	Amount owed by customer to bank

ANSWERS TO ACTIVITIES

Answer 11.3

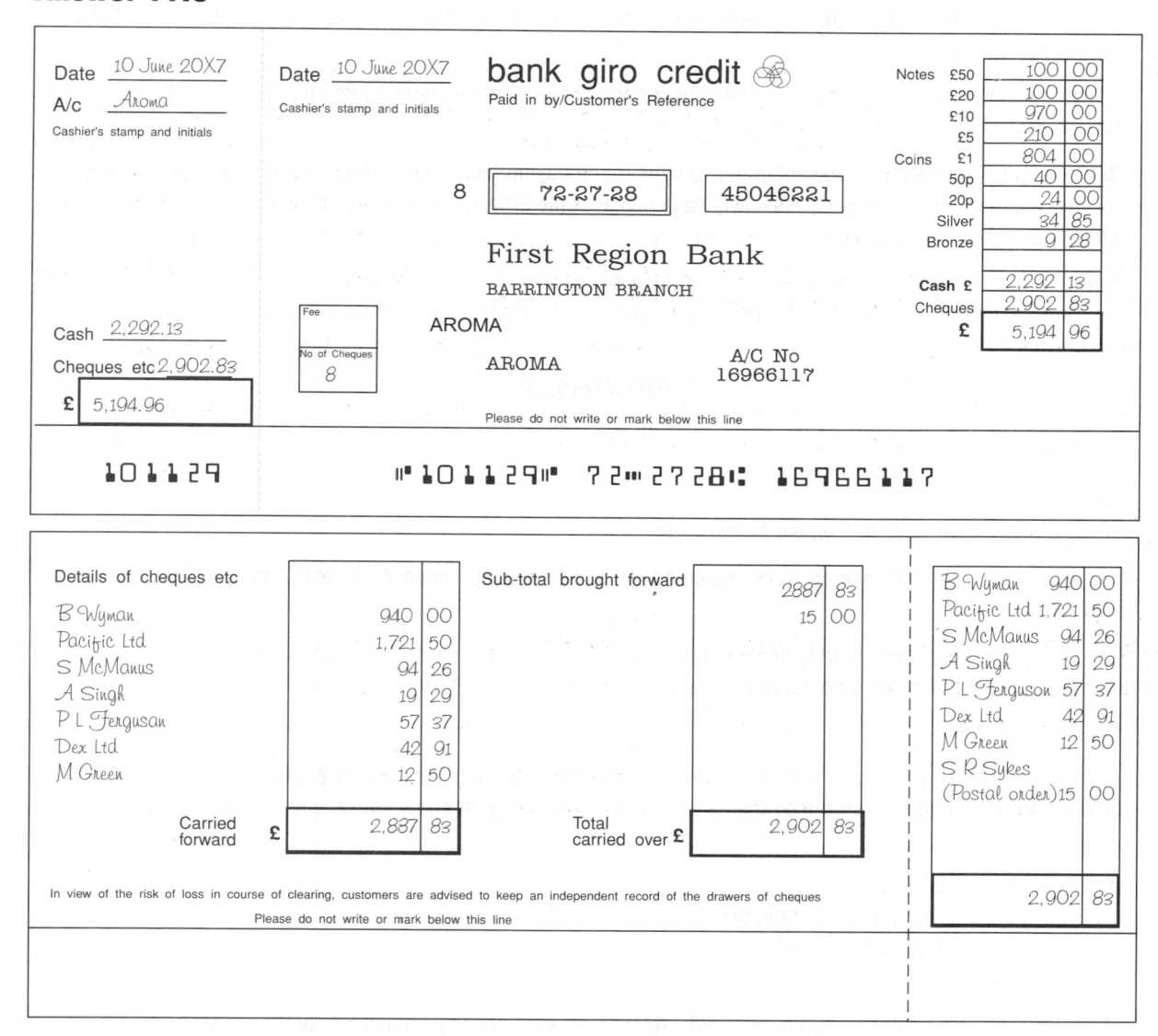

Date 10 June 20X7	Date 10 June 20X7	**bank giro credit**	Notes £50	100	00
A/c Aroma	Cashier's stamp and initials	Paid in by/Customer's Reference	£20	100	00
Cashier's stamp and initials			£10	970	00
			£5	210	00
		8 72-27-28 45046221	Coins £1	804	00
			50p	40	00
		First Region Bank	20p	24	00
		BARRINGTON BRANCH	Silver	34	85
Cash 2,292.13	Fee	AROMA	Bronze	9	28
Cheques etc 2,902.83	No of Cheques	AROMA A/C No	Cash £	2,292	13
£ 5,194.96	8	16966117	Cheques	2,902	83
			£	5,194	96

101129   101129 72-2728: 16966117

Details of cheques etc			Sub-total brought forward	2887	83	B Wyman	940	00
B Wyman	940	00		15	00	Pacific Ltd	1,721	50
Pacific Ltd	1,721	50				S McManus	94	26
S McManus	94	26				A Singh	19	29
A Singh	19	29				P L Ferguson	57	37
P L Ferguson	57	37				Dex Ltd	42	91
Dex Ltd	42	91				M Green	12	50
M Green	12	50				S R Sykes		
						(Postal order)	15	00
Carried forward £	2,837	83	Total carried over £	2,902	83		2,902	83

In view of the risk of loss in course of clearing, customers are advised to keep an independent record of the drawers of cheques

Please do not write or mark below this line

Answer 11.4

(a) The words on each of the cheques have been written by the bank in order to indicate why the cheques have not been 'paid'. The fact that the cheques cannot be paid means that the bank will have debited the amounts of the returned cheques from the firm's bank account. Action should be taken as follows.

First cheque. These words mean simply that the cheque has not been signed by the drawer (our customer). We should return the cheque to our customer, asking him either to sign it or to issue a new cheque.

ANSWERS TO ACTIVITIES

Second cheque. In this case, the cheque has been paid in to the bank before its due date: before the date written on the cheque. Since this cheque has been given a date after the date it was received by the firm, it is called a 'post dated' cheque.

Unless we want to ask the customer to send us a fresh cheque with an earlier date on it, we will have to wait until the due date of the cheque and try to pay it in again then.

Third cheque. The bank has presented this cheque to the paying bank (the drawer's bank) but that bank has declined to honour it. Most businesses will have had at some time customers who have run into financial difficulties, and this may have happened here.

It may be necessary to make further enquiries if we do not already have knowledge of the customer's difficulties. If we are not able to secure payment from the customer, we may have to instruct our solicitor to help us to recover the debt.

(b)
MEMORANDUM

To: A Smith
     General Manager
From: A Technician
Subject: *Cheques returned unpaid by the bank*

7 May 20X7

You asked about the returned cheques shown on the bank statement dated 2 May 20X7 and the bank charges relating to them.

Two of the three cheques should clearly not have been paid in to the bank. One of these had no drawer's signature and another was a post-dated cheque.

Recommendation

A checklist should be prepared for use by the staff member preparing cheques for banking. A brief check list will be more easily used and memorised than a lengthy list. The checklist should cover the following points as a minimum.

(i)   Is the cheque 'in date'?
(ii) Is payee name/endorsement in order?
(iii) Do words and figures agree?
(iv) Is it signed?

The third cheque was returned with the words 'refer to drawer', possibly indicating that the customer is in financial difficulties. The possibility that from time to time difficulties in recovering some debts will involve some cheques being returned unpaid is something which a business may just have to accept. A business may avoid some of these problems by being careful to whom it sells on credit. However, problems may still arise where customers who were thought to be creditworthy unexpectedly ran into financial difficulties later on.

Recommendation

The sales ledger department (the credit controller) should be informed of all cheques returned as 'refer to drawer'. If such items are occurring frequently it may be time to review the credit policy of the business.

Answer 11.5

(a)

Day	Cash/cheques sales £		Credit card sales £	Total for day £	Total for week so far £
Monday	696.97	(684.08 + 37.05 − 24.16)	104.28	801.25	801.25
Tuesday	479.82	(504.27 + 12.60 − 37.05)	202.96	682.78	1,484.03
Wednesday	698.21	(691.41 + 19.40 − 12.60)	86.91	785.12	2,269.15
Thursday	742.64	(729.62 + 32.42 − 19.40)	291.41	1,034.05	3,303.20
Friday	834.99	(840.50 + 26.91 − 32.42)	300.89	1,135.88	4,439.08
	3,452.63		986.45	4,439.08	
Total per till summaries				4,439.28	
Difference (not investigated)				0.20	

(b)

```
┌─────────────────────────────────────────────────────────────────────┐
│  ┌──────────────────────────────────────────┐                       │
│  │ HAVE YOU IMPRINTED THE SUMMARY           │                       │
│  │ WITH YOUR RETAILER'S CARD?               │                       │
│  └──────────────────────────────────────────┘                       │
│                                                                     │
│  BANK Processing (White) copy of       ┌──────────┬──────────────┐  │
│  Summary with your Vouchers in         │  ITEMS   │   AMOUNT     │  │
│  correct order:                        ├──────────┼──────────────┤  │
│  1. SUMMARY                            │          │              │  │
│  2. SALES VOUCHERS                     │    3     │  124  : 17   │  │
│  3. REFUND VOUCHERS                    │          │              │  │
│  KEEP Retailer's copies (Blue & Yellow)├──────────┼──────────────┤  │
│  NO MORE THAN 200 Vouchers to each     │    1     │   37  : 26   │  │
│  Summary                               │          │              │  │
│  DO NOT USE Staples, Pins, Paper Clips ├──────────┼──────────────┤  │
│                                         │  DATE   │  TOTAL       │  │
│                                         │29.11.X7 │   86  : 91   │  │
│                                         │         │   £          │  │
│                                        └──────────┴──────────────┘  │
│                                                                     │
│  First Region Bank     BANKING                                      │
│  FASTPASS              SUMMARY               RETAILER'S SIGNATURE   │
│                                                                     │
│  ┌─────────────────────────────────────────────────────────────┐    │
│  │ COMPLETE THIS SUMMARY FOR EVERY DEPOSIT OF SALES VOUCHERS   │    │
│  │ AND ENTER THE TOTAL ON YOUR NORMAL CURRENT ACCOUNT          │    │
│  │ PAYING-IN SLIP                                              │    │
│  └─────────────────────────────────────────────────────────────┘    │
└─────────────────────────────────────────────────────────────────────┘
```

(c) The total should be entered on the usual current account paying-in slip. The top and processing copies of the summary will be handed over at the bank with the credit card vouchers and the rest of the day's takings. The middle copy will be kept by Aroma for their records in case a query arises.

ANSWERS TO ACTIVITIES

Answer 11.6

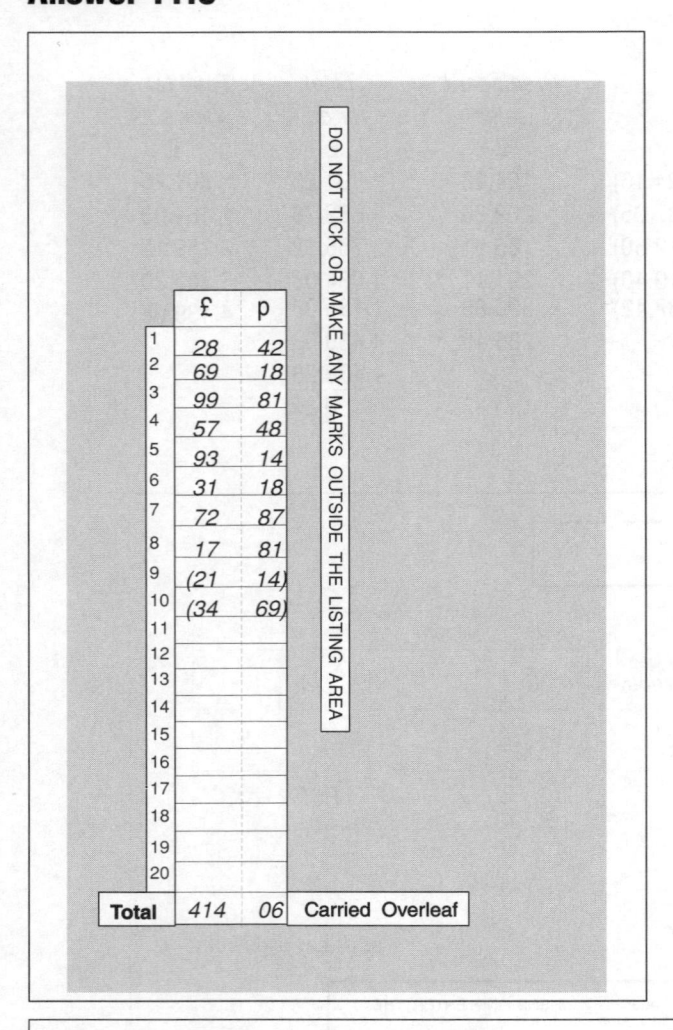

DO NOT TICK OR MAKE ANY MARKS OUTSIDE THE LISTING AREA

	£	p
1	28	42
2	69	18
3	99	81
4	57	48
5	93	14
6	31	18
7	72	87
8	17	81
9	(21	14)
10	(34	69)
11		
12		
13		
14		
15		
16		
17		
18		
19		
20		
Total	414	06	Carried Overleaf

HAVE YOU IMPRINTED THE SUMMARY WITH YOUR RETAILER'S CARD?

BANK Processing (White) copy of Summary with your Vouchers in correct order:
1. SUMMARY
2. SALES VOUCHERS
3. REFUND VOUCHERS
KEEP Retailer's copies (Blue & Yellow)
NO MORE THAN 200 Vouchers to each Summary
DO NOT USE Staples, Pins, Paper Clips

	ITEMS	AMOUNT	
SALES VOUCHERS (LISTED OVERLEAF)	8	469	89
LESS REFUND VOUCHERS	2	(55	83)
DATE 22.5.X7	TOTAL £	414 :	06

SUMMARY - RETAILER'S COPY

Southern Bank **BANKING**
FASTPASS **SUMMARY**

RETAILER'S SIGNATURE

COMPLETE THIS SUMMARY FOR EVERY DEPOSIT OF SALES VOUCHERS AND ENTER THE TOTAL ON YOUR NORMAL CURRENT ACCOUNT PAYING-IN SLIP

ANSWERS TO ACTIVITIES

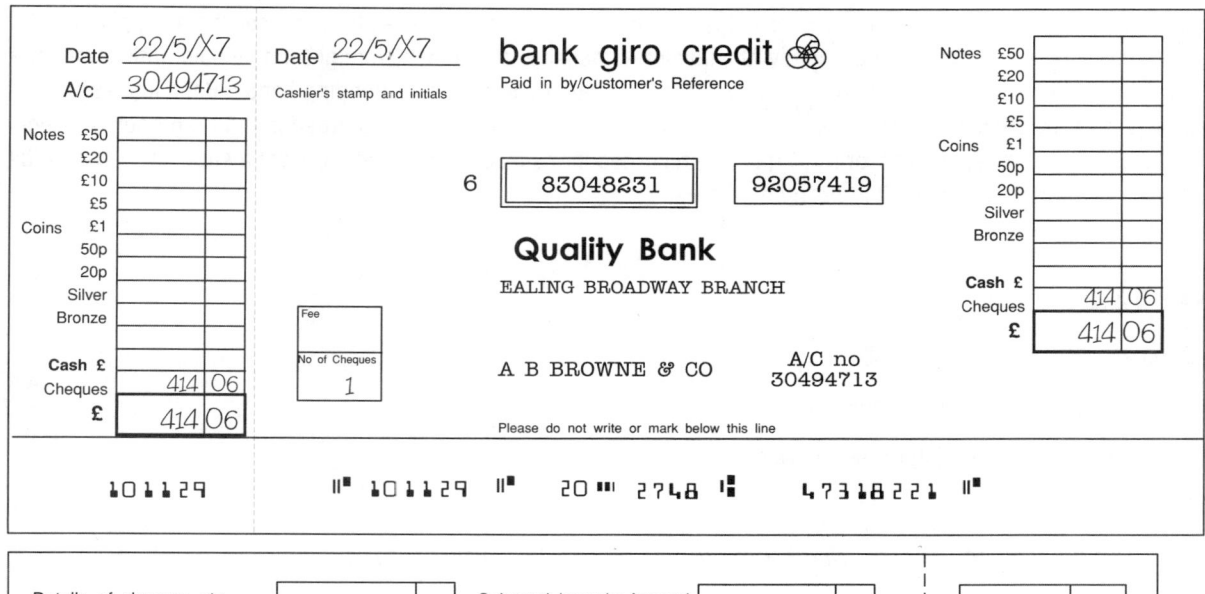

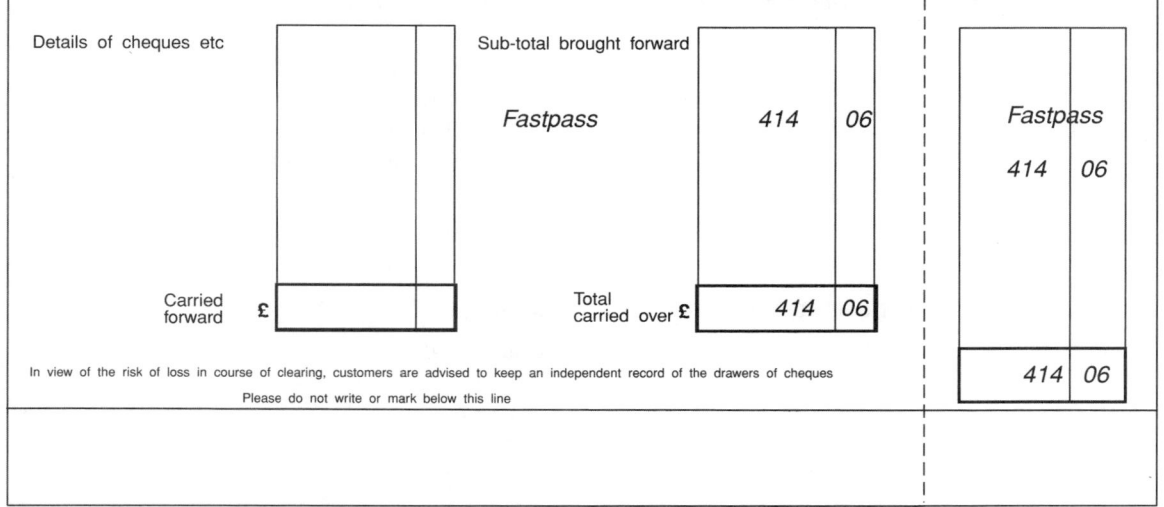

[Bank giro credit slip filled in with: Date 22/5/X7, A/c 30494713, Date 22/5/X7, 6, 83048231, 92057419, Quality Bank, EALING BROADWAY BRANCH, A B BROWNE & CO, A/C no 30494713, No of Cheques 1, Cash £ Cheques 414 06, £ 414 06. Right side: Cash £ Cheques 414 06, £ 414 06. MICR line: 101129 101129 20 2748 47318221. Counterfoil: Fastpass 414 06, Total carried over £ 414 06, Fastpass 414 06, 414 06.]

Chapter 12

Answer 12.1

Tutorial note. The cash book records money received and money paid. If something does not involve money coming into or going out of the business, it will not result in an entry in the cash book.

The following will not be entered in the cash book.

(c) Supplier's invoice
(d) Credit note
(e) Debit note

ANSWERS TO ACTIVITIES

A cheque received (a) and a payment from sales ledger customers (b) comprise receipts. But receiving a supplier's invoice (c) is not a receipt or payment of money: the invoice establishes a debt, which might not be paid until some time later. Similarly, issuing (d) a credit note or (e) a debit note does not involve money changing hands. Bank interest received (f) is paid (by the bank) when debited to the bank account, and needs to be recorded in the cash book. A fixed asset has been sold and the payment for it (g) must be recorded in the cash book. A refund from a supplier (h) would be included as it is a monetary item (ie it is *not* a credit note).

Answer 12.2

(a) £405.26 + £715.22 = £1,120.48.

(b) (i) 11.00am to 1.00pm (see working)

    (ii) 12.00 noon to 2.00pm (see working)

Working

Two hour period	Number of sales	Value of sales £
9.00 - 11.00	43	618.66
10.00 - 12.00	64	1,638.24
11.00 - 1.00	76 Highest (i)	1,954.17
12.00 - 2.00	65	2,005.76 Highest (ii)
1.00 - 3.00	45	1,616.37
2.00 - 4.00	54	873.05
3.00 - 5.00	72	1,120.48

(c) Total sales can be calculated from two-hour periods as in the working for (b).

Period	Value of sales £
9.00 - 11.00	618.66
11.00 - 1.00	1,954.17
1.00 - 3.00	1,616.37
3.00 - 5.00	1,120.48
Total sales	5,309.68
Add float	25.00
Less credit card and cheque sales	(319.25)
Total in till	5,015.43

Answer 12.3

(a) Assuming that the times at which the members of staff concerned took over the till are precisely as stated compared with the times on the till's own clock, we can calculate the amounts expected to be counted in the till at each change of duty.

ANSWERS TO ACTIVITIES

	Expected £		Actual £	Difference £
11.00 am	643.66	(£618.66 + £25.00)	625.66	– 18.00
3.00 pm	4,214.20	(£618.66 + £1,954.17 + £1,616.37 + £25.00)	4,196.20	– 18.00

At both 11.00am and 3.00pm the cash counted is £18.00 short. It would appear that a shortage of £18.00 occurred while John Walton was operating the till and that an excess of 58p occurred between 3.00pm and 5.00pm while Ali Alaqat was on duty. This has led to a net shortage of £17.42 at the close of business.

(b) On each change of staff duty, a report could be obtained from the cash register giving a subtotal of sales for the day up to that time. This total could be added to the amount of the float at the start of the day to give a figure for the amount expected in the till at that time. Preferably, the subtotal should be obtained after the till operators have written down their own count. Otherwise the till operators may be tempted not to bother to carry out their own count.

Answer 12.4

(a)

Cash received sheet   Number... 1523

Date	Name	Account No.	Amount £
20.4.X7	Jill's Kitchen Co	J211	492.70
20.4.X7	G Edwards & Son	E102	242.98
21.4.X7	Crystal Water Co	C101	892.76
21.4.X7	H M Customs & Excise	1600	487.50
21.4.X7	Green Gourmet Co	G105	500.00
22.4.X7	BRM Motors	1720	1,700.00
22.4.X7	Jennan Tonic Ltd	J110	1,920.70
23.4.X7	Oliver's Organic Foods	O301	400.00
23.4.X7	Parkers Preserves Ltd	P002	3,208.00
24.4.X7	Pennine Springs Ltd	P004	4,920.75
	Total	1000	14,765.39

(b) The cash receipts will be recorded on the debit side of the cash book, probably on a single line showing the cash received sheet number.

ANSWERS TO ACTIVITIES

Answer 12.5

AROMA POSTING SUMMARY		WEEK COMMENCING 20.4.X7	
ACCOUNT	NO	DEBIT	CREDIT
Cash account	1000	14,765.39	
Sales ledger control account	1200		12,577.89
VAT account	1600		487.50
Disposal of fixed assets	1720		1,700.00
Totals		14,765.39	14,765.39

Answer 12.6

(a)

ARIA ENTERPRISES

RECEIPTS

Date	Narrative	Folio	Discount allowed	Receipt total	VAT	Debtors	Cash sales	Other
05-Feb	Carmen Carpets	SL0075	112.50	2,137.50		2,137.50		
08-Feb	Placido Players	SL0553		42.00	6.25		35.75	
11-Feb	Mehta Metronomes	SL0712		543.27		543.27		
14-Feb	Luciano Lighting	SL0009	19.00	361.00		361.00		
15-Feb	Tosca Tents	SL0473		4,000.00	595.74		3,404.26	
15-Feb	Magic Flute Instruments	SL0338	475.00	9,025.00		9,025.00		
	Bank interest	INT270 CR		42.01				42.01
	Sale of delivery van	FAD028 CR		2,500.00				2,500.00
	Totals		606.50	18,650.78	601.99	12,066.77	3,440.01	2,542.01
			DIS340 DR SLC040 CR	CAB010 DR	VAT094 CR	SLC040 CR	SAL200 CR	

530

(b)

ARIA ENTERPRISES

CASH BOOK RECEIPTS POSTING SUMMARY 15 FEBRUARY

Narrative	Nominal ledger account	DR	CR
		£	£
Cash	CAB010	18,650.78	
Sales discounts allowed	DIS340	606.50	
VAT control	VAT094		601.99
Sales ledger control	SLC040		12,066.77
	SLC040		606.50
Sales	SAL200		3,440.01
Interest received	INT270		42.01
Fixed asset disposal	FAD028		2,500.00
		19,257.28	19,257.28

```
                                    CASH                                    CAB 010
                                     £                                         £
15 Feb   Bal b/d            76,959.00
         Cash book          18,650.78

                            VAT CONTROL ACCOUNT                              VAT 094
                                     £                                         £
                                                 15 Feb   Bal b/d         10,500.00
                                                          Cash book          601.99

                         SALES LEDGER CONTROL ACCOUNT                        SLC 040
                                     £                                         £
15 Feb   bal b/d           152,744.00            15 Feb   Cash book       12,066.77
                                                          Cash book          606.50

                          SALES DISCOUNTS ALLOWED                            DIS 340
                                     £                                         £
15 Feb   Bal b/d             7,050.00
         Cash book             606.50

                                    SALES                                    SAL 200
                                     £                                         £
                                                 15 Feb   Bal b/d        372,771.00
                                                          Cash book        3,440.01

                             INTEREST RECEIVED                               INT 270
                                     £                                         £
                                                 15 Feb   Cash book           42.01
```

ANSWERS TO ACTIVITIES

	FIXED ASSET DISPOSALS		FAD 028
£			£
	15 Feb	Cash book	2,500.00

Chapter 13

Answer 13.1

AROMA

CHEQUE REQUISITION FORM

DATE: 20 JUNE 20X7

Please draw a cheque on the business's bank account:

PAYABLE TO: ARTHUR DALEY

AMOUNT: £500

REASON: SECOND HAND DELIVERY VAN

Please tick as appropriate

Invoice/receipt to follow	✓
No invoice or receipt	
Other evidence attached	

Send cheque to: KRIS ANTHEMUM

Signature: *K Anthemum*

Position: PROPRIETOR

Answer 13.2

(a)

Ref	Amount £	Due date (30 days)	Payment date 25.7 £	1.8 £	8.8 £	15.8 £
133097	984.10	21.7	984.10			
CN 01711	(942.42)	-	(942.42)			
133142	6,975.27	28.7	6,975.27			
133179	2,474.19	2.8		2,474.19		
133200	1,709.94	4.8		1,709.94		
133224	2,788.50	7.8		2,788.50		
133275	670.83	11.8			670.83	
133309	1,888.66	14.8			1,888.66	
133324	524.96	16.8				524.96
133394	2,004.92	16.8				2,004.92
133441	879.22	18.8				879.22
133619	1,424.67	21.8				1,424.67
CN 01794	(404.88)		(404.88)			
	20,977.96		6,612.07	6,972.63	2,559.49	4,833.77

Note. Invoice 133660 for £1,424.67 will be paid on 22 August. Credit notes are taken as early as possible. No settlement discounts are due.

(b)

Ref	£	Best discount available (%)	£	Payment date 25.7 £	1.8 £	8.8 £	15.8 £
133097	984.10		-	984.10			
CN 01711	(942.42)		-	(942.42)			
133142	6,975.27		-	6,975.27			
133179	2,474.19		-		2,474.19		
133200	1,709.94		-		1,709.94		
133224	2,788.50		-		2,788.50		
133275	670.83	(1)	6.71	664.12			
133309	1,888.66	(1)	18.89	1,869.77			
133324	524.96	(1)	5.25	519.71			
133394	2,004.92	(1)	20.05	1,984.87			
133441	879.22	(2)	17.58	861.64			
133619	1,424.67	(2)	28.49	1,396.18			
CN 01794	(404.88)		-	(404.88)			
133660	1,424.67	(2)	28.49	1,396.18			
	22,402.63		125.46	15,304.54	6,972.63	-	-

Note. Credit notes are taken as early as possible.

ANSWERS TO ACTIVITIES

Answer 13.3

(a) The following errors or discrepancies are apparent.

    (i) The payment made on 8 October is not reflected in the statement. This is probably because the payment was in transit when the statement was prepared.

    (ii) Invoice 50311 (2.9.X7) is shown on the statement as £662.54 instead of £642.54.

    (iii) Invoice 50449 (9.9.X7) is shown on the statement as £357.42 instead of £354.72.

    (iv) Credit note 7211 (13.9.X7) for £864.75 is not shown on the statement.

(b) (i) The items over thirty days old and remaining unpaid as at 15 October 20X7 are as follows.

Date	Details	Amount £
7.9.X7	Invoice 50411	6,997.21
9.9.X7	Invoice 50449	354.72
11.9.X7	Invoice 50457	3,428.88
13.9.X7	Credit note 7211	(864.75)
Total payment to be made		9,916.06

(ii)

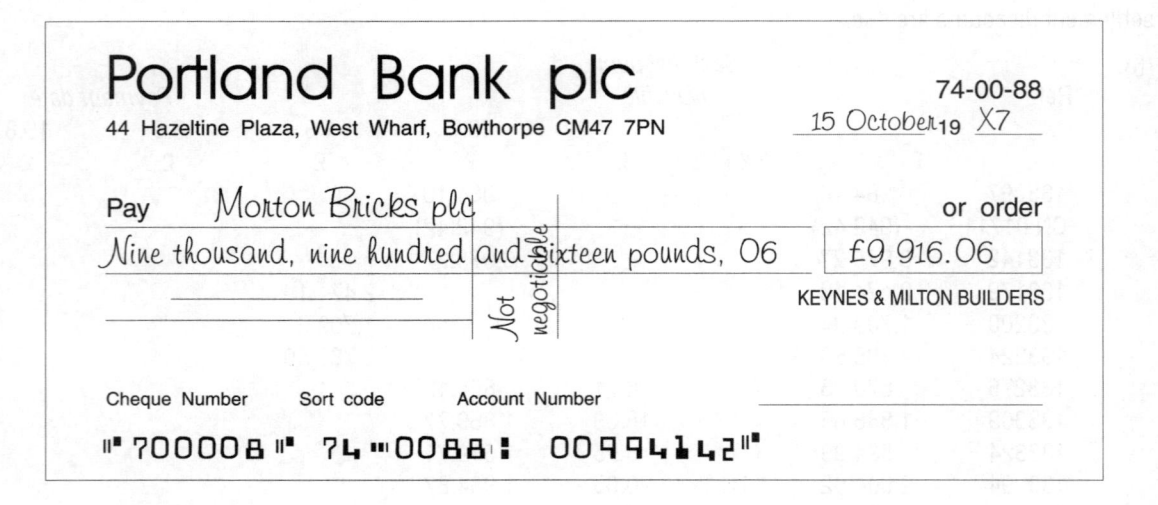

Portland Bank plc
74-00-88
44 Hazeltine Plaza, West Wharf, Bowthorpe CM47 7PN
15 October 19 X7

Pay Morton Bricks plc or order
Nine thousand, nine hundred and sixteen pounds, 06   £9,916.06

Not negotiable

KEYNES & MILTON BUILDERS

Cheque Number Sort code Account Number

700008 74-0088 0099442

Answer 13.4

(a) **Recommended method: cash**

This is a small business payment which should be paid out of petty cash for the sake of convenience.

(b) **Recommended method: standing order**

A standing order is convenient for regular fixed payments. Once the standing order instruction is made, the bank will ensure that all payments are made on the due dates and will stop making payments at the date specified in the instruction. Some finance companies may insist on a standing order being set up, as it is convenient for them to receive instalments regularly without having to issue payment requests or reminders.

(c) **Recommended method: by cheque at the bank**, accompanied by the bill and completed bank giro credit form. The bank clerk will stamp the bill as evidence that the payment was made.

Paying by cheque is safer than paying by cash and is more usual for such a large payment. Handing the cheque over at the bank will be convenient and evidence of payment will be obtained. If the payment is made at a bank other than that at which Aroma holds an account, the bank receiving the payment will probably make a small charge for processing it.

An alternative method is to send a crossed cheque by post, enclosing the payment counterfoil.

(d) **Recommended method: direct debit mandate**

The direct debit mandate will allow the Council to debit the amounts due direct from Aroma's bank account on the due dates. The mandate will be effective until it is cancelled. The Council must inform Aroma in advance of the amounts it will be debiting.

(e) **Recommended method: credit card or charge card**

Payment by credit card or charge card avoids the need to pay immediately by cash or cheque. If Kris's personal card is used, he will claim payment later from Aroma, which may pay him by cheque or with his monthly salary payment. If a business credit or charge card is used, Aroma will be responsible for paying the amounts shown on the monthly statement.

(f) **Recommended method: banker's draft**

A banker's draft cannot be stopped or cancelled once it is issued. Being effectively like a cheque drawn on the bank itself, it is generally accepted as being as good as cash. It is therefore most likely to be accepted by Selham Motors.

Answer 13.5

(a)

Aroma

4 The Boulevard
Market Town
MT 3AB
Telephone: 01279 33942
Fax: 01279 33920

REMITTANCE ADVICE

Supplier account number

FO 11

Date of payment: 2 June 20X7

Feathers Limited
247 Marconi Road
Chelmsford, Essex CM1 4PQ

Invoice/ credit note date	Details	Invoices £	Credit notes £	Payment amount £
30.3.X7	Invoice 07114	87.42		87.42
6.4.X7	Credit note CR084		167.14	(167.14)
7.4.X7	Invoice 07241	292.23		292.23
9.4.X7	Invoice 07249	851.80		851.80
14.4.X7	Invoice 07302	165.87		165.87
22.4.X7	Credit note CR087		118.96	(118.96)
22.4.X7	Invoice 07487	494.68		494.68
28.4.X7	Credit note CR099		87.42	(87.42)
7.5.X7	Invoice 07714	116.25		116.25
	Total payment			1,634.73

Aroma

4 The Boulevard
Market Town
MT2 3AB
Telephone: 01279 33942
Fax: 01279 33920

REMITTANCE ADVICE

Supplier account number

FO 17

Date of payment: 2 June 20X7

The Furniture People
4 Kane Street
Northampton NN3 4SR

Invoice/ credit note date	Details	Invoices £	Credit notes £	Payment amount £
2.4.X7	Invoice 734282	4,397.18		4,397.18
23.4.X7	Invoice 735110	7,215.72		7,215.72
27.4.X7	Invoice 735192	990.43		990.43
27.4.X7	Invoice 735204	1,459.00		1,459.00
4.5.X7	Credit note 274221		1,107.33	(1,107.33)
	Total payment			12,955.00

ANSWERS TO ACTIVITIES

(b) The total payments to be made are as follows.

	£
Feathers Ltd	1,634.73
The Furniture People	12,955.00
Total	14,589.73

Answer 13.6

(a)

Portland Bank plc
7 The Square, Bishop's Stortford, Hertfordshire CM23 1NP
74-98-76
2 June 20 X7

Pay Feathers Limited or order
One thousand, six hundred and thirty-four pounds 73   £1,634.73
A/c payee
FOR AND ON BEHALF OF AROMA

Cheque Number   Sort code   Account Number
720088   74-9876   64196419

Portland Bank plc
7 The Square, Bishop's Stortford, Hertfordshire CM23 1NP
74-98-76
2 June 20 X7

Pay The Furniture People or order
Twelve thousand, nine hundred and fifty-five pounds only   £12,955.00
A/c payee
FOR AND ON BEHALF OF AROMA

Cheque Number   Sort code   Account Number
720089   74-9876   64196419

(b) The cheque to Feathers Ltd requires the signatures of two directors; the cheque to The Furniture People requires the signature of the Chairman or the Managing Director and that of one other director. I would take the cheques for signature (together with invoices, remittance advices and any other supporting documentation) to K Anthemum (Chairman). Neither of the other two directors (J Knight and J Mackie) are in today, but I would ask J Knight, who is in tomorrow, to sign the cheques as early as possible. In the meantime, I would keep all documents in the safe overnight for security.

ANSWERS TO ACTIVITIES

(c) I would stamp the invoices to indicate that payment of the invoice has been approved and made, and on what date. In some firms, a sticker may be used for this purpose. This procedure provides a record of the approval of the payment for later reference and may help to prevent an invoice being paid twice in error.

Chapter 14

Answer 14.1

(a) As a matter of physical security, using only **one cheque book** at a time minimises the risk that a cheque book will fall into the wrong hands. Cheque books which have not yet been started should be locked securely in a safe, as should the current cheque book when it is not in use.

Using only one cheque book at a time also makes it simpler to keep a check on the sequence of cheques being issued. Cheques will be issued and entered in the cash book consecutively.

(b) Entering the number of all cheques in the cash book even if **cancelled** makes it easier to check that all payments by cheque have been entered. It also means that the cash book will provide a record of all cheques in case of later queries or when checking the bank statement with the cash book.

(c) If cancelled cheques are not retained, anyone carrying out checks (for example, an internal or external auditor) cannot be sure what has happened to cheques which are recorded as having been cancelled. There is a risk that someone has taken the cheque with the intention of misusing it even though it has been recorded as cancelled. **Retaining cancelled cheques** provides conclusive evidence that the cheque has not fallen into the wrong hands.

(d) This is an example of **segregation of duties**. It will be less tempting for an employee to act dishonestly if he knows that related aspects of transactions which he deals with are handled by somebody else.

(e) Payments by **standing order or direct debit** will probably appear on the bank statement before they are entered into the cash book. It is not acceptable simply to transfer the details of payments made from the bank statement to the cash book, since the wrong payments may have been made by the bank as the result of some error. The bank may have made a payment even though the standing order or direct debit mandate has been cancelled, or the company may have failed to cancel a mandate which should have been cancelled. It is therefore a good idea to check that any standing order or direct debit payments which *have* been made *should* have been made before the details are entered in the cash book.

Answer 14.2

Both (a) and (b) are FALSE.

The cash book records

- money received by the business
- money paid by the business

The name 'cash book' is still used even though money may be in the form of cheques or other media.

We record cheque payments in the cash book as soon as possible after we issue the cheques: (a) is therefore false. Payments could be very difficult to keep track of if we waited until the cheque was presented before recording the payment.

A standing order is a payment like any other, and needs to be recorded in the cash book regardless of whether we have yet received the benefit: (b) is therefore also false.

Answer 14.3

(a) When a cheque is being written by hand, the writer may make an error. A computer-printed cheque might similarly have been printed incorrectly. Rather than making an alteration (which must be signed by the cheque signatories), it is generally better to **cancel** the cheque. The writer may do this by writing a line through the whole cheque and writing the word 'CANCELLED' across it.

There may be a good reason for cancelling a cheque even if it has been completed correctly. For example, it may be decided before the cheque is sent that a different amount should be paid to the supplier.

(b) Payment of a cheque may be **stopped** after it has been sent out by issuing an instruction to the bank. This instruction tells the bank not to pay the cheque, and when a collecting bank attempts to clear the cheque our bank will decline to honour it. A reversing entry will need to be made in the cash book.

If it is discovered that a cheque has been lost in the post, then stopping payment is a sensible precaution against the possibility that someone will attempt to present the cheque fraudulently. Most banks will accept a stop instruction by telephone, although this should be confirmed in writing to the bank. The bank will generally make a charge for stopping a cheque.

(c) A **paid cheque** is one which has been cleared through the bank account. The paid cheque will either be retained by the drawer's bank or sent to the drawer.

Answer 14.4

Receipts Payments

Date	Details	Discount	Cash	Bank	Date	Details	Discount	Cash	Bank
4.5	Balance b/d		224		4.5	Balance b/d			336
4.5	Bank		50		4.5	Cash withdrawal			50
6.5	Cash sales		45		5.5	R Hill	12		108
8.5	H Larkin	20		180	7.5	Telephone			210
9.5	D Randle			482	8.5	Honour Ltd			135
		20	319	662			12		839
9.5	Balance c/d			117	9.5	Balance c/d		319	
		20	319	839			12	319	839
10.5	Balance b/d		319		10.5	Balance b/d			177

ANSWERS TO ACTIVITIES

Answer 14.5

(a)

ARIA ENTERPRISES

PAYMENTS

Date	Narrative	Folio	Discount received	Payment total	VAT	Creditors	Salaries	O'heads	Fixed assets	Sundry expenses
1-Feb	Smallsoft Software	PL0054	110.00	2,090.00		2,090.00				
2-Feb	Mailhouse Ltd	PL0467		569.02		569.02				
2-Feb	Champagne (cash)			65.00	9.68					55.32
4-Feb	Stationery Box	PL0503	250.00	4,750.00		4,750.00				
5-Feb	Pacific Computers Ltd			32,894.00					32,894.00	
8-Feb	PR Reps Ltd	PL0004		5,501.40		5,501.40				
9-Feb	Champagne (cash)			19.95	2.97					16.98
9-Feb	Flowers R Us Ltd	PL0962	1.75	33.25		33.25				
10-Feb	BG (for 3 Spring Street)			178.99				178.99		
13-Feb	Window cleaner (cash)			25.00	3.72					21.28
14-Feb	Jan/Feb salaries			46,987.65			46,987.65			
14-Feb	CopyRight Ltd	PL0775		36.48		36.48				
15-Feb	Data Warehouse Ltd	PL0087		10,237.95		10,237.95				
	London Electricity (HO)			1,016.00				1,016.00		
			361.75	104,404.69	16.37	23,218.10	46,987.65	1,194.99	32,894.00	93.58
			PLC110 DR	CAB010 CR	VAT094 DR	PLC110 DR	WAG510 DR	UTI470 DR	FAC020 DR	SUN490 DR
			DIS350 CR							

(b)

ARIA ENTERPRISES

CASH BOOK PAYMENTS POSTING SUMMARY 15 FEBRUARY

Narrative	Nominal ledger account	DR	CR
		£	£
Cash	**CAB010**		104,404.69
Purchase discounts	**DIS350**		361.75
VAT control	**VAT094**	16.37	
Purchase ledger control	**PLC110**	361.75	
	PLC110	23,218.10	
Salaries	**WAG510**	46,987.65	
Utility costs	**UTI470**	1,194.99	
Fixed asset cost	**FAC020**	32,894.00	
Sundry expenses	**SUN490**	93.58	
		104,766.44	104,766.44

```
                             CASH                                CAB 010
                              £                                    £
15 Feb   Bal b/d          95,609.78 | 15 Feb   Cash book       104,404.69

                          VAT CONTROL                            VAT 094
                              £                                    £
15 Feb   Cash book            16.37 | 15 Feb   Bal b/d          11,102.00

                        SUNDRY EXPENSES                          SUN 490
                              £                                    £
15 Feb   Bal b/d             567.92 |
         Cash book            93.58 |

                       FIXED ASSET COST                          FAC 020
                              £                                    £
15 Feb   Bal b/d         272,972.00 |
         Cash book        32,894.00 |

                         UTILITY COSTS                           UTI 470
                              £                                    £
15 Feb   Bal b/d           1,509.72 |
         Cash book         1,194.99 |

                           SALARIES                              WAG 510
                              £                                    £
15 Feb   Bal b/d          45,207.69 |
         Cash book        46,987.65 |
```

ANSWERS TO ACTIVITIES

		PURCHASE DISCOUNTS RECEIVED			DIS 350
	£				£
		15 Feb	Bal b/d		279.48
			Cash book		361.75

		PURCHASE LEDGER CONTROL			PLC 110
		£			£
15 Feb	Cash book	23,218.10	15 Feb	Bal b/d	112,221.80
	Cash book discount	361.75			

Answer 14.6

(a)

Cheque number	Date 20X7	Payee	Amount £	
400602	1 May	Cash	127.00	
400603	3 May	ACM Crushers Ltd	2,012.42	
400604	3 May	Benzade Ltd	101.24	
400605	3 May	Quaygate Ltd	905.50	(£205.00 + £700.50)
400606	10 May	ACM Crushers Ltd	8,739.29	(£7,018.00 + £1,721.29)
400607	10 May	Benzade Ltd	94.27	
400608	17 May	Gadd Ltd	713.50	(£621.00 + £92.50)
400609	24 May	Benzade Ltd	414.36	(£172.19 + £242.17)
400610	31 May	ACM Crushers Ltd	982.00	
400611	31 May	Gadd Ltd	1,927.91	
400612	31 May	Quaygate Ltd	401.15	

(b) Payments

Date 20X7	Details	Cheque nos/ref	Amount £	
1 May	Petty cash	400602	127.00	
3 May	Purchase ledger	400603-605	3,019.16	(W1)
10 May	Purchase ledger	400606-607	8,833.56	(W2)
15 May	Turnmead Ltd	Standing order	192.00	
17 May	Purchase ledger	400608	713.50	
24 May	Purchase ledger	400609	414.36	
29 May	May salaries	BACS	5,842.45	
30 May	Icarus Ltd	Standing order	342.00	
31 May	Purchase ledger	400610-612	3,311.06	(W3)
			22,795.09	

Workings

1   £2,012.42 + £101.24 + £905.50 = £3,019.16

2   £8,739.29 + £94.27 = £8,833.56

3   £982.00 + £1,927.91 + £401.45 = £3,311.06

ANSWERS TO ACTIVITIES

Chapter 15

Answer 15.1

Expense item	Amount	Direct recipient	Acceptable?
Portable air conditioning unit	£75.99	Sam Gardner, office manager	No – exceeds £25 limit
Coffee filters for office coffee machine	£2.99	Raj Devi, PA	Yes
Bunch of flowers for Valentine's day	£18.00	Orlando Orseo, Sales	No – not an **office** expense
Metro ticket to Plastics Today conference	£2.60	Orlando Orseo, Sales	Yes

Answer 15.2

Reasons for not adopting the 'kitty box' suggestion

1 An open box is not a safe place physically for cash - it could easily get lost or stolen.

2 'Dipping in' means that there are no checks that the expenditure is authorised and for a valid reason.

3 A float of £30 in the kitty box means that, in theory, £30 can be spent on one item of expenditure. This breaches the £25 limit on individual items of petty cash expense.

4 Usually petty cash can only be paid out against a receipt. The 'kitty box' suggests that payment can be made without a receipt. This is only permissible with the authority of the Administration Manager.

Answer 15.3

(a) There is no receipt and no authorisation, therefore you cannot yet pay this claim. Raj should be asked to obtain authorisation from the Administration Manager.

(b) This is less than £10.00 and supported by a valid receipt. Therefore you can authorise this payment yourself, provided the tea bags were for office use.

(c) Even though this payment has been authorised, it is over the individual payment limit of £25. Therefore it cannot be paid out of petty cash. Alternative methods of payment can be offered, eg cheque.

(d) This is an office expense, supported by a valid receipt and below your £10 limit. Therefore you can authorise the payment yourself.

(e) This is below the £25 limit and has been authorised by the Administration Manager, therefore you can pay this claim.

(f) Although this has a valid receipt, it is over your £10 authorisation limit. Therefore Raj will need to obtain authorisation from the Administration Manager before payment can be made.

(g) There is no receipt and so the claim will need to be authorised by the Administration manager before you can pay it.

ANSWERS TO ACTIVITIES

Answer 15.4

The receipts total £73.46, which means that there is £76.54 (£150 – £73.46) left in the box. To bring it back to £150, a top up of £73.46 is needed.

Answer 15.5

	No 101
Petty Cash Voucher	
	Date 14.12.X7
Postage	6	25
	6	25
Signature: *A Clarke*	
Authorised by: *Petty Cashier*	

	No 102
Petty Cash Voucher	
	Date 14.12.X7
Rail ticket	7	50
	7	50
Signature:	
Authorised by: *Petty Cashier*	

Answer 15.6

You are not able to complete vouchers for any of the items in this exercise.

(a) The cost of an employee's daily travel to work is not an expense of the business.

(b) This request exceeds the £25.00 limit applying to petty cash disbursements. The bill should be paid from the main bank account.

(c) No receipt will be available and the request should therefore be referred to the Administration Manager.

(d) The sum exceeds your £10.00 authorisation limit and should be referred to the Administration Manager.

ANSWERS TO ACTIVITIES

Answer 15.7

				Analysis of payments		
Date	Details	Voucher No	Total £	Travel £	Postage £	Sundry £
20X7						
15.12	Gratuity	103	5.00			5.00
15.12	Coffee, tea and sugar	104	15.40			15.40

Answer 15.8 and 15.9

See Page 546

Answer 15.10

(a) and (c) See Page 546.

(b) The amount of the cheque requisition is payments (£87.26) less receipts (£44.18).

Cheque requisition

Date 18.12.X7

Payable to Cash

Amount £43.08

Details Petty cash imprest float

Signed Petty Cashier

ANSWERS TO ACTIVITIES

PETTY CASH BOOK

Receipts					Payments			Analysis of payments				
Details	Net receipt £	VAT £	Total £	Date	Details	Voucher No	Total £	Travel £	Postage £	Stationery £	Repairs £	Sundry £	VAT £
Balance b/d			150.00	20X7 14.12	Postage	101	6.25		6.25				
Cash sale	24.80	4.34	29.14	14.12	Travel	102	7.50	7.50					
				15.12	Sundry	103	5.00					5.00	
				15.12	Sundry	104	15.40					15.40	
Telephone	1.60	0.28	1.88	16.12	Stationery	105	10.81			9.20			1.61
				17.12	Sundry	106	5.17					4.40	0.77
				17.12	Repairs	107	22.09				18.80		3.29
				17.12	Stationery	108	4.23			3.60			0.63
				17.12	Sundry	109	2.82					2.40	0.42
Cash sale	11.20	1.96	13.16	18.12	Sundry	110	7.99			1.20		5.60	1.19
Cash book			43.08		Balance c/d	-	150.00						
	37.60	6.58	237.26				237.26	7.50	6.25	14.00	18.80	32.80	7.91
Balance b/d			150.00	21.12									

546

Chapter 16

Answer 16.1

Employees may prefer to be paid in cash because:

- it's what they're used to
- they don't need to have a bank or building society account
- they can spend some of their money straight away without waiting for a cheque to clear
- they know how much they have been paid with absolute certainty
- they can immediately give part of their wages to whoever does the housekeeping, even if that person does not have a bank or building society account
- they may not trust banks or building societies, and/or perceive them as expensive
- they get paid weekly (whereas cashless pay is more often monthly) and they find it easier to budget for a week at a time than a longer period

Answer 16.2

NAME	NET WAGE £	NET WAGE p	£20	£10	£5	£2	£1	50p	20p	10p	5p	2p	1p
Bigg	120	12	6							1		1	
Little	36	05	1	1	1		1				1		
Large	129	71	6		1	2		1	1				1
Small	87	04	4		1	1						2	
Stout	276	94	13	1	1		1	1	2			2	
Thynne	110	25	5	1					1		1		
Fatt	89	71	4		1	2		1	1				1
Skinnie	122	43	6			1			2			1	1
VALUE	972	25	£900	£30	£25	£12	£2	£1.50	£1.40	10p	10p	12p	3p
NUMBER			45	3	5	6	2	3	7	1	2	6	3

Note. As well as calculating each employee's note and coin requirements, you must **check** your calculations by making sure that the totals for each denomination add up to the total of net wages.

ANSWERS TO ACTIVITIES

Answer 16.3

(a) Gina seems likely to be **self-employed** as she works for several businesses. She should, therefore, be responsible for her own income tax and NICs. However it would be **good business practice** for her to provide an **invoice** with her **business name** and **address** on it. The Inland Revenue would certainly want these details if they ever **investigated** your company's affairs, so that they could ensure that Gina is declaring her income and paying tax. You should recommend this to the accounts department manager who authorises these payments.

(b) Jo should be asked to sign a **form** expressly authorising the payroll department to deduct the £100 advance from her net pay at the end of the month. It is always best to make arrangements like this crystal clear to avoid disputes.

(c) Lewis Taylor is a **casual worker**. As he is a full-time student, it is possible that he has no taxable income, but his part-time work may provide him with high enough earnings to be subject to tax and NICs. He should certainly sign a receipt for his earnings, giving his name and address, as this will be needed by the Inland Revenue. If he knows his NI number, he should also provide that.

Answer 16.4

This is a small workforce and as the company is new it will want to save as much money as possible on overheads. It will also be looking for a method of payment which will be acceptable to the employees and secure. A software company's employees are likely to be comfortable with new technology; the majority probably already have current accounts with banks or building societies.

Bearing all this in mind:

Payment by	Advantages	Disadvantages
Cash	• Employees get immediate access to pay	• Old fashioned • Time consuming • Expensive • Security risk to company and employees
Cheque	• More secure than cash • Simple system to set up and operate • Not too time consuming to operate in a small company, especially if cheques are printed automatically	• Risk of fraud and theft for company • Cheques can get lost • Delay for employees in getting cleared funds • More payments to check on bank statement • Not as modern as direct credit • Could mean high bank charges

ANSWERS TO ACTIVITIES

Payment by	Advantages	Disadvantages
Direct Credit	• Up to date, projects right image for a software company • Quick • Secure • Hardware probably already in use in company • Integrates well with the rest of the accounting system • Helps cashflow management for company • Cleared funds on pay day for employees, even when off sick or on holiday	• Direct access could be expensive because of the cost of the BACSTEL link (a software company would probably have all the hardware needed) and the low number of payments • Indirect access might still be expensive compared with cheques

Assuming that a cost comparison shows that direct credit would be cheaper than cheque payment (or very little more expensive), this seems the best choice for this company. If it would be too expensive, then cheque payment would be much more satisfactory than cash payment.

Answer 16.5

	Dr £	Cr £
Gross wages expense, administrative staff	102,531	
Gross wages expense, sales & marketing staff	226,704	
Gross wages expense, production staff	1,067,895	
Wages control		1,397,130
Employer's NIC expense	104,782	
Wages control		104,782
Employer's pension contributions expense	41,728	
Wages control		41,728
Wages control	79,588	
Pension fund creditor (£41,728 + £37,860)		79,588
Wages control	540,437	
PAYE & NIC creditor (£351,826 + £104,782 + £83,829)		540,437
Wages control	10,180	
GAYE creditor		10,180
Wages control	903,893	
Bank (asset)		903,893
Wages control	9,542	
Season ticket loans (asset)		9,542

ANSWERS TO ACTIVITIES

WAGES CONTROL

	£		£
PAYE & NIC creditor	540,437	Gross wages expense	1,397,130
Pension fund creditor	79,588	Employer's NIC expense	104,782
GAYE creditor	10,180	Employer's pension contributions	
Bank	903,893	Expense	41,728
Season ticket loans	9,542		
	1,543,640		1,543,640

Answer 16.6

The average payment is found by adding all the monthly totals together (which gives £13,050) and dividing this by 12.

£13,050 ÷ 12 = £1,087.50 monthly

So Aroma can pay quarterly, as it is a small employer.

Answer 16.7

	£	£
Income Tax		40,000
less refund		(500)
		39,500
Employees' NICs	7,000	
Employer's NICs	14,000	
		21,000
Total payable		60,500

In the payslip P30B an amount of £39,500 would be allocated to Income Tax, and £21,000 to net NICs.

Chapter 17

Answer 17.1

True

Answer 17.2

(a) No

(b) Your advertisement is not an offer, but an 'invitation to make an offer'. It invites other parties to make an offer to purchase.

Jenson makes an offer to purchase the car for £3,000 which you reject, by making a 'counter-offer' to sell the vehicle to him for £3,500. He can accept or reject your counter-offer. He rejects it. At this point there is no contract between you and Jenson.

You then reach agreement with Eddie to sell the car to him; at this point a contract comes into force between you and Eddie. Jenson cannot therefore successfully sue you for breach of contract as there is no contract between you and him at any point.

Answer 17.3

(a) No

(b) Your newspaper advertisement is not an offer for sale but an invitation to make an offer. You make an offer when you offer to sell the goods to Ajax for £550. In offering £480, he makes a counter-offer. This has the effect of terminating your offer. An acceptance of an offer must be unqualified acceptance of all the terms of the offer. Therefore when the telephone call ends there is no contract and no open offer. Thus Ajax's subsequent order is an offer to purchase which you are free to accept or reject. You are not bound to sell him the goods at £550 per batch.

Answer 17.4

(a) No

(b) For an agreement to be valid there must be offer and acceptance. Each must be communicated to the other party. There must be some action on the part of the 'offeree' (the person to whom the offer is made) to indicate acceptance. The offeror cannot impose acceptance merely because the offeree does not reject the goods.

Goods sent to a person who did not request them are not 'accepted' merely because he does not return them to the sender. Silence cannot constitute acceptance. (The Unsolicited Goods and Services Act 1971 also addresses this area of the law.)

Answer 17.5

(a) No

(b) Acceptance of an offer must be unqualified acceptance. Sally has stipulated that the CD players must be delivered by Saturday and, because she is introducing a new term into the contract, her purported acceptance is not valid.

Answer 17.6

(a) No

(b) The advertisement in the magazine is an invitation to make an offer. It is not an offer which is capable of being accepted. When Billy rings up to order 30 units, he is making an offer to purchase the goods. Super Sounds Ltd does not have to accept that offer.

ANSWERS TO ACTIVITIES

Answer 17.7

(a) 16 August

(b) Where it is within the contemplation of the parties that acceptance might be made by using the post, the acceptance is complete and effective as soon as a letter of acceptance is posted. This means that the contract is also complete at that time. This is referred to as the postal rule.

Answer 17.8

(a) No

(b) The offer to supply smoke alarms at £2.20 each has been withdrawn (revoked) before acceptance and that revocation was actually received by Great Fires. Once an offer is revoked, it is no longer open for acceptance.

Answer 17.9

(a) Yes

(b) Although the advertisement is an invitation to make an offer, there is an agreement between Wang and the retailer, consisting of offer and acceptance. (It could be said that the store assistant's offer to supply the PC by the next day is a legal offer accepted by Wang when he completes the order form, but it is more likely that Wang's completion of the order form is an offer which is legally accepted when the store accept the order form for fulfilment of the order.)

Answer 17.10

(a) No
(b) Contracts of sale are between the buyer and the seller, not between the buyer and the manufacturer.

Answer 17.11

S 18 rule 1 states that if the contract is unconditional and the goods are specific or identified, property passes when the contract is made. If this applies, it does not matter that the seller has not yet delivered the goods or that the buyer has not yet paid for them.

Rule 2 states that where there is a contract for the sale of specific goods and the seller is bound to do something to the goods for the purpose of putting them into a deliverable state, the property does not pass until the thing is done and the buyer has notice that it has been done.

In this case, rule 2 applies and so property in the goods (ownership) has not passed. Risk of ownership has therefore not passed either, and the action will fail.

Answer 17.12

An action for the price.

Index

INDEX

Acceptance	453
Acceptance and rejection of goods or services	462
Acceptance of an offer	454
Acceptance subject to contract	454
Advantages and disadvantages of paying by cheque	344
Advertisement	453
Age analysis of creditors	174
Age analysis of debtors	193
Agreement	450
Allowance	22
Amending the supplier record	166
Analysed cash book	310
Analysing payments	370
Analysis of purchases	89
Analysis of sales	74
Appearance and finish	459
Archive records	417
Archiving	229
Archiving information	229
Authorisation	331, 389
Authorisation limits	389
Authorised	139, 431
Authorised signatures	339
Automatic payment methods	174
BACS	174, 224, 247, 270, 338, 349
BACSTEL	435
Bailor/bailee relationship	280
Balance forward	167
Balancing off	410
Bank giro credit	436
Bank giro credit form	358
Bank of England	277
Banker	279
Bankers Automated Clearing Services (BACS)	349
Banker's draft	246, 269, 338, 350
Banker's drafts	303
Banking	
cash	281
credit card transactions	297
system	276
Banking and EFTPOS	301
Banking cash	281
Banking cheques	285
Banking plastic card transactions	291
Batch processing	93
Block codes	17
Building society cheque	269
Bulk banking	290
Bureau	435
Business	99
Business letter	196
Cancelled cheques	371
Capital and revenue items	321
Carriage paid	14
Cash	338
Cash account	111
Cash book	370
Cash discount	51, 340
Cash flow	205, 249
Cash flow problems	224
Cash on delivery	14
Cash payment	429
Cash received sheets	315
Cash registers	311
Central bank	277
CHAPS	247, 270, 338, 357
Charge card	267, 355
Chased for payment	217
Checking suppliers' invoices and credit notes	55
Checks on petty cash	396
Checks over payments	173
Cheque	338
Cheque books	338
Cheque for a company	256
Cheque guarantee card	257
Cheque payment	433
Cheque requisition form	333
Cheques	338
CIF	14
Civil law	450
Clearing or retail banks	277
Clearing system	277
Coding	17
Coding data	17
Coinage Acts	249
Coinage analysis	429
Commercial agreements	452
Communicated to the offeror	454
Company credit card or charge card	338
Company credit or charge cards	355
Completeness	370
Completeness check	393

555

INDEX

Completion statement	242
Computer	36
Computer cheques	172
Computerisation of payments recording	380
Computerised systems	92
Confidential	433
Consideration	452
Continuation file	225
Contra entries	175
Contra entries with the sales ledger	175
Contract	451
Contract law	451
Contracts for the sale of goods	457
Contracts of employment	451
Control list	371
Controls over payments	330
Controls over recording payments	369
Counter-offer	454
Counting cash	282
Courtesy	216
Covering letter	358
Credit card receipt	262
Credit card summaries	291
Credit card vouchers	291
Credit control	205
Credit limits	35
Credit note	32, 59, 342
Credit notes	201
Credit rating	206
Creditor management policies	223
Criminal action	451
Criminal law	450
Crossings on cheques	254
Customer	279
Customer records	138
Customer terms	206
Damaged	88
Data Protection Act 1998	470
Data protection principles	471
Day book totals	81
Dealing with creditors' queries	216
Debit balances	164
Debit cards	267
Debt collection letter	204
Debtor/creditor relationship	280
Debtors' queries	198

Deed	455
Deed of covenant	455
Delete any supplier record	166
Deleting or destroying information	231
Demands for payment	203
Direct access	435
Direct credit	435
Direct debit	247, 338
Direct debits	269
Discount	20, 51
Discounts	223, 340
Discounts allowed	310
Discounts and early payment	223
Discounts received	170, 371
Discrepancies	58
Dishonoured cheques	257
Dishonoured for payment	289
Dividing the ledger	167
Documentation to go out with payments	358
Documenting goods and services received	48
Double entry	117
Double entry recording of sales	111
'Double entry' system	81
Durability	459
E & OE	14
Economic trends	248
EFTPOS	268, 301
Electronic cash registers	243
Electronic funds transfer	356
Electronic transfer	435
Employees' NIC contributions	443
Employer's costs	438
Employer's NIC contributions	443
Endorsement	253
in blank	254
Evidence of payment	246
Ex works	14
Exempt items	23
Expenses claim forms	335
Expenses day book	91
Expenses not yet incurred	394
Faceted codes	18
Facsimile ('fax') machines	198
False description	459
Faulty	88

556

INDEX

Fidelity insurance	250
Filing and retention of suppliers' statements	216
Fitness of goods for a disclosed purpose	460
Float	283, 410
Floor limit	265
FOB	14
Forgery	249, 255
Formation of a contract	451
Fraud	50, 369, 433
Freedom from minor defects	459
Frequency of reconciling supplier statements	216

G

Giving change	243
Goods received	48
Gross pay	437, 439

H

Handing cash over	431
Hierarchical codes	18
Hire purchase	352
HM Customs & Excise	112

I

Implied terms	458
Imprest amount	390, 415
Imprest system	390
Indirect access	435
In-house store cards	267
Inland Revenue	431, 438
Insufficient funds	289
Insurance premiums	352
Intention to create legal relations	452
Invitation to make an offer	453
IOUs and petty cash	396

K

Key account customers	207

L

Law of contract	450
Legal aspects of cheques	252
Legal relationship (banker/customer)	280
Legal standing of a receipt	245
Legally binding	452
Letter of enquiry	5
Lien	462
Limiting the size of petty cash payments	389
Lost cheques	345

M

Mail Transfer (MT)	356
Mail transfer and telegraphic transfer	338
Main ledger code	334
Maintaining supplier records	165
Management of creditors	222
Mandate	256
Manual postings	375
Memorandum accounts	92, 137
Methods of payment	171, 338
Mistake	396
Money consideration	457
Mortgagor/mortgagee relationship	281

N

Net pay	426
Net wages	438
Netting off	175
New supplier account	165
NICs	431, 436
Night safes	251

O

Objective of creditor management	223
Offer	452
Offer and acceptance	452
Open item	166
Open item method	152
Opening a new ledger account	165
Opening files	225
Operational balances	277
Order form	358
Ordering money	429
Other creditors	164

P

P30B	442
Partnership cheques	256
Passing of property and risk	461
PAYE	431, 436
Paying-in slip	281, 287, 291
Payment in cash	429
Payment out of petty cash	431
Payments	
by banker's draft	350
by cash	338
by other methods	355
Payments by banker's draft	350
Payments by cheque	338

INDEX

Payments by standing order and direct debit	352
Payments on account	154
Payments to suppliers	171
Payroll ledger accounts	437
Payslip	427
Penalties	223
Personal accounts for creditors	92
Personal accounts for debtors	81
Petty cash advances	395
Petty cash book	310, 415
Petty cash box	388
Petty cash vouchers	392
Petty cashier	388
Plastic cards	260
Possession	461
Postal rule	454
Post-dated cheques	256
Posting cash payments	375
Posting petty cash	410
Posting purchase returns	169
Posting summary	416
Postings summary	322
Practical tips in creditor management	224
Preparing cheques	339
Price	457
Price extensions	56
Privacy	470
Profit	99
Proforma	14
Pro-forma invoice	358
Proforma wages control account	440
Promptness	216
Property	461
Purchase day book	87
Purchase ledger	168
Purchase ledger control account	117
Purchase order	9, 43
Purchase returns	169
Purchase returns day book	88
Purchases and returns	119
Purpose of petty cash	387

Quotation	5

Real remedies	462
Rebate	22
Receipts	242, 389

Receiving money into petty cash	397
Reconciling items	215
Recording goods received	48
Recording petty cash payments	400
Recording purchases and cash paid	168
Recording receipts of money into petty cash	404
Recording transactions in personal accounts	92
Rejection	454
Relationship between banker and customer	279
Remedies against the buyer	462
Remedies against the goods	462
Reminders	204
Remittance advice	184, 239
Remittance advices	172, 358
Rental payments	352
Retail receipts	242
Retaining information	228
Retention of records	170
Retention of title	461
Retention policy	228
Returned cheques	382
Revocation	454
Right of resale	463
Right to sell the goods	458
Romalpa	461
Round sum payments	154

Safes	250
Safety	459
Sale by sample	460
Sale of goods	451, 457
remedies	462
Sale or return	88
Sales and debtors	318
Sales day book	73
Sales ledger	81
Sales ledger control account	111, 144
Sales ledger postings	136
Sales order set	12
Sales returns day book	78
Satisfactory quality	459
Seasonal trends	248
Security	249, 339, 388
Security and control of petty cash	388
Security guards	251
Security problems	433
Segregate duties	238

INDEX

Selecting items for payment	172
Sellers' order forms	9
Seller's title	458
Sequence codes	17
Service book	49
Services received	49
Settlement discount	340
Sharing information	224
Short informal report	197
Significant digit codes	18
Social, domestic and family arrangements	452
Special endorsement	254
Spreadsheet	78, 92
Spreadsheets	78
Stale cheque	256
Standing order	247, 338, 352
Standing orders	269
Statements of account	182
Stolen cheques and cheque guarantee cards	290
Stoppage in transit	462
Stopping cheques	345
Strong box	251
Summary voucher	291, 294
Supplier records	165
Supplier statement reconciliations	214
Suppliers' statements of account	212
Supply of information	453
Supply of services	457

Telegraphic Transfer (TT)	356
Termination of offer	454
Terms of credit	223
Theft	250, 396, 433
Three column cash book	374
Till receipts	242, 243
Time of performance	458
Timing and methods of payments	337
Timing of receipts	247
Topping up the float	410
Topping up the imprest	391
Tort	451
Trade creditors	164
Trade Descriptions Act 1968	459
Trade-in arrangement	457
Transaction processing	142
Transactions	450
Types of business purchase	47
Types of receipt from customers	247

Unclaimed wages	431
Unqualified agreement	454
Unsolicited	454
Updating the records	437

VAT (Value Added Tax)	23, 112, 223, 371, 405
VAT and purchases	118
VAT receipts	389
Voucher numbers	393

What makes a contract	451
What makes a valid contract	451
Written receipts	246

INDEX

See overleaf for information on other
BPP products and how to order

AAT Order

To BPP Professional Education, Aldine Place, London W12 8AW
Tel: 020 8740 2211. Fax: 020 8740 1184
E-mail: Publishing@bpp.com Web:www.bpp.com

Mr/Mrs/Ms (Full name)
Daytime delivery address
Postcode
Daytime Tel
E-mail

	5/03 Texts	5/03 Kits	Special offer	8/03 Passcards	Tapes
FOUNDATION (£14.95 except as indicated)				Foundation	
Units 1 & 2 Receipts and Payments	☐	☐	Foundation Sage Bookeeping and Excel Spreadsheets CD-ROM free if ordering all Foundation Text and Kits, including Units 21 and 22/23	£6.95 ☐	£10.00 ☐
Unit 3 Ledger Balances and Initial Trial Balance	☐	☐			
Unit 4 Supplying Information for Mgmt Control	☐	☐			
Unit 21 Working with Computers (£9.95) (6/03)	☐	☐			
Unit 22/23 Healthy Workplace/Personal Effectiveness (£9.95)	☐	☐			
Sage and Excel for Foundation (CD-ROM £9.95)	☐				
INTERMEDIATE (£9.95 except as indicated)					
Unit 5 Financial Records and Accounts	☐	☐		£5.95 ☐	£10.00 ☐
Unit 6/7 Costs and Reports (Combined Text £14.95)	☐				
Unit 6 Costs and Revenues		☐		£5.95 ☐	£10.00 ☐
Unit 7 Reports and Returns		☐		£5.95 ☐	
TECHNICIAN (£9.95 except as indicated)					
Unit 8/9 Managing Performance and Controlling Resources	☐	☐		£5.95 ☐	£10.00 ☐
Spreadsheets for Technician (CD-ROM)	☐		Spreadsheets for Technicians CD-ROM free if take Unit 8/9 Text and Kit		
Unit 10 Core Managing Systems and People (£14.95)	☐	☐		£5.95 ☐	£10.00 ☐
Unit 11 Option Financial Statements (A/c Practice)	☐	☐		£5.95 ☐	
Unit 12 Option Financial Statements (Central Govnmt)	☐	☐			
Unit 15 Option Cash Management and Credit Control	☐	☐		£5.95 ☐	
Unit 17 Option Implementing Audit Procedures	☐	☐		£5.95 ☐	
Unit 18 Option Business Tax (FA03)|8/03 Text & Kit	☐	☐			
Unit 19 Option Personal Tax (FA 03)|8/03 Text & Kit	☐	☐			
TECHNICIAN 2002 (£9.95)					
Unit 18 Option Business Tax FA02 (8/02 Text & Kit	☐	☐			
Unit 19 Option Personal Tax FA02 (8/02 Text & Kit)	☐	☐			
SUBTOTAL	£	£		£	£

We aim to deliver to all UK addresses inside 5 working days; a signature will be required. Orders to all EU addresses should be delivered within 6 working days. All other orders to overseas addresses should be delivered within 8 working days. * Europe includes the Republic of Ireland and the Channel Islands.

TOTAL FOR PRODUCTS £ _____

POSTAGE & PACKING

Texts/Kits	First	Each extra
UK	£3.00	£3.00
Europe*	£6.00	£4.00
Rest of world	£20.00	£10.00

Passcards		
UK	£2.00	£1.00
Europe*	£3.00	£2.00
Rest of world	£8.00	£8.00

Tapes		
UK	£2.00	£1.00
Europe*	£3.00	£2.00
Rest of world	£8.00	£8.00

TOTAL FOR POSTAGE & PACKING £ _____
(Max £12 Texts/Kits/Passcards - deliveries in UK)

Grand Total (Cheques to *BPP Professional Education*)
I enclose a cheque for (incl. Postage) £ _____
Or charge to Access/Visa/Switch
Card Number ☐☐☐☐ ☐☐☐☐ ☐☐☐☐ ☐☐☐☐
Expiry date _____ Start Date _____
Issue Number (Switch Only) _____
Signature _____

See overleaf for information on other
BPP products and how to order

AAT Order

To BPP Professional Education, Aldine Place, London W12 8AW
Tel: 020 8740 2211. Fax: 020 8740 1184
E-mail: Publishing@bpp.com Web: www.bpp.com

Mr/Mrs/Ms (Full name)

Daytime delivery address

Postcode

Daytime Tel   E-mail

OTHER MATERIAL FOR AAT STUDENTS	8/03 Texts	3/03 Text

FOUNDATION (£5.95)
Basic Mathematics ☐

INTERMEDIATE (£5.95)
Basic Bookkeeping (for students exempt from Foundation) ☐

FOR ALL STUDENTS (£5.95)
Building Your Portfolio (old standards) ☐
Building Your Portfolio (new standards) ☐

£ ☐   £ ☐

TOTAL FOR PRODUCTS £ ☐

POSTAGE & PACKING

Texts/Kits	First	Each extra
UK	£3.00	£3.00
Europe*	£6.00	£4.00
Rest of world	£20.00	£10.00

Passcards		
UK	£2.00	£1.00
Europe*	£3.00	£2.00
Rest of world	£8.00	£8.00

Tapes		
UK	£2.00	£1.00
Europe*	£3.00	£2.00
Rest of world	£8.00	£8.00

TOTAL FOR POSTAGE & PACKING £ ☐
(Max £12 Texts/Kits/Passcards - deliveries in UK)

Grand Total (Cheques to *BPP Professional Education*)
I enclose a cheque for (incl. Postage) £ ☐
Or charge to Access/Visa/Switch
Card Number ☐☐☐☐☐☐☐☐☐☐☐☐☐☐☐☐

Expiry date ☐☐☐☐   Start Date ☐☐☐☐

Issue Number (Switch Only) ☐☐

Signature

We aim to deliver to all UK addresses inside 5 working days; a signature will be required. Orders to all EU addresses should be delivered within 6 working days. All other orders to overseas addresses should be delivered within 8 working days. * Europe includes the Republic of Ireland and the Channel Islands.

Review Form & Free Prize Draw – Units 1 and 2 Recording income and receipts and Making and recording payments (5/03)

All original review forms from the entire BPP range, completed with genuine comments, will be entered into one of two draws on 31 January 2004 and 31 July 2004. The names on the first four forms picked out on each occasion will be sent a cheque for £50.

Name: _____   Address: _____

How have you used this Interactive Text?
(Tick one box only)
☐ Home study (book only)
☐ On a course: college _____
☐ With 'correspondence' package
☐ Other _____

Why did you decide to purchase this Interactive Text? *(Tick one box only)*
☐ Have used BPP Texts in the past
☐ Recommendation by friend/colleague
☐ Recommendation by a lecturer at college
☐ Saw advertising
☐ Other _____

During the past six months do you recall seeing/receiving any of the following?
(Tick as many boxes as are relevant)
☐ Our advertisement in *Accounting Technician* magazine
☐ Our advertisement in *Pass*
☐ Our brochure with a letter through the post

Which (if any) aspects of our advertising do you find useful?
(Tick as many boxes as are relevant)
☐ Prices and publication dates of new editions
☐ Information on Interactive Text content
☐ Facility to order books off-the-page
☐ None of the above

Have you used the companion Assessment Kit for this subject?   ☐ Yes   ☐ No

Your ratings, comments and suggestions would be appreciated on the following areas

	Very useful	Useful	Not useful
Introduction	☐	☐	☐
Chapter contents lists	☐	☐	☐
Examples	☐	☐	☐
Activities and answers	☐	☐	☐
Key learning points	☐	☐	☐
Quick quizzes and answers	☐	☐	☐

	Excellent	Good	Adequate	Poor
Overall opinion of this Text	☐	☐	☐	☐

Do you intend to continue using BPP Interactive Texts/Assessment Kits?   ☐ Yes   ☐ No

Please note any further comments and suggestions/errors on the reverse of this page.

The BPP author of this edition can be e-mailed at: **janiceross@bpp.com**

Please return this form to: Janice Ross, BPP Professional Education, **FREEPOST, London, W12 8BR**

Review Form & Free Prize Draw (continued)

Please note any further comments and suggestions/errors below

Free Prize Draw Rules

1. Closing date for 31 January 2004 draw is 31 December 2003. Closing date for 31 July 2004 draw is 30 June 2004.
2. Restricted to entries with UK and Eire addresses only. BPP employees, their families and business associates are excluded.
3. No purchase necessary. Entry forms are available upon request from BPP Professional Education. No more than one entry per title, per person. Draw restricted to persons aged 16 and over.
4. Winners will be notified by post and receive their cheques not later than 6 weeks after the relevant draw date.
5. The decision of the promoter in all matters is final and binding. No correspondence will be entered into.